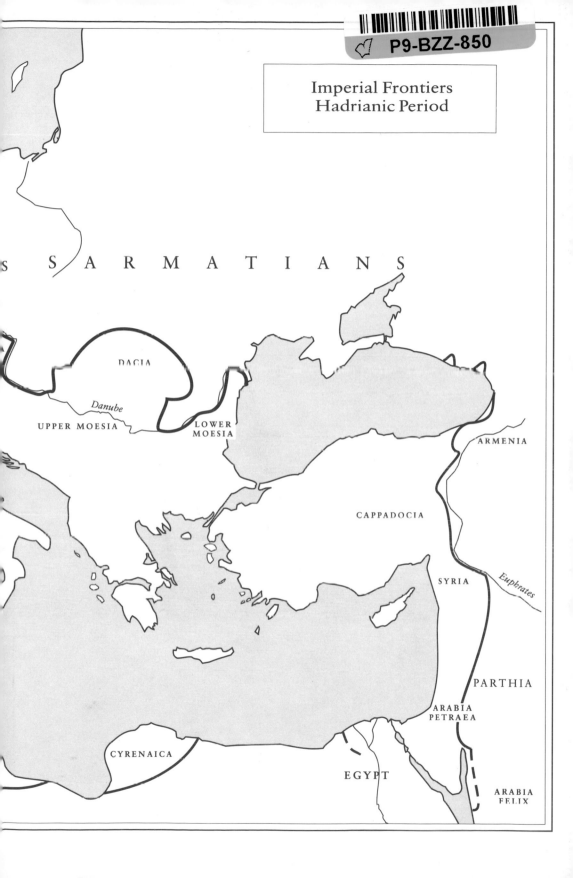

Imperial Frontiers
Hadrianic Period

s S A R M A T I A N S

DACIA

Danube

UPPER MOESIA

LOWER
MOESIA

ARMENIA

CAPPADOCIA

SYRIA

Euphrates

PARTHIA

ARABIA
PETRAEA

CYRENAICA

EGYPT

ARABIA
FELIX

THE REACH OF ROME

THE
REACH OF ROME

A History of
the Roman Imperial Frontier
1st–5th Centuries AD

DEREK WILLIAMS

St. Martin's Press ❧ New York

Library of Congress Cataloging-in-Publication Data

Williams, Derek.
    The Reach of Rome / Derek Williams.
        p.   cm.
    ISBN 0-312-15631-6
    1. Rome—Boundaries—History.   2. Limes (Roman
boundary)—History.   3. Fortification—Rome.
4. Military art and science—Rome.   I. Title.
DG59.A2W56   1997
937—dc21   97-8191
                                                    CIP

First published in Great Britain by
Constable and Company Limited

First U.S. Edition: July 1997

10   9   8   7   6   5   4   3   2   1

To our grandchildren
Alex, Elly and Becky

CONTENTS

LIST OF MAPS AND DIAGRAMS

Maps and diagrams drawn by John Mitchell

LIST OF PHOTOGRAPHS

All photographs by the author

Acknowledgements

Among many to whom I am in debt, precedence must be given to the organisers of and contributors to the Congresses of Roman Frontier Studies and the publishers of the successive volumes of their proceedings, almost all of which have been drawn upon, some extensively. The foundations of our subject lie even deeper, at the level of local archaeology and the regional antiquarian journals; but it was the Congresses which brought together scholars at international level, allowing an empire-wide view of the frontiers to emerge from the national fragments at last. A glance at my footnotes will show that their papers are the heart of the frontier discussions in this book.

I would like to thank all authors of works mentioned in my text or notes. I am especially grateful to the general editors of the *British Archaeological Reports*, Oxford, their individual authors, and editors of the *colloquia*, conferences or collected articles. This valuable series has highlighted the work of some of the most able scholars of our day in archaeological and related fields.

A number of distinguished works, not mentioned in my notes, have been of general value. These include: S. L. Dyson's *The Creation of the Roman Frontier* (Princeton, 1985), which provides essential background on European frontier formation during the Republican period; F. Millar and others, *Das Römische Reich und seine Nachbarn* (Frankfurt, 1966), which places the empire in its surroundings; J. B. Campbell, *The Emperor and the Roman Army* (Oxford, 1984) on the relationship between soldiers and centre; *Roman Civilization, Sourcebook 2, the Empire* (New York, 1966) in which N. Lewis and M. Reinhold present and translate a wealth of source material;

E. Luttwak's *The Grand Strategy of the Roman Empire* (Baltimore, 1976), an influential treatment of achievement in diplomacy and war; R. Martin's *Tacitus* (London, 1981), which enriches our view of Rome's most memorable historian; C. R. Whittaker's *Frontiers of the Roman Empire: A Social and Economic Study* (Baltimore, 1994), which makes a notable contribution to the subject's theoretical background; and Stephen Johnson's fine study of the military and paramilitary scene in 3rd- and 4th-century Western Europe, *Late Roman Fortifications* (London, 1983).

In the matter of translation from the modern languages I accept responsibility for all passages quoted but wish especially to thank Miss Muriel E. Hammond for assistance with a significant number of the reports and papers in German. Regarding the ancient languages, I owe a debt to the editors, publishers, textual scholars and translators of the Oxford Classical, Teubner and Budé series; and, above all, to the Loeb Classical Library, whose Greek and Latin texts often provided the basis for my own translations used throughout this book. The Loeb English versions, by scholars far more accomplished than myself, offered a frequent reassurance for my parallel efforts. In general, however, I have leaned further towards free translation. My objective has been to produce flexible renderings and to adapt these into a fluent narrative. I apologise for telescoping texts and occasionally combining passages into composite quotations. Nevertheless I have tried, like all sincere translators, not to lose the essence of the originals.

The ancient sources most frequently quoted are Dio Cassius' *History of Rome*, the principal works of Tacitus, the *Augustan History*, Ammianus Marcellinus' *History*, Strabo's *Geographica* and Pliny's *Natural History*. These are available for wider reading in the Loeb Classical Library and, in several instances, in the Penguin Classics editions. A number of the minor sources are still unavailable in translated form.

O. Seek's edition of the *Notitia Dignitatum* (Berlin, 1896); the *Theodosian Code* (trans. C. Pharr; Princeton, 1952); Zosimus' *New History* (San Antonio, 1967) and *de Rebus Bellicis* (ed. M. W. C. Hassall; London, 1979) are among the source books consulted. Chapter and page numbers in Gibbon's *Decline and Fall* refer to the 1811 edition, which chanced to be the version of that great work at my disposal.

Quotations from *Fossatum Africae* are by kind permission of its publisher, Arts et Métiers Graphiques, Paris.

I am indebted beyond measure to Caroline Davidson, literary agent, whose perceptive and thoughtful comment on my original draft resulted in extensive reshaping and necessary improvements. Also to Dr Andrew Dalby for careful reading and helpful suggestion. Their structural recommendations exercised a decisive influence on the book's final form. Susan Trevelyan's and Anne Charvet's searching and constructive reading of the typescript yielded a torrent of improvements. All have been immensely helpful, but the book would not have seen daylight were it not for Carol O'Brien, of Constable and Co., whose readiness to back an outsider to the academic field was an act of perspicacity and pluck of which I hope my efforts will prove worthy.

I would next like to thank the president, secretary and librarians of the Society for the Promotion of Roman Studies, London, within whose walls and with whose volumes on loan I have passed happy hours; and whose collection of books was the key to the production of this one. I also wish to thank Kathy Clark and Samantha Hopkins for lifting my ungainly manuscript to the level of a clean, clear typescript and for unremitting vigilance regarding errors.

On a more personal note, it gives me pleasure to thank Professor J. A. Robinson of Syracuse University for encouragement and counsel. His inspiration in tracing and telephoning me, following an almost forty-year loss of contact, led to the renewal of an old friendship coinciding precisely with the writing of this book.

I have abiding gratitude and fondness for the memory of my teachers at the best of schools and the greatest of universities. At the Royal Grammar School, Newcastle upon Tyne, Sydney Middlebrook gave me the love of history and Maurice Guy Robinson of letters; Hugh Owen, H. N. Smith and James Herdman equipped me with the ancient and modern languages and Donald Meaken the geographical grasp, without any one of which I would not have dared attack this summit. At Corpus Christi College, Cambridge, Patrick Bury extended and deepened the historical sense. Bruce Dickens, an eminent Anglo-Saxonist, gave encouragement to my interest in Romano-British studies, then little more than a hobby. Michael McCrum, in addition to friendly support, helped greatly in opening my eyes to the Classical world of the Mediterranean, not least by recommending me to the British School at Athens. Alas, of all these fine teachers only the last now survives. It is a sad consequence of writing a book late in life that so many to whom one owes so much are no longer here to be thanked.

Though my father too did not live to see this book, I owe him and my mother infinite gratitude for their long, loving and patient support, reaching back to youthful days, with many a dawn call for outings to Hadrian's Wall and car rides to and from Roman locations.

Lastly, I thank Olive. It has been her struggle to maintain me, our small house and very large garden through more than two years entirely devoted to writing, which made that writing possible. For the sacrifices and losses it has cost, I am deeply sorry.

It has proved tricky to find a just balance for our subject, owing largely to the gap between my two pillars of wisdom: ancient literature and modern archaeology. The written sources are finite. The likelihood that manuscripts will be discovered is now small and what we have is so mulled over that little remains to be said. By contrast field investigation's scope is almost infinite and the available sites will never be fully dug. This means that the archaeology of the imperial boundary is forever under sail yet never reaches port. Anyone who bases history upon it knows that what he writes will require continual updating. Indeed it is an incentive not to write at all.

A second problem is the unevenness of information available from the specialised literature, on which our study largely depends. Research on the European frontier greatly outweighs that on the combined frontiers of Asia and Africa. The Roman imperial boundary's main sectors passed through or fringed on eight countries in present-day Europe, where its interest is generally acknowledged; and nine in the Islamic world, where it is generally not. There are regions where secretiveness, xenophobia or ferment seem almost to be ways of life. Any critic of the frontier scholar's efforts must remember that these involve several states which could presently be called unstable, or unfriendly towards the West. The Kurdish problem alone restricts access to the pertinent parts of three. Fortunately, political changes open doors as well as close them. Something is now known about all sectors of the imperial frontier and much about some of them. Though a more definitive story may yet need several decades of research (which in turn requires a context of stability and international goodwill not presently foreseeable) a provisional account, accessible to the general reader, is nevertheless overdue.

Introduction

Boundaries are basic. Because we live by exploiting the natural world, territorial control and the exclusion of rivals are perpetual themes in human and animal behaviour. All territories have edges, defining the space within which the owner's needs are met or beyond which he accepts the strength of others. To have meaning, these edges must be recognisable. A bird may indicate them by singing, a wolf by urinating. We, whose dominant sense is sight, mark them visually. And since it requires time to exploit territory, we have long sought to signpost our margins in durable ways, avoiding the need to prowl them incessantly.

As well as manifest remains like earthen dykes or ditches, the world must be criss-crossed by boundaries no longer detectable because they consisted of natural features like streams and ridges, plus more transient signals like felled trees, sticks stuck in the ground and painted stones. Their messages were nevertheless the same: to assert ownership and forbid intrusion. In the Middle Ages a border was called march (German *Mark*, Italian *marcha*), because it was originally marked. Related words include marquis or margrave, but also market and merchant, for frontiers beget business, each side supplying what is rare to the other.

There are sound reasons for marking rather than guarding a frontier. Essentially, this is because the longest line of any territory is its outside edge. Were guards to be deployed along the entire length, unacceptably large numbers would be absorbed and too few left within. In practice manned frontiers awaited the development of standing armies. Even then, the great majority of states rejected peripheral defence on the grounds that it offered poor return on large investment. The need to spread along a defended line in order to cover all approaches is a grave disadvantage, for an attacker will bring maximum numbers to bear at the point of assault. In terms of place and time the initiative will be his. Expensive equipment like barriers, signalling systems and road networks are therefore needed to restore the balance in the defender's favour.

By contrast, one who defends from inside a territory needs few formal works and may even dispense with a regular army, providing the time required by the invader to advance toward the centre is sufficient to muster reserves or summon a militia. Above all, units held centrally can counter-attack with undivided force. Only in this way can a defender regain the initiative. Therefore, on grounds both of number of soldiers and effectiveness of response, most defensive strategies have been based on reaction against specific threats rather than on general exclusion, and have deployed their strength not on boundaries, but somewhere between edge and centre. Distance between frontier and capital has often been related to mobilisation time.

The Roman emperors' commitment to a manned and fortified frontier is, thus, a historical oddity. Indeed, any form of static defence ran counter to Rome's own legacy, which was one of aggressive, mobile warfare. Why, during the first century of our era, did she reverse her traditional strategy in favour of a hedgehog position, untried before and largely rejected by subsequent ages? Such are the questions to be answered.

Meanwhile, many will be surprised that a defensive work of this character even existed, let alone that it encircled the empire, an area the size of the United States together with Alaska. This was a mighty work. Though for the most part it did not consist of walls like Hadrian's, the normal arrangement was a barrier of some sort: man-made, natural or both, with the entire army dispersed along it. The result was a guarded line, comparable in role to the Great Wall of China: a frontier of interdiction, which had also something in common with the iron curtains of our own century. It represented a division between richer and poorer, somewhat resembling a First-world/Third-world interface. None of these is a precise comparison, for history offers few frontiers to which the Roman can be related. Only an inborn conviction of invincibility would allow the caesars to follow this peculiar course and to waive the advantages of concentrated strikepower and centralised response. Indeed, at the time of the frontier's formation and during most of the early empire, their conviction was supported by the fact that there was no enemy dangerous enough to merit a retaliatory blow such as the combined strength of the legions might inflict.

What advantages were offered by a frontier of this type? First, precise definition and total protection, allowing economic development right up to the border line. This is an idea opposed to that of marches, which were in effect no man's lands, expendable shields offered by each side to the other. Secondly, such a frontier meant that internal fortifications were superfluous. What need of walls with an empire walled? This is quite contrary to the pessimism of the medieval approach, which put a wall round every town, a tower alongside every church, a castle at every key point and a sword or bow in every hand. Thirdly, since all were protected by a ring of steel, Rome's civilian subjects could remain unarmed, live without fear and follow profitable pursuits. To create an empire which was as safe half-a-mile behind the frontier as in the Roman Forum, within which walls and weapons were extraneous, was surely antiquity's greatest feat. In this respect, Rome's was a superlative achievement – as long as the frontier held.

One cannot doubt that the Romans would have regarded the marcher concept as an anarchic overlap of backward peoples, unworthy of the mistress of the world. By contrast Roman frontiers were crisp and efficient. The army was a masterful user of terrain. Boundary decisions were generally more thoughtful than those of modern empires, whose lines were ruled on maps, throwing together incompatible tribes or religions. Being under tight military control, Rome's were never freebooter frontiers run by miners, trappers or outlaws. Nor were they strained by a torrent of homesteaders and prospectors. The imperial boundaries seem benign in comparison with the contact zones of recent centuries. Human and ecological disasters most commonly occur at cultural and economic divides, of which the decimation of the American Indian, the enslavement of the African, the destruction of Aztec and Inca, the near-extinction of the North American bison and the Siberian fur animals are prominent examples. Rome was far from blameless, but instances of interfacial brutality were relatively fewer and their scale smaller. A world without barriers is a noble goal, but pending man's fitness to achieve it, firm frontiers, disciplined and clear, have undeniable advantages.

And yet one must be emphatic in denying that the imperial frontier was created with these advantages in mind; or that the empire's way of protecting itself was arrived at by rational considerations of cost and benefit. Rather its merits were bonuses of a system whose origins lay in suspicion and fear, which evolved haphazardly and was perpetuated by complacency and drift. Though it stabilised the environs of Classical antiquity, though it would help preserve the *pax Romana* for nearly four centuries; there was a cost. This boundary fixation, this obsession with territoriality carried the seeds of downfall. In the long term the state of mind generated by safe borders would dull Rome's fighting spirit and hasten the death sentence which the processes of history have placed on all empires. The seeming impregnability of these frontiers would create a bulwark myth, a ring of false confidence within which experience of warfare lapsed and military invention dwindled.

The remarkable concept of *moenia mundi*, the world's walls, a universal shelter belt girding the entirety of civilised mankind, a mantelet behind which the Mediterranean condition could be applied beyond the Alps and the Euphrates; its inception, growth and consequences are the meaning and substance of our story.

Hadlow
Kent
March 1996

'See this small one, tiptoe on
The green foothills of the years,
Views a younger world than yours;
When you go down, he'll be the tall one.'

C. DAY LEWIS

THE REACH OF ROME

CHAPTER 1

Augustus:
The Advice

Rome was already seven centuries old at the dissolution of the Republic and her empire substantially in place when her first emperor took the purple. In step with long and glorious achievements both in war and diplomacy, there had grown assumptions of Rome's omnipotence and eternity, coupled with the belief that her outward march had no limits save those which ocean, unprofitable climate and terrain might impose. Despite the calamity of the civil wars, which had brought Augustus to the throne, confidence towards the outside world remained unshaken. Ideas of appeasement, or of passivity as a principle of statecraft, ran counter to Rome's experience and were alien to her thinking. The corollary – a defended frontier – was equally unthinkable. Frontiers were needed to hold ground and keep the peace, but they were seen as temporary, as pausing places, or as startlines for future advance. Frontiers in the sense of stoplines, fixed and final, guarded and fortified, were as yet unfamiliar to Romans. Nor, till expansion faltered, would they begin to form.

The very nature of the Republic had made it unlikely that Rome's borderlands would be placed under permanent military control, simply because the principle of permanence was not applied to military matters. The Senate, the Republic's ruling body, was an aristocratic assembly, based on power-sharing, but haunted by the fear that some of its members might use the military machine to seize more than their fair share. This meant that there would be no such thing as professional generals or standing armies. Senators were entrusted with commands for strictly defined objectives and armies raised for single campaigns. Units would be retained to guard new conquests only if a specific danger threatened and only for as long as danger lasted. The non-existence of permanent armed forces told against fixed frontiers in a practical sense as surely as Rome's history of glorious expansion denied them psychologically.

This expansion had been fitful. Frontiers were where the last campaign ended. Any given moment might reveal provinces half won and lands in limbo, while the army which captured them was disbanded, its officers' commissions terminated and attention turned to other theatres. Meanwhile, *de facto* boundaries were secured by treaties with the new neighbours, cemented by the installation of pro-Roman chieftains, bribery, the awarding of commercial privileges, the creation of evacuated zones, the dismantling of fortifications and similar devices. Friendly tribes might retain their weapons and be paid to watch those that were unfriendly. Behind all such measures was the threat of reprisal, and a stern reputation to back it.

Along the Asian borders were a number of small states known as 'friends of the Roman people'.[1] The rapid campaigns and sweeping settlements of Pompey had disposed of Alexander the Great's near-eastern territories, annexing Syria as a Roman province and leaving much of the remainder under Rome's protection, though still in the hands of local rulers. This screen of dependencies across Armenia and what is now eastern Turkey, with outliers to the south, formed a buffer between Rome and her rival Parthia (Iran). With occasional assistance these allies could look after the frontier in their own areas, providing a solution of sorts for the empire's eastern flank. It was nevertheless a temporary solution. The caretaker kingdoms were not strong and sometimes not even staunch. In due course they would be absorbed into the Roman empire. Meanwhile, with Parthia presently quiescent, imperial attention could focus on the European theatres; and it is to them we must look for the frontier's inception.

So, by 27 BC, the year of Augustus' accession, Rome had formed the habit of expansion, but had not yet reached geographical limits which might modify that habit. His reign would be crucial to the frontier idea, for during it Rome encountered these limits and the influences which guided her towards perimeter defence were first felt. The origin of the frontier in its full and formal sense thus coincided almost exactly with the beginning of the empire, though the emergence of actual boundary works still lay some decades ahead.

The civil wars had ended on a dangerous note. On the winning side alone sixty legions stood combat-ready: a factor which compelled an urgent and radical review of the army's future. Augustus decided to retain twenty-eight, while the remainder would be demobilised and settled in colonies. By this act the West's first professional standing army, consisting of 150,000 legionaries and a similar number of auxiliaries, was created. Length of service was set at sixteen years, later increased to twenty.

However, a standing army did not mean that formal, garrisoned frontiers must follow. On the contrary, an empire protected along its edges, rather than by armies held in the interior was unprecedented. Nor was there some strategic reason, peculiar to early imperial Rome, why precedent should now be broken. The pointer to the future lay not just in the new army's formation but in its deployment, which was politically influenced. The historian Dio Cassius of Nicaea, writing in the 3rd century, tells us of Augustus that 'Before the least sign of trouble he made haste to discharge some of the soldiers and to scatter most of the others.'[2]

In this last phrase lay far-reaching consequences. 'Scattering the soldiers' meant confining the army to the outer provinces, with all legions posted as far as possible both from Rome and (in as much as the strategic situation allowed) from each other. Though Augustus had no notion of its outcome, the seeds of a frontier army were already being sown. Should a durable type of frontier now evolve, the existence of a standing army, stationed round the empire's edge, ensured that there would be the permanent means to guard it. This would in turn shape the frontier's character, distinguishing it from prehistoric dykes and ditchworks, which were unmanned and fulfilled a delineational rather than a truly defensive role. The new demobilisation terms reinforced these tendencies. Veteran colonies would be predominantly in the outer provinces where land was more readily available. In effect this created a frontier reserve, made resolute by men protecting their own homes.

We need not look far to explain the army's dispersal. It expressed Augustus' distrust of soldiers and of ambitious men who might suborn them. By keeping the legions close to the borders their energies could be directed toward foreign enemies; and keeping them far from each other would ensure that no overwhelming force could be assembled which might threaten the throne. While caution was understandable in the aftermath of civil war, Augustus' arrangements would long outlive him. In this matter of deployment, all the early and many of the late emperors would follow his lead; not in deference to Augustus' memory, but because they shared his fears. It says little for Rome's constitutional development that centuries were to pass without resolution of the principate's most basic problems: uncertainty regarding control of the army and absence of a universally accepted formula for succession to the throne. Fear of usurpation would dominate imperial thinking till the end and ensure that this early decision to scatter the army, based on suspicion rather than strategy, established the norm. The forces remained dispersed for at least two hundred years. There was no home army, no Italian command or centrally based reserve. Frontiers were reinforced only by borrowing from other frontiers, campaigns made possible only by weakening frontier garrisons. If seriously challenged, Rome would be unable to respond with the authority of a unified force. Fortunately, the need to cope with major incursions was still far distant.

Augustus' disposition of the legions was matched by his manipulation of the provinces: 'Of these he retained the most powerful on the grounds that they were insecure, either with enemies on their borders or themselves capable of rebellion. But his real purpose was that he alone should have arms and maintain soldiers.'[3] In short Augustus kept the outer, returning the inner provinces to the Senate. It was, as Dio states, a muted way of making himself commander-in-chief, for the army would be stationed only in the outer provinces which would be governed and administered by the emperor's appointees. At the same time it established his hold over foreign affairs and decisions of peace or war. Finally it meant that the future frontier would be under direct, imperial authority. This is a factor of some importance for the shape of our story. Unfashionable as it may be to reckon history in terms of kings or caesars, ours must especially emphasise Rome's rulers, for military and frontier responsibility was exclusively theirs. In Tacitus' words: 'Since Augustus so arranged it, the emperors alone earned the blame and praise for Rome's distant wars.'[4]

The division of territory into what Dio called the 'Senate's share' and 'Caesar's share' was accompanied by a ban on senators even visiting a frontier province without imperial permission: a clear indication that Augustus considered dissident senators and mutinous soldiers as the likeliest ingredients of conspiracy. To this we must add the rider that the Senate, with its centuries of experience, remained indispensable; and the emperors continued to rely on it for their senior officials, including provincial governors and legionary commanders. More broadly, partition of the provinces begins a divergence between inner and outer, in which the majority of Roman subjects become unfamiliar with the frontiers, unused to the sight of soldiers, incapable of self-protection and dependent for their safety on the remoter provincials.

In contrast with his revolutionary reforms of army and state, Augustus' view of the world – and of Roman claims to it – appears traditional. Evidence may be produced for his admiration of Alexander the Great, as well as for 'all who had uplifted Rome from her modest past to her glorious present'.[5] It can be deduced from Augustan literature that unlimited dominion was seen as a destiny decreed by heaven; or that the world was Rome's birthright, of which the empire was merely the part she found convenient to occupy.[6] But it will suffice to consider the facts of the reign: Egypt annexed, the Spanish conquest concluded, the Alpine lands and Balkans taken in hand: in short more territory acquired than by any other individual in Rome's history. Nor is there evidence that Augustus was seeking limits to the *imperium*. Though his armies had brought the Danube within reach, there was apparently no hurry to invest it as a frontier. On the contrary, his goals lay in yet more heroic projects, in still more aggressive and fluid warfare.

Next would be the conquest of Germany, initially to the Elbe. It was led by the emperor's stepsons: Drusus, who died on campaign, and then Tiberius. Sixteen years' struggle in mire and forest, amphibious landings and spectacular marches were rewarded with a succession of victories. A bold project, sometimes called the Bohemian Plan, was mooted as a culminating blow. Tiberius would cross the Danube heading north, snip off what is now the western end of the Czech Republic, descend into the German plain and join hands with an army group advancing eastwards from the Rhine. We may guess this would have brought the empire to a line through modern Vienna–Prague–Dresden–Magdeburg–Hamburg that would have been straighter and shorter than the Rhine–Danube axis. But nothing requires the assumption of either as a prospective frontier. The so-called Bohemian Plan may have been only one step in a larger offensive.

None would be implemented. Shortly before commencement of operations, a revolt erupted in Tiberius' rear and spread rapidly across the Balkans. To quell it required over half Rome's fighting strength, which became tied up for three years in a dangerous, mountain war. Meanwhile it seemed to Augustus that northern Germany, west of the Elbe, was sufficiently pacified to allow its organisation in legal and fiscal terms. The governor entrusted with this task was from the fringe of the imperial family: P. Quintillius Varus, jurist and administrator, experienced only in the mature provinces and a military novice. But Germany was unready for civilian rule, with its infrastructure of roads and forts incomplete and the army disinclined to winter far inside the conquered territory. Accordingly, in AD 9, at the end of his first summer in the new province, Varus and his party turned back toward the Rhine. The column consisted of three legions and auxiliaries with families, servants and a lengthy baggage-train. Poor intelligence and gullible leadership allowed it to be inveigled from its course. The large contingent of German auxiliaries then deserted. Varus struggled on through drenching rain. The German soldiers, augmented by all who could be mustered from the surrounding tribes, returned to ambush the column. In a three-day running fight the legions were eroded and the entire company annihilated at a location now believed to be ten miles northwest of Osnabrück. Varus and his staff chose suicide. Romans called it the Varian Disaster, also known as the battle of the Teutoburg Forest.

This calamity, closely following the Illyrican revolt, deeply disheartened the ageing Augustus. It carried the warning that there were two sorts of provincial: those already accustomed to taxes and laws, like the Greeks and Egyptians; and those recently wild and free, like the Illyricans and Germans. What is more, there were two kinds of land and two sorts of warfare. The developed state, with its roads, cities, organised army and central government had been captured relatively easily. The attacker could use the roads and strike towards the heart. The defender had no choice but to accept the sort of set-piece encounter at which Rome excelled. But what of trackless, townless countries, where authority was nebulous and the enemy dispersed and concealed? One recalls 146 BC, the astonishing year in which Rome encompassed the destruction of Carthage and Corinth and two empires tumbled ready-made into her lap. Such days were gone. Though Germany promised an agriculture comparable to Gaul's and a recruiting ground second to none, hostility was implacable and the developmental problems daunting.

The old emperor lived five years with the remorse of the Varian Disaster. In the summer of AD 14, after eating figs from his own garden fed to him by the empress Livia, his condition worsened; and the *amici* (counsellors) and other notables were summoned:

> Sending for his colleagues he gave them his instructions, finally adding, 'I found Rome brick, I leave it marble': meaning not merely the state of its buildings, but of the empire generally. Then, mockingly, he asked for a round of applause (as may be given to a comic actor at the conclusion of some mime): so ridiculing most tellingly the puny span of man.[7]

Thus he died on 19 August, by which month posterity remembers him. The death was concealed until Tiberius could be brought back from a visit to Dalmatia. On returning, he requested that documents be read to the Senate. These consisted of three notebooks, 'all written by Augustus in his own hand'.[8] The first contained instructions for the funeral. The second recorded all he had accomplished. 'The third was a statement of national resources, including the armed forces, the taxes to be levied and so on.'

This third part suggests the crudity of the imperial machine as well as its secretiveness, hinting as it does that the vital facts of empire were known only to the emperor and perhaps carried about his person. Be that as it may, there was a twist in the tail, for the final sentence contained Augustus' last admonition to his successors. Tacitus, with characteristic compression, puts this into five famous words: *consilium coercendi intra terminos imperii* (advice that the empire should be kept within its existing boundaries). Dio enlarges: 'His advice was that we should be content with what we now possessed. Under no circumstances should we seek to expand the empire. It would be difficult to defend and we might lose what we already had.'[9] This was an astonishing turnabout and a comment of immeasurable importance for the future frontier. The imperialist had recanted. After a reign which had cut broad swaths into the *barbaricum*,[10] the inference was that such things might never be seen again. For five stirring centuries Rome had taught her children that legions marched. Now the emperor's parting words were that they should sit. It was hardly an inspirational codicil to the Augustan age.

Augustus' advice put Tiberius in a quandary. On the one hand he saw his stepfather's dying wish as sacrosanct, or at least found it convenient to say so. For he too was older and wiser. Few knew better that Germany meant 'more forests, deeper swamps and an ever-savage enemy'.[11] On the other hand the Varian Disaster had left Rome baying for blood. A war of revenge had in fact been unleashed in Augustus' last year, and was now unstoppable. In command was Germanicus, Drusus' son, spurred by the wish to vindicate his father and restore Rome's honour. He too would spend three years in Germany. Writing to Tiberius he expressed the belief that given one more summer he could end resistance for ever. But Tiberius was tiring. The German war had gone on for twenty-eight years and was clearly repeating itself. Though Romans were defeating Germans, Rome was not defeating Germany. Tiberius was fond of saying that the deified Augustus had sent him nine times into Germania,[12] which added up to at least six years' field experience. During that time he must have come to realise how open-ended the task was, must have known that fresh tribes were still trickling down from the inexhaustible reservoir of the north,[13] and seen how the simultaneous effort on the Rhine and in the Balkans had exhausted the army; how even Roman shoulders lacked strength to carry the undeveloped world of central and eastern Europe.

As for Germanicus, he would have to make do with a Triumph, a coin issue, the consulate and a governorship in the East. As for the Germans: 'they could be left to their own, internal struggles'.[14] As for public opinion and the dream of endless empire: Tiberius replied with the tired comment, 'there have been successes enough already'.[15]

The subject of Germania was dropped. No one spoke of abandoning claims. No one announced the war's conclusion. Germanicus was simply recalled and not replaced. The army wintered on the Rhine but did not recross in the spring. Instead of patriotic fervour, silence now settled over the German front. Yet this was a meaningful silence, and from it the Roman imperial frontier imperceptibly grew. Imperceptibly, because the armistice was still being played to the public as a lull in attack rather than a commitment to defence. For the army too the adjustment would be gradual. All in all it is not surprising that the organisation of the Rhine's left bank into an efficient, tightly guarded frontier spread over fifty years. The Danubian armies followed suit. Tents were stowed and substantial buildings slowly replaced them as the norm of military life. Fort ramparts and turreted gates rose and villages sprouted outside them. Out of the security which is the soldier's gift to the civilian and the enterprise which is the civilian's gift to the soldier, towns will grow and small economic miracles will begin.

How suitable would Rhine and Danube be as frontiers? It is unlikely that the Roman psyche found difficulty in accepting them. In the Styx legend, myth had anticipated history. The custom of mounting grotesque figures, known as *termini*, on bridges suggests an ancient connection between Terminus, god of boundaries, and running water. The Tiber itself had been a prehistoric divide between nine tribal territories; and streams would later be the boundaries of Italy's eleven departments. In the 2nd century BC the Po was the Roman republic's border, as was the Rubicon[16] between Italy and Nearer Gaul. Most obviously, the Rhine and Danube were already the *de facto* edges of existing provinces, the former equipped with forts in connection with the German War. Their promotion to imperial frontiers can be seen as part of an evolution. On the other hand, the merit of river frontiers may be questioned on practical grounds. The spread of plant, animal and human species have seldom been halted by rivers. Rather they have tended to unify; to create civilisations, such as that of the Nile, and regions, such as the Rhineland; or economic unities, as expressed in the English 'side' (e.g. Merseyside, Tyneside). How do they compare in defensive potential with other natural obstacles? Seas, deserts, mountains and rivers, even marshes and thicket, all deter and delay. But hindrance is only half the matter. In practice, a river is the easiest obstacle to garrison. Water supply compared with a desert and food delivery compared with a mountain top are obvious advantages. A good, defensible river will be broader than the range of hand-thrown missiles, normally unfordable, difficult to swim, requiring engineering work to bridge and allowing ample time to anticipate an enemy's crossing by boat or raft. A river 100 yards wide begins to qualify, one of 150 yards is acceptable. Rhine and Danube are commonly three times this width. In the above senses, the Rhine offers a serviceable frontier from the moment of its debouch from the Alps. The Danube swells more gradually, but after receiving the flow of the Inn and several adjacent streams, it, too, becomes broad. It is Europe's longest river.[17] Herodotus called it 'the greatest river known to us'.[18] Together Rhine and Danube offer a defensible line from North Sea to Black Sea of

1,650 miles (2,750 km). The relatively short stretch where the Danube's headwaters are narrow is reinforced by the central Alps.

Given Roman technical superiority over those on the far bank, this was an obstacle which, suitably equipped with forts and a surveillance system, could be used to great advantage. The Roman navy would intercept intruders and float reinforcements quickly downstream. Related to this was the necessity for supplies, especially of groceries[19] and building materials. Land transport was the bane of the ancient world, with military destinies yoked to the lumbering ox-cart.[20] Due to the fodder requirement of draught animals it was uneconomical to move grain more than fifty miles. Apparently, it cost less to ship cargoes the entire length of the Mediterranean than to haul them seventy-five miles overland. This was an impasse which only two centuries of canal building, the railway age and the internal combustion engine would eventually break.

Returning to Augustus' *consilium*: we have seen that Tiberius considered it binding, and shunned foreign ventures, 'arranging external matters by diplomacy rather than weaponry'.[21] What of subsequent emperors? How permanent would the abandonment of expansion be? In the sense of indefinite expansion, no one would return to that illusion. In the sense of conquering Germany, that too was an enterprise no one would again take seriously. But in more limited adventures Augustus' last wish would be breached as often as observed. The maintenance of a steady-state empire cannot be regarded as a policy norm for more than a century yet. Meanwhile, there will be a mixture, even an alternation, of expansionist and non-expansionist emperors. But seldom if ever will there be a non-expansionist public. Rome's long, emotional legacy will incline her toward dreams of glory for many years to come. From now on an emperor seeking instant popularity will need only signal a resumption of the offensive to obtain it. In effect it will be insecure caesars who choose this course: for example Caligula, whose invasion of Britain halted at Boulogne; and Nero, whose drive for the Caspian Gates ended as abruptly as his life. And yet, despite imperial and public lack of interest in frontiers, the river barrier continued to strengthen. Once begun the process would become automatic, for those who command idle armies are always eager to put them to work and soldiers are seldom slow to improve their own protection.

In sum, Augustus and Tiberius bequeathed an army of 28 legions (each of 6,000 men), plus a like number of auxiliaries: about a third of a million men in all, who were, or would be, posted permanently to the empire's edges. Deployment followed something like the following pattern: Rhine 8 legions, Middle Danube 6, Lower Danube 2, Syria 4, Asia Minor 2, Egypt 2, Africa 1 and Spain 3. When Egypt and Spain had settled down, their legions too would be moved toward the frontiers. The auxiliaries, lower paid and of varying weaponry and ethnic origins, were light infantry and cavalry units, usually of 500 men. Besides adding flexibility to Roman tactics, they helped screen the larger units and reduce legionary casualties. The *auxilia*'s importance will grow as the frontier develops.

Facing these forces, with varying degrees of docility were, in Europe, from North Sea to Middle Danube, Germans; and from the Middle to Lower Danube, Sarmatians, a tribal group originating from the Eurasian steppe. In Asia were various Iranian peoples, principally the Parthians, plus the Arabian tribes; and in Africa Hamitic natives of the Ethiopian and Berber nations.

The army remained a quality instrument based on high standards of discipline and training; but only time would tell whether complacency and the custodial role corroded its fighting qualities. Rome's diplomatic talents had not deserted her. Foremost was co-option, her gift for merger with the nations in her path, of advancing by gathering support along the way. Nothing had been so essential, for it took more manpower by far than that born within Rome's city boundaries to acquire such territories. As Tacitus put it, '*provinciarum sanguine provincias vinci*'[22] (It is by provincial blood that provinces are won). We will see that this is also how they were held.

The frontiers were presently quiet. But such was the sea of peoples surrounding the empire that their large-scale mobilisation or concerted attack would have left its defenders hopelessly outnumbered. Augustus and his successors were able to make do with an army of modest size only because Rome's enemies were unlikely to achieve grand alliances or inter-racial combinations. Again to quote Tacitus: 'Nor have we weapon stronger against the strong than this: that they share no common purpose.'[23] 'Long may it last this – if not love for us – at least detestation of each other. Fortune grants us nothing greater than our enemies' disunity.'[24]

Thanks to the success of her soldiers and diplomats, Rome had expanded toward the limit of her strength, and now looked out onto largely hostile surroundings. Could she keep what she had won? Was she right to set foot on the path of rigid territorial integrity, to create a walled garden and exclude the rest of the world? Would internal difficulties and the inconsistencies of the Caesars allow her to make the best of this course? Or would the imperial frontier prove to be a Maginot Line, with all its dangers and delusions?

CHAPTER 2

Vespasian:
A Frontier Emerging

AUGUSTUS' ADVICE STOOD for almost thirty years till its first emphatic overturn in the invasion of Britain by his step-grandson, Claudius, in AD 43. This resumption of the offensive was doubtless applauded by a Roman public hungry for victory and the lavish celebrations it entailed. Nevertheless the problems which flowed from the British venture warn us against assuming that the strategic decisions of the early emperors will invariably be sagacious, or that the process of frontier creation will be positive and smooth.

Britain was not what she seemed. Smiling toward the Continent, her southward aspect masked a time-wasting Wales and a perilous and profitless north. Once committed, pride would forbid withdrawal, condemning the army to a century-long search for a line on which to stand. Britain would be Rome's least judicious choice of province, whose thriftlessness is emphasised by the fact that the Channel had provided an excellent frontier from the first. In crossing it Rome rejected Gaul as the northwestern limit of her dominion and with it the safety of salt water, from across which the Britons in any case posed no threat.

The lure of Britain lay not in strategic advantage but in newsworthiness: the romance and mystery of the place itself, as well as the stir created by extending Roman rule across 'outer ocean'. Caesar had shown it to be so. After his visit (ninety-seven years earlier) the Senate voted a twenty-day thanksgiving for the army's safe return. This was the sort of acclaim Claudius craved. With his stammer, his limp and his former role as the imperial family fool, this son and brother of successful generals needed successes of his own. But though the invasion would win him laurels, its end was less easy to predict. How much of Britain should Rome take; and where might a halting place be found?

The campaign was conducted by Aulus Plautius with four legions, of which the youthful Vespasian commanded one. While the main force crossed the Thames in the vicinity of future London, Vespasian overran the south and south-west, reducing some of the Celtic world's most formidable forts through his mastery of artillery.[1] It seems likely that he found in Exeter – as Plautius did in Lincoln – a suitable base; and that between these points a line of sorts was formed.

This is the Fosse Way, a later name for the strategic road which was soon to link the two fortresses. It would follow an already ancient track, one of the prehistoric ridge ways which avoided the thicket and mire of the valley bottoms by clinging to higher ground. What is to history 'the Fosse Way' is to geography 'the Limestone Ridge'. Yet surprisingly, in plain language, the feature is nameless, being more a concept than an entity. In fact it consists of four groups of hills,[2] with gaps between. Faithful to the slanting grain of England's structure, this discontinuous line runs south-west–north-east for 210 miles, from the south of Devon to north of Grantham, not far short of the highly defensible site of Lincoln itself. Faithful also to the gentleness of English topography, it is seldom higher than one thousand feet and often much lower; in places so low that the road or rail traveller crosses it without noticing.

Why did Plautius halt on this overlong and not overstrong line enclosing less than a third of Britain? Was this where the emperor had decided the province would end, or simply where the offensive ran out of steam? Was it a stopping place, a pausing place or a stalling place? The standard view has tended to be deferential to Rome: that the Fosse Way was the boundary of Roman Britain as Claudius saw it, that Plautius halted according to plan, that his instructions were to establish a definitive frontier on this line, that the province would be developed within it and treaties would guarantee peace outside it. Such opinions were perhaps encouraged by Roman frontier studies, which wanted there to be a frontier. Little has been found to support it: no dyke or ditch (despite the name 'fosse'), no signal towers and some big gaps between forts (though these may be filled by future finds). Further, no continuing effort was made to strengthen the position; and, of course, it was militarily unrealistic: too long, sited on a weak feature, without river backing; and its left flank uncomfortably close to the upland zones of Hereford and Gwent.

Whether plan or improvisation, the line ran Exeter–Honiton–Ilchester–Bath–Circencester (then, following today's A249) Bourton on the Water–Stow on the Wold, east of Leamington Spa, passing between Rugby and Coventry to Leicester (then following the A46) to Newark and Lincoln. Accepting that timber forts leave few traces and allowing for lost locations and urban overlay, this is a poor lot, both in terms of proven remains and worthwhileness of visiting. An exception is the Lunt, near Coventry Airport; cavalry fort and probable forward post of the Fosse Way scheme. Its AD 60–80 phase has been excavated and impressively reconstructed, despite limited means.[3]

Two other sites, marginally worth visiting, are Martinhoe and Old Burrow, on the north Devon coast either side of Lynmouth. These outposts watched the coast of Wales, 16–20 miles distant; from which the Silurian tribe glared back across the Bristol Channel. The fortlets, 80-foot square, are easily traceable. The residue of bonfires suggests signal contact with naval ships. Especially when evoked by appropriate weather, these clifftops are strong in margin-of-empire mood; with the Welsh shore mysteriously distant, while purple Exmoor looms to the rear. Thus far, dangerous and intractable lands were excluded. A step further and this would change: a more northerly stopline would have unfavourable terrain both in front and behind.

For the moment, let us leave the army deployed along its ridge and follow Vespasian's fortunes which, under Claudius' successor Nero, would be subject to melodramatic swings.

In Greece, as a member of the imperial entourage, he committed the most appalling *faux-pas*, either by walking out in the middle or falling asleep during the course of one of Nero's recitals. The upshot was total disfavour and dismissal from Court. He then fled to some obscure country town, where he went into hiding in fear of his life. But in the end he was offered a province and an army command.[4]

The province was Judaea. The command, to crush the Jewish rebellion of AD 67. 'In the end' meant at the age of fifty-eight, twenty-three years after he had last seen service in Britain. Why this sudden recall; this amnesty, so seldom offered by the unmerciful Nero? Because artillery was needed to oust the Jews from their walled cities; and someone remembered Vespasian's record against the mighty earthworks of southern Britain.

In AD 68 Vespasian directed the reduction of Jotapata, in northern Judaea, and began preparations for the siege of Jerusalem. Meanwhile, in Rome, time was running out for the line of Augustus. Disowned by the army and deserted by the guard, Nero chose suicide, inaugurating the desperate struggle known as the 'Year of the Four Emperors' (AD 69). Now Vespasian, safe in the east, could wait while the western claimants killed each other. When the time was right he would intervene decisively as *restitutor orbis*, putter-to-rights of a Roman world gone wrong. Such was the improbable path to power of T. Flavius Vespasianus who, in the ten years remaining to him as emperor, would do much to bring the army's blurred role into focus and make Rome's vague frontiers cogent and secure.

To the questions of empire Vespasian would apply the test of common sense. He tended to accept courses on which the state was already embarked, not questioning their rightness or wrongness, but whether they were well or badly implemented. Rome had decided to have fixed and formal frontiers: then let them work properly and be defended thoroughly. Along the eastern borders petty princedoms were proving incompatible with systematic control: then get rid of them and put in the Roman army. Money had been spent on invading Britain: then finish the job. Though not perhaps deep, here at least was straight thinking.

Among previous emperors we discern a curious, common factor: the absence of sons. Though there was neither rule nor clear precedent for succession, availability of a natural heir would certainly have eased this anxious process. Fortunately Vespasian was well supplied and now insisted that the Senate designate Titus and Domitian as 'caesars', a title which will increasingly mean 'heir apparent'.[5]

Having resolved the succession, Vespasian hastened to disembroil an empire turned inside out by civil war. Everywhere garrisons which had been withdrawn to fight for one or other of the contestants had left their frontiers bare. Heavy drafts out of Britain emboldened the tribes to void treaties, so sealing the Fosse Way's fate as a viable line and ending any illusion that peace might be maintained by sitting on a fence and hoping those outside would behave. Far worse, forts had been destroyed along the entire European waterfront from delta to delta. Batavia (the Netherlands) was in revolt; while the Chattans, opposite the Middle Rhine, and the Dacians, a Sarmatian people facing the Lower Danube, were crossing unhindered. Nothing better demonstrated Rome's grip than the result of relaxing it.

There was also a war to finish in Judaea, with Vespasian personally committed to the outcome and his elder son Titus now in charge of it. Thirty years of age, generous and glamorous where his father was homespun and stolid, Titus was nevertheless a ruthless commander. He had learned his father's artillery techniques and would push them to the limit. Jerusalem was reduced to rubble and its defenders to slavery.

The Jewish War demonstrates much about Roman views on fixed defences. The Romans saw siege as an aspect of offensive warfare. This is unlike our own view, moulded by the Middle Ages, when walls were strong in relation to ways of assailing them, making siege a waiting game. The difference is expressed in language. For example, the French *siège* means sitting. In Latin the word normally used was *oppugnatio*, an assault on. To the Romans, as we have seen, it was almost mandatory to attack, and by the same token to despise fixed defences, arising from a long tradition of aggressive warfare and an experience (in relation to the Greek and Carthaginian colonies) of town walls against which they had always prevailed. As the time approaches for the empire to adopt the defensive, these prejudices would not only make adaptation doubly difficult, but ensure that fixed frontiers were slow to gain acceptance in the public mind.

Judaea now provides a frontier which was both a prototype and a demonstration of how the concept of defended borders had, in some instances, predated Roman thinking. Indeed after so long on the attack it was inevitable that when the time came to defend, Rome would need to learn from others. The traditional limits of the Israelite domain, 'from Dan to Beer Sheba',[6] remind us that settlement had ended on the northern edge of the Negev desert, there yielding to herd folk, the Amalekites and Edomites; and that this had been a borderland since the early bronze age (3rd millennium BC) against 'the children of the east (who had) entered into the land to destroy it'.[7] Biblical references imply that from Solomonic times (9th century BC) defence consisted of towers along the desert's edge, backed by walled or palisaded towns. Though Old Testament boundaries are somewhat elastic, we may take the traditional limit of arable land and today's 8-inch rainfall isohyet as guides to the region of perennial protection, north of a line between the southern Dead Sea and the Mediterranean coast at Gaza.

It is probable that on the completion of Titus' campaign it was decided to reject the badlands of the Negev and Sinai as inoperable in terms of Roman taxation (assessed on cultivated fields or property and organised in relation to fixed communities) and to revive the anciently defended border against nomad tribes who might be expected to continue their habit of encroaching northwards in time of drought. This frontier would be 75 Roman miles (69 miles, 110 km) in length and run from the Dead Sea to the Mediterranean perhaps 15 miles south of Gaza. It consisted of a line of forts and towers, without continuous barrier such as ditch, mound or wall. Walking the northern Negev in the late 1950s, Professor Mordechai Gichon of Tel Aviv University discovered the remains of some seven forts, thirteen fortlets and two dozen block houses or road stations, by no means a final count. This does however include the supplements of later centuries, giving little idea of original strength. The works were of local stone, with walls of squared blocks and rubble core. Advantageous ground was used, such as south-facing slopes or the northern banks of streams. Lookout towers were ranged on hilltops behind and in front of the line, up to three miles inside 'enemy territory'. This allowed forts to be sited in valleys with limited visibility, but where water was most available and food could be grown. Other towers guarded fields, wells and link roads. Some foundations are without doorways, implying entrance at upper floor level by means of a retractable ladder. By the early 1970s Professor Gichon had listed 'over a hundred towers with Roman or Byzantine pottery', though 'only one had been excavated at the time of writing'.[8]

In Europe, Vespasian surveyed the ruin resulting from neglect of the Rhine and Danube defences in the months following Nero's suicide. Evidently both rivers had been crossed almost at will, with the Roman mound-and-stockade forts on the nearer banks burnt and trampled by German and Dacian. Now they would be rebuilt in stone: made strong, fireproof and rainproof, ending the need for constant repair to washed-out earthwork and wasting woodwork. It was a symbolic as well as a practical step. By substituting masonry for timber, the permanent for the makeshift, Rome was giving notice that she was here to stay. To the army it was a signal which said 'this far and no further'; a promise of home and peace to soldiers who had known only tents and lulls.

Refortification on the 1,700-mile line of the long rivers was too big a project to be entered lightly. It can only have reflected a deliberate decision not just to hold existing ground but to resist acquiring new. Thousands of legionaries now became instant quarrymen, masons, brickmakers, limemakers and tilers; hundreds of sailors became bargees and lightermen. The rivers plan asked for new forts, roads, bridges and ports as well as the rebuilding of old. Continued by Vespasian's sons it would occupy the rest of the century, quickening the riparian frontiers towards their 2nd-century condition, when legions would be approximately a hundred miles apart, auxiliary units fifteen miles,[9] with a fine mesh of fortlets and watchtowers between; so placing every part of the bank under surveillance, with assistance never far away.

Siting forts was tricky, especially between Basle and Mainz and on parts of the Hungarian Danube, where inundation and riverbed movement were common. Many prehistoric sites were reused, especially on the Danube where Roman fort names often include the Celtic *dunum* (fortified place). Their pre-Roman origins gave promise of freedom from flood. Similarly, Roman strategic roads usually followed iron age riverbank tracks, while ports were takeovers of native moorings and ferry crossings. Where there had been sole reliance on river traffic it was now doubled by road. The Danube's calmer reaches and the Upper Rhine regularly froze from December to February,[10] and there were drops in level prior to freeze and during drought. Danger was then compounded, since streams became most fordable by the barbarians when least navigable by the Roman navy. The rivers were now bridged, or the bridges restored, opposite all legionary fortresses, sometimes with a fort on the far side to guard the bridgehead. Treaties with tribes adjacent to the eastern banks were mended.

On the Lower Rhine, the double fortress of Vetera (Xanten), a focus of mutiny, was rebuilt on a new site at single-legion size. There were now four legions: at Nijmegen, Xanten, Neuss and Bonn. The fleet, considerably strengthened, had its headquarters at Altburg, two miles south of Cologne. The Upper Rhine also had four legions: two at Mainz and one each at Strasbourg and Windisch (Switzerland). For some time the Mainz legions had looked enviously at fertile pockets on the German side, which promised better food supply than the hilly hinterland on their own. For this reason they had built forts across the river, on the lower Main and Neckar. These were restored by Vespasian and their number increased, probably reflecting a decision to keep a closer watch on the Chattan tribe, in view of what was about to follow.

The great crook in the European frontier, caused by the Rhine's sharp turn at Basle, had proved irksome to troop movement and obstructive to the functioning of the Rhine–Danube axis as a strategic whole. In 73–4 Vespasian's general, Cornelius Clemens, annexed the southwestern corner of Germany, so opening a direct route from Strasbourg to Augsburg and the Upper Danube. A road was built during the remainder of the decade, reducing the Basle detour by 150 miles. This, plus completion of the riverbank roads, would mean a continuous highway from North Sea to Black Sea, anticipating Europe's motorway ambitions by nineteen centuries. The move may be seen not as a reversion to Augustan expansion but a limited act of frontier rectification. Even so, it would not be as limited as Vespasian hoped. The new road needed protection from the restive Chattans to its north, which involved a deepening commitment on the Main and Neckar. An even better corner-cutting operation, from Mainz to the Danube, would then beckon.

On the Upper Danube legions were still deemed unnecessary. The frontier faced a thinly peopled area, while to its south the Eastern Alps provided a strong shield for Italy. Accordingly this 350-mile stretch was covered only by the auxiliary armies of Raetia (Bavaria) and Noricum (Austria) with a thin line of infantry cohorts and cavalry wings. These were now augmented by reinforcing Claudius' forts on the Danube headwaters and adding others, further down, at Linz, Wallsee, Mautern, Traismaur, Zwentendorf, Zeiselmaur, Klosterneuburg, and so on. It is interesting how many of those Austrian town and village names include *maur*[11] in memory of Roman masonry or of later walls which used it. In two of these instances medieval castles follow fort outlines and in four cases churches stand over the former *principiae* (headquarters buildings) which contained the regimental chapels, forming a religious link of long duration. Such associations, plus the even more obvious one of continuous occupation from that day to this, typify the Roman frontier in continental Europe; though unbroken ties are less common elsewhere.

Beginning a few miles above Vienna was the province of Illyricum.

This was now divided into Dalmatia (western Croatia) and the frontier province of Pannonia (eastern Austria, western Hungary), whose forts would be the origin of three national capitals to be: Vienna, Budapest and Belgrade. From now on Pannonia would be a key province: midway on the Danube, facing two directions of attack[12] and commanding the passes across the Julian Alps, sole eastern gateway to Italy. Here were the ingredients of dilemma: for while the external responsibilities of the new province merited an establishment of four legions, internal security suggested none. Though Pannonia had come out in Vespasian's favour during the struggle for succession, her position on the road to Rome was perfect for participation in the politics of *coup d'état*. Vespasian compromised and gave her two.

A fort was now built at Vindobona, whose first syllable gave its German name Wien (Vienna). The garrison here was British: *ala I Flavia Britannica milliaria*, a crack cavalry wing, a thousand strong and double normal size. Because of rapids above, Vienna was a traffic terminus and also offered an island, which facilitated bridging. Across river it faces what is today the Marchfeld,[13] a plain narrowing northwards into the Moravian Gap, making it the perfect base for rapid response against the southeastern Germans. The fort would be enlarged into a legionary fortress at a later date, its walls surviving as the city walls for many centuries, with medieval Vienna crowding inside. The local legionary base and Pannonia's capital was, however, Carnuntum, fifteen miles downstream from Vienna and almost opposite the Morava's entry into the Danube. A Tiberian foundation, now rebuilt in stone, it lies near the village of Petronell, under wheatfields through which aerial scrutiny shows buildings and streets. Below Carnuntum the Middle Danube may have had five or six auxiliary forts, including one under today's Budapest, also a future legionary base. All coincided with road ends linking ultimately with Italy. Vespasian would increase the forts to about ten.

The Lower Danube's defences remained backward. Vespasian divided Moesia into two provinces, Upper and Lower; an inevitable reform given the 500-mile length of its river frontage. Two legions were already in today's Bulgaria, at Novae (near Svishtov) and Oescus (near Gigen), only 55 miles apart. These faced Dacia (Transylvania), a direction dark with menace. Like most sites on the Bulgarian-Romanian Danube, they are worth viewing; though here we enter the later Eastern Empire, beneath whose subsequent fortifications most earlier structures lie hidden. Down river to the Black Sea, the best part of 300 miles, there was as yet no legionary fortress. Lower Moesia (today's Romanian Black Sea province of Dobruja) still relied on naval patrols from Noviodunum (Ghergina), just above the delta. Construction of the riverside road was now in hand and the auxiliary army was boosted to some fifteen forts containing 7,500 men. To see this in perspective: the two Rhine commands each had more than six times that number to guard half the mileage. Though improvements were in hand, this was still a corner of the empire whose neglect was proportional to distance from the centre.

Finally, there is the delta, forty-five miles in length between the branching of the main stream and the Black Sea coast. Here, held between three main arms, lie seventeen hundred square miles of egret-haunted, willow-hung wetland, with endless lagoons and winding streams. The northern channel, now the Romanian–Moldovan border, is presently biggest; but the nearer, St George Channel, was almost certainly the imperial frontier,[14] controlled from the rising ground to the south and based on the fort of Salsovia (Mahmudia). The actual delta offered few firm sites and was doubtless malarial.

South of the Danube mouths the frontier should have crossed the Black Sea to the Pontic port of Trapezus (Trabzon, Turkey), east of which lay Armenia. Such a maritime line did not however exist, even in theory. To patrol half a sea made little sense and the Black Sea fleet needed a foothold at the eastern end in case of trouble in that unstable region. Nero had muddied the water by seeking to revive Caesar's dream of the Black Sea as a Roman lake. The venture languished on his death and Vespasian did not revive it. He would nevertheless leave a detachment at Harmozica, near Tbilisi. From this base the army would patrol as far as the Caspian, as suggested by the discovery of the name of a centurion of *legio XII Fulminata*, carved on a hillside near Baku, in Azerbaijan.[15] Nineteen hundred miles in a straight line from Italy, this is the easternmost doodle of imperial Rome.

In support of Harmozica Vespasian probably retained the auxiliary fort at Apsarus (Gonio, near Batumi) at the Black Sea's eastern extremity, and also those of Sebastopolis (Sukhumi) and Phasis (south of today's Poti).[16] Here was a trio of strongpoints which could control peacetime trade and wartime supply, initiating the policy of holding the eastern Black Sea by a semicircle of coastal forts, a day's sail apart, projecting deep into barbarian territory and supported by sea. The headquarters of the Black Sea fleet had been advanced from Tomis to Trapezus in order to be closer to the Armenian theatre and this arrangement was retained.

Vespasian's most memorable achievement was as architect of Rome's eastern frontier. In this he was spurred both by knowledge of Parthian recovery and his own experience of the east, with its ramshackle defensive arrangements. The sector can best be seen in halves: Asia Minor and Syria, with their different geographies. They also faced different neighbours: Armenia in the north and Parthia in the south; though in the sense that Armenia was commonly under Parthian control, these were aspects of one problem. It will be useful to describe these adversaries, as well as the Roman provinces facing them.

The Parthian empire was larger than today's Iran, for it included what is now Iraq and Afghanistan. One may wonder why much the same empire was called different things at different times: Median, Persian, Parthian and Iranian. This is due to the successive supremacy of parts over the whole. The adjective Iranian may be used to describe general characteristics. Confusing to the modern reader is the absence of Arabs from the Tigris-Euphrates basin. Here were the Parthian provinces of Babylonia and Assyria, corresponding to today's southern and northern Iraq. Assyria[17] shared a common frontier with Roman Syria.

Confusing too is the absence of Turks from Asia Minor. Armenia, anciently bigger than the modern republic of that name, included the eastern quarter of present Turkey. Racially and linguistically Iranian, Armenia is comparable to Tibet in standing above and striving to be free of its two big neighbours. Both coveted this mountain country, not for its intrinsic worth, but to overlook the other. Though a longstanding bone of contention, Armenia was only the back door between the two empires. The front was via the Euphrates, a direct route which could feed and water large armies. Invasion via the Tigris was more difficult but nevertheless feasible.

In summary, here were empires of roughly equal strength, neither sufficiently powerful to eliminate the other. Both were able defenders and each empire's centre was beyond the other's reach. Parthia proper (today's Iran) is a mountainous land, especially uninviting to an attacker from the west. Her decisive arm was heavy cavalry. Selective breeding had produced mounts which could not only carry armoured men but wear chain mail themselves. This, plus the development of mounted archery, had been the making of Parthian imperialism, keeping the steppe nomads at bay and allowing the unification of extensive lands. But Parthia also had her share of disadvantage. Her rival provinces, restless for independence or ascendancy, frustrated the triumph of central power. And yet the Parthians commanded deference, the only outside civilisation with which Rome had direct contact and the only neighbour of whom they never used the word barbaricum. Above all they were respected as enemies:

> Those smash-and-grab peoples, who have been such a bane to us, I would count rather as thieves than enemies. Alone among men the Parthian bears the name of 'enemy of the Roman people' in a manner we must never hold in contempt; as is well illustrated by the defeats of Crassus and Mark Antony . . .[18]

The clash of Rome and Parthia had lost the meaning it had when, at Salamis and Marathon, the West's future hung by a thread. Especially fruitless was the prolonged head-butting of the two rams over the Armenian ewe. For their part, the Romans never forgot the glamour of Alexander the Great, augmented by that of Pompey. Through long tradition, glory dwelt in the east, where laurels were greenest and revenge sweetest. But while the Orient remained an ultimate focus for Roman megalomania, war was in fact rare.[19] Expeditions were costly and required much preparation, while raids were debarred by drought and distance. The norm was therefore peace, though peace without trust.

At the western end of this cold war lay Asia Minor, entirely under Roman ownership except for its eastern extremity. The interior, superficially Hellenised but racially Iranian, had consisted of small kingdoms, leftovers from the empire of Alexander. Last to be annexed had been Cappadocia, which passed into Tiberius' hands in AD 17. This dry plateau and mountain was neglected and undermanned, its contact with Armenia being managed by the intermediate, 'friendly kingdoms' of Commagene and Lesser Armenia. Beyond was Armenia proper: 'ambiguous Armenia',[20] in and out of Parthia's pocket.

Such was the Cappadocia which awaited Vespasian's attention: fifty years in Roman hands, still void of roads and legions, yet central to a strategy long overdue for definition. Here a frontier must be made from scratch: comparable to those of Europe, which already had a three-generation lead. A surviving 'friendly kingdom' impeded the project. Commagene was still responsible for that part of the Euphrates which faced the invasion route via the Tigris. Typically, its defensive arrangements probably consisted of a walled capital, in this case Samosata (Samsat, Turkey), a royal bodyguard and a part-time army on call in emergency. Vespasian doubtless believed that if the eastern frontier were to be firmly held this meant full-time soldiers under direct control. Re-annexation[21] of this small ally would allow a Roman river frontage all the way down to Syria.

The distance across Anatolia, from Black Sea to Syrian border, is some 300 miles. Three ranges lie crosswise (see Map 1). The Pontic Range, climbing steeply from the Black Sea coast, is the highest, with peaks at 10,000 and passes up to 6,000 feet, blocked from four to five months by snow. Next is the Central or Anti-Taurus and finally the southern or Kurdish Taurus, both over 6,000 feet, with peaks rather higher. The Euphrates, rising in the region of Erzurum, flows westwards in the trough between the first and second of these chains. It then swings south, carving deep clefts through the Anti-Taurus and Kurdish Taurus. These gorges are the most spectacular features along the edges of the Roman world; and also the most impregnable. Their depth is as great as 1,300 feet, falling in a series of terraces, sometimes wide, sometimes sheer and narrow. Though in scale only a quarter of the Grand Canyon, the impression is not dissimilar. It is this south-flowing part of the Euphrates, from approximately Erzincan to the Syrian border (two thirds of the distance across Anatolia) which offered Vespasian a defence against the east to make military mouths water.

There were nevertheless snags. The height of the canyon's rim made it irksome of access and intensely cold in winter. On the river below, white water rendered long stretches unnavigable and there would be no Euphrates Fleet in support. Further the gorges are inter-mittent, with many side valleys and fords. Water levels are subject to sharp rises and falls. In short the Turkish Euphrates has neither the continuity nor dependability of Rhine and Danube, though it offered a spectacular basis for defence. Legionary fortresses could plug the gaps between the main ranges, auxiliary forts the lesser valleys. A trunk road would be indispensable, but due to gradient and snowdrift it could not always follow the river closely. Loops and spur roads would be essential, though these too would be exposed to snow.

The frontier across eastern Asia Minor, though among the most stirring, is one of the least studied, owing to geographical factors and the long closure of eastern Turkey to outsiders. Hasty forays by nineteenth-century British consuls were followed by Freya Stark's, overland and by raft, described by that distinguished traveller in her *Rome on the Euphrates* (1966). Though the pace of investigation has since quickened, it remains the preserve of the intrepid individual, often on foot; and results have been modest. Does this reflect the scarcity of seekers or of things sought? Certainly, by contrast with other frontiers there seems a curious shortage of remains such as forts, fortlets, watchtowers and milestones. Aerial survey might answer the question, but military governors seldom welcome it.

> The physical remains of the Roman frontier in Cappadocia have proved elusive, indeed it is probably safe to say that they are amongst the least substantial traces of any frontier in the empire. No aerial survey has been carried out. Travel conditions are not always easy and sometimes recall the fears expressed by Wm. Camden[22] on approaching the central sector of Hadrian's Wall in 1598.[23]

T. B. Mitford's method of walk and talk is a homely but sound approach to field survey,[24] allowing time to look, think and glean information from those encountered *en route*. As Dr Mitford says, some have doubted there was a formal frontier across Turkey at all: a view dispelled in no small measure by his own contributions in identifying the main road system and the outline of a fortified scheme.

> Doubt has continued to surround the very existence of an ordered frontier comparable in length with the German but facing an organised and formidable enemy; garrisoned ultimately by four legions and enduring without substantial modification from Vespasian to Justinian. Discussion has been hesitant, identification haphazard.[25]

The major military road from the Black Sea to the present Turkish-Syrian border was begun by Vespasian and finished by his sons. High mountains dictated divergences of up to twenty-five miles from the river. The surviving map of the Roman empire, the Peutinger Table (now in the Austrian National Library, Vienna), shows it and lists stations. Assuming these were forts and the usual seven miles apart, some are recognisable on the ground and some are not; few have been matched to their ancient names and none excavated. Though in theory plottable, uneven terrain and water supply resulted in erratic spacing. In the north, between the Black Sea and the Euphrates' southward turn, the frontier is presumed to have been the road itself. Unfortunately, on this stretch, no part of the present-day road is demonstrably Roman, though this is not to say that none existed. The paving, for which Roman roads are famous, tended only to be laid on prestigious stretches. In remoter regions roads were often surfaced with tamped gravel or packed stone fragments, materials which may be indistinguishable from those of later ages.

As for the general principle of a road frontier, we will find this common enough. It is in fact likely that the idea of the outermost road of an exterior province serving as its boundary was the starting point of most cross-country (non-riverine) frontier stretches; and that more elaborate patterns, including various sorts of man-made barrier, evolved from it. This is compatible with Roman traditions of land survey, in which plot boundaries consisted of perimeter paths. Frontier roads would normally be patrolled, equipped with watch-towers and backed by forts, making them simultaneous lines of control, surveillance and defence. Whether running behind a river, an overland barrier, or constituting the frontier itself, roads were indispensable for supply and tactical movement. They also allowed strategic movement, since emergencies on one frontier were normally met by reinforcement from another. This is why arterial roads would in due course run from Rhine delta to Danube delta and from Black to Red Sea. Internally, feeder roads would connect each frontier with the imperial network so that, at least theoretically, every military unit was road-linked to its commander-in-chief on the Palatine Hill: all in all a remarkable accomplishment. However, in the case of the presumed road between the Black Sea and Upper Euphrates, the lack of tower and fort remains, as well as the absence of milestones, continue to keep us guessing about the true nature of this 120-mile stretch.

Trapezus (modern Trabzon) is, then, the presumed start on the Asian continent of a Roman frontier which will not see salt water again till its termination at Aqaba, nearly 900 miles distant.[26] In origin a Greek colony, Trabzon's upper town, enclosed by Justinianic walls, contains the ruins of a Byzantine palace and several churches.

This sad corner of West-in-East was the last capital of East Rome for here, protected by sea and mountain, the Comneni family held out until 1461, eight years after Constantinople's fall. So it may be said that this is where the last spark of Rome was extinguished, 2,214 years after the legendary birth of Romulus. Trabzon hung on, a ghost of Byzantium, till exorcised by the Greek exodus of 1918, though in romantic eyes haunted yet.[27]

From ricefields and nut orchards the southbound road rises steeply to the Pass of Zigana at 6,200 feet. In the trough beyond was the base at Satala, where Vespasian put his new legion, *XVI Flavia*, commanding the approach to Armenia via modern Leninakan. Its Byzantine walls, like battered dental crowns encasing Roman stumps, beckon the would-be excavator. After a long gap of 250 land- and river-miles comes a second legionary fortress, Melitene (Malatya), facing the Murat. No site better exemplifies the Pandora's box of eastern archaeology. The Vespasianic fortress, occupied and altered during much of the Roman period, was rebuilt by Justinian. Destroyed by the Persians it was taken by the Arabs, retaken by the Byzantines and redestroyed by the Seljuk Turks. It was then occupied by the Armenians, captured by the Mongols and ravaged again by Tamerlane in 1395. It fell to the Ottomans in 1575 but was destroyed again during the war with Mehemet Ali in 1838. Of course, such 'destructions' are seldom total. Each seals in a part of the last. But even assuming excavation to high standards: which level would have priority, which would be preserved, which displayed?

Beyond Melitene lay two, ford-controlling fortresses: Samosata (Samsat), capital of the recently annexed Commagene, in the southern foothills of the Kurdish Taurus; and Zeugma, where the Euphrates emerges onto the Syrian plain. These blocked approaches toward Antioch and the Mediterranean. Samosata is now under the waters of the Atatürk barrage, with neither the old capital nor the fortress of *legio XVI Flavia firma* archaeologically investigated. Both on the Euphrates and the Lower Danube, dams (or rather the lakes they create) are engulfing uncounted remains. Uncounted in the sense that while some are inundated without being excavated, others are lost before they have even been found.

Prior to descending into the Syrian plain let us try to sum up on Anatolia's defensive scheme. The gorges remain a mystery. That they were the backbone of the defensive position seems clear from the military installations which punctuate them and the road which shadows them. Yet proof of tactical control remains in short supply. We must assume tower chains, since the gorge's lip offers stupendous views toward Armenia while legionary bases and forts lie in the valleys below. The evidence of almost all other frontier sectors points to the fundamentality of watchtower surveillance. On the other hand we must remember that on the Roman side 400 miles of thinly peopled country lay behind this border before the rich province of Asia[28] was reached. Raids were of less consequence than on other frontiers and Armenia had no special reputation for inflicting them. The real danger, from Parthia, was big but rare. Surveillance might therefore have been less essential than on other frontiers.

Roman Syria, though then including today's Lebanon and a bite of southern Turkey, was without the large triangle of land between Euphrates and Tigris which is northeast Syria today. This would not pass into Roman ownership until a later period. The capital Antioch (today's Antakya, in Turkey) and the northwest corner generally was a populous region, richer then than now. Syria was a mercantile land, formerly the centre of seafaring Phoenicia but also, in an inland sense, a crossroads between Anatolia and the Levant, Mesopotamia and the Mediterranean. South-eastwards begins the desert, widening rapidly to 750 miles between the Gulfs of Persia and Aqaba. It can be crossed only via the stepping stone of the Palmyran oasis and then with difficulty. The Parthian pendulum oscillated slowly, casting its intermittent shadow across the region. Augustus had placed a large army in the Syrian province. This consisted of four legions, together the queen in Rome's eastern chess game. The worries of Syria's governor were many: proud Parthia, the never-to-be-reconciled Jews, the ambiguous Palmyrenes, the bickering bedouin, plus allied kingdoms of varying constancy. His four legions did not man a frontier (it would perhaps have been difficult to decide which way to face) but sat in the middle of a Syria whose citizens were themselves fickle and riot-prone.

The Syrians were a part-Hellenised, Semitic people whose language, Syriac, is a recognisable descendant of Hebrew and parent of Arabic. The upper class spoke Greek. Before Roman annexation in 64 BC, Syria had been the heart of the Seleucid empire[29] and Antioch its capital. During this period population pressure had pushed farming into the desert fringes and protection from nomad raids was needed even before the province became Roman. Thus, from an eastward direction, Roman Syria faced two dissimilar dangers: the

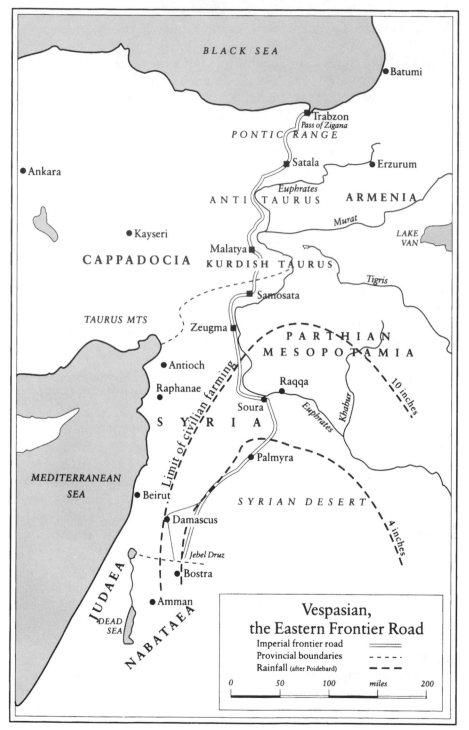

BLACK SEA

• Batumi

Trabzon
Pass of Zigana

PONTIC RANGE

• Ankara

Satala

• Erzurum

Euphrates

ANTI TAURUS   ARMENIA

Murat

LAKE
VAN

• Kayseri

CAPPADOCIA   Malatya

KURDISH TAURUS

Tigris

Samosata

TAURUS MTS   Zeugma

PARTHIAN
MESOPOTAMIA

Limit of civilian farming

• Antioch

Raphanae
•

S   Y   R   I   A   Raqqa

Soura

Euphrates   *Khabur*   *10 inches*

MEDITERRANEAN
SEA

• Palmyra

SYRIAN DESERT

• Beirut

Damascus
•

Jebel Druz

4 inches

JUDAEA

Bostra
•

DEAD
SEA

• Amman

NABATAEA

Vespasian,
the Eastern Frontier Road

Imperial frontier road
Provincial boundaries
Rainfall (after Poidebard)

0   50   100   *miles*   200

Parthian, occasional but large, and the nomad, continual but small. The response was two levels of defence: patrolling the desert's edges – an auxiliary function – with the legions held centrally in reserve. Regarding the latter, this created a situation which was the common soldier's dream: stationing in cities. Since no fortress is known from ancient writ or has been discovered on the ground, it can only be presumed that the legions lived in military enclaves within built-up areas, not easily distinguishable from other remains and in most cases now hidden under modern cities. This is in striking contrast to the northern armies in their 'cowtowns' of leather tents and wooden duckboards. Not surprisingly the Syrian legions won themselves the worst press in the Roman army. Thus Fronto, later 2nd century:

> The Antioch garrison, more often in the bars than in the ranks, spent their time applauding actors. Horses were shaggy from neglect, riders expertly groomed; horses saddled with goosedown cushions, riders better dressed than armed. Few could mount without puffing and blowing and most threw spears about as well as a child throws toys. Gambling was frequent; sleep undisturbed by guard duties, unless it was guarding the wine cups![30]

Twelve years prior to Vespasian this balmy spell had been broken by the arrival of Domitius Corbulo, Nero's ablest general who, in expectation of a Parthian attack via Armenia, marched some units up to the freezing Anatolian plateau and moved others up to the line of the Syrian Euphrates; which he defended by adapting river craft as gunboats, moored at strategic points: ready-made forts, pending the building of real ones. Tacitus tells us that as part of his rearward defences Corbulo 'built forts to protect key water sources behind the line of the river, destroying unprotected wells by filling them with sand'.[31] Here we have a blueprint for the Syrian frontier, soon to receive Vespasian's attention. He would follow Corbulo's plan, using the river against Parthia (as far as its course allowed) and water-hole control as the means to command the desert and its wayward tribes.

The Euphrates, flowing into the Syrian plain, was navigable and wide: a good defensible line except for one drawback and that without remedy; before long, its direction changes from south to southeastward. This made it a retreating frontier and one of diminishing utility, passing all too soon into Parthian territory. Accordingly it was decided that the frontier must bid the Euphrates farewell at Sura

(Souriya, a little west of today's Raqqa) and strike overland, south to Palmyra, then southwest to Bostra (Busra), beyond which Roman territory ended (Nabataea, now Jordan, being still an independent state). So the Euphrates, having obliged Rome for 250 miles now shifted peremptorily into Parthia, ensuring by this removal that the larger part of Syria's frontier would be overland and across desert. In view of the desert's width and severity it would not be an ineffectual boundary, though in all respects different from that further north. Regarding its character we must turn to a pioneering figure in the story of the frontier's redemption from obscurity.

Antoine Poidebard, S.J. (1878–1955), was born in Lyons and entered the Jesuit order at nineteen. He was sent to Armenia on missionary work, returning to France in 1914 as a chaplain on the Western Front, ending the war in the chaos of the post-revolutionary Caucasus. Seeking quieter goals, he attended the University of St Joseph, Beirut, receiving a chair in 1924. Two influences shaped his destinies. The first was the Syrian Mandate. In 1920 the League of Nations had awarded the trusteeship of Syria with Lebanon to France; and, to Britain, Iraq, Jordan and Palestine, former provinces of the Ottoman empire considered not yet ready for independence. All would remain in quasi-colonial status till the late 1940s. Here was a region of incalculable importance for the study of antiquity, under Western administrations for the first time since the crusades.

The other influence on Poidebard would be aerial photography. Its birth had arisen from the simultaneous, late-nineteenth-century enthusiasms for photography and ballooning. War transformed novelty into necessity. A memorable product of the First World War was the work of O. G. S. Crawford (1866–1957), an archaeologist who brought his experience as Royal Flying Corps observer to solving the basic problems of aerial analysis in the post-war period.[32] It had long been evident how low lighting emphasised relief, revealing old features with a clarity entirely new. The biggest bonus remained to be realised. From the early 1920s Crawford began to understand the differential drying of disturbed ground and the differential growth of plants in response to it, with vegetation lusher above former hollows or ditches and sparser above walls or mounds. In the Middle East, parch marks and their opposite, crop marks, are especially pronounced during seasons of transition and can give a striking picture of what lies beneath. Roads show clearly, though for another reason. The great majority of desert is not sand and dune but gravel, stones and boulders, often strewn over a firm surface. Here Roman roads were usually created simply by clearing away the stony litter, using the larger rocks as kerbing. Roaming camels still follow them, less hard on their pads than the natural desert, so that their surfaces are freshly trodden and more visible in turn.

Responding to the opportunity of the mandate, grasping the potential of the aeroplane and resolving to teach himself photography from scratch, Père Poidebard badgered the colonial government for support in conducting a general aerial survey. With the cooperation of the French Air Force he would eventually complete 250 missions, mainly in a Potez 25 reconnaissance biplane with open cockpits. This aircraft could fly slowly and land almost anywhere. On one occasion, at zero altitude and on the verge of stalling, Poidebard claimed to have read a Roman milestone in flight! He did not set out with a mission to find a frontier. Initially, the flying Jesuit had little notion of what he might find. He began by photographing the Syrian *tels* (occupation mounds). Soon he was able to distinguish roads, some leading eastward, into the desert. Then watchtower foundations and fort walls began to appear through the sand. Finally hydraulic works were identified: reservoirs, dams, channels, aqueducts and the former fields by which the army supported itself on the desert's margins. What was emerging was quite unlike the European frontiers, based upon the unmistakable lines of rivers. These works were diffused, forming a web of surveillance based upon a network of secondary roads. Though the official boundary was probably the main road closest to the enemy (the patrolled highway Sura–Palmyra–Bostra), it had little validity in military terms. Unlike a river, a desert is not a linear obstacle, but a barrier in depth, able to wear down the invader by worsening his waterlessness day after day. The defender has no need to fight on a line. Rather he lets the width of the desert fight for him.

There is a second element which makes desert frontiers unlike others and that is nomadism. Here again, the desert does not lend itself to delineation. Its extent changes with the seasons. Its margins are vague and so are its people. To impose prohibition of movement across some arbitrary line is a declaration of war upon nomadism. In view of Parthian influence in the desert's eastern half, Rome naturally wanted a friendly population in the western section. On the other hand, unlimited freedom for the bedouin is a prescription for trouble, especially where grazing and farming meet. Fortunately the solution to the nomad problem and the Parthian problem was much the same: oasis control, which at one level could be used as a stick to beat the bedouin, at another to block a major enemy by destroying his water supply.

It will be clear that both types of countermeasure favoured the use of auxiliaries. Not only were they cheaper and more mobile but it would be easier to feed small units under desert conditions. The general rule seems to have been that garrisons should support themselves, except in grain and perhaps meat. Depending on circumstances even these might be in part farmed by soldiers or their dependants, in part purchased (or levied in lieu of taxes) from farmers not far distant. But here were garrisons well beyond the normal limits of farming. How were they fed? A brief answer is that the army disposed of a workforce sufficient to create catchment and irrigation systems in regions not considered worthwhile for civilian farming. The visitor, seeing evidence of this cultivation where none exists today, may assume either climatic change or regional decline. Neither need be the case. Roman army agriculture was, in today's parlance, subsidised; not in the sense of grants but in the provision of initial works and free labour. What is more it did not have to show a profit. In bad times shortage could be averted by outside supply or the temporary reduction of garrisons.

Poidebard was the first to recognise that in arid regions a Roman frontier can be related to a modern rainfall map.[33] The frontier which he revealed consisted of a patrolled zone with a road network, some 65 miles deep, its guardposts roughly 10 miles apart and larger posts or forts every 30 miles. Side roads penetrated tribal areas for maximum surveillance. A 10-inch annual rainfall, the normal minimum of civilian dry farming, gives an inward limit for this zone. Eight inches, considered the minimum to support a military unit, gives a theoretical outward limit. In fact, however, the easternmost extent of control here takes us as far as the 4-inch isohyet: an achievement which may be explained in terms of irrigation and water storage, reduced patrolling in summer, special supply arrangements like purchase of meat from the nomads and assistance from the Palmyran oasis. Such was the desert screen implemented by the *auxilia*. It freed the legions, supervised nomad movements and regulated the caravans which entered imperial territory from Parthia via Palmyra.

Poidebard's aerial surveys covered two zones and yielded two books. The first, in 1925–32, scanned a diagonal band of 110-mile width from the southwestern to the northeastern corners of modern Syria, from which came his classic exposition of the desert frontier, *La Trace de Rome dans le Désert de Syrie* (Paris, 1934).[34] The second, in 1934–42, examined the more northerly stretch of frontier and hinterland where the Euphrates protected Syria's most populous area, described in *Le Limes de Chalcis* (Paris, 1945). These prompted less follow-up than Poidebard's memory deserves: a reflection in part of relations between Syria and the West, in part of problems inherent in the techniques themselves. Aerial photography emphasises the final stage of a site and is best suited to late periods. The long tenure of these eastern frontiers – developed throughout the imperial era, then taken over by the Byzantine empire – plus the even greater antiquity of the region generally, embarrass the photo-interpreter with a profusion of data. In fairness to Poidebard, he did much to prove his aerial observations on the ground; supporting them with site visits, study and deep thought. After all, his surveys took only 550 flying hours, his books 20 years. Nevertheless it will require decades to complete these findings. Poidebard opened the door on Rome's desert frontiers, but it remains for archaeology's big battalions to follow and for others to attempt a final synthesis.

· With the desert patrolled by auxiliaries, Vespasian was free to station the eastern legions on his new Euphrates frontier, much as those of Europe already occupied key points on the long rivers. The northernmost, at Satala, facing Armenia, was manned by a newly formed legion. Three of the Syrian four were posted far from the bars and bordellos of their erstwhile cities, at Melitene, Samosata and Zeugma. The fourth and more fortunate, *VI Ferrata* (the Ironclad), remained to counter internal unrest, being placed just north of today's Lebanese border at Raphanae, between that unruly trio of cities: Antioch, Jerusalem and Palmyra. The latter name means Palm City and was probably the biblical Tadmor. It was a caravan centre which lived by exploiting its position at the heart of wilderness midway between Parthia and the Mediterranean. Its existence made the Syrian desert just feasible as an invasion route: 'Palmyra, nobly situated, is known for her fertility and hot springs. The fields are encircled by a vast sea of sand, as if nature had isolated her from the rest of the world, giving her a destiny of her own between two great empires and always, at the first hint of trouble, attracting the attention of both.'[35] Long an independent state, Palmyra had been seized by a shrewd Tiberius and handed back by a contrary Caligula.

She now seems to have been reannexed by Vespasian. However, Rome continued to give careful handling to a people whose experience of desert warfare was crucial to her, employing the Palmyran camel corps to patrol the region, despite an empire-wide ban on the use of auxiliaries in their own countries. Despite all, the Syrian frontier would in a less local sense be among the empire's most stable, with only one war between Parthia and Rome during the century following Vespasian's restructuring.

Appropriately, it is toward the end of this same Flavian period that a new word emerges by which Roman authors and modern scholars describe the frontier system under whose protection the empire is now passing. The word is *limes*, plural *limites*, from which we have the identical French word and the English limit. The words *terminus* (boundary) or *finis* (border) had previously been used. These would continue to describe other sorts of boundaries, for example between provinces. As the Rhine and Danube became frontiers the word *ripa* (river bank) had already begun to take on the meaning of a riverine frontier. *Limes* now describes a fortified frontier of cross-country type. Apart from temporary arrangements none had existed until recent events brought the army to the Fosse Way, the Black Forest and the Syrian Desert.

Limes may originate from the adjectives *limosus* (muddy) and *limus* (sideways, crosswise) whose senses converge in the idea of a field path, later a boundary between holdings in the standard blocs of one hundred plots as laid out by Roman surveyors. The connection between these and the imperial frontier becomes clearer when one remembers that the empire's earliest overland boundaries were based on transverse roads, fronting the *barbaricum*. Though roads through insecure or recently conquered regions normally had lookouts and forts, it became customary to double a frontier road's protection by reducing fort intervals from a day's to half a day's march (from 15 to 7 Roman miles), at any rate in Europe. Most definitions of the term *limes* are based on a passing remark by the 4th-century historian Spartianus, who speaks of 'places where the barbarians are divided from us not by rivers but by *limites*',[36] though ancient sources do not make it clear whether *limes* referred to the actual line or the entire defensive system. Modern opinion tends to concur with the *Dizionario Epigraphico* in favouring the wider interpretation; for it is not a method of boundary marking but a strategy which gives the Roman frontier its distinctive character. However this distinction is not invariably respected by modern commentators, who often use the word *limes* to describe all the empire's exterior frontiers, whether overland or riverine.

The existence of the *limes* as a fortified frontier for the defence of the Roman empire (not to be confused with modern notions of a frontier as a precise line marked by boundary stones or other means) first appears in literary usage around AD 97 in Tacitus, *Agricola*, 41, and similarly in *Germania*, 29. The essential element is considered to be a road which followed the frontier, branching toward the interior in such a way that the entire road network of the empire was ultimately linked with its frontier. The second indispensable element is the group of works associated with the frontier's manning for the purposes of defence and the control of movement across the boundary.'[37]

It is not of course known how the word *limes* was pronounced.[38]

The Roman stone fort also dominates from this period onwards. Rectangular with rounded corners, like a playing card; following the outline and layout of its parent, the marching camp; varying in size and dimensions according to establishment and local tradition; this now appears along all the Roman borderlands. With the army (29 legions and a similar complement of auxiliaries) totalling some 350,000, the number of legionary fortresses and auxiliary forts required to house them must have been at least 500. Allowing for changes of station, division of units and rebuilding, the total number of fort remains finally scattered round the imperial edges can hardly have been less than 1,500, excluding fortlets and temporary camps. Today we see them, sometimes outlined by surviving walls or mounds, sometimes as platforms from which the stones have been robbed and sometimes faintly, in the ghostly images of aerial photographs. A few, less than 5%, are partly excavated or restored, open to the public and adequately protected; though of these not one in the entire circuit of the former Roman empire is totally excavated and on view. Many are sealed under cities and may never be seen. Many are safe under soil or sand and may be seen one day. Many are presently threatened or will succumb to the unquiet decades ahead. Many have been destroyed already, though since ground always retains some imprint of its disturbance, absolute erasure is rare. So, across lands never unified before or since, among the random marks of accidental events, the circles and sinuosities of other cultures, there shows this constant, self-assured shape; the stamp of Rome on the passport of the past.

Vespasian did not decide what kind of frontier Rome would have. This had been shaped by circumstance and its evolution was well advanced by the time he took the purple. The rightness of its direction seemed to be confirmed by the Year of the Four Emperors, whose internal events lent strength to the principle that the army should continue to be split up and whose external consequences demonstrated that the frontier should be strengthened and sealed. In the same year, the Batavian revolt – when German soldiers again put loyalty to tribe above loyalty to Rome – had convinced Vespasian that auxiliary units should never be allowed to serve in their regions of origin. Accordingly there began the military diaspora so characteristic of the Roman frontier, with Gauls in Africa, Africans on the Danube, Spaniards in the east, Orientals in the west, every type of provincial on every province's frontier except his own; a tangle of postings so complex that one wonders who kept track of it. In practice little changed. Though units arrived as foreigners, subsequent recruitment was local. Within three generations these aliens, now with local mothers and grandmothers, became natives again. In fact there is no known instance of auxiliary mutiny after this time. Vespasian also recognised the auxiliary army's value as plugging material for the frontier. Henceforward the business of day-to-day regulation will be theirs. They will become the *gendarmerie* of the empire's edges and keepers of its gates; not only policing the frontier and administering the formalities at checkpoints and crossings, but also defending it and retaliating to trouble. The legions, though often stationed on the line, will remain aloof from its chores, spending their time in training or the construction of forts, roads and bridges. Their function is deterrence, strategic intervention and the provision of drafts for occasional wars in other theatres.

Turning to considerations of grand strategy, there are three ways in which a country may defend itself. One is to offer no formal resistance but to vex by guerrilla means: an option for the weak against the strong, which we may discount in the case of the empire at the height of its power. This leaves a choice of two: spreading force along a front or gathering it in the rear; putting one's strength on the line or concealing it. In nature these approaches are exemplified by the oyster and the peach. The oyster presents an unwelcoming shell, but having struggled to lever it open you will find it is internally defenceless and can be swallowed without even cooking or chewing. The peach is inviting, but the hard and spiky stone will jar the teeth of whoever bites deeply, and the kernel is seldom damaged. The great majority of nations have evolved along peach lines. Rome, like China, is among the few powers which preferred preventive to reactive defence, a crustaceous to a membranous frontier. Whatever might prove best in the long run, this was the course which seemed right to Vespasian and, as far as we are aware, to most of his thinking contemporaries. He pursued it with vigour and good sense, achieving much in the last decade of a life whose best years had been wasted because of a trivial and imagined slight to Nero's vanity.

A few, prescient words of Tacitus come to mind. Though he wrote them of Tiberius, the comment applies far better to the state of the Roman world at Vespasian's death: 'An empire enclosed by remote rivers. Legions, provinces, fleets: the whole system interlinked.'[39] Careenage is the process of beaching a ship, turning her over, scouring, recaulking and repainting her hull before returning her leakproof to the water. This Vespasian applied to the empire. He found Rome ripped in four and left her single, secure and sound. His final achievement was to die a natural death, a destiny denied seven of his eight predecessors.[40]

CHAPTER 3

Domitian:
Sour Prizes

In AD 79 Vespasian was succeeded by the dashing and generous Titus. The new emperor was popular not only for his military record but as a spender and giver of games; releasing in a rush of largesse the hoarded proceeds of his father's thrift. It is easy to be liked while the money lasts. It was, however, Titus who did not last. At only forty-two years of age, his health gave way. In a parting glimpse we see him[1] borne off in a litter, groaning that fate was about to rob him of his best years because of a single sin: a liaison with his brother's wife, the future empress Domitia. The destruction of Jerusalem apparently counted for less.

Before introducing Titus' successor it is appropriate to recall that history knows nothing more curious than the Roman imperial throne, both for the personalities of those who sat on it and the wildly varying effect which the act of sitting seemed to have upon men previously normal. The experience transformed Nero from a courteous youth into a fickle tyrant. By contrast, its main influence upon Vespasian and Titus was to emphasise their amiability. Next came Domitian, the quiet younger brother. On him the effect would be demonic, releasing paranoia and jealousy so intense that it could be fatal for anyone in public life to do well or even show promise. Thus the Roman state would enter a phase of numbing mediocrity in which none dared fail and all feared to succeed.

Parallel with these events was the deepening involvement in Britain. The Fosse Way had proved ineffectual and, in Wales and the Pennines, Nero's and Vespasian's governors grappled with the consequences. Boudicca's rebellion and troop reductions during the Year of the Four Emperors retarded remedy. In AD 78 Vespasian, who had won his spurs in the British enterprise and was loath to see it fail, despatched Julius Agricola with orders to bring the entire island under control. Why should Vespasian seek total subjugation despite the north's slight value? A realistic reason lay in defence costs. Augustus' completion of the conquest of Spain to its northwestern extremity had allowed the virtual demilitarisation of the Iberian peninsula; a formula which could be applied to a Britain grossly overgarrisoned in relation to her worth. A profitable province was one which did not need a frontier. Most costly was one with an enemy still at large in it.

So, 134 years after Caesar and thirty-six after Claudius disembarked in Kent, Roman eyes turned at last to the far north. Agricola's memorable summer of AD 80 put southern Scotland[2] behind him and the Highlands in front. The rising curtain revealed a surprise: the Forth–Clyde isthmus, offering a defensive line of 35 miles, seven times shorter than the Fosse Way. A second surprise was the nearness of Ireland, which Agricola saw from the Rhinns of Galloway, only 25 miles distant.

An embarrassment of options thus arose. A close view of Argyll made it clear that the Highlands would be harder to crack than anticipated. On the other hand, to seal off northern Scotland at the isthmus, or to invade Ireland, now seemed unexpectedly easy. Uncertainty was protracted by the death of Titus in September 81. Though in mid-campaign Agricola was obliged to await fresh orders, for war was an imperial prerogative and each new emperor must confirm or veto it. To crown all, Domitian had decided on an expedition of his own across the Middle Rhine against the troublesome Chattans. He would lead in person; and naturally had first call on troops. Some 25% of British units were therefore transferred to Germany. Only then did Agricola receive clear orders to proceed with the conquest of all Scotland: the sterner task with the weaker force.

The depleted army now advanced up Strathmore into the northeast, provoking the tribes to take the field at Mons Graupius.[3] The Britons were routed, with ten thousand dead, though the terrain and the onset of dusk allowed twice that number to escape. It was an inconclusive battle, fought too late in the day and too late in the season. Few believe that with a reduced force and so much ill-digested country to his rear, Agricola could in any case have taken and held the Highlands and Islands. He was now recalled, a doomed man, for glamour and glory were attached to his victory and Domitian had earned none. The Chattan campaign had been a propaganda flop, the enemy merely retreating into the forest and memories of Quintillius Varus forbidding deep pursuit. After two or at most three seasons Domitian was forced to break off and dash to the Lower Danube, where Decebalus of Dacia (today's Romania) had launched the first of his attacks.

Both the Scottish and German wars produced frontiers. Sallustius Lucullus, Agricola's probable successor, guarded the recent gains with forts, though none is certain north of Stracathro.[4] These probably included the so-called 'glen-blocking forts', earlier attributed to Agricola. Here Fendoch, at the mouth of the Sma' Glen,[5] is the most romantically sited. Its grassy platform is still visible by the burn while, on the ridge above, a ring-shaped mound marks the site of a watchtower which peeped into Breadalbane. This Highland frontier across Stirling, Perthshire and Angus, consisting of forts sealing the main exits from mountain to plain, was now briefly the front line of the empire. Nine such forts along a 120-mile line between Clyde and Angus are presently known. However, their dispositions imply a holding rather than a long-term intention. Rome's preference was for a strong frontier, hard up against a weak, empty, or evacuated zone; not one on the downhill side of an enemy still impenitent and strong.

At about the same time a line of different character was established along the road between the rivers Forth and Tay, the present A9. This amounts to a second defensive screen, ten miles south of the mountain edge, thought to have shielded a friendly Fife against attack from the Highlands. It consisted of a series of roadside watchtowers, almost certainly through cleared forest. Their sites were long known on the Gask Ridge, between Kinkell Bridge and Perth, at half- to one-mile intervals over a fifteen-mile distance; but aerial surveys during the 1980s have doubled the supposed length. Such wooden towers were supported on four stout posts and must have resembled the sort of structure we today associate with prison compounds or forest fire lookouts. Each was surrounded by a mound and ditch, usually circular, 25 or 30 yards across; the only visible feature today. They are not always easy to spot and some are in thick plantations.

During the late 80s, then, the frontier's centre was Perth, with its most sensitive spot fifteen miles inland, at Dunkeld; where the River Tay, emerging from peat to pasture, offers a notable chink in the Highland armour. Here work was begun on a new legionary fortress, Pinnata Castra (Inchtuthil), whose Latin name[6] suggests a virgin site and seems to mean 'turreted fortresses'.[7] Though its situation,[8] on a spur above the river, is striking, there is little to be seen above ground. Construction was of timber. Nevertheless, Inchtuthil provided a challenge almost unique in the empire to disinter a fortress dating from a single period on an undisturbed site; accepted by Sir Ian Richmond and St Joseph between the early 1950s and the former's untimely death in 1965. The 52-acre fortress, with its seven miles of exterior and interior walls, was found to have been destroyed just before completion. This was a planned demolition, carried out as part of an orderly withdrawal. Bent nails, yanked out by claw-hammer, littered the site. Everything of value or utility was removed and burned, broken or buried. A million unused nails, weighing eleven tons, were concealed in pits.

What we are witnessing, following Agricola's recall in 84 or 85, is a step-by-step shrinkage of Roman Scotland. First to go was the northernmost fort, Stracathro, a full forty miles short of the Graupius battlefield and eighty short of Agricola's furthest point north. Then, around AD 87, comes the abandonment of Inchtuthil and other Perthshire positions, including the watchtower line some two years later. Enlargement of Agricola's fort at Newstead[9] now spells a movement of the army's centre of gravity from northern to southern Scotland. The reason is plain. Units were still being filched by Domitian. This southward shift in Britain echoes a larger shift in the continental fulcrum from Rhine to Danube. Indeed the outbreak of war with Decebalus led to the withdrawal of an entire legion, *II Adiutrix*,[10] reducing the British legions to three and bidding a final adieu to any hope of subjugating the entire island.

Before following Domitian's dash to the Danube let us assess the results of his Chattan campaign. In prestige terms it had been a fiasco. Though he could, like Claudius, have visited Britain and reaped the triumph of a 600-mile advance, the emperor had staked his reputation on a much-heralded venture, which faded unspectacularly away. Sequins were stitched to this dowdy dress by the decreeing of two new provinces, Upper and Lower Germany, with capitals at Mainz and Cologne. These had been part of Gallia Belgica (eastern

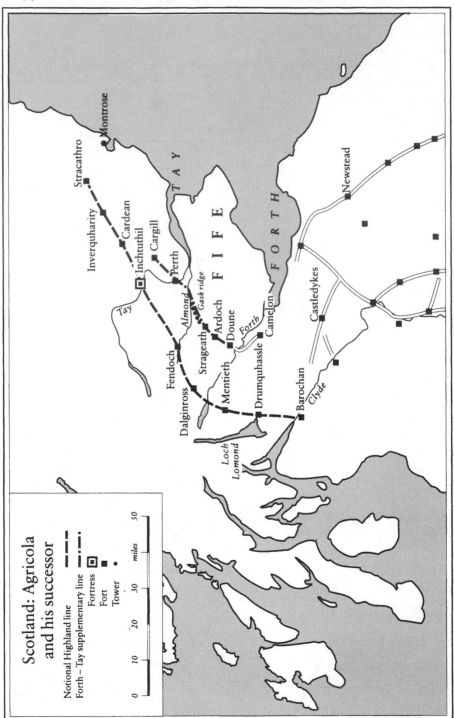

Scotland: Agricola
and his successor

Notional Highland line
Forth – Tay supplementary line
Fortress
Fort
Tower

miles
0   10   20   30   50

Montrose
Stracathro
Inverquharity
Cardean
Cargill
Inchtuthil
Perth
T A Y
Tay
Almond
Gask ridge
F I F E
F O R T H
Newstead
Strageath
Ardoch
Doune
Forth
Camelon
Castledykes
Fendoch
Dalginross
Mentieth
Drumquhassle
Barochan
Clyde
Loch
Lomond

Gaul). In fact they comprised little more than the western Rhine bank, which the army had occupied since the time of Augustus. It was nevertheless an ingenious twist to win two German provinces with the pen!

Ironically, the Chattan foray would produce more tangible results than Agricola's forlorn glories in North Britain. Sufficient ground was gained to link up with the Black Forest, annexed by Vespasian, allowing a much improved version of the Rhine–Danube shortcut. Furthermore it engendered a useful blueprint for cross-country frontiers under European conditions. Fighting had been in forest along a front often consisting of a cleared strip with guardposts, not unlike the Gask Ridge and predating it by five years. From this emerged the first of Rome's *limites* known to have been based on a patrolled track with watchtowers: a precise, man-made line, with little resemblance to the in-depth defence of Syria's desert edge. The Rhine–Danube overland frontier adapted rivers, ridges and areas of dense thicket into a single scheme (see map 3). No one could argue it as a line of great natural strength. Its ridges seldom exceed a few hundred feet, its rivers are of moderate width and sometimes the terrain offers no advantage at all. Fortunately most of its course lay through a lightly peopled, heavily wooded landscape, where tribal disturbances were rare and migrational stresses slight. From the Rhine's confluence with the Lahn (just above Coblenz) the frontier struck south-east to pick up the crest of the Taunus Range, following it at 1,200–1,800 feet round the north of Frankfurt. From here it looped further north, as far as today's Pohlheim, to include the fertile Wetterau corridor before turning south to join the Main at Gross Krotzenburg, twelve miles east of Frankfurt's centre. Then, for about fifteen miles, the Main itself became the frontier, up to the village of Worth, where the line left the river. It now continued southwards across the Odenwald to join the Neckar, whose course it followed upstream into the Swabian Jura, finally joining existing forts on the Upper Danube established by Claudius.

The original works consisted of wooden towers, intervisible down long lanes of cleared forest or along patrolled river banks; supported by the turf and timber forts of the auxiliary army at intervals of several miles, soon to be linked by road. Traces of plaited screen or wickerwork hurdling have been found, seemingly used as an occasional frontier fence.[11] Though flimsy and temporary, such obstacles might delay intruders sufficiently for a patrol to intervene.

These works would be elaborated and strengthened with the passage of time, the frontier itself later being extended slightly at its northern end and the southern half completely realigned. This was to mean abandoning the Odenwald stretch in favour of a line running further eastwards, eventually reaching the Danube near Regensburg, 150 miles further downriver. In its final form[12] the line reached 310 miles long, with more than 60 forts and 900 signal towers; arguably Europe's most extensive archaeological monument. Owing to duplication created by changes of route, the number of forts was actually nearer 100 and of towers perhaps 1,500, though not simultaneously manned. The frontier was to be held for almost two centuries, shortening the journey to the Danube by ten days.

Almost unmentioned in ancient literature, a detailed picture of the frontier's workings is provided by archaeology. Yet till the last century this was a feature swallowed by time, its memory faded even from folk consciousness. Only in the Bavarian sector, approaching the Danube, was it dimly remembered in the name *Teufelsmauer* (Devil's Wall). The Prussian Academy's offer in 1748 of a prize for the best thesis on the extent of Roman penetration into Germany suggests the frontier's whereabouts were then still largely guesswork. Throughout the nineteenth century the growth of local history societies produced a rash of digging, in which evidence was often destroyed in the search for coins or showcase objects. By mid-century the universities were arguing that the effort should be coordinated and professionally led; but it was not until forty years later that the Reichstag voted funds for the establishment of a Reichslimeskommission (Imperial Frontier Commission) for this purpose.

Theodor Mommsen (1817–1903) was its first director; an awesome scholar and perhaps the greatest of all Romanists. At seventy-five he was still so active – and national enthusiasm so great – that during his nine remaining years the entire frontier was located and sufficiently excavated to reveal the system in outline. Such an effort by a nation in pursuit of its past had never been seen before. Mommsen divided the frontier into fifteen stretches based on local administrative boundaries, each under a 'stretch commissar'. The assault was conducted along a 500 km front by the largest battery of excavators, surveyors and historians ever mustered; bulked out by numerous amateurs, with a variety of specialists on call. By 1901, thirty-four forts were on partial display to an excited public.

In 1903, however, with less than half its goals achieved, the storm of pick and shovel abated. Like most scientific enquiry it was proving open-ended. Moreover the techniques of archaeology – originally developed for drier lands – were advancing rapidly and the advances served not to expedite but to retard the schedule. These involved concentration upon perishable materials and the shadowy evidence they bequeathed, especially the residues of rotted timber, including stains in the soil and negative features, such as cavities. Since all early watchtowers and many interior fort buildings were of wood, this was evidence of some magnitude. For these reasons excavation slowed and there were even calls for the re-examination of sites already dug. The decision was taken by Ernst Fabricius (1857–1942), the Commission's second director, to suspend excavation and concentrate on evaluating data which had poured in from the field.

If the bringing to light of the Rhine–Danube overland frontier was Mommsen's monument, the bringing of it to print was Fabricius'. This was the Commission's report[13] on the Upper German–Raetian frontier, so called after the provinces it guarded. Like the excavations, this was to prove a longer task than expected. The last of its fourteen volumes was not published till 1937. All in all it had been a remarkable feat, both at dig and desk. Students of other Roman frontiers doffed their mortar-boards. In 1928 a prominent hillock on Hadrian's Wall was named Mons Fabricius[14] in honour of the achievement. Meanwhile, excavation had been resumed, continuing steadily between the wars and from the late 1940s to the present.

This then was a frontier won from oblivion. Whereas along those ever-busy waterways of Rhine and Danube so much has been lost to flood and river shift, stone stealing and the neglect of insensible centuries, here were extensive stretches preserved by loneliness and forest. It does not however mean that the visitor will be greeted by mighty works or that his children can clamber over battlements. The remains are much reduced by time. Like other Roman frontiers, this was the outback of antiquity and these its outworks; the unenviable station of poor, part-Romanised auxiliary soldiers and their families. Therefore, as the author of a guidebook warns: 'Do not set out with false expectations. You will find no high-standing ruins or remarkable art works. Sometimes you may be hard put to find anything at all.'[15] These are golden rules for Roman frontiers: often lonely places, whose remains cannot compete in grandeur with those of Rome's inner provinces, nor with the cathedrals, castles, palaces and mosques

of later ages. Often, however, such deficiencies are compensated for
by beauty or majesty of setting and a sense of standing on one
of history's momentous divides. Roman Germany shares this sense.
Typically, the traces are in the form of earthen mounds, ditch outlines, tower bases, wall foundations and so on, sometimes scattered
and fragmentary. At its best in cavernous forest or among mile on
mile of silent hills, this frontier strikingly evokes the mood (as one
imagines it) of a little altered landscape, facing a *barbaricum* which
stretched awesomely and infinitely eastwards.

Most concentrated, in terms of scenic and archaeological interest,
is the Taunus Range. The Germans have done good work with the
in situ reconstruction of specimen watchtowers and other features.
The Kastell Saalburg (twelve miles north of Frankfurt) is a rebuilt
cohort fort with a complete circuit of walls, ditches, gates, a headquarters building and museum, plus specimen granary, workshop
and barrack block. Reconstructions are on original foundations,
mainly carried out between 1898 and 1907, at the suggestion of
Wilhelm II. The outer walls were raised from a surviving height of
six to their present fourteen feet. A short walk northwestwards brings
one to the actual frontier line, marked by a stone of recent origin
inscribed *Limes Imperii Romani* ('frontier of the Roman Empire').
On the German *limes* as a whole there are some three dozen
museums, mainly in small towns near the frontier's course. Though
sites and footpaths are well signposted, good maps and the assistance
of a guidebook are advisable. Helpful items are on sale at local
bookshops and the Saalburg Fort.

Events suggest that the Dacian incursion was towards the Black
Sea. Near today's Bucarest–Constantza highway, about 110 miles
south of the Carpathians and 35 from the coast, is the Romanian
village of Adamklissi. On a flat-topped hill just north of the village
stands a large memorial or 'altar', about 18 feet high and 40 feet
square, inscribed with the names of Roman dead. They are mainly
from western parts of the empire and may point to the destruction
of one of the Lower German legions brought to Moesia by Domitian.
Twelve miles east is a different kind of monument. This is the
empire's first frontier earthwork or *vallum*.[16] It ran from the Danube
at Axiopolis (Rashova) east by southeast to Tomis (Constantza).
Here the river approaches to within thirty miles of the Black Sea and
the corridor, formed by its running almost parallel with the coast,
was sealed at the narrowest point, creating a second defensive line

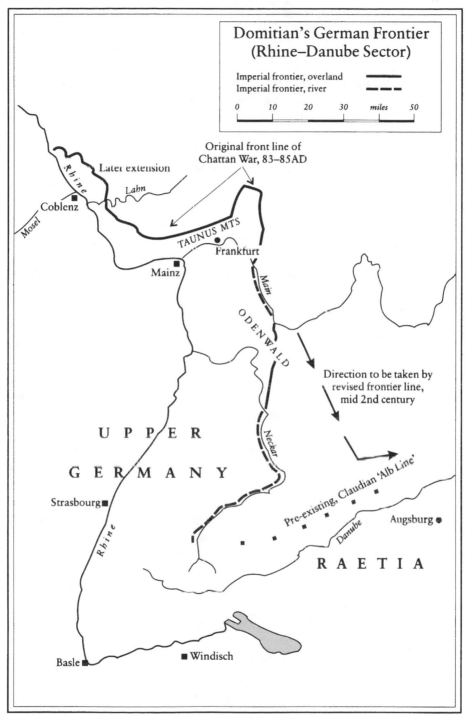

**Domitian's German Frontier
(Rhine–Danube Sector)**

Imperial frontier, overland ———
Imperial frontier, river – – –

0   10   20   30   *miles*   50

Original front line of
Chattan War, 83–85AD

Later extension

Rhine

Lahn

Mosel

Coblenz

TAUNUS MTS

Frankfurt

Mainz

Main

O D E N W A L D

Direction to be taken by
revised frontier line,
mid 2nd century

U P P E R

Neckar

G E R M A N Y

Strasbourg

Rhine

Pre-existing, Claudian 'Alb Line'

Danube

Augsburg

R A E T I A

Basle   Windisch

within the Lower Danube and behind its delta. Indeed this is so natural a location for a blocking wall that in the immediate vicinity there are three, two of earth and one of stone; a source of confusion, now seemingly resolved.

The so-called Small Earthwork, oldest and most eroded, is of barbarian origin and prehistoric date. The relationship of ditch to mound obliges us to assume that it faced the opposite way, controlling access from the direction of Bulgaria and Greece. The Great Earthwork is tentatively attributed to Domitian. Though much weathered, its mound is still in places eight or nine feet high, with a deep ditch on the eastern and a shallow one on the western side. The latter was presumably an additional source of turf and soil. Its earth and timber forts, indeed the whole system, seem hastily built. Defending from the direction of the delta, it would be of special value against the Dacians, who had evidently crossed the Danube somewhere near the last bend. Tomis lay just outside the earthwork's direct route toward the sea, but a loop was constructed to take in the city. The Stone Wall, its masonry much robbed, also faces the delta. It has been dated, by an inscription in Old Slavonic, to the Byzantine emperor John Tzimisces,[17] 10th century AD. The three walls follow different courses, sometimes close together, sometimes a few miles apart. On one occasion the Domitianic and Byzantine versions actually cross over. The ensemble, mistakenly known as 'Trajan's Dykes', was once regarded as a single concept with a triple line. An attempt to unravel the tangle was made by C. Schuchardt in 1917,[18] his excavations aided by the first aerial photographs of a Roman frontier; another bonus of military reconnaissance. Little has been published since and detailed information remains scarce.

In Germany we identified woven fencing as the first, tentative sign of a continuous barrier applied to a Roman overland frontier. Here, a few years later, was the same idea in substantial form. Of course dykes were nothing new. Iron age Europe abounded in them. A trench was dug and the upcast thrown into a mound, the combined ditch depth and mound height forming an obstacle or boundary. They were not, however, especially strong. The Celts had largely abandoned them in favour of hillforts or the *murus Gallicus*.[19] The difference is that Domitian's earthwork had thirty forts behind it, one per Roman mile, which immediately distinguishes it from iron age dykes. In other words it was a manned obstacle whose purpose, like most of Rome's overland frontiers, was less against attack than

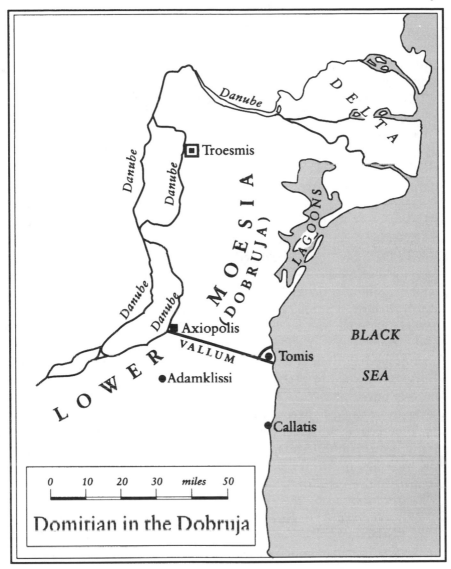

Domitian in the Dobruja

as an aid to patrolling and a deterrent to infiltration. Attack would be met by the fort garrisons on level and open ground in front of the obstacle. We fight our enemies, said Tacitus, 'not with mounds and ditches, but men and weapons'.[20] Such was Domitian's supposed contribution to bolting the Lower Danube door.

His worries were not yet over. A rebellion by Antoninus Saturninus, commander of the two-legion garrison at Mainz, spurred him back to the Rhine. This would spell the end of troop concentrations in time of peace. Augustus had begun the dispersal of the legions, Vespasian had broken up the Syrian cluster of four, and now Domitian forbade even two. It was a principle based not on strategy but on suspicion. The mutiny, though swiftly suppressed, was followed by yet more Chattan misbehaviour. At this juncture, Rhenish problems were again overtaken by Danubian. We have seen how the Lower Danube is overshadowed by the Carpathians. On the Middle Danube a comparable threat is posed by the mountains of Slovakia, which dominate the river for over a hundred miles. This was the south-eastern extremity of the German lands and home of the Marcommanic tribe; an area little disturbed by the Augustan campaigns and long regarded as stable. Now mischief erupted from this corner, encouraged doubtless by Decebalus and the knowledge that the emperor was again preoccupied with the Chattans. Domitian had now reigned nine years in an accelerating nightmare of hopes and reverses, rushing between Rhine and Danube in a manner prophetic of later centuries. Such was the fate of an emperor upon whose father and brother Mars had never frowned. These setbacks, plus the treachery of Saturninus, now served to tip him into near-madness, leading to the terror of the last six years and climaxing in his contract-killing, organised by the empress Domitia.

Though Tacitus, in his *Life of Julius Agricola*, tries hard to infer that Britain was a key zone of operations,[21] his own later works make it clear that imperial destinies lay elsewhere: in Rome itself, on the Rhine and Danube, and of these increasingly the latter. Britain was a side-show, opened because Claudius needed a success and reopened because of Vespasian's personal attachment. This led Agricola far out along a branch which would only support military adventures provided that the tree itself was secure. The progressive paring down of the British legions shows how far Rome had moved from the strike-where-she-liked situation of the later Republic, to one of rob-Peter-to-pay-Paul. Frontier armies were on call to other frontiers.

Expansion in one direction depended on peace in others; and fronts must henceforth be treated not in terms of prestige but of precedence. The initiative was gradually slipping from Rome's hands. Decebalus had pulled the string and Domitian had been forced to jump. Scotland's fate had been determined in Romania.

CHAPTER 4

Trajan:
Triumph and Trouble

ARMED FRONTIERS point to stability. They suggest that if someone
has bothered to create them he must wish to keep to them. On the
other hand it was part of the imperial inheritance that each emperor
should have absolute power in external affairs; and neither a frontier's apparent permanence nor the value of its works was seen to
override his right to scrap it. What might influence a decision to do
so? We must accept as a constant of the early empire that no propaganda points would be scored by digging ditches, manning watchtowers or hiding behind rivers. To judge from the continuing
popularity of war, public opinion still saw the defensive as un-
Roman. For an emperor who courted popularity, frontier security
could not compete with winning battles.

And yet frontiers were proving indispensable. They were a coagu-
lant, staunching the bleeding at the edges suffered by all land empires.
They were a remedy for misadventure. Should a campaign misfire it
could be dismissed with a boundary. If an emperor chose war in one
direction, frontiers would protect him in others. Their formation was
easy, war increasingly difficult. By the late 1st century the shortage
of avenues for expansion and the normalisation of most foreign
relationships were together providing the context for the emergence
of an empire with stable limits.

As a result, frontiers had been quietly forming for eighty years.
The process seems to have required no sustained, central initiative.
It was normal for units to strengthen their stations and for men

in exposed positions to improve their protection, and natural that provincial governors, with paid workforces of soldiers and sailors, should seek to keep them occupied. Though prompted by a nod from the Palatine, the frontiers were moving toward permanence of their own accord. The gradual conversion of the military from a culture of heroism to one of custodianship, the growth of public acceptance and the strengthening of the imperial defences were all advancing hand in hand. True to the nature of slow processes the frontier concept would eventually take deep root and become accepted as the norm of empire, as an aspect even of Rome's eternity.

It is presumably because the idea of an armed frontier grew in so muted a manner, because it sidled into the Roman scheme and took decades to develop, that it was rarely questioned. In the century ahead some of Rome's ablest leaders will condone, without apparent qualm or criticism, a strategy to which the ancient world's future had become almost accidentally attached. While many an emperor assessed his predecessor's actions with a searching eye, the frontier as a long-term principle seemed no man's doing. It was the product of drift, in which all had acquiesced and all took for granted. The principate continued therefore to be guided by conflicting principles: a general move toward frontier-making, punctuated by individual attempts to gain glory. Though normalisation was the rule, the emperor who would reject it in favour of war at least once was never far away. Nevertheless, despite the fact that caesars continued to be mesmerised by battlefield success, from the time of Augustus none of their expeditions had been of major consequence. Distance, resistance, and the discovery that advance in one theatre meant cutbacks in others, were all moderating factors. Germany and Parthia remained big prizes, but they were also big risks. Britain (a substitute Germany) and Armenia (a poor man's Parthia) had provided exercise for the army but without great recompense. In sum, the tendency was to foster a circumvallate empire, now nearing its final extent, coexisting with exceptions in the form of foreign campaigns numbering one or two per reign: each emperor's gesture, as it were, to the fighting centuries of Rome's past. It is clear that for an end to this contradiction and for total devotion to fixed frontiers we must await a man of peace. Other than Tiberius there had to date been none. We have recognised only Vespasian as an active champion of the defended periphery, though he too was embroiled in the battle for Britain.

With Trajan's principate (AD 98–117), official interest in the frontier touches an historic low and we return to the view that an army's meaning lies not in deterrence but in war. His ventures will entail the drafting of reserves from the frontiers in large numbers. However, as Domitian's discomfiture had shown, it was crucial that while the imperial back was turned all other parts of the line should hold. In this sense even Trajan, arch-proponent of the attack, was now dependent on the frontiers. Despite their downgrading in terms of military priority, no alternative idea for holding ground and no other way of denying it to the enemy emerges from this reign.

The main events of the early reign are the Dacian Wars of 101–105. For these our main source is Trajan's Column, whose marble spiral tells the story in twenty-three ascending bands of sculptural reliefs. Dacia approximated to today's Romania, minus the Black Sea province of Dobruja. Its heartland was Transylvania, encircled by the 8,000-foot Carpathians: one of nature's most perfect strongholds and a perpetual taunt to the Lower Danube frontier (see map 5). The Dacians were of Sarmatian origin: a steppe people who, around 300 BC, had braved the passes to find this favourable and fertile land. A cultural miracle followed, by which, in less than four centuries, nomads were transformed into farmers, with high standards of craftsmanship and metalwork, a money economy and (in a mixture of Greek and Roman characters) the beginnings of literacy. Finally, the first century of our era saw the rise of a centralised kingdom with ominous military potential. Dacia could now be called the most developed nation-state in Europe outside the Mediterranean; probably the only one. We will recall the inconclusive clashes between Domitian and Decebalus in 85–92. Following Trajan's accession (in AD 98 and already in his early forties) Dio comments that 'he could see how Dacian power and pride were continuing to grow'.[1] Accordingly a pre-emptive attack was launched in the spring of 101, at which point the Column's narrative begins. Though its account of the wars need not detain us, several frontier matters are connected; none more than the frieze's remarkable opening scene. This is a view of an imperial *ripa* or riverbank frontier; the only such picture we possess.

The viewpoint is as if from a boat on the Danube, looking towards the Roman bank. On it stands a pair of guardposts: square or oblong, two-storeyed, stone-built blockhouses with pitched roofs, each surrounded by a ring of pointed stakes. Next come three watch-and-signal towers, probably three-storeyed and enclosed by similar palisades. They have wooden balconies and from each a long firebrand slants skywards. These are alight, suggesting the hours of darkness. Near the first tower is a huge, square logpile consisting of twelve layers each of twelve stout timbers. This is too big for signalling. Its probable function was as a bonfire to be lit in the event of an unauthorised night-time crossing; the ancient equivalent of a searchlight. The pile's symmetry, the number of logs, plus the inference that there was one per three towers, could suggest a regulation arrangement to light up the river in the event of nocturnal emergency. Nearby, also, are hay or strawstacks, providing material for smoke signals. Four auxiliary foot soldiers, in knee breeches and with oval shields, patrol the bank. Archaeology suggests that the distance between Middle Danube watchtowers may have varied between four hundred yards and two or three miles, depending on local visibility and apprehensions.[2] The periodicity of two guardposts followed by three towers cannot be taken literally. The frieze's first band, slanting upwards from its flat base, tapers in gradually and the designer was obliged to put the shorter buildings first.

The wars spanned five years, ending with the destruction of the enemy's capital, Sarmizegetusa, the suicide of the king and Dacia's conversion to a Roman province. Following an initial Roman victory Decebalus accepted a demeaning treaty, but hostilities were resumed a year later on the grounds that he was failing to honour it. During the lull Trajan's engineers had been flat out on two of the imperial frontier's most famous projects. The first was a permanent bridge across the Danube between Upper Moesia and Dacia designed by Apollodorus of Damascus. The bridging point was Drobeta (Turnu Severin, Romania) between today's Serbian and Romanian banks and just below the Iron Gates gorges, where routes branched northwards toward the key passes into Transylvania. At almost a kilometre (1,087 yards, including approaches), this would be the longest permanent bridge in antiquity.

The second project is scarcely less remarkable: the restoration and widening of the cliff road through the Iron Gates of Orsova. This deep, limestone gorge, eighty miles long, formed by the Danube cutting through the southern Carpathians, separates the Middle Danube of Hungary and Serbia from the Lower Danube of Romania and Bulgaria. Within its echoing walls the river narrowed from over 600 yards to a mere fifty, with a corresponding rush of current.

Today these whirling waters are stilled and their level raised by the dam of the Djerdap power station, whose reservoir the gorge has become. During the Roman period the ravine presented so great an obstacle that the Pannonian and Moesian fleets were out of contact. It also impeded efforts to build a continuous frontier road. Tiberius, Claudius and Domitian all attempted to cut a path into the vertical face on today's Serbian side. They finally created a throughway of sorts, though only six feet wide, of which the inner half was a rock ledge and the outer half planking, supported on timber brackets keyed into the cliff from joist holes below.[3] We may suppose that by Trajan's day the wooden part had been stripped away by spring floods and the crashing ice for which the gorge was infamous. It was a link he must mend, for his main entry points to Dacia were at either end of it. Accordingly, over a distance of twelve miles, in the sheerest part of the canyon, the three-foot ledge was widened to six feet, producing a rock road to withstand the river's worst and dependent on wooden cantilevering for its safety rail only. The ledge and its accompanying beam holes were well preserved before the reservoir engulfed them.

Dio's account of the interim treaty is revealing on the matter of deserters and the defection of skilled men: 'Henceforward Decebalus must align himself with Roman policy, cease to harbour deserters and desist from employing fugitives from within the empire; for the biggest and best part of his army had been made up of those enticed from Roman territory.'[4] It seems that Roman soldiers, veterans and engineers fought for Decebalus in scandalous numbers, organising his defences, equipping him with ordnance and building his war machine. The motive was no doubt gainful employment rather than hatred of Rome. Since the ancient world had not invented political viewpoints in our sense, there was little ideological basis for treason. Nor was there much basis for loyalty among those of non-Roman ethnic origin, the majority of the empire's subjects. Provincials, especially from the outer provinces; soldiers, especially from the auxiliary army,[5] as well as fugitives from justice or injustice, could, it seems, be attracted to leave imperial territory, provided that this did not mean committing themselves to a *barbaricum* in which murder or enslavement were the likely outcomes. The existence of a wealthy, stable, neighbouring state created a counter-magnet, drawing soldiers and frontiersmen in numbers hurtful to Roman authority and pride, as the prominence of this question on Trajan's agenda proves.

Comparing the first and last scenes on the Column, we are reminded of the frontier Trajan had given up and the one which he would now take on. With Dacia's annexation those stretches of the Danube that form today's border between Romania and Bulgaria were no longer the empire's edge. Their stations were now evacuated, save some five garrisons left in place as a small reserve. Most, including the legions at Ratiaria and Oescus, were posted elsewhere. A precisely defined, closely guarded river bank with first-class communications, improved for the best part of a century, would now be exchanged for something hitherto untried.

Transylvania – a saucer with the Carpathians its rim – is, as we have said, nature's perfect fortress. But natural defences do not always suit human defenders. High mountains are difficult to supply and in winter impossible to garrison. What is more, the Carpathians do not form a single ridge but are a tangle of peaks, thirty-five to fifty-five miles deep. The Roman army had no experience of high-altitude defence. In all senses, 300 inbending river miles bartered for 500 outbending mountain miles was no bargain at all. Like Claudius and Britain, the impulse had been to conquer, then to think about how the conquest might be held.

The elements of frontier control had by now resolved into ten: a natural barrier where available; a man-made barrier where necessary; a line of forts; fortlets; watchtowers, with their associated signal system; a frontier road; the legionary fortresses; the veteran colonies; an outer screen of diplomacy; and the fleet. The fortlets provided garrisons for the towers and in peacetime regulated passage through the frontier. In time of trouble the watchtowers alerted the forts, the fort garrisons moved to intercept, the barriers slowed the attackers and the roads speeded the defenders. The legionary fortresses housed the reserve, the veteran colonies provided extra back-up, the forward operations gathered intelligence and the navy guarded the rivers and coasts. To these we must add an eleventh factor: the logistics of supply, which governed the other ten. During our own time Switzerland has ameliorated the problems of mountain defence by bringing tunnelling and the development of her specialized railway system to a fine art. But without such capabilities Trajan would be obliged to defend Transylvania by some rearrangement of the usual elements. Of these a strong, natural barrier existed. A man-made barrier was therefore unnecessary, except for a short stretch of earth *vallum* in the west to safeguard Dacia's important goldfields.[6] Forts would continue to be indispensable, though Transylvania's shape encouraged their construction not in a line but in two concentric circles, with three legions at the centre. The outer ring of forts would largely be sited in the last main valleys before the foothills began. Transylvania's internal rivers were discontinuous, or too swift-flowing for systematic naval patrol. Since diplomatic prospects had been poisoned by war, progress in that direction would be unlikely. This leaves towers as the only means to control the actual mountain zone. Nevertheless they would be used imaginatively and the plan would work. While some towers were spread laterally, as on Rhine or Danube, to keep contact and cover gaps between forts, the great majority was arranged in depth, on spurs and hilltops in front of the forts, forming surveillance networks which are the essential feature of the Carpathian frontier.

Under this scheme, individual signal towers would be placed at widely varying intervals (300–4,000 yards) depending on topography, but with a collective view reaching as far as twenty miles into the mountains. The classic grouping was V-shaped, spreading over various peaks and ridges toward the enemy and tapering back to a receiving post, usually on a hill above the mother fort. The latter lay in a valley, often without its own view forward; but information from the towers would be passed from hilltop to hilltop and finally beamed down from the receiving post to the garrison commander. The typical fort defended a twenty-mile width and controlled a forward 'view' ten to fifteen miles into the mountains.

The principle was most intensively applied to the north, towards modern-day Lviv and the western Ukraine. Here the Somesh, with its steep and twisting valley, is an imperfect river frontier in the conventional sense; but it was an ideal base line for intervention and pass blocking, provided that its garrisons could be alerted in time. In northwestern Transylvania some forty stone towers and two earthen fortlets are known to have lain forwards of the Moigrad and Bologa forts. N. Gudea's diagram[7] of the latter shows twelve towers relaying signals from a depth of seventeen miles into the Carpathians, which were then 'bounced' from a receiving station on Mount Bologii, above the fort. Another system, focused on Buciumi, consisted of thirteen towers beaming signals a distance of between five and seven miles, back to the mother fort in a valley below. Some fifty watchtowers radiated from the fort of Tihau. In the north-east the fort of Brinconveneshti appears to have controlled a similar group. Remains

consist largely of stone foundations but timber towers probably pre-
ceded them. Such networks did not spring into immediate being but
evolved through several reigns, reaching full development a century
later. It is, however, fair to suppose that they began with Trajan,
since his forts could do little without them.

Before 1880 the frontiers of the Dacian province were thought to
have lain in the internal valleys. Systematic research started late,
with the foundation of the archaeological section of the Romanian
Academy in 1949. This began a period of emphasis on forts and
their excavation. In the 1960s, however, under the direction of S.
Ferenczi of the University of Cluj, students walking a seventy-mile
arc of the Carpathians identified 128 Roman watchtower sites;[8] and
the uncovering of the immense surveillance blanket has continued
since.

So, around Transylvania, we see the beginnings of a unique frontier. This was not a crest line. It could better be described as antenni-
form or feeler frontier, using smallest manpower for deepest
vigilance. Its custody was almost certainly in the hands of the
numeri.[9] These part-Romanised contingents were now being
recruited from tribes close outside the imperial borders. They func-
tioned as auxiliary to the Auxiliaries. Like modern 'guest workers'
from third-world countries, their pay and expectations were the
lowest, which was just as well, for life in these towers must have
been hard and lonely.

Of the three legions stationed in Dacia, two would be withdrawn
in little more than a decade; leaving only *XIII Gemina* at Apulum,
close to the goldfields. The total garrison would be like Britain's:
about 30,000–40,000 or ten per cent of the Roman army. In terms
both of getting and holding territory the bargain days were over.

Though Dacia's mines would more than pay for a garrison of this
size one must ask, more generally, how the remotest provinces found
the means to fund the largest armies. Britain, as we have said, had
a tenth of the empire's soldiery, but not a fiftieth of its treasury.
Assuming taxation to have been primarily directed toward feeding
the local units, who supplied the specie for their salaries? The fact
is we know little about how government expenditure worked, how
incomings were balanced against requirements, or in what measure
the emperors tapped the senatorial to pay for the armed provinces.
Doubtless emperors were more dependent on the Senate than we
think.

Upriver from Dacia the Danube's reach by Belgrade was still in contact with barbarian territory and remained fully guarded. So did the 150-mile stretch from Belgrade through the Iron Gates. Though now Roman on both sides, the latter remained a sensitive area, not only because of Trajan's new works but because of another important mining area, around Bor and Mount Kosmai (Serbia). Downriver toward the Black Sea the Danube continued as the imperial frontier and was progressively reinforced. As befits the main access corridor between the Eurasian steppe and Europe proper, Lower Moesia (the Dobruja) begins to take on the aspect of a bastion, remaining so throughout the Roman and most of the Byzantine periods. Along the 225-mile water frontage to the delta there would soon be two legions and sixteen or seventeen auxiliary units in forts roughly fifteen miles apart, plus several garrisons behind the line and substantial naval units. Domitian's earth wall across the interior was abandoned.

The Dobruja's garrison now numbered some 20,000 men and there is interesting evidence of its need for civilian support. Without sufficient farmers the *annona* (corn levy) could not feed the soldiers; nor could the supply of recruits be maintained. Normally a civilian population already existed behind the European frontiers and grew with them. But for centuries the Pontic coast had been a no man's land, so troubled by raids that few dared work it. Cultivation, according to Ovid,[10] had been feasible only within sprinting distance of town walls. But now, with so large a garrison to ensure security, there was no reason for this state of affairs to continue. Accordingly, farming families were drafted in from Roman Thrace (Bulgaria), their names soon appearing on inscriptions from the *vici* of forts.[11] Rarely are we given so clear a demonstration that the imperial frontier was neither self-contained nor self-perpetuating.

The Dacian conquest had removed a thorn lodged for half a century in Rome's side. Though a salient, or outward-bulging frontier is never ideal, the tenure of Dacia put the security of all imperial territory from Budapest to the Black Sea on a sounder footing. It was a prow of safety projected 250 miles into the *barbaricum* (see map 5), with the flanking tribes now themselves outflanked. In this strategic sense the new province would continue to be an asset throughout the 165 years in which Rome had the strength to hold it. In particular the result of Trajan's victory was sixty years of almost unbroken peace in this quadrant of empire; a peace which made the prosperity of the second century possible, for that period both begins and ends with eruption on the Middle Danube. More generally, the 2nd century will be prosperous but not dynamic. The empire will remain 95% agricultural. There will be little invention or technical progress. Growth of wealth will continue to be stifled by the absence of ideas about ways of creating it. Like the empire, the army now entered comfortable middle age. Trajan had given it a shake, kicking it out of its camps and up the Carpathians; demonstrating to a watchful outside world that there was life in it yet. But the period showed no advances in the techniques of war, only military conservatism: a disinclination to change, in tactics or weaponry, confirmed by the seeming invincibility of Rome's arms and the inviolability of her borders. Prosperity now reached toward the frontiers, even accumulated there; for the presence of a third of a million soldiers and their dependants, by far the empire's biggest wage-earning group, guaranteed a living for farmers, artisans and entrepreneurs. Perhaps the most ominous, long-term effect was that the differential between the outer provinces and the inner barbarian lands would grow. At first it had been slight, with little economic strain, as between the United States and Canada. But gradually it was tending to resemble that between the United States and Mexico. The frontier was becoming a focus for envy.

In hailing Trajan, we say farewell to Cornelius Tacitus. His probable span was AD 56–120, though we have no firm dates for his life and few for his works. However, his writing is retrospective, covering nothing later than Agricola's death in 93. Though by no means an historian of the imperial frontier (for none existed) Tacitus remains the most searching analyst of an empire whose edges may be glimpsed intermittently by the light of his descriptive flash and intuitional flare. Impatient of detail, his insights go further than fact: to perceptions of character and motive which shaped Rome's destiny. Supreme stylist, master of the historiographic art in an age when the writing of history was an art form, we will miss the crackle of his sentences, his tart summations and brilliant verdicts.

Trajan was from Italica, near Seville; a relaxed, liberal and approachable man whose popularity both with the army and the citizens of Rome was beyond question. His ward Hadrian was twenty-three years his junior and his country cousin from the same Spanish town. The boy's father died when he was ten and Trajan became his guardian. In due course his mother sent him to Rome, where he was laughed at for his provincial accent, lost his head at the sight of so much glamour, overspent his allowance and incurred his guardian's wrath. He began secretly to loathe Trajan, to envy his easy popularity, despise his inconsiderable intellect and detest his adventurist policies. He served in both Dacian Wars and upon their conclusion was given special responsibility for organising the victory festivities. In the light of his misgivings regarding the war, to be put in charge of its glorification, including celebrations lasting over a year, four triumphal arches and seven commemorative coin issues, must have been bitter medicine. Thereafter he was rewarded with the governorship of Pannonia, the key frontier province. Recognition at last? Not quite.

In about 103 Trajan had divided Pannonia into Upper and Lower (*Superior* and *Inferior*). This was because the two stretches of the Danube (before and after the bend at Budapest) faced different directions, with different enemies requiring different handling. Here was the great divide of Rome's European frontier, where the Suebic or southern Germans met the Iazyges or northernmost Sarmatians;[12] and where the barbarians of the woodland met those of the grassland.

Of these newly created commands it was Lower Pannonia which fell to Hadrian: perhaps the smallest frontier province of all, its insignificance heightened by the glamorous governorships on either side. Hadrian had only one legion. He governed a strip barely thirty miles deep, bordering the river between Budapest and Belgrade. Here the Danube flows mainly southwards. Across it the Iazyges, settled there by Rome and now three parts surrounded by her territory, were relatively quiet. Hereabouts the Danube was marshy and malarial, making it less vulnerable to attack but less pleasant to defend. All in all governorship of this new, one-legion province, was not an overwhelming honour. It faced a tribe of horse thieves. Its capital, Aquincum (Budapest), was rudely equipped, for the governor of Upper Pannonia had inherited the administration, leaving Hadrian the task of creating his own.

Upper Pannonia also stole the limelight in constructional terms. Vindobona (Vienna) and Brigetio (on the river, forty miles west of Budapest) were now given legionary fortresses, built in stone from scratch. Nevertheless Hadrian was able to foster a project peculiarly his own. This was his governor's palace, on an island in the Danube now called Hajógyar (Shipbuilders' Island). Discovered in 1851, lost under a shipyard, rediscovered during the Second World War but not understood till its excavation in the 1950s, this was a large and lavish villa, centrally heated, decorated in painted stucco and including as its reception room a striking, domed rotunda of 220-foot diameter.[13] Extravagant, certainly; but also revealing of the man who would be the most individualistic of Roman emperors.

The palace suggests that Hadrian was no longer a nervous youth in Trajan's shadow. Now, at thirty-one years, we sense a quart-sized governor in a pint-sized province. Moreover, the building was remarkable for its symbolism. Being on an island, some hundreds of yards forward of the legionary camp, it was projected as it were into the *barbaricum*, or at least to the last inch of imperial territory. Significantly, the gubernatorial quarters, as well as the public rooms, were on the north or barbarian-facing side. Here Hadrian could entertain in viceregal splendour, conduct business, walk in the gardens, eat, sleep and wake within view of the Iazygian horsemen on their east Hungarian grassland: the beginning of that endless steppe, regarded by Romans as akin to desert or ocean. This is in marked contrast to provinces like Britain, whose governor's palace (in Cannon Street, London) was far removed in miles and mood from its frontier. Defiant in midstream, it implies that the young Hadrian was already a devotee of metaphor, proclaiming that Romanity is not something diluted by distance, but a principle as valid on the empire's edge as in the Roman forum.

Returning to Trajan: the Column has shown him in victory. The totality of his success and the richness of his booty have seemed to belie the Varian warning, the Augustan advice and the Tiberian caution, as if there were no longer a price to be paid for overstepping the limits of Roman strength. Trajan had drawn the better part of twelve legions into the Dacian conflict and by and large the line elsewhere had held. Was this because Rome was stronger than ever; or was Trajan merely a gambler on a winning streak? His next flutter would also pay handsomely – and for small outlay.

It seems that during the Dacian Wars, Trajan had left instructions to his governor of Syria that upon the death of Rabbel II he should march into the latter's kingdom; and indeed, during the year of Decebalus' defeat and suicide, the last ruler of the last free state on the Mediterranean shore died in bed. This was Nabataea, whose territory corresponded to modern Jordan, plus some of Gaza and Sinai, with influence reaching part way down the Red Sea. Annexation, accomplished by A. Cornelius Palma, was smooth and unopposed, signifying a final closing of the Roman ring and representing almost the last move of the century-long game in which friendly Near Eastern kingdoms were quietly removed from the board and their vague defensive arrangements replaced with firm, Roman-run frontiers. Here, however, firmness would be relative; for on her eastern side Nabataea, like Syria, faded into featureless desert, with little on which to base precise definition.

The Nabataeans were Arabs and their language Arabic. More exactly, they were descended from a north Arabian tribe which had moved into biblical Edom during the 6th–4th centuries BC. In the Roman period relatively few Arabs had strayed beyond the Arabian peninsula. Strabo recognised three groups: the western Arabs 'who share Egypt east of the Nile with others'; the northern Arabs (Nabataeans, plus bedouin tribes of the Syrian Desert); and the southern Arabs of Arabia proper.[14] This last (today's Saudi Arabia, plus the territory on her fringes) was known as *Arabia Felix* (Arabia the Blest).

Though Arabs monopolised trade between India and the West, this lock was picked early in Augustus' reign, when an anonymous Roman castaway fetched up on the west coast of India. His story was tested by a Greek navigator Hippalus who, in about AD, 45 discovered the timing of the monsoonal gales, so opening the Indian Ocean to western prows, causing a flurry of sails in the ports on the Roman (i.e. Egyptian) side of the Red Sea and a business boom in Alexandria. Strabo tells us that from only one of these ports (Myos Hormos) 120 vessels were setting out for India every year.

The Nabataeans had been quick to profit from this spice rush by stepping up operations at their emporium of Leucê Comê,[15] some 240 miles down the Hejazi coast, usually placed at El Haura. We are told by the *Periplus of the Erythraean Sea*[16] that a Roman centurion was stationed there, levying a 25% duty on imported items,[17] which suggests a customs union between Nabataea and Rome. This outpost would henceforth mark the empire's southeastern extremity. A few miles inland, on the road to Medina, eleven soldiers' names are cut into two rocks, one of which was seemingly a watchtower base. Though in Greek characters, these are Arab-sounding, suggesting Roman *auxilia* or *numeri*.[18] Trajan re-dug a canal (built by Augustus) between the Nile and Clysma (Suez) and it is likely that he now put a fleet into the Red Sea.[19] There was as yet no need to fortify the Egyptian coast.

Such was the situation in this quiet corner of the Roman world, with the Arabs occupying today's Arabia, plus Jordan and adjacent fringes: a minor people awaiting their place in history. Returning to Nabataea, this was a land of transit and a wealthy one: crossroads of long-haul camel traffic from Parthia and the shorter journey between Red Sea and Mediterranean. The monsoons brought the merchantmen into the Red Sea in winter and goods must be transferred to northern ports for the spring sailings. Crucial to this movement was the Kings' Highway, running from Aqaba to the Syrian border at Bostra and branching to Gaza; an ancient road whose name is preserved in the Old Testament.[20]

Nabataea's capital and most famous creation was Petra, which would sleep in its chasm until the astonished Swiss explorer Burckhardt stumbled into it in 1812. He found a ghost city, much as antiquity had left it, with cliff-carved façades and rock-cut chambers. Westerners were transfixed by the haunting lithographs of David Roberts, who visited Petra during his tour of Egypt and the Holy Land in 1839. To many it remains their favourite Middle Eastern site. Petra's name would be incorporated into that of Trajan's new province Arabia Petraea, though this could be taken as a pun, for the land is rocky indeed. It was however rejected as the capital, which was established at Bustra (Bosra), today just inside modern Syria; a choice perhaps explained by a view which saw Arabia as an adjunct of the Syrian province. *Legio VI Ferrata* ('the iron legion') was now stationed there.

The legion would spend several seasons upgrading the Kings' Highway into a paved road, the best in the East. Its fame is suggested by numerous milestones, replaced successively, of which several hundred have been found along the 250-mile length in groups of up to nine. The road is traceable in many places and well preserved in some. At the turn of the century a five-mile stretch was found with its top-dressing of cinder and clay still in place,[21] reminding us that the horseshoe had not been invented and stone surfaces required padding to protect animals' feet. The care given to the project was clearly connected with the memory of Trajan's father, Marcus Ulpius Traianus, who had built the road up to the border on the Syrian side. Now, with the Flavian road across Asia Minor, the existing Syrian network, and finally this highway (renamed the *Via Nova Traiana*), there was a continuous artery from Black Sea to Red Sea, from Trebizond to Aqaba.

We have seen Nabataea as a land of commercial transit. It was also one of climatic transition. This is clear in Jordan today, in places over 200 miles wide but with almost all settlement confined to a western strip of only twenty-five miles. While Amman may hope for twelve inches annually, rainfall dwindles eastwards to as little as two. Further south the contrast is even more abrupt. However, the limits of grazing have always varied, from year to year and age to age. Though it seems that up to the time of annexation Nabataea enjoyed a slightly better rainfall than today's, drought was slowly increasing. Accordingly, nomadic pressures against the settled zone would grow during the 2nd and 3rd centuries, though they were not yet serious. Parthia would never be a direct threat to the Arabian province, due to the waterless width between. The desert here is not sandy. It rises slowly toward 2,000 feet: in the north by a series of black, basaltic plains, in the south by long terraces of reddish lava. Much is *hammada* or rocky plateau, fanged with flints, execrable walking and generally avoided by man and beast. Here roads are *pistes aménagées*, the *aménagement* consisting of the surface clearance of sharp stones, as noted by Poidebard in Syria. Since all ages have used this simple method it is not always easy to be sure which roads were Roman.

Regarding defence, Arabia Petraea is a clear example of the Roman takeover of existing arrangements. The Nabataeans had controlled the desert by watchtowers, inherited in turn from the Moabite Kingdom, again demonstrating that this ubiquitous tool for securing the empire's edge was not Roman in origin. The towers had been of large, rough, drystone masonry, often with barrack accommodation within a walled enclosure and supplied by reservoir or cistern. They would now be commandeered by the Roman army, repaired or rebuilt and extended eastward until, by the 4th century, they constituted a major surveillance network, not unlike the Syrian, reaching fifteen or twenty miles into the desert: a zone of control but not a line of exclusion; allowing the nomads to enter the province in time of drought but ensuring that their movements would be supervised.

It was probably not until the 3rd century that the word Saracen[22] began to be used to distinguish marauding bedouin from Romanised Arabs. So Ammian, an ex-soldier with personal experience of the eastern frontier, writes of them in the late 4th century:

> . . . the Saracens, whom it gives us no pleasure to choose either as friend or foe, ranging near and far, destroying whatever was to

.hand in a remarkably short time: as hungry hawks sighting prey from on high swoop, strike and fly off all in one [. . .]

They fight as equals, half-naked, in thigh-length cloaks of coloured wool, travelling long distances on swift horses and slim camels, alike in tranquil or troubled times. None holds a plough, tends a tree or tills soil; but all wander homelessly, without shelter or laws, covering wide spaces, unable long to endure the same sky or sun.

So they live, always on the move. Even their wives are on temporary lease. Although in token of marriage a prospective wife may offer her husband a spear and tent by way of dowry, she retains the right to leave him after an arranged time if she wishes. And you would not believe with what abandon both sexes give themselves to lovemaking. They wander so incessantly that a woman marries in one place, has children in another and brings them up in yet another, all without stopping. They live on game and milk, herbs and such birds as they are able to snare; and we have met many who were quite ignorant of grain and wine. So much for this unhappy breed.[23]

There was another border zone inherited from the Nabataeans: their frontier with Palestine. In Chapter 2 we saw how, after suppressing the Jewish revolt, Titus revived Judaea's southern defensive line, which had faced the nomads of the Negev since at least the age of Solomon. With the annexation of Nabataea the Negev passed into Roman hands: a signal, one might expect, for Trajan to abolish its frontier. There is however no evidence for abandonment until the next reign. Rome had, for the first time, incorporated a desert within her boundaries and apparently the *limes Palaestinae* was for a time kept on as an 'interior frontier', by which places considered not worth occupying were sealed off and watched around the rim. To restate the defensive problems of Roman Arabia: these lay largely in the future. With only one legion and a like number of auxiliaries, the province was at present lightly defended by a watchtower screen along the desert's edge. Though the *Via Nova* was guarded, there is little likelihood that it served as a frontier. Indeed it was unsuited to do so, since it ran through the farming zone rather than outside it.

It is time to introduce an unforgettable character in the story of *limes* research; not least because he was born on the Roman frontier and returned to it nearly seventy years later via the Great Wall of

China. This conundrum is resolved in the career of Aurel Stein (1862–1943). Born in Budapest, from 1900 he made explorations in China and, towards the end of his long life, turned to the British mandated territories of Transjordan and Iraq, where he would take up a challenge comparable to Poidebard's in Syria.

A student of oriental languages, Stein accepted a post in India; and from there, in 1900, led the first of four Central Asian expeditions. Between the wars he also explored extensively in Iran. He died in Kabul in October 1943 at the age of eighty-three. Of present interest is his work in the Tarim Basin, beyond Tibet, exploring and excavating over its 1,200-mile width. At Lop Nor he uncovered rolls of raw silk, preserved in the dry sand. Subsequently he traced an ancient camel route through Chinese Turkestan to the commencement of Russian territory. These apparently random discoveries seemed to add up to a hypothesis: that he had found the first part of the fabled Silk Road. Not unnaturally his imagination turned towards Syria where the Roman frontier – in many ways the mirror image of the Chinese – awaited the arrival of the fabulous filament, a pound of which was said by Pliny to be worth a pound of gold.[24]

So matters rested for a quarter century, while Stein's tireless spirit drove him toward other goals. But by 1929 he was in touch with Poidebard and in 1934 reviewed *La Trace de Rome* for English-speaking journals. Ceding Syria to the French, Stein recognised the parallel possibilities of the adjacent British dependencies. Like Poidebard and Crawford he recognised that this period, with air forces stationed in the mandated territories, offered an unrepeatable chance to study aspects of Western heritage in countries that would soon return to the East. In 1938, after almost a decade of string-pulling and at the eleventh hour, with war clouds gathering, he was able to achieve a 700-mile survey along a diagonal line from the Gulf of Aqaba to northern Iraq. He flew in a Vickers Wellesley bomber but was later allocated the Vincent: a smaller, slower biplane, more suited to photographic work. He also followed some of his observations by ground visits, though there was no time for excavation.

Stein, now seventy-seven, was flying in open cockpits, bouncing in unsuitable vehicles over unspeakable surfaces and sleeping out in the freezing desert nights. He was, moreover, an Orientalist rather than a Romanist. He was alone, rushed, underequipped and oversti-mulated. He misinterpreted many sites. His *Report*,[25] written in 1940, was backed by insufficient knowledge of other Roman frontiers. Even his theory regarding the Silk Road would not stand the test of time.[26] But his photos recorded hundreds of works, many Roman and most unknown, of which some have since been destroyed and others damaged or deteriorated. Certain areas, notably in Iraq, have been closed to aerial survey ever since.

In this sense Stein's *limes* legacy, snatched in his declining years, just before war began and the mandates ended, has the stamp of greatness. But a series of disappointments ensued. Stein left Amman in May 1939, returned to England and then sailed for India. All the negatives of his aerial photographs had been left with the Royal Air Force in the Middle East, a repository Stein naïvely believed more secure than sea travel during those precarious months. However he did have with him two prints of each photograph. Four years later, before his final exit to Kabul, he deposited these in a suitcase, together with one typescript copy of his *Report* at his bank, the Srinagar branch of the Imperial Bank of India. Some years after his death this suitcase would be returned to England, where it came into the hands of Stein's executor Kenneth Mason, professor of geography at Oxford, who passed the contents to an appropriate expert, Sir Mortimer Wheeler. Yet these two men would soon be dead, and the majority of the photos would be lost without trace, presumably when Wheeler's effects were disposed of. Fortunately, a minority of aerials, from Iraq only, had found their way to the British Museum, and these survive. Similarly, the ground photographs, though of lesser importance, had been left with the India Office and they too are preserved. But most damaging of all, the negatives left in Baghdad and Amman were routinely destroyed, along with almost the entire RAF Middle Eastern archive from the inter-war years. So, in a complex fiasco, part of Stein's Iraqi coverage and his entire Jordanian aerial record were lost. His *Limes* Report remained unread. Gossip even had it that a spiteful and eccentric widow had sequestrated the manuscript. But its author was a lifelong bachelor and the malign Lady Stein did not exist.

In the late 1970s Dr David Kennedy of Sheffield University found the main body of Stein's papers stored in the Bodleian Library, Oxford, in a hundred cardboard boxes. Luckily the cache included the original of the report, with handwritten emendations. This would at last be published, along with the best of the surviving photographs, forty-two years after it was written. It is of great interest still. Owing to the survival of Iraqi rather than Jordanian photos, the northern sector of the survey remains the more valuable, not least because it covers the most unfamiliar of Roman frontiers.[27]

In subsequent years the balance of knowledge has swung back into Jordan's favour as a site for research. While Iraq, following the murder of Feisal II, slid into xenophobia, Jordan remained under saner guidance. As a result it has become a favoured quadrant of the Roman marches for investigation, especially by a younger generation of American and British scholars, with the blessing of a vigorous Jordanian Department of Antiquities, yielding commensurate informational rewards. Most notable has been the *limes Arabicus* survey, beginning in the late 1970s, sponsored by the University of North Carolina. Fieldwork includes interesting signalling experiments between tower sites.[28] Here results showed how information could be relayed from a twenty-mile spread of towers to a fort in a few minutes. Torch signals were visible by night for over twelve miles.

In Roman frontier studies much ink has flowed on the question of signalling methods and codes. Why, one may ask, are they so important? The answer lies in numbers. Towers were common to almost the entire edge of empire and were sometimes ranged in considerable depth. A total of ten thousand may not be an exaggeration for the frontier as a whole. Even given a manning level of only two per tower, with just two watches, this could involve nearly a fifth of the Roman auxiliary army, with perhaps a comparable number servicing the towers, patrolling between them or guarding them. Ignoring other calls on the army's time, this suggests a strategic division of 40% of auxiliaries devoted to surveillance and 60% to response. As the link between these two groups, signalling obviously affected the daily lives of many.

Because towers are vulnerable to small arms fire, today's observers prefer to lie low. But in antiquity a frontier bristling with towers was a show of strength and a warning that intrusion would be opposed. This display of tower power especially characterised nervous frontiers like those of Britain and Germany, facing enemies reputedly strong. On the other hand fewer towers could imply confidence or the success of other methods of control.

Regarding signalling theory, Vegetius (late 4th century AD) specified 'fire by night and smoke by day'[29] as the two basic methods, but goes on to speak of waving a wooden torch, hoisting flags and blowing bugles. A bugle or conch mouthpiece has been found in a forward location on the German frontier. The use of mirrors made of polished metal was especially likely in sunny climes, as is suggested by the names of at least two frontier posts in Africa.[30] Vegetius offers little help on the information conveyed. While some have favoured a refined system we must bear in mind the non-existence of telescopes, vulnerability to bad light, the lack of sophistication of the auxiliary soldier, irregular distances between towers and the many variables of the frontier as a whole. Elaborate signalling techniques and the existence of an army-wide system are therefore matters of doubt. Perhaps 'intrusion!' and 'message received' were the sum of the signal towers' vocabulary; and less urgent detail was carried by runners or despatch riders.

Trajan's Nabataean venture proved popular and successful. No blood was spilt and few fortifications built; though this is not to say that Jordan has few to show. These are largely of the 3rd and 4th centuries, when the Arabian province would have three legions and a large auxiliary force. As Dr Parker puts it: 'Scholars of the Roman frontier, digging postholes and foundations in Germany and Britain, were stunned by the military structures which dotted the Arabian frontier, such as forts and watchtowers standing to nearly their original height.'[31] These include world-class examples, some now tottering and in need of consolidation. For example Qasr[32] el Hallabat, late Roman-Byzantine, with walls twelve feet high, twenty-five miles east by north-east of Amman. The late Roman-medieval Qasr el Azraq is seventy miles east of Amman. In 1916 the Emir Feisal's army wintered in this oasis and T. E. Lawrence occupied one of the fort's guardrooms. Qasr el Aseikin, a hilltop fort above Azraq, lies six miles to the north-east. Way out on Route 30, two thirds of the way to the Iraqi border and fourteen miles north-west of pump station 4 (on the disused IPC pipeline) is Qasr Burqu, a large watchtower still over thirty feet high, which perhaps had four storeys.

Some sixty miles south of Amman, between the main road and Kerak, is El Lejjun, a 4th-century legionary base, with low-standing but complete remains. This is a rare site, abandoned in the 6th century and almost untouched till the twentieth, with a potential for study greater than Inchtuthil's. Above it is the fort of Khirbet[33] el Fityan, clearly the receiving station for the fortress and in fact the gathering centre used in the signalling experiment. Ten miles north-east is the late-period cavalry fort of Qasr B'shir: one of the best in the Roman world, its walls almost intact and its south-west tower preserved to the roof (off-road vehicle and local guidance advised).

Five miles south of Lejjun is another thirty-foot tower, Qasr Abu Rubka. Eight miles east of Petra was the frontier town of Udruh, whose southern wall still stands to twenty feet. The ruins probably conceal a late fortress, guarding the *Via Nova*, though the road is difficult to trace in this sector and the town was built over during the Islamic period. Nor is there visible trace of the fortress at Aqaba (Aila). Stein suggested it may be under the mound still called Aila, close to the tip of the Gulf. Twenty-five miles east of Aqaba is the incomparable Wadi Rum.[34] Though without notable remains this is Roman frontier country *par excellence*, with a majesty to match the Euphrates gorges.

Our scene now shifts to southern Scotland where, in or about AD 105, Rome suffered some major setback. All we know is that the key fort of Newstead (near Melrose) and five or six others were burnt, with destruction as far south as Corbridge. Coincidence with the second Dacian War suggests that troop withdrawals had brought the army of Britain below safety level. Whatever happened, the result was momentous, for it would shape Roman thinking on what might be retained of Britain and what rescinded, for centuries to come. The immediate response was to fall back to the Tyne Gap and set up a line across that sixty-mile isthmus, towards which the long neck of England's north finally narrows. It was an overdue decision. Having stalled in Scotland a decade since, it was time to abjure that profitless portion; though what might then have been accomplished deftly and discreetly was now done clumsily and ingloriously: a lesson which would not be lost on Hadrian, then engaged in arranging the Dacian victory festivities.

The Tyne Gap is the dent made by Tyne and Eden in the Pennine flanks and divides that range from the Cheviots, its northern extension. The valley of the South Tyne, back to back with that of the Irthing (an Eden tributary), opens a pleasant, east–west corridor through melancholy moorland, widening at either end. Stretched supply lines had plagued the Scottish venture. By contrast, the fertility of the Solway plain, lower Eden and Tyne, plus river access from both coasts, were strong attractions. Thanks, furthermore, to Agricola, the basis for a frontier existed already in the form of a fortified road from Carlisle to Corbridge; with forts at either end and two between. The original intention had not been to join North to Irish Seas but merely to cross-link the two south to north invasion routes, today's A68 (Dere Street) and the A6 at Carlisle.

Agricola's road would now be upgraded and extended westwards to the coast; its defences increased to at least six large and as many small forts. Whether it was also continued eastward down the Tyne is a question slow to be solved. The road is known by its Saxon name, the Stanegate: i.e. of stone and a gate to the west. It was first proposed as a *limes* by R. G. Collingwood (1889–1943), Wayneflete professor of metaphysical philosophy at Oxford, whose life and learning remind us that Roman frontier studies need not mean narrowness of view. In his memorable first volume of the *Oxford History of Britain*[35] he suggested a Trajanic line similar to that between Rhine and Danube, with forts sited at the normal European frontier specification of seven miles. The roadside towers, which would make his German comparison more exact, have not been found; but despite this and other drawbacks Collingwood's thesis still stands and the Stanegate may cautiously be accepted as Rome's third attempt to form a British frontier. Since it was to last only twenty years the Stanegate would never be elaborately developed and its forts remained earth and timber. The majority are known only through aerial photography or soundings; though there are visible exceptions, like the fortlet at Haltwhistle Burn. The road is still traceable in places. Visitors may consider it poor recompense for the loss of Scotland.

Consolation is to be had at Chesterholm (Vindolanda), now a famous site, one and a half miles north of Bardon Mill (Northumberland). Approaching from the west the modern roadway overlies the Stanegate and the broken shaft of one of its milestones is passed. Under the later *vicus* (civilian settlement) is an even earlier establishment from the time of Domitian. The Trajanic fort was built on the spur beyond, though the visible remains are of later date. The Stanegate rounds its northern foot, with an intact but uninscribed milestone, delightfully *in situ*. Here we are in a charming glen with restricted views to either side. On high ground, less than a mile to the east, the earthen perimeter of Barcombe signal tower may be seen in the corner of an evacuated British village. This was Vindolanda's eyes, a receiving station similar in function to Khirbet el Fityan or to those on the Carpathian frontier.

Vindolanda is a monument to the Birley family: with three careers (father's and sons') devoted to Roman researches. Eric Birley (1905–1995), sometime owner of Chesterholm, donated the site to the nation. But this is only his second memorial; for the first is surely the Congresses of Roman Frontier Studies, which met at his instigation in

Newcastle, 1949; and has reconvened in one or other of the former frontier provinces every few years since. Without its published work our picture would be halved and the residue scattered among the fifteen or more countries whose scholars regularly contribute. The Birley achievement is of high order, in both local and international fields.

In 1973 Robin Birley, digging to Trajanic levels just outside the fort, came upon the first of over two hundred wooden fragments covered with Latin handwriting. The excitement of this find must be seen in the light of centuries of epigraphic discovery which has tended to widen our knowledge while deepening it little in a human sense. The formality of stone, the reserve of coins, the muteness of the military: all share a reluctance to speak personally, in the way our media-minded age takes for granted. This is why a site like Pompeii, with its vivid sense of people, achieves world fame while frontier forts lie in lonely fields. At least the Birleys have redeemed Vindolanda. The fragments were buried deeply, seemingly in a rubbish dump of the Trajanic fort, which underlaps the walls presently visible. They had been waterlogged and the fading and blurring of the ink presented exceptional difficulties. Evidence for the 1973–75 excavations were not published till 1983.[36] An official document, deciphered from twelve related pieces, tells of many soldiers assigned to workshop duties; suggesting some major job like fort enlargement. Almost certainly this was the end-phase of a winter programme, for we will see that such a workforce may not have been available in summer. 'April 25th: in the workshops 343 men. Of these 12 cobblers, 18 bathhouse builders [. . .] for lead [. . .] hospital [. . .] in the kilns [. . .] for clay [. . .] plasterers [. . .] for hardcore.' Were these visiting legionaries; or does it mean that auxiliary soldiers had by now developed secondary or winter skills as specialists in a craft, beside their primary function of guarding the frontier?

There were also fragments of letters between officers, all spending a sizeable proportion of content in greetings, commendations, requests or acknowledgements. While this illustrates the importance of contacts and favours in the Roman scheme – reminiscent of some oriental societies today – it does of course mean that many precious fragments are devoted to soft rather than hard information. 'A friend sent me fifty oysters from Cordonovi [. . .]'[37] 'I have sent you . . . pairs of socks from Sattua, two pairs of sandals and two of underpants. Greet Tetricus and all our messmates, with whom I hope you live in good fortune.' These results were of palaeographic interest; but after a long wait for publication the yield in general terms was modest. Excavation continued, however, with more texts published.[38] By now the total number of fragments had risen almost to a thousand; and though some were blank or illegible the quality of information was rising too. There were letters concerning supplies, requests for leave, even an appeal for clemency by a 'foreigner': perhaps meaning that a volunteer from another province expected punishment to be less harsh than for a locally levied recruit:[39] '[. . .] do not let me, innocent and an overseas man, be beaten till I bleed – even if I did do wrong [. . .]' Over two hundred names have so far accumulated, of which more than thirty are Roman citizens, seven Greek, six or seven German and many Celtic. One officer, discussing British fighting methods, uses the diminutive *brittunculi* (the Britlets) giving us a national equivalent of *homunculus* (manikin), *graeculus* (Greekling) and other known disparagements.

During the 1988 excavations a muster list for the fort's garrison was disinterred. It is a document of unique interest.

18th May
1st Cohort Tungrians,[40] Julius Verecundus commanding.

Total strength (including
6 centurions) 752

Absent:
Attached to the Governor's Guard
at the office of Ferox[41] .... 46 men
At Coria [Corbridge] .... 337 men (with 2 centurions)
In London............................ 1 centurion
Various others .... 26 men (with 2 centurions)
At [illegible] .... 46 men

Total absent .... 456 men

Present strength remaining .... 296 (with 1 centurion)

Of these, sick 15
             injured 6
             eye ailments 10
Total................................ 31

Balance present and fit for
active duties .... 256 (including 1 centurion)

One's first reaction – as also to the large number assigned to work-shop duties – is to wonder how the frontier got guarded at all. Secondly, here is clear evidence for a view long dawning: that a standard-sized unit fitting neatly into a regulation-built fort and dedi-cated to the specific duties of that fort, is a theoretical proposition only. This cohort was 50% over-strength in the first place, raising the spectre that our estimates for the army as a whole might be wildly wide of the mark. Thirdly, postings to lonely outposts were not always as stern or as final as they might seem. The governor's bodyguard, a thousand men drawn from various units in rotation, was usually stationed in London! Nor was the bracing life of a frontiersman invariably healthy. One in ten was on the sick list.

Much correspondence concerned quartermastery, with building materials, timber, premade wooden objects, hides and textiles all mentioned. References to food supplies include venison, pork, ham, cereals, sour wine and beer; but luxury clothing items, tableware, honey or mead, spices and olives are also listed. Surprisingly perhaps in those troubled times, there are references to the presence of women and children. Most interesting of all is a correspondence between two ladies:[42] parts of letters from a Claudia Severa, wife of Aelius, commander of a neighbouring fort, to Sulpicia Lepidana, whose husband was prefect at Vindolanda. These appear to have been writ-ten by secretaries, with greetings added by the correspondent herself. Hand and language are refined.

> Claudia Severa to her Lepidana, greetings. Come to us, I pray you, on the third before the ides of September.[43] I beg you most warmly to come, for your being here will make my day. All the very best to your Cerialis. Aelius and our little boy send their love. I'll be waiting. Goodbye sister, my dearest soul . . .

This touching note conveys the feelings of an army wife, alone in a lonely outpost, reaching out along the frontier to solitary women in other forts, seven, fourteen, even twenty-one miles away. Its senti-ments suggest how infrequent and precious such contacts must have been. Given the distances, two neighbours on either side and one toward the south were a likely limit to Claudia's social world for five years, a cohort commander's normal term.

We know little else of the officers' wives on frontiers. Common to all forts was the commander's house (praetorium). It was two-storeyed, often with a ground-plan of fifteen or twenty rooms, centrally heated, with kitchen and bath suite, obviously suitable for a family and servants. Though in the midst of a crowded fort it faced inwards onto a tranquil courtyard or small garden. Junior officers' families may have shared the accommodation. The *praetorium* was a standard part of a fort, even in the wildest places; as for example at Fendoch, in the very jaws of the Scottish Highlands. Even so we are unsure when this began, or under what circumstances it was thought safe for Roman women to live on the world's margins. The existence of a commandant's house does not necessarily mean it was fully occupied from the first. In the post-expansion phase, however, it seems likely that security was normally considered adequate. Security was apparently not the only criterion. Tacitus records a clash in the Senate during Tiberius' reign. Ostensibly it concerned governors' wives – indeed it arose from a debate about the governorship of Africa – but it is full of army references and could easily be applied to officers' wives a generation later.

During the debate Severus Caecina moved that no provincial governor should be accompanied by his wife, declaring: 'Though I myself have a wife and six children whom I love dearly, while I have served forty years in various provinces she has always been left behind in Italy. The old rule[44] which forbade our dragging women abroad was a sound one. The feminine influence is toward luxury in peace, timidity in war and indecision in business. Their presence turns a Roman march into a barbarian ramble. Lack of resolve and staying power are not alas the only failings of the fair sex. Given a chance they reveal themselves as intriguing, ambitious and hard as nails. Soon they are flaunting themselves among the ranks and the centurions are dancing attendance. There was recently a case of a woman taking drill parades and directing manoeuvres! And is it not true that whenever an official gets into trouble for corruption, the real trouble turns out to be his wife? For it is toward her that the seediest of provincials gravitate; and it is she who fiddles the books. So there are two governors to salute in the street, two governmental offices to be paid for: and, depend on it, it will be from hers that the perverse and domineering orders stream. Make no mistake, they who were once held in check by law have broken their chains and rule supreme: in the home, in the courts and now in the army!'

But Caecina's was a minority view. Romans were increasingly confident in their empire and relaxed in their attitudes to public service:

> A few senators listened with approval. Most protested that these opinions were not relevant to a debate on who should govern Africa. Severus was answered by Valerius Massalinus who maintained that the law prohibiting women had existed because the harsh circumstances of the Republic had made it unavoidable. But under today's conditions it was less than fair to say that because a few women had forgotten their place, husbands in general should be deprived of their wives. Similarly it would be a mistake if the frail sex were to be left at home, prey to the temptations of their frailty and the appetites of others. All who speak of righting wrongs in the provinces might remember the scandals in the capital [. . .][45]

By such arguments Caecina's motion was sidetracked.

Returning to the commander's house: this covered some 6% of a fort's interior and its accommodation was roughly equivalent to the barrack space allotted eighty men. A private soldier would simply not have had room to keep a woman in the fort, even had it been allowed. Officially, a serving auxiliary below the rank of centurion was not even permitted to marry. But love could, without too much difficulty, find a way. Marriage would be valid under native custom and children could be legitimised on the ending of their father's time with the colours. Many liaisons were therefore contracted locally, though what the arrangements were for living out is unknown.[46] While citizenship was granted to auxiliary soldiers on discharge, the privilege did not extend to their wives.

So much for our resumé of Trajan's activities in Britain: a theatre at which he was never present and in which we may guess that he was little interested. Seven years now passed between the dramatic events which included the defeat of Decebalus, the annexation of Arabia, the evacuation of Scotland; and the beginning of another drama, provoked by another adventurer. Parthia, presently considered weak, had accepted Trajan's right to nominate her king. But in 112 the nobles defiantly elected one Chosroes, a candidate of their own. To make matters worse Chosroes tried to shore up his position by instigating an anti-Roman coup in Armenia and installing a puppet king. The coup misfired, leaving the pro-Roman party in control of half the country. This was a signal for rebellion in Parthia's eastern provinces. Though these events gave Trajan ample leverage he decided on the continuation of diplomacy by more strenuous means: marching on Armenia, deposing Chosroes' puppet and annexing his kingdom. The downhill road into a divided Parthia lay open.

Here was a fateful juncture. Eighty-seven years earlier, on the day of Augustus' funeral, the advice to halt Rome's outward march had been read to a surprised Senate. Most subsequent emperors appeared to ignore it, but when all was said and done the only substantial acquisition in the century following had been Britain; and she was of questionable worth. More specifically, Augustus had declined to poach from Parthia. He accepted an equilibrium, with the upper Euphrates as its fulcrum. This was a policy rejected only by Nero. Vespasian, by instigating an eastern frontier, had invested in it heavily. Which course would Trajan now follow? Dio believed his weakness was for grandeur and this governed the choice he was about to make.[47] Given his extrovert nature and love of popularity, there is little doubt Trajan had relished both fighting the Dacian Wars and spending its spoils on triumphs and monuments. But excitement faded as the routines of peace returned. Had this left him with a sense of anticlimax, with dreams still unfulfilled; and might these be strong enough to tempt him into a last gamble, the greatest left to Roman arms?

In the spring of 115 Trajan swept south, overrunning northern Mesopotamia. His aim was to detach what we now call Iraq from Iran, taking the valley for Rome and leaving Parthia the mountains. As border cities toppled the emperor's popularity surged. Once again where Trajan led Hadrian followed, more than ever convinced he was marching to a deluded drum. How could these territories be defended? Conquest of the Land of the Two Rivers would open a 600-mile frontier, facing an enemy always on higher ground. Rome would never find the strength to destroy Parthia's heartland and, unless she did, could not win outright.

Yet win Trajan did. His planning was excellent. Ships built in the Kurdish foothills were then transported in sections by wagon. A powerful fleet thus appeared on the Tigris in a treeless region where the Parthians least expected it. 'Trajan advanced as far as Babylon, for Parthia was weakened by internal conflict and still in the throes of civil war. He then crossed the Tigris and entered Ctesiphon,[48] where the soldiers saluted him as victor and hailed him as *Parthicus*.

In addition to other honours the Senate voted him the privilege of celebrating Triumphs in perpetuity.'[49] Chosroes was put to flight. For Trajan it had been a career-crowning campaign. He was a general who had never lost; who had won both in the West and East; who had conquered more territory than anyone since Augustus; who had added six provinces to the empire;[50] and who had brought Rome to her eastern high tide at the head of the Persian Gulf.

There now followed a pause for sightseeing. Trajan was sixty-three years old.

> After taking Ctesiphon he expressed the wish to sail downriver to the Gulf. On seeing the ocean and a ship setting out for the Indies, he said 'I would certainly have gone there too had I been younger'; and he began to brood about the Indians and ask about them, rating Alexander the Great lucky to have gone that far. On the other hand he wished it to be known that his own gains were greater than Alexander's; indeed he wrote to the Senate to this effect.[51]

After musing on that sunny strand, Trajan turned back toward Ctesiphon, where his army was resting. But first a brief stop in Babylon to view the deathplace of Alexander, whose star had been extinguished there more than four centuries earlier: 'offering sacrifices to his spirit in the very room where he breathed his last'. It was in this setting, heavy with symbolism, that bad news arrived:

> In Rome a triumphal arch had been put in hand and people were already discussing meeting him on the road, exceptionally far from the city. However Trajan would never see Rome again. His exploits were over and he was about to lose what he had taken. For while he was away at the Gulf all the newly occupied territories burst into flame and garrisons were put either to flight or the sword. The news was brought him at Babylon which he had visited because of its fame, though there were only ruins to be seen.[52]

The coming year would witness a calamitous run on Trajan's fortunes. The Parthian, still unbeaten, holding the long line of foothills east of the Tigris, had been able from that base to foment rebellion behind the entirety of Trajan's overstretched front. His generals managed a partial recovery and a patched-up armistice. Trajan himself commanded at the siege of Hatra,[53] perhaps the severest trouble spot, but after an exhausting campaign failed to take the town.

Rome's adversity was Israel's opportunity. That nation's fervour, quenched in the homeland by Vespasian and Titus, now burst out in other provinces where there were Jewish communities: first at Cyrene[54] but spreading soon to Egypt and Cyprus. According to Dio almost a quarter of a million perished. Here was an innate weakness of peripheral defence: internal catastrophe, unrelieved by an army stationed on distant frontiers. But this was no time for reappraisal. The pattern pointed to Syria as the next flashpoint, the place most crucial to Trajan's rear. He hurried there.

But now a third disaster. In Antioch Trajan suffered a severe stroke. It was decided to repatriate him by sea. His ship put in at Selinus, not far along the coast of Asia Minor, where he died. His ashes were taken on to Rome and deposited in the chamber at the base of his Column.

Hadrian was free at last. He must move cautiously against the memory of a man still universally loved. But twenty years' frustration were at an end. Humiliation in the East opened the door to a new beginning. For Hadrian had something to say which would scarcely be acceptable to Roman ears, his task made possible only because recent events in Parthia had proved him right. This was that the time had come for the empire to go over to the defensive. A message, one may think, essentially the same as that of Augustus; for to assert that Rome must cease to expand is no different from saying that the empire must keep within its boundaries. The difference is that Augustus said it posthumously. He did not have to face the Roman people; and what he said was binding on no one. He merely left advice, which his successors were free to follow or ignore. It is quite another matter to say it at the outset, to make it a plank of policy and to translate it into fact.

CHAPTER 5

Hadrian:
'Britain will be a monument for us'

WE ARE NOT EVEN SURE that Hadrian was Trajan's rightful successor. The *optimus princeps* (styled by the Senate 'best emperor of all') had shirked the duty of naming his heir. Nonetheless it was Hadrian's fortune to have been created governor of Syria; and as such not only to be in Antioch with Trajan at the time of his stroke, close to the scene of his death and first to hear of it; but also heir to the command of the formidable army still assembled for the Parthian war. Reality was easing his path to the throne. What of legality? This hung on a directive, supposedly dictated by the dying Trajan during his last journey along the Cyprus-facing coast and sent back to Antioch just before the end. But the empress Plotina travelled with her husband and scandal preferred that she was in love with Hadrian and had forged the signature.

Regarding sources for this reign, it begins in the twilight of second- or third-hand evidence: the synopses and summaries of later centuries, which add little of substance. Dio Cassius remains faithful, but he too writes from another age, and we see him through the bleary window of John Xiphilinus, a Byzantine editor who abridged part of his work. However, a new door opens in the shape of a collection of imperial biographies, also of 4th-century authorship, called the *Augustan History*.[1] These start with Hadrian and continue with portraits of thirty subsequent emperors or pretenders, ending 150 years later. They constitute the sole historical account of parts of the 2nd and 3rd centuries. Alas, they are a dwindling asset, their second half descending into crudity and bogusness. Fortunately the problems of this perplexing book need not trouble us here. Hadrian's biography is a fine piece of work. With its detailed account of his thinking and motives it offers an insight into the psyche of this complex and contradictory emperor such as the student of antiquity is seldom granted. One may ask whether the quirks of character on which it dwells were relevant to the shaping of frontiers. But Hadrian's was an extraordinary case and we will argue that they were. Indeed there are peculiarities of foreign policy and frontier development which we believe inexplicable except in terms of Hadrian's temperament and personal obsessions.

Dio tells us he was charming and pleasant, tall, elegant and strongly built. He was often kind and lenient. Gibbon's judgement that 'the ruling passions of his soul were curiosity and vanity'[2] is an oversimplification. To these we must add an array of outstanding gifts and powers. Of his memory and comprehension for example: 'After a quick scan he could repeat obscurest chapter and verse from his head. Incredibly, he could write, dictate, listen and converse all at once. His grasp of the national exchequer was as total as the careful housewife her kitchen.'[3] And Dio: 'His intellectual pretensions were boundless. He enjoyed every kind of challenge, boasting that there was nothing relating to peace or war, public or private life, about which he was not well informed.'[4]

Hadrian was the most mentally active and perhaps the most intelligent of all Rome's rulers. He was almost certainly the most vain. It was said that he wrote his own 'biography', then arranged publication in the name of a civil servant who had to pretend the book was his own.[5] To this we must add jealousy. Not, as with Domitian, of success in government or generalship, but in the fields of creativity and learning, which he came to regard as his own. This was harmless in itself. But his envy of others' achievements was extreme and led to the downfall of many. For whoever must outdo everyone will always be in collision with someone. Indeed such was his character that he was jealous even of the dead. He "abolished" Homer![6] From this and other stories comes an impression of paradox: on the one hand a 'renaissance' figure, excelling in many fields; on the other so full of foibles that each credit is cancelled by a debit. The outcome was contrariness:

He studied poetry and literature. He excelled in mathematics and painting. He boasted of his prowess as a flautist and singer. He was a great voluptuary and wrote many verses, including love poems, on sensuous themes. By contrast he was an expert swordsman and conversant with all aspects of armament. He was at once austere and amiable, grave and gay, hesitant and impulsive, thrifty and generous, secretive and frank, cruel and clement; and always and in all ways wayward.[7]

The arts both of war and peace were represented in the empire-wide journeys which would characterise his reign. Those to the armies of the frontiers have naturally been stressed by military historians, but the time spent in Greece and Egypt on unmilitary pursuits was in fact greater. These voyages of self-discovery are relived in the follies and pleasances of the imperial villa at Tivoli. There can be few instances of human complexity more remarkable than that Hadrian's Villa and Hadrian's Wall should have sprung from the same brain.

There exists, however, a feat of design surpassing both: the Pantheon, greatest of all Roman buildings to survive. The first edifice of this name and on this site was dedicated in 27 BC by Marcus Agrippa, friend and lieutenant of Augustus. This temple, of modest size and conventional shape, had been gutted by fire in AD 80. Confusingly, the porch still bears Agrippa's name. It was not until 1892 that a French surveyor, Georges Chadanne, inspecting the fabric, discovered that the upper core was of bricks date-stamped within two or three years on either side of AD 123 which, as we will see, was the first full building season of Hadrian's Wall. It is now accepted that Hadrian was the Pantheon's architect and that it was he who produced the idea of combining a Greek portico with a Roman dome.[8] And what a dome! It is still the world's largest, with a diameter 30 inches greater than St Peter's. By contrast another of his masterworks was a disaster. In Jerusalem Hadrian placed his temple of Jupiter on the site of Solomon's Temple. This sensational sacrilege cost yet another revolt and a needless one; an episode that suggests a quest for symbolism and monumentality far beyond the limits of sound judgement.

If Hadrian the artist is a behavioural riddle, what of Hadrian the successor to Trajan? He was an acute sufferer from what might be called the famous father complex; and it is in reaction to his predecessor that we may understand him best. Trajan made war. Hadrian turned to peace. Trajan won territories. Hadrian would relinquish them. 'He abandoned all conquests east of the Euphrates and Tigris (see map 13), following what he was fond of calling the example of Cato, who had argued that if the Macedonians could not be held as subjects they should be set free.'[9] Allowing Armenia, Mesopotamia, Assyria and Babylonia to revert to Parthia was a gesture easier made than justified. It must have rocked the empire. Hadrian then swung his guns towards Dacia. However, this case was different. Not only had there been noble toil to take it; there had already been an eleven-year commitment to holding it. Eutropius gives a glimpse of the misgivings which Hadrian's swerves in foreign policy were now creating:

> Similarly in the matter of Dacia, Hadrian's advisors were at pains to dissuade him from handing over so many Roman citizens to the barbarians; for in the wake of Trajan's conquest a large number of immigrants had poured in from all over the empire, filling the human vacuum created by the long wars with Decebalus.[10]

The fact that Dacian gold production was by then in full swing may have dulcified this decision.

In a further group of measures Trajan's games and other observances were phased out and his theatres quietly closed. Hadrian's spite then focused upon those who had shone in his predecessor's service, including the architect Apollodorus, whose Danube bridge was now slighted. Dio comments tersely that 'Hadrian, fearing it might be used by the barbarians to cross into Moesia, had the superstructure removed.'[11] It was of course correct that bridges may be used both ways. However, no other bridge was dismantled. So Apollodorus' celebrated structure lingered as a row of empty piers. Four centuries later Procopius mentions its remnant as 'totally destroyed by flood and neglect'.[12]

More overt still was Hadrian's attack on the military establishment. In his year of accession four former consuls were executed on conspiracy charges. All had been generals under Trajan. They included Cornelius Palma, who annexed Arabia in 106. Lucius Quietus, a hero of the Dacian Wars, was dismissed and murdered.[13] Hadrian believed he could best outshine Trajan's memory by eclipsing him on the military side. He therefore sought to outdo his predecessor in everything short of actually making war: in his grip on the army, his grasp of its problems and his quest for its allegiance; involving himself in a constant vying with Trajan's reputation for soldierliness. This was complicated by the peculiar problem of Hadrian's reign: that peace meant an under-employed army. Since neither war nor inaction was acceptable, he was driven to devise alternatives such as manoeuvres and drill, which he implemented with obsessive zeal. An even more meaningful answer to military idleness would lie in frontier construction.

There were now 29 legions numbering some 175,000 men; slightly over 400 auxiliary cohorts and cavalry regiments,[14] plus an unknown number of *numeri*, giving an army of perhaps 225,000. Added to these were ten fleets, the Praetorian Guard and several urban cohorts for interior duties. A 2nd-century total for the armed forces of 450,000–500,000 thus seems feasible. Assuming a population of 60 million, the ratio of soldiers to civilians was perhaps 1:120 or 8%. Though remarkably close to 1992 ratios,[15] we must remember that modern technology allows big reductions. In any other terms Rome's army was still small in relation to responsibilities. Thanks to superior organisation this number would continue to be adequate, provided that no significant change in the *barbaricum* upset the balance.

Implementation of Hadrian's policy of non-aggression would depend on the goodwill of an army angered by his abandonment of provinces won with their blood. Farsighted officers must have feared what conversion from a fighting force to a guard force might mean. On this we have no contemporary comment, but the strictures (forty years later) of the finger-wagging Fronto:

> From the territories Trajan had taken and which needed to be organised, Hadrian simply withdrew the army. Entire provinces were handed back on a plate. Then he diverted his armies with war games rather than the real thing. But lack of combat leads to lack of courage. As with all activity, but most of all with war, to sit still is to seize up.[16]

No truer comment on imperial frontier policy may be found in the entirety of ancient literature.

Regarding Hadrian's legendary journeys: no other emperor travelled as long or as far. The years 120–131, between his 44th and 55th birthdays, were largely spent criss-crossing the empire. Of this it is probable that only two years were in the western provinces and that 75% was in the eastern Mediterranean. There, though he visited Arabia and revisited Syria, most time was passed in Greece and Egypt.

However, his first journey was unplanned. It arose from an invasion by the Rhoxolans, a steppe tribe from outside the Danube delta. Unable to force the river, they were deflected into the Romanian plain, where archaeology confirms the destruction of four forts near the future Bucarest. This was land won by Trajan between the Danube and Carpathians. It seems likely that Hadrian, fresh to the purple, hurried to the scene because he wished to demonstrate how such an incident could be peacefully resolved. It transpired that the problem was only one of ruffled feathers; and that 'when the Rhoxolan king complained that his stipend had been reduced Hadrian arranged an amicable renegotiation.'[17] Extortion was a pillar of iron age diplomacy. Rome was not of course an entirely helpless victim. All her subsidies had strings attached, such as keeping the peace, acceptance of supervision and sometimes supplying recruits. However, Hadrian's proposal must have amazed the barbarians as much as it shocked the Romans. Not only would the stipend be increased, but Rome would rescind the territory the Rhoxolans had just devastated, allowing them into the tongue of territory stretching from the Pontic region to a point 300 miles up the Danube's northern side. Clearly Hadrian had been caught off balance, forced in the first year of what was planned as a peaceful reign to rush to the aid of a province he had never wanted, there to haggle over a strip of Trajan's territory with the king of a trivial tribe. We must assume the upset caused him to behave emotionally, producing a decision that makes no strategic sense.

Six years later Hadrian made a reappraisal visit to Dacia. It seems he had decided to make amends by building new defences to protect the injured flank. This would be a road-and-fort line, to close off the western end of the corridor which his earlier diplomacy had opened, so strengthening what remained of the link between Transylvania and the rest of Roman territory. The chosen route was that of the Olt (Alutanus), about ninety miles west of today's Bucarest. A medium-size river, the south-flowing Olt cuts through the Carpathians to emerge on the Romanian plain, entering the Danube at a right angle.

The Olt Line would be 150 miles long, running from Islaz on the Danube to the village of Boita, just under the Turnu Rossu (Red Tower) Pass (see map 18). It would follow the west bank of the Olt, except for some thirty-five miles in the northern or mountain sector. Eighteen known forts were already linked by a road locally known as 'Trajan's Way'. The road and a few of the forts originated from the Dacian Wars, but the whole was now upgraded and extended by Hadrian. The southern forts, built where Danubian mud has buried all sources of stone, are of brick. These were first noted in 1691 by Count Luigi Marsigli, an Italian military engineer in the service of Austria-Hungary.[18] Systematic investigation began in the 1960s. In the northern sector, the Olt plunges through a defile only marginally less spectacular than the Danube gorges. Here Trajan's Way left the river to take an easier route (see map 18). This loop was still in use and continued to take the heavy traffic. However, Hadrian now ordered a new, rock-cut road to be driven through the defile, a feat equal to that of the Iron Gates project and closely resembling it. Today the ledge is obscured by rockfall and by a railway line which commandeered its course.

Was the defile road a snook cocked at Trajan's Danube gorge road, only 120 miles away? It is even possible that the engineering challenge influenced Hadrian's choice of the Olt in the first place. By and large it was a bad choice. The line's southern half could be said to be on the right side of the wrong river: wrong in the sense that its forts were largely blind to an oncoming enemy, for the 'enemy' bank is the higher. In its northern half, among 6,000-foot mountains, it is difficult to see why defence was needed at all. However, the project did make work for idle hands as well as providing a secure road in and out of Transylvania.

The Dacian province was now divided into three, creating specialised commands, each related to different requirement. Lower Dacia, south of the Carpathians, was protected by the Olt Line. Upper Dacia, the southern half of Transylvania, with the single remaining legion, had the safeguarding of the goldfields as its priority. Dacia Porolissensis was now constituted to defend the northern arc of the Carpathians. It was an armed camp, with fifteen auxiliary units and many *numeri*. Napoca (Cluj) was its capital, but Hadrian established an advanced headquarters forty miles further north at Porolissum (Moigrad) from which the province took its name. Here two forts and a small town were shielded behind a two-and-a-half-mile earth rampart, later strengthened into a double stone wall with towers and fortlets.[19]

Porolissum was central to the Somesh river, along which lay a line of forts at seven-mile intervals. The valley is narrow, with foothills rising steeply to 2,000 feet, obscuring the view toward the northwest

Carpathian range beyond. Originally the Somesh and Upper Somesh were thought to be the front line. However, since many of the forts are on the north side it could not have been designed as a defended riverbank in the usual sense, but as a line of interception whose garrisons, alerted by signal towers, could advance and bar the passes. Tower foundations were first discovered in these foothills in 1882. Ferenczi and his students found them to be 600 yards to 2¼ miles apart, depending on topography.[20] So much for the Somesh frontier, begun by Trajan and reorganised by Hadrian, who doubtless thought it a poor substitute for the broad, deep Danube. Nevertheless he left Dacia well organised and tactically sound. Its frontier would hold for a long time yet; even allowing the posting of the units to other fronts during the century ahead.[21] By his division into specialised commands and establishment of a front-line headquarters, Hadrian anticipated two defensive principles of a late empire, over a century and a half before they were generally applied.

Here we may broach a matter connected with the Middle and Lower Danube, though not attributable with certainty to Hadrian. These are three Roman roads, running outside the imperial limits. One departed from Aquincum (Budapest) heading east across the Iazygian grasslands of eastern Hungary to re-enter the empire via the Somesh valley into Dacia Porolissensis, after a passage of 200 miles through barbarian territory. The second, 100 miles further south, ran east from Lugio (Dunaszakcso) on the Danube, along today's Pecs–Szeged–Arad axis, entering southern Transylvania via the Muresh valley. These provided direct links between Pannonia and Dacia, avoiding a tedious detour by way of Belgrade. A third road, across the comparable dent in Roman territory on the other side of Transylvania, ran between the northeastern Carpathians and the Black Sea. This crossed southern Moldova to the Roman controlled port of Tyras, beyond the Danube mouths.[22] Little is known of these routes: when built, how defended, under what circumstances used, or when abandoned. Obviously they depended on tribal goodwill. We assume road and outpost concessions were granted for cash, like oil leases or the tenancy of overseas bases today.

Let us pursue Hadrian up the Danube where his policy was simply to continue that of his predecessors, closing gaps and decreasing distances between forts. Stretches facing thickly forested and hilly areas were considered less at risk than those facing populous valleys or plains. The Vienna–Bratislava reach, opposite the wide valley of

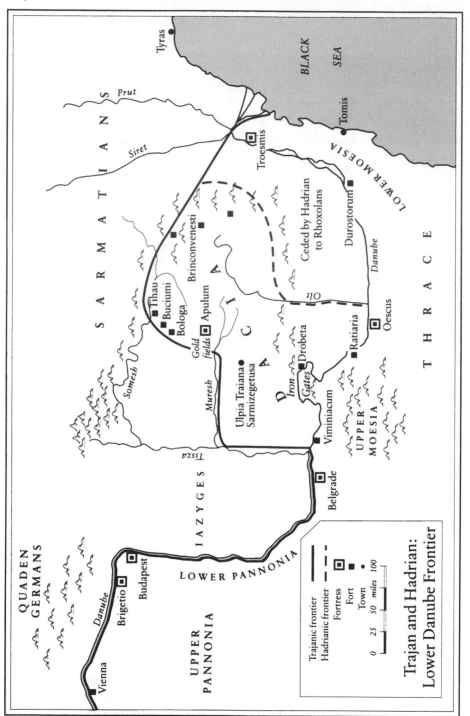

Trajan and Hadrian:
Lower Danube Frontier

Trajanic frontier
Hadrianic frontier
Fortress
Fort
Town

0   25   50   100
         miles

the March (Morava) was of special concern. Nor was this much reduced in the direction of Budapest, where the Slovakian plain widens to a depth of forty miles. Three legions guarded this 150-mile frontage.

On the Roman side a long-term problem was emerging. It had been inevitable from the first day the eagles reached the rivers that numerous camps, plus the commercial opportunities which great waterways offer, would be a formula for urban growth, sometimes of the mushroom kind. It was inevitable too that such towns, under the barbarians' noses, would in due course require extra protection. This might take the form of a screen of far-bank forts, or at least an early-warning system of watchtowers on the barbarian side. Such measures would in turn encourage the economic penetration of the far bank.

The Lower Austrian–Czechoslovakian sphere had long attracted Roman traders. It is rich in signs of cross-river activity, much of it dating to the early 2nd century. Roman roof tiles have been found widely in Czechoslovakia, especially along the south-flowing Danube tributaries: for ninety miles up the March, for example, and 100 miles up the Váh. These must have come from Roman-style constructions, but whether Roman or built by Rome for local notables is difficult to say. Since the 1960s, however, many sites of Roman character have been discovered on the barbarian side of the Danube: nearly forty in Lower Austria, Moravia, Slovakia and western Hungary; some close to the river but others up to a hundred miles inside barbarian territory. A number contain a mixture of Roman and German buildings, suggesting militarily supported supply bases, connected with long-distance commerce inside barbarian territory.[23] Most are of Hadrianic date.[24]

A general surmise could be that Hadrian was sanctioning a peaceful penetration of the Bohemian region, by commercial and diplomatic means. This was more ambitious than the normal activities of freelance traders. Tiles and other building materials produced at legionary factories, the lay-out of structures, and the presence of small garrisons, all prove official involvement. The drive was not begun by Hadrian but its momentum greatly increased during his reign. The spade seldom reveals motives; and it is an open question whether it was his intention to thaw the *barbaricum* and reduce dangerous differences of wealth, or whether it was merely the exploitation of local conditions. Army involvement suggests policy, though the absence of evidence for comparable initiatives on other frontiers could point to commercial opportunism.

In the early summer of 129 Hadrian was probably in the east Pontic region. With Vespasian's abandonment of Armenia its importance had increased, being once again the meeting point of Roman and Parthian influences. At the Black Sea's eastern extremity was the puppet kingdom of Colchis, with a Roman garrison at Apsarus; and it was probably Hadrian who decided to put in five auxiliary units and enlarge the fort. Apsarus (Gonia), a Georgian citadel on Roman foundations, is five miles north of Batumi and close to the Cherokhi river (Accampsis) which, as legend has it, the Argonauts penetrated in the final stage of their quest for the Golden Fleece. The present ruin has sixteen towers with walls fifteen feet high and is of stone-work bigger and rougher than normal Roman standards, except for the southeast corner where older masonry appears to have been reused. At almost eleven acres it is unusually big for an auxiliary fort, being over half the size of a legionary fortress.

Of greater interest is the visit to Arabia. This was the province annexed on Trajan's orders; and Hadrian had done away with the unfortunate general who carried them out. He did not, however, seek to be rid of the province itself, presumably regarding it as within Rome's proper sphere. On the other hand he could not bring himself to show it favour. The capital Bostra Traiana was ignored in favour of Petra which Hadrian, in tit-for-tat fashion, renamed Petra Hadriana. Another snub – this time to the army of Arabia – is implied by the coinage. Hadrian's unique series, commemorating ten provincial armies, ignored this province; though it included his native Spain, by then a military backwater.

On the Rhine, Hadrian's approach to riverine defence was conventional and without sign of a cross-river penetration such as we have seen into Bohemia. In fact his visit of 122 is mainly memorable for a measure which sealed the frontier more tightly. The *Augustan History* says that 'Hadrian shut out the barbarians with tall stakes, set deep into the ground and fastened together in the manner of a mural fence [*in modum muralis saepis*],'[25] referring to Domitian's overland frontier across southern Germany, which shielded the lately annexed regions of the Wetterau and Black Forest and allowed a short cut to the Upper Danube. It consisted of a patrolled road linked by watchtowers and backed by forts. The towers were wooden, though in some sectors ground floors were of dry-stone walling, braced by internal crossbeams and packed with earth. This produced a solid cube, perhaps twelve feet high, resistant to fire or ram. Upon this stood the usable part of the tower: a rest-room with observation deck above. The door was thus removed from ground level and was accessible by means of a retractable ladder.[26] Many tower sites can be found in the forest, usually consisting of a mound surrounded by ring ditch. The *limes* included smallish, widely spaced forts, with watchtowers 700–1,000 yards apart, facing a densely forested, little populated corner of Germany, from which no major attack had so far arisen.

The palisade which Hadrian now put in hand was a reinforcement of this frontier and its enduring hallmark, leaving a stamp on place-names[27] and in the language.[28] Light stakes or palings had a long tradition of army usage, mainly for emergency protection. Hadrian's would be a heavyweight version: a single row of tall, stout, upright posts, sharpened at the top and backed by cross-battening. They were made of trunks rather than branches, ten inches across and spaced a few inches apart, so an intruder could be seen between them but would be unable to squeeze through. The palisade stood a few yards in front of the watchtowers, which could look over it while protected by it.

The German pale has been called the first of Rome's closed, man-made frontiers; and with minor exceptions this is correct. It was not, however, totally closed, for as with all Roman frontiers, there were guarded gates. The palisade would be applied to some 200 miles of Upper Germany, except where the rivers Main and Neckar fronted the line. Its construction would involve the cutting and placing of the best part of a million uprights. Nonetheless, it was cannily conceived. This was Rome's forest frontier, and the raw materials were everywhere to hand. Erecting the posts could be combined with the need to create a field of view by tree-felling for at least 200 yards in front of the towers. Cleared and depopulated strips were a universal frontier feature. If people were not excluded from the zone of surveillance there would be frequent false alarms. Though the palisade could be pierced by determined men with spade or fire, it would be effective against trespass or small raids. However, even oak, standing in damp soil, has less than a twenty-year life before rotting at ground level. The placement and replacement of a million staves would certainly keep the men busy.

Hadrian proceeded downriver. Doubtless a warm welcome

awaited him in Cologne from the Lower German governor, A. Platorius Nepos: a kindly man who had befriended the awkward and oversensitive youth when he was being taken less than seriously by Trajan's circle. His reward had been Lower Germany, the province graced by the heroism of Augustus' stepsons. It was about to be followed by the ultimate honour of the imperial career structure: the governorship of Britain.

The custom of posting the best men to Europe's farthest corner had arisen during the previous century, both because of Britain's peculiar glamour and because, with peace on the Rhine, the action had shifted there. Only Trajan, who moved the action elsewhere, sent Britain second-raters. Hadrian, as usual, reversed Trajanic practice. His present governor was Q. Pompeius Falco, an eminent trouble-shooter. An inscription[29] tells us that Falco previously commanded the Lower Danube, a frequent flashpoint. Hadrian had sent him, probably in 118, to restore the northern marches where 'the Britons were out of control'.[30] He would later be despatched to the most troublesome spot of all, as implementer of Hadrian's final solution to the Judaean question. In Britain Falco may have been mauled, for another of Fronto's letters contains the remark: 'In Hadrian's day, how many of our soldiers were killed by the Jews, how many by the Britons!'[31] Puzzlingly, no archaeological record of a border catastrophe early in Hadrian's reign exists. But whatever went wrong it is likely Falco righted it, for failure would hardly have been followed by a mission to Jerusalem. In all probability then, the year 122 found Britain in a condition of uneasy peace, with an army low in morale and numbers still drawn down as a result of Trajan's wars; with Falco as the outgoing and Nepos as the incoming governor.

For some time Hadrian had been considering an ultimate solution of another kind: to the 75-year-long search for a British frontier. Light has been shed on this by an exciting discovery, though how much we cannot yet tell. Again it is at Vindolanda where persistence, skill and good fortune have broken the crust of military archaeology to find fresh bread within. The trove, uncovered during the 1992 digging season, consists of remnants of a 50-square-yard timber building of fifty rooms, some with painted walls, dated to the 120s. What can explain so noble a residence in the wilds of Northumberland other than to house the imperial party during the visit of 122? Since such a building would require a year to construct and decorate we may be sure something big had been mooted for some time; and since it was central to and only a mile behind the future site of Hadrian's Wall we may suppose that the line had been preselected. In other words Falco's officers, acting on imperial instructions, had already reconnoitred a route and awaited the emperor's approval.

So Hadrian embarked for Britain, probably accompanied by Nepos and *Legio VI Victrix*, on the first imperial visit since Claudius.

> Thereupon, having reformed the army of the Rhine in regal manner, he set out for Britain where he put many things to rights and was the first to build a wall, eighty miles in length, by which barbarians and Romans should be divided.[32]

Such is the sole, written evidence for the building of Hadrian's Wall and for his purpose in building it. Furthermore these four words 'by which barbarians and Romans should be divided'[33] are the only Roman statement of a frontier intention we have. We will remember, from a moment ago, this same source on the subject of the palisade: 'he shut out[34] the barbarians with tall stakes'. Dividing and shutting out are evidently the *Augustan History*'s view of a frontier's function: a means of dismissing and sealing off the barbarians who would then, in the words of Tiberius, 'be left to their own feuds'.[35] This sits ill with what we have just seen on the Middle Danube, where peaceful penetration was in full swing. A conclusion could be that Hadrian's biographer was not expressing Hadrian's opinion but that of his own, more pessimistic age.

A clearer course is to compare the *Augustan History*'s definition with the modern view, which generally speaking does not maintain that 2nd-century borders were intended for total containment, except in wartime. They had two purposes, reflected in their two sorts of garrison. The fort dwellers (the larger part) were devoted to combat readiness. Their job was to deter and defend. Thus far there is no disagreement with the *Augustan History*. The difference lies in the fortlet dwellers, who manned the towers and gates, and had the day-to-day work of running the frontier. They were dedicated not to separation but to regulation: supervising the contacts between Roman and barbarian. In short they were not unlike the custodians of a modern frontier, where surveillance, policing, customs and immigration are all part of normal routine. This dual but flexible nature of a frontier, defensible in war but an influence for normalisation in peace, will also apply to Hadrian's Wall.

What precedent was there for a stone wall of this length; and how far did the legions' experience equip them to build it? Iron age Europe has numerous precursors in the form of boundary dykes and defensive earthworks. In the Aegean some, like the long walls between Athens and Piraeus, had already been translated into stone.[36] None, however, is more than a few miles long. Shorter still, though stronger and more elaborate, were the Hellenistic city walls which Alexander's successors had left abundantly in the Near East. Hadrian's Wall would embody aspects of them all: the length of prehistoric dykes, the width and general style of early Greek stone walls, plus something of the sophistication of late Greek urban ramparts. But none of these was a true precedent in terms of ambition. Here was a wall which would fortify not a town but a province. It is the scale that was new, not just to imperial frontiers but to the West generally and indeed to all the Near and Middle Eastern countries within its purview.

There *was* a precedent, even so. Unfortunately we have evidence neither for nor against the case that Hadrian modelled his wall on the Great Wall of China. Here we are in the realm of surmise, though not entirely wild. First the Chinese wall already existed, its earliest version predating Hadrian by four centuries. Secondly, a word for China in Latin, a broadly correct grasp of her location by classical geographers and the extensive importation of Chinese silk, imply at least a background knowledge of that country. Thirdly there is the often remarked similarity of appearance and setting, the central sector of Hadrian's Wall resembling the Great Wall in miniature. Fourthly we have Hadrian's insatiable curiosity and fascination with the exotic. Finally there was the common predicament of both empires, enclosed by the envy of backward peoples and seeking protection against them. Though the balance of probability seems to favour Hadrian's having some notion of that mighty work, as well as the temperament to respond to it, the canons of historicity forbid us further speculation.

However, precedent is one thing, experience another. The army had never built a long wall. City walls had been discontinued over a century earlier. What need of them when the caesars had ringed the Roman world? Military installations were of course walled. But at this period fort ramparts were earth-backed, in effect mounds with exterior stone facing. The stone requirement (and the number of masons and plasterers per legion) was probably smaller than might be imagined. In particular the existence of a body of skills to build an extended, concrete-bonded, weather-resistant stone wall over rough and steep ground is open to question.

Another matter for caution is the extent to which our thinking is coloured by the defensive works of later periods. For reasons of cost long walls can rarely be as strong as short ones. Had Hadrian's Wall been defended with the intensity of a medieval castle it would have required thousands of men to the mile, able to concentrate on the parapet in large numbers. On much of Hadrian's Wall only two sentries could cross over. We are talking not about defence against mighty onslaughts, but a patrolled cordon, an aid to policing and the maintenance of quiet. A wall may be seen as a labour-saving device, requiring fewer men for surveillance than an 'open' frontier. In time of war battles might be fought; but this would be on open ground, in front of the barrier.

Hadrian's relocation of the British frontier involved moving Trajan's line from the bottom to the top of the same valley and anchoring it to salt water at either end. Trajan's road and Hadrian's ridge keep company for many miles. A short, uphill walk takes us from one to the other. But there is a major transition, from pleasant to dramatic scenery and from passive to commanding ground. How had Trajan's officers missed so strong a siting? In all probability they had rejected that waterless and windy ridge in favour of the valley, with its faster communications and more realistic means of supply. A more valid question is why Hadrian did not choose to upgrade the existing arrangements, as he had done in Germany and Transylvania. Clearly he had something more ambitious in view.

How was the Wall conceived? The Vindolanda discovery suggests visualisation from the centre outwards, rather than from one or other end. This seems to be supported by the less confident alignments west of Gilsland[37] and the afterthinking east of Newcastle. Though we must now dismiss the idea of Hadrian seeing his Wall in a flash of inspiration, it remains feasible that the line of cliffs known as the Whin Sill, so close to his residence, excited his imagination regarding how striking an impression might be achieved. In any case it would not be the choice of route which surprised those concerned but the ambitious specifications and materials. After forty years of penny-pinching, the army of Britain was ill prepared to find itself in a money-no-object situation, as well as ill qualified for the role of innovative builder.

Is it possible that the 'crisis' of the years preceding was exaggerated to excuse an escalating budget? We will recall the absence of archaeological record for disaster during Falco's governorship. If this were so dangerous a time, why expose all three legions to prolonged risk; for a general whose legions are building a wall is like an admiral whose ships are in dock. The legions would be guarded by the auxiliary regiments while working. Yet there is evidence that auxiliaries were posted out of Britain during this period.[38] If none of this suggests peril, we may wonder whether Hadrian came to Britain with a crisis in mind and produced a monument to solve it, or whether he came with a monument in mind and produced a crisis to justify it.

It is difficult to guess the Wall's budget, since the workforce consisted of soldiers who were paid in any case. This has led some to suppose that all military works were free. But here were logistics far beyond the army's unaided capability. Lavish specification and awkward siting meant a haulage problem (with its consequent call on civilians, carts and animals) so large that this may have become the controlling factor, dictating the entire programme and many of its modifications. It is thought that basic construction took two and a half seasons, during which the original ten-foot width, building westwards from Newcastle, was reduced to eight. Since this was only a moderate gain (the same number of facing stones being required) it is assumed that height was reduced also, perhaps by three feet.

The quirks of geology, which make pink cities of Chester, Carlisle and Glasgow and yellow ones of York, Newcastle and Edinburgh are encountered too on Hadrian's Wall. In leaving the yellow sandstone, the builders also left the limestone, essential for the Wall's concrete core. West of the change to red rock (five miles inside the Cumbrian border) the Wall was built of turf, to be replaced in stone during the decade following, when time could be given to carting lime as far as twenty miles westwards.

Actual construction was in the hands of the three legions in Britain. Though some forty-four temporary camps have been identified close to the Wall, it has not proved possible to detect a sequence of construction camps or to separate these from earlier or later works. It is assumed that the legions returned to their bases every autumn.[39] In the case of *II Augusta* at Caerleon, in south Wales, this would mean a three-week march.

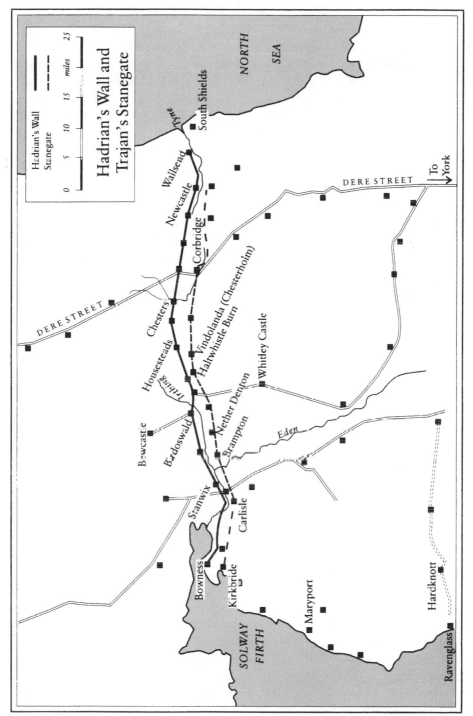

Hadrian's Wall and
Trajan's Stanegate

Hadrian's Wall
Stanegate

miles

0 5 10 15 20 25

NORTH SEA

South Shields

Tyne

Wallsend

Newcastle

Corbridge

DERE STREET

To York

Chesters

Vindolanda (Chesterholm)

Haltwhistle Burn

Whitley Castle

Housesteads

Irthing

Nether Denton

Bewcastle

Birdoswald

Brampton

Eden

Stanwix

Carlisle

Bowness

Kirkbride

Maryport

SOLWAY FIRTH

Hardknott

Ravenglass

Choice of line followed the principle that frontiers should seek to avoid partitioning tribal territory. An exception was a Brigantian enclave in today's Dumfriesshire. A fragment of Britain's largest tribe had seemingly strayed northwestwards from its Pennine homeland and rounded the Solway Firth. The placing of three outpost forts beyond the Wall's western sector to protect these sundered subjects was seemingly the price Hadrian paid for Brigantian acquiescence. However, this theory is slenderly based, on a single altar to the goddess Brigantia found at Birrens, north of Carlisle.

Our account cannot proceed without some detail of the works. First, the dimensions of the Wall itself: 73½ miles (80 Roman miles, 113 km) in length and usually 8–10 feet (2m.40–3m.25) in width. Height can only be conjectured. A common estimate is 15 feet (4m.60) to the sentry walk, with a five-foot parapet, giving a northern face of 20 feet. This is based on the lower part of a flight of steps and also on the dimensions of the ditch which fronted the Wall, assuming a sentry on the parapet could see into it and over the counterscarp beyond. Fortlets were attached to the Wall's southern side each Roman mile and watchtowers built into the structure every third of a mile. These are known as milecastles and turrets.

Impressive statistics may be mustered for the materials used. Perhaps 30 million facing stones were quarried, fetched, shaped and laid. The core materials (stone-rubble and mortar) represent some 75% of the wall's bulk at ten feet wide and 65% at eight feet wide. Estimates of a million cubic yards have been made for the combined stone requirement.[40] When a 40-foot-long trial section of Wall was reconstructed at Vindolanda it was found that 800 gallons (3,637 litres) of water per day were needed to mix the mortar. Since the Wall follows a ridgetop route for much of its course, water had generally to be transported uphill by draft animal. The water required by up to 30 gangs, mixing concrete throughout 2½ working seasons would be in the order of 10 million gallons (nearly a million tons) for the basic Wall and perhaps 15 million gallons for the entire building process.

Enormous quantities of charcoal or timber would be required as fuel for lime making, plus scaffolding poles and planks for wooden buildings, turret floors and roofs, all of which once more points to the need for bulk movement of materials, not always available in the Wall's proximity. Thrift seems quite alien to the Wall's concept, unlike that of the German palisade, reminding us of the *Augustan History*'s comment that Hadrian was at once stingy and extravagant. Stingy, perhaps, when his motive was practical; extravagant when it was monumental. Possibly a million cubic yards of soil were shifted. A large V-shaped ditch was dug in front of the Wall, except where it is sited on clifftops. Behind the Wall lay an entirely novel earthwork, known as the *Vallum*. This also consists of a ditch, but with a mound on either side, placed widely to give a thirty-foot berm between ditch and mounds. The *Vallum* is inscriptionless and inscrutable, its mystery deepened by the absence of any comparable work on other parts of the imperial frontier. While most agree that it defined the rearward boundary of an exclusion zone, its many peculiarities are still debated.

The Wall's western terminus is Bowness, on the southern shore of the Solway, at a point where it is no longer fordable. Beyond here the danger of seaborne attack from southwestern Scotland was considered sufficient to warrant extension down the Cumbrian coast in the form of a line of forts, fortlets and watchtowers, spaced as on the Wall, though without the barrier itself. The Wall was perhaps commanded from the large fort at Stanwix, near Carlisle, central to the line if these coastal defences are included. Its senior officer was responsible to the legate of the nearest legion, *VI Victrix*, at York. In the east the Wall originally began at Newcastle, nine miles from the sea, but was extended four miles downstream to Wallsend, where a doubling of the Tyne's width made crossing difficult. Here the first (or last) yards of Wall sloped into the Tyne at a spot later occupied by the Swan Hunter shipyard.

At about the same time, a fundamental change of plan involved relocating the Wall's main garrison. The initial intention had been to leave all fighting units on the Stanegate, whose installations were kept open for that purpose. It was now decided to insert fourteen forts into the line of the Wall, lengths of which had to be demolished to receive them. This was presumably to ensure a readier response to attack; but it is not known what prompted the decision or who was involved. By now the emperor was probably in Greece, his remoteness from the scene suggesting that the idea arose in Britain. The usual explanation is that the change of plan was prompted by native hostility to the Wall, though it may have been logistical. The original programme was carried through in AD 122–124, the *Vallum* built and forts added by 128, but the replacement of the turf section

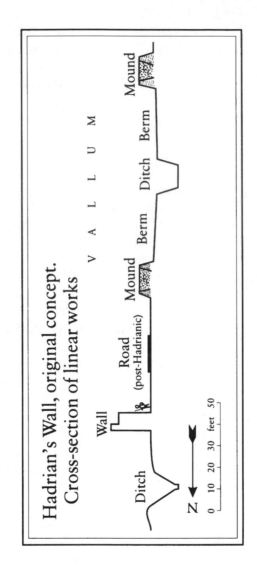

Hadrian's Wall, original concept.
Cross-section of linear works

and completion of the coastal defences probably dragged on until Hadrian's death in 138.

The total garrison has been put at 5,500 cavalry and 13,000 infantry; but with further discoveries in the west this might be scaled up to a total of 20,000 in all. Of these perhaps 12,000 were on the Wall and the rest in forward, flanking or rearward locations. This gives an approximate figure of 160 men to the mile, while the German overland frontier probably had no more than 100. The theoretical reason for a stronger barrier – that fewer would be needed to guard it – does not seem to have been achieved.

It is still common to underrate civilians and regard them as dependants of the Roman army. This has coloured our view of the *vici* ('villages') adjacent to all Roman forts, which popular myth still sees as the haunt of taverners and hangers-on. Until lately they were thought to have been nurseries for the forts, where soldiers were born, married and retired; sons succeeding fathers with the colours. Recent thinking prompts a third view: that fort and *vicus* were two parts of a working unit, the latter as it were an industrial suburb of the former. We now know that a *vicus* was built as part of the official plan. Military establishments required blacksmiths, carpenters, clothiers and bootmakers as normal aspects of functioning. More sociable relationships naturally followed, but opinion now rejects the idea of a closed cycle of birth, recruitment and death. Many veterans retired to towns or moved south to be replaced by boys from local farms and villages.[41] In this period military service may be regarded as the road to improvement rather than a treadmill of the generations. Both Housesteads and Vindolanda have extensively excavated *vici*, with sizeable areas on view.

While not denying the importance of villa development in the south, archaeology now stresses the native farms. These differed little from pre-Roman days. It is thought that an agricultural population of two million (larger than at the Norman Conquest) lived and farmed in iron age manner throughout the Roman occupation, usually in villages of round huts or on isolated farms. Though their methods were less productive, numbers so outweighed the villas that they must be considered the larger producer by far. Peace, roads, markets and the requirement to pay taxes provided a spur, nowhere more than in the Wall's vicinity. During the 1970s, aerial reconnaissance over the Solway region revealed more and larger native farms than had been dreamed: with 82 sites on the Scottish and 183 on the Cumbrian or Roman side.[42] These findings suggest the impact on agriculture of 20,000 soldiers and ultimately perhaps 40,000 civilians, concentrated in the Wall zone.

The *Vallum* demands further comment. It runs parallel with the Wall and usually close behind, except in the central sector where it shuns the crags. Its course is normally straight. It had a deep, wide, flat-bottomed ditch of a type unknown to Roman fieldworks. Earth from this was built into two identical mounds, steep sided and flat topped. Normally mounds are close to ditches, so that one's height augments the other's depth. Here they are widely spaced. To add to the puzzle, the *Vallum* is indifferent to defensive ground, passing close under hillocks or slopes to left or right. These facts have led commentators to conclude that it was not a military work and therefore its purpose must have been delineational. But the scale seems disproportionate. It is a very large earthwork. Were it not for the Wall's proximity it would be internationally famous. Collingwood consulted an engineering contractor who estimated it had taken a million man-days in soil shifting alone;[43] a high price to warn trespassers, when a ditch one tenth of the size, or a wooden fence, would have made the point.

The *Vallum* may be seen in the light of another peculiarity: the absence of a road in Hadrian's scheme. The Stanegate, usually about a mile away, was too far to be a useful service road. We seek in vain for a flexible link between installations. There is one, but it was built after Hadrian's death. An added irony is that Nepos, among many appointments, had been superintendent of Italian highways.[44]

A *limes* without road and a *Vallum* of vague purpose. Are these thoughts eligible for marriage? Was the *Vallum* intended as a road; in fact two, for its thirty-foot-wide, well-drained berms would have made excellent, concealed gallops for the switching of cavalry between threatened points? Was one berm designated for rapid deployment, the other for wheeled traffic and civilians?[45] Such might have been Hadrian's notion. But in practice the *Vallum* was a white elephant. Its alignments were too rigid for a useful service function. Doubtless it was a monumental nuisance. It would soon be modified and in due course abandoned. So the *Vallum* keeps its secret. Archaeology seems to have given it up; scholarship to have grounded on the reef of delineation. Perhaps one has looked too long at the works and not long enough at their designer. The Roman frontier was a remote place, run by commonsense soldiers, normally spared the

oddities of the caesars. Its students are accustomed to seeking commonsense answers. They are unprepared for the squandering of a
million man-hours on a Hadrianic caprice.

The scale of the western coastal defences is also open to question.
This was Rome's first saltwater frontier, for the Black Sea coastal
forts faced inland. Recent findings have obliged a revision of the
system's length. Instead of running only to St Bees Head it may have
reached as far south as Millom: sixty miles instead of thirty-five.
Beyond Workington this coast no longer faces Scotland but Ireland,
from which there is no record of trouble; and its forts no longer
defended the flank of Hadrian's Wall but the Lake District, whose
terrain was its own defence. A coastal line of almost three times the
length dictated by strategic necessity, absorbing perhaps 4,000 men,
could suggest the same, inflated importance shared by all the Wall's
components.

There are other examples of overprovision. At river crossings the
Hadrianic bridges were unnecessarily strong, with close-spaced piers,
suggesting that the Wall was actually carried over the water. Later
bridges on the same sites were normal road bridges: in one case
timber replacing stone, in another three piers replacing eight. What
purpose had there been in taking so massive a burden across three
rivers whose bridges, with parapets and end-towers, provided ample
defence? Was the army's time being put to practical or theatrical
effect?

Regarding turrets, we must first question their number. We should
then ask whether their design was most related to how well they
would see, or how well they looked. It will be remembered that
Trajan's Carpathian and Jordanian defences rested on watchtower
screens, reaching far beyond the forts. As in all things, an opposite
path was trodden by Hadrian. The turrets were included in the main
line: 140 of them, two between each milecastle, recessed into the
rampart's rear and standing perhaps to twice its height. If ranged in
front of the Wall, at points of maximum vantage, far fewer would
have been needed. They are spaced to a formula, with slight regard
to topography, duplicating each other's view and overlapping each
other's signalling range. We must conclude that fieldcraft was not
uppermost in this concept. Like the bridges, the turrets enhanced the
Wall's visual impact. Their design seems to satisfy an ornamental
rather than a practical criterion. Again, each milecastle had an
impressive, arched gate, giving access through the Wall. Gates were

normal, but provision of over a hundred[46] makes no sense. Was this bombast, like 'Thebes of a hundred gates'? Was it an architect enlivening a blank façade? Or were they part of some grandiose tactical experiment?

The Wall itself was unusual in its freestandingness, for as we have said fort walls of this period had a stone exterior face backed by an earthen ramp. These were cheaper to build and more stable; while their sole disadvantage, that they took up space within the fort, would not apply to a linear barrier. They defied battering ram and sapper. Their tops were accessible from behind at any point. In an emergency soldiers did not have to queue to climb steps. The advantage of a freestanding wall is clear: it looks better. From which angle: for obviously the front view is the same in either instance? A wall is best seen axially, looking along it, the view in fact of those who are manning it. It is from this angle that the snaking line and the succession of turret-crowned crests excites the eye. Here then is thinking unheard of on other frontier stretches: that visual effect should dominate the design and that this should be aimed at Romans as much as barbarians. Given such grandiloquent intentions it will come as no surprise to hear the Wall was whitewashed![47] This has been deduced from residues on the underside of facing stones, where the mixture of lime plaster and water trickled and was hidden from the weather.[48]

In the dedication to his treatise on architecture Vitruvius expressed his ideal for a public building: 'that the greatness of our power might be matched by the distinction and authority of our buildings'.[49] Similarly the younger Pliny, in a letter to Trajan, argues that 'projects worthy of your immortal name combine usefulness with magnificence.'[50] Until Hadrian, no such claim could be made for frontier works. They had been built by soldiers to frugal budgets and backwoods standards. The Wall changes all this. 'Britain' (as an earlier governor said to his men before the battle with Queen Boudicca) 'will be a noble monument for us!'[51] So it would be for Hadrian.

In proposing the Wall as a work in which utility was subordinated to display and symbolism, let us remember that Hadrian's record in that direction includes Tivoli, which a modern biographer calls: 'this colossal fantasy, this dream in three dimensions [. . .] no less than three quarters of the size of Rome itself'.[52] His mausoleum, now the Castel Sant' Angelo, deliberately faces Augustus' tomb across the Tiber, echoing it yet far outdoing it in grandeur. Hadrian loved to place buildings in opposition, so that one idea confronted another. His governor's palace at Budapest is a forceful example: a gesture, confronting the nullity of the outside lands with the majesty of Rome.

This scarp across Britain between North Sea and Atlantic, ultimate edge of Roman rule, was an irresistible setting for the opposition of ideas in which Hadrian excelled. Northwards it confronted the barbarian, southwards it was juxtaposed with the feeble remnant of Trajan's frontier; sideways it spoke to the army of Britain of pride restored. Most of all it served notice that there would be no further offensives. It would impress the northern tribes, but also mollify them, making it clear that Rome had no further ambitions in their direction. Why waste such a frontier by further advance?

Hadrian's Wall may be understood as a statement, comparable yet opposite to Trajan's Column. These two are the most famous military monuments of western antiquity. Though one stands at the empire's heart and the other on its rim, they are related if one sees them as the signposting of divergent courses in foreign policy, contrary attitudes to the helmsmanship of empire.

And yet, while Hadrian's character offers clues to the whims of the Wall, nothing prepares us for the flaws on which construction was based. This consisted of facing stones front and rear, with a rubble and concrete core. The facing stones are unusually long (12–18 inches) with a rectangular face at one end and tapering to a pointed root at the other. They were laid as 'headers',[53] with long axis across the Wall's line: the rectangular end being the actual facing, the tapering end pointing inwards toward the centre. The object was that the facing stone's root should bond with the Wall's concrete core, like tooth into gum.

Concrete is mortar, mixed with stones. Mortar, normally made from lime, sand and water, is highly fissile. But in a proper concrete mix the stones prevent cracks from running. On the other hand large stones, like those in the core of Hadrian's Wall (ranging from fist- to head-size), can prevent crack formation only partially; for splits will occur between the pieces and zigzag among them. Here, since small stones were not sufficiently used, the result is not a true concrete. The characteristic core material was merely mortar poured among coarse rubble or coarse rubble plopped into mortar. There is another weakness of mortar. On exposure to air its gripping element, quicklime, gradually reverts to chalk. Though there are ways of managing the instability of mortar[54] none is more important than that the building itself should be stable and not structurally dependent on lime's adhesive power. In furniture this is comparable to reliance on carpentry rather than glue. Here the Wall's weakness is in the shape and balance of its facing stones. By chiselling them to taper inwards, the masons ensured that they were front-heavy and would tend to topple outwards if the Wall's interior weakened.

In the European iron age, drystone walling, strong enough for defence, had relied on throughstones, tie-beams or metal cramps. Hellenistic walls had largely used clay and rubble cores, whose outward thrust was held by interior crosswalls or compartments. Hadrian's Wall represents a transitional phase: an advance on its Celtic or Hellenistic predecessors in the sense of being *opus caementicum* (concrete work), but demonstrating a poor grasp of the nature of concrete. During the later empire we will see true concrete walls whose strength lay in the solid concrete core, with a facing of lightweight stone blocks which merely kept out the weather; much as our bathroom tiles have a waterproofing rather than a structural role. Such walls were still two centuries away. In the case of Hadrian's it was not the core but the badly balanced facing stones that were the structural element while mortars, themselves of variable quality, were intended to counter outward collapse. Over a century earlier Vitruvius had complained that:

> Our impatient workmen have a care for the facings only, filling the intervening space with a lot of broken stone and mortar, thrown in higgledy-piggledy. This has the effect of dividing what should be a unified structure into three: the two faces and the core. No wall based on rubble, however finished on the outside, can escape time's revenge. In due course the mortar dries out, the lime and sand part company, the rubble loosens and the wall becomes a ruin. Such walls will not last more than eighty years.[55]

This forecast falls uncannily close to the repairs undertaken some eighty-six years later by Septimius Severus, in a rebuild so total that until the nineteenth century the Wall was believed to be his. The overhaul had a number of objectives including the reduction of turrets and blocking of gates, but in some stretches there is evidence of rebuilding from the ground and the use of improved mortars, based on limestones from further afield.[56]

Vitruvius recommended that the two faces of large ramparts be cross-tied by means of charred timbers. Also that the structure be compartmentalised by interior walls, linking one or other face to the core: 'So the burden of rubble will be distributed in pockets and its weight will never combine into a mass sufficient to thrust out the base.'[57] Neither technique was used in Hadrian's Wall. There it is more likely that the weight of the facing stones caused the upper courses (first to be attacked by weather) to peel outwards, especially on the northern or parapet side. Remembering the Pantheon, a masterclass of building skills, it is amazing that Hadrian should have accepted unsound specifications for the Wall's construction. It reveals him as a gentleman architect, heavily dependent on others for implementation and technical advice. We may assume that the quality of advice between Rome and Vindolanda varied extremely. When all was said and done, the emperor had no choice but to leave his enterprise in the hands of men who had neither built nor even seen a freestanding wall of this style or scale.

Turning to strategy, the Wall's purpose seems essentially defensive. Would it otherwise have been sighted on high ridges and unassailable clifftops? An ambiguity arises from its combination of guarding and fighting garrisons, which has led to confusing terms like 'the offensive–defensive'. Though it is true that a minority sat on the wall while a majority trained to sally forth from it, these are tactical matters. Strategically the Wall, like all walls – indeed like all frontier works – was a passive concept. But perhaps these definitions were rendered academic by events; or, more precisely, by non-events. Shielded in the east behind friendly alliances, in the centre behind crags, in the west behind outposts and on the coast behind brine, the cohorts awaited their call in vain. Decades passed without emergency. The Wall would suffer only two major upsets in the next two and a half centuries. Even then its vulnerability would be to troop withdrawals for service elsewhere rather than to direct attack.

What of the Wall today? In its central sector, over the dragon's back of the Whin Sill, the works have survived more visibly than in any other part of the empire's frontier. They stand to shoulder-height for miles on end, Western antiquity's lengthiest relic in stone (save the Roman roads) and Britain's premier historical monument. The English cathedrals, the Welsh castles, the noble houses: other countries have comparable treasures. Hadrian's Wall is unique.

However, it does not outdo other frontiers in all respects. It is, for one thing, among the shortest. Forts and towers in the East and

North Africa are better preserved. The standards of museums, site reconstruction and display are generally higher in Germany. Nor is the Wall alone among imperial frontiers in running through stirring country. It is only when we add all factors (atmosphere, setting, accessibility, preservation, time documented, research done, literature published, as well as the grandeur of the monument itself) that Hadrian's Wall is seen to be incomparable.

Alas, after faring well for fifteen centuries, the Wall underwent a catastrophe comparable to the dissolution of the monasteries as an act of English vandalism. In 1745 Field Marshal Wade, who had brought roads to the Highlands,[58] was charged with the interception of Charles Edward Stuart. Quartered at Newcastle, he suffered the humiliation of being slow to move his ordnance when the Young Pretender thrust into England via Carlisle. In a gesture of self-justification he proposed a new, east–west highway on the most direct course possible: the unwavering line of Hadrian's Wall. Beginning soon after Wade's death in 1751, the roadmakers razed twenty-seven miles of tumbled wall, spreading its stones as their hardcore. So they continued to Shield-on-the-Wall, five miles short of half-way, at the cost of most of the eastern sector. Fortunately some one and a half valuable miles were saved where the road diverted to take the North Tyne's medieval crossing at Chollerford. However, final deliverance does not come till milecastle 33, where the high crags begin and the road could not follow. Much of the best lies westwards from here, intermittently for some fifteen miles. The walk, beginning at Housesteads fort and heading west, is the best in England. The *Vallum* is impressive for most of the seven-mile section from Shield to Haltwhistle Burn. But so great is the number of books that it would be repetitive to list locations. For these we recommend the latest edition of the Collingwood Bruce, *Handbook to the Roman Wall* and the Ordnance Survey map of Hadrian's Wall.

Few Wall watchers visit the Cumbrian coast and there is not a great deal to bring them. Its happiest survival is ten miles back from the shore: Hardknott Castle, guarding the road from the naval station at Ravenglass to Ambleside. This is a well-preserved fort standing on a spur above Eskdale, one of England's loveliest valleys, and close under the Scafell range. When the weather is right this is among the imperial frontier's most magical locations.

As Romania remembers Trajan, so the north of England recalls Hadrian: the Hadrian hairdressing salon, the Hadrian supermarket, the Hadrian laundrette. Such confidence in the Wall's authorship is recent. It was not till 1910 that the weight of evidence began to tilt in Hadrian's favour. Before then it had been 'the Roman Wall' and earlier yet 'the Pict Wall'. Confusion was confounded by the existence of three, seemingly successive frontiers; Wall, turf wall and *Vallum*, assumed to be the work of different emperors. By bequeathing us a boundary as it were in triplicate, Hadrian so perplexed posterity that history awarded him the booby prize: attributing the *Vallum* to him and the Wall to Septimius (197–211), its repairer and revisionist.

Enlightenment began with F. J. Haverfield, who excavated on the Wall for a decade from 1893. It was calculated, by his pupil R. G. Collingwood, that the Wall's works cover an area of sixteen square miles; and that to examine this by the total excavation method (established during the nineteenth century and perfected by General A. H. Pitt-Rivers) would take two thousand years![59] The answer was selective excavation, as evolved in response to the same problem by the Reichslimeskommission. Its then director, General O. von Sarwey, was invited to view the Wall and offer advice. Haverfield returned the visit. So began an Anglo-German frontier *entente* which, despite two wars, would in the end generate much – perhaps most – of our knowledge. Henceforward Haverfield and his successor Gerald Simpson would apply the new approach, selecting spot sites with specific dating questions in mind. One lay just inside Cumbria, slightly west of the Birdoswald fort, where a chance realignment had preserved some 2,000 yards of turf wall, elsewhere demolished when replaced in stone. By excavating the corresponding turf- and stone-wall milecastles, Simpson revealed both to be Hadrianic. This was typical of the inter-war findings: ditch, stone wall, turf wall, forts and *Vallum* all being proved to have their origin in the decade of Hadrian's visit. The second puzzle – their sequence within that decade – could then begin to be unravelled.

Beyond lies a third set of questions, perhaps unanswerable, related to the modifications and policy changes which typified the building phase; errors enough for recrimination between designer and project manager to last the rest of their days. Nepos left Britain at the end of a normal four-year term in 126. Did his worsening relationship with the emperor originate from this period? The *Augustan History* tells us only that: 'Especially Hadrian came to detest Platorius Nepos, of whom he had once been so fond [. . .]'[60]

Or did it arise later, fuelled by the paranoia which eventually engulfed all Hadrian's relationships? 'He gave generously to friends; and yet he was always willing to listen to whispers against them and in the end came to believe nearly all of them enemies; even the closest; even those, like Nepos, who had served him in the highest offices.'[61] The poison worked mutually. Hadrian attempted to reverse it by visiting Nepos' sickbed. But his kindness came too late and we are left with a last, sad glimpse of Hadrian waiting at the door of Nepos' house, while his old friend pretended to be too ill, or not at home.

Having come to believe all friends enemies, Hadrian too would die a lonely man. But the story of his contribution to the frontier has not yet run its course; for an important part, fully one third of the imperial circuit, awaits our attention still.

CHAPTER 6

Africa:
The Limits of the Possible

Agricultural abundance, defended at paltry cost, may seem an unachievable formula for a frontier province; yet Egypt offered it. Nevertheless, when Augustus annexed Cleopatra's kingdom he saw the Nile as a larder so rich that he must set three legions to guard against its seizure by potential rivals. The garrison was thus largely deployed to counter unrest either from within the empire, or from Egypt herself. As time passed and suspicion receded, he withdrew a legion and by Hadrian's time only one remained: *XXII Deiotariana*, stationed near the capital, Alexandria. Were it not for that city's deplorable public order record even this would have been unnecessary.

In fact, Egypt was almost impregnable. Apart from Alexandria there are no good anchorages and harbourless coasts stretch far in either direction. 'The Nile, ambling through its immense amplitude of space,'[1] is safer still. On the left is the Western Desert where, despite a few oases, waterpoints are up to 180 miles apart. No trans-Saharan route begins or ends here. Between the Nile and the Dead Sea is the Eastern Desert, with few wells and 6,000-foot mountains. To the south it is a simple matter to block the Nile's narrowing corridor. Upriver lay Ethiopia and beyond her the Sudd, a weedy swamp unpenetrated till 1860, severing Egypt from the rest of Africa and confirming her Mediterraneanness.

Well over 500 miles to the south, at Syenê, was Egypt's only land frontier then considered worth guarding; and that lightly. This faced the northern part of Ethiopia, today's Sudan: 'As for the Ethiopians, they are good neither for war nor much else, as is demonstrated by the fact that Egypt can be watched by only three cohorts and even these are under strength!'[2] Pliny specifies the location of their forts: 'The Nile enters Egyptian territory at Syenê, a peninsula a mile round where, on the Arabian side, the forts are situated[3] and off which lie the four islands of Philae, 600 (Roman) miles upstream from where the delta begins.'[4] In short he locates the *de iure* frontier at Syenê (now an island facing the town of Aswan) whose Roman name was Elephanta. This he describes as 'four miles below the last cataract [. . . the] extreme limit of navigation in Egypt and terminus for Ethiopian vessels, except those which can be dismantled for portage round the rapids.'[5] The *de facto* frontier was clearly the natural barrier of the cataract, whose deafening succession of torrents was stilled by the Aswan low dam, placed just above it in 1902. Behind is now a lake with more islands, including Agilkiya, to which the temples of submerged Philae were transferred. A few miles further is the high dam and for 500 miles south of it Lake Nasser. Frontier knowledge is ill served by such heavy losses within the contact area.

During Augustus' reign the geographer Strabo visited Egypt as guest of its prefect, his friend Aelius Gallus, ascending the Nile to the limit of Roman territory. He described Syenê as being on the tropic of Cancer, 'for at midday the sun shines down deep wells to the water at the bottom'.[6] Though the tropic is in fact forty miles further, the cataract was and would remain Rome's southernmost frontier. Strabo's description conveys his sense of standing at a decisive, cultural barrier and close to the known world's end; for it was believed that beyond Ethiopia lay only the earth-encircling ocean. The Nile was thought to rise in the High Atlas of southern Morocco and flow eastwards, turning north into the Sudan and thence to Egypt, with the African continent scarcely a third of its actual length. Strabo adds: 'Because of the bareness and remoteness of their country, the Ethiopians lead a miserable and largely itinerant life; whereas with the Egyptians the opposite is true',[7] prompting his reflection that 'The edges of the inhabited world must, because of their heat or cold, be inferior to the temperate part, as is clear from the life-style of the people and their lack of bare necessities. They lead a hard, nomadic life and go almost naked.'[8]

But Strabo underestimated the Ethiopians. Soon Augustus despatched Gallus on an expedition into *Arabia Felix*. Taking advantage of his absence, Candace, their queen, 'a masculine sort of woman with one eye',[9] stormed downriver, overwhelming Syenê and taking much booty. In reply a Roman column under Gaius Petronius penetrated some 500 miles upriver to Napata, her northern capital.[10] The queen capitulated, ceding thirty leagues[11] of river to Rome. This strip now became a Roman protectorate known as the Triacontaschœnus (Thirty Leagues Land) reduced by Augustus to a more manageable twelve leagues (sixty-six miles), the Dodekaschœnus. It was a military buffer zone, held by a string of small outposts above the cataract and dependent on the forts just below it. Under these arrangements, with little more than the three cohorts specified by Strabo, the Nile frontier would remain inviolate for 250 years.[12]

At sea the Alexandrine fleet's main duty was to escort grain convoys to Italy. The Nile was patrolled by a separate unit, the *potamophylacia* (river watch), whose station above the cataract at Hiera Sykaminos is not attested until the 3rd century. We have seen how Rome controlled a substantial share of the India trade through the Red Sea ports. From north to south these were Myos Hormos (just south of the Gulf of Suez), Leukos Limen (Quseir) and Berenikê (Bernice), at each of which was an auxiliary unit. The road from the Nile to the Red Sea ran eastwards from the bend below Luxor. Part way were gold and beryl mines, plus the famous porphyry quarries at Wadi Hammamat. Via the coast came topaz and pearls, as well as Indian spices and other luxuries; traffic which required the provision of road patrols, with way stations at the watering points;[13] though this protection was against banditry rather than an external danger.

Following Egypt's other shoreline, westwards from Alexandria, one may hardly leave that city's outskirts without awareness of the Western Desert. In the four-hundred-mile stretch from here to Tobruk we see something quite new to our picture of the imperial frontier: no defences or military presence of any kind. This was an open door onto the Mediterranean coast from the eastern Sahara. But it was a deserted coast and a desolate Sahara, with little to defend and no one to oppose.

Before continuing westwards let us glance toward the greatest of all deserts whose presence dictated how much of Africa Rome could have. It was surprisingly little, for Roman North Africa was not a fiftieth part of the Dark Continent overall. Though her rule extended over its entire width, penetration southwards was rarely more than a hundred miles and often only thirty. History has no example of so long a frontier for so modest a holding. In defence of this 2,000-mile-wide strip, the desert solved a larger but created a smaller problem. On the one hand its vastness vetoed the passage of armies and made the Sahara Rome's safest borderline. On the other hand (except for the Nile banks and three barren patches along the Mediterranean coast) the desert begins gradually. This is a transitional zone and the home of transitional peoples. Though it is generally true that the empire died with the rainfall and the *barbaricum* began with the drought, even Saharans cannot live without pasture and their search for it would blur any boundary Rome might set.

The Berbers were (and still are) the indigenous Saharans. From about 10,000 BC they were driven toward the Mediterranean by desiccation; then, much later, back toward the desert fringes by the arrival of Greek and Phoenician settlers. The word *berber* is not recorded in antiquity, but is probably from the Latin *barbarus* (barbarian). It occurs on the Horn of Africa in the placename Berbera, perhaps also reflecting a Roman contact. Be that as it may the Berbers – known by a variety of tribal names – were the principal threat to Roman North Africa, though rarely more than a nuisance, aggravated by distance and problems inseparable from nomadism.

Westwards from Egypt is the country now called Libya. Here confusion in naming arises, because in Latin *Libya* was used for Africa generally, while *Africa* denoted Tunisia. Accepting the word in the modern sense, it seems that nature intended Libya to be two, for its habitable parts consist of twin protuberances, pushed far enough north to catch the winter rain. Of these the Romans called the eastern Cyrenaica, after its principal city Cyrene; and the Greeks the Pentapolis,[14] whose five original cities (later increasing to thirteen) were spread between today's Tobruk and Benghazi. The western part was Tripolitania, named after its three original cities. Separating Cyrenaica from Tripolitania is the Gulf of Sirte, which recedes far enough southwards to be almost rainless. Here desert again reaches sea and there was a hiatus in the imperial frontier. The two Libyas would not be united until the present century when, after 400 years under Turkey, Italy acquired them in the war of 1911–12. Even then physical linkage would await the construction of Mussolini's ambitious highway, the Litoranea Libica, which closed the 500-mile gap at last.

In any ancient context, however, Cyrenaica and Tripolitania must be seen separately. From the north they resembled two islands, the passage between them shunned by sailors due to dangerous shoals and onshore winds. Their separateness was emphasised by that major cultural partition of the empire, the linguistic divide between Latin and Greek, which fell across Africa at Arae Philaenorum, fifteen miles west of today's El Agheila.[15] Cyrenaica was decisively Greek. Her five cities, colonised from the island of Thera (Santorini) in the 7th century BC, were the only ancient Greek foundations on African soil. They would later be ruled by a branch of the Ptolemies. But control was tenuous, for the waterless way from Alexandria, 'twenty days for a man travelling light',[16] was too long for an army to cross without risk. When in 96 BC the last king, Apion, willed Cyrenaica to Rome, the Senate refused it; relenting twenty years later only because the harbours were being used by pirates. The territory was attached to Crete, and throughout the Principate it continued as part of that senatorial province. Tripolitania, though also isolated, was easier to reach from the western side and for this reason had come under Carthaginian dominance, passing to Rome after the Second Punic War and eventually being administered as part of the African province.

In Hadrian's time there seems to have been little concern regarding the external security of either Cyrenaica or Tripolitania. The Ptolemies had left Cyrene and her sister cities equipped with strong walls. The only danger – a minor one – lay in the direction of the Gulf of Sirte where tribes, migrating to the shore, were sometimes deflected northeastwards toward the nearer of the two green islands. Despite Cyrenaica's being part of an ostensibly 'unarmed province', there was already at least one fort[17] covering the Sirte direction and more would follow. In the case of Tripolitania, there is no evidence for a military garrison before the late 2nd century. The arming of Libya would largely await that rarity: an emperor interested in Africa, for this was the non-priority continent, where much could be taken and little given. In any case neither of Libya's parts would compare as a producer with Egypt. At twenty miles from the coast the eight-inch rainfall limit, minimum for dry farming without irrigational works, is passed. Though Tripolitania has been proposed as a terminus for trans-Saharan commerce,[18] there is still no firm evidence that such traffic existed, and contacts with 'black Africa' remain likeliest at the continent's extremities: via the Red Sea and Morocco.[19]

Let us follow the edge of Roman territory westwards from Libya where, in today's northern Tunisia, we will find a Roman bargain greater than Egypt and even closer to home. The province of Africa, expropriated after the overthrow of Carthage, with its two hundred cities and superabundant wheatfields, had been described by Josephus as, 'This third part of the world, which feeds the city of Rome for eight months of the year and submits cheerfully to taxation, though only a single legion is stationed in its midst.'[20] Southward wheat gave way to olives, whose oil lit and washed half the empire. It was a corner we will call 'vital Africa', to whose bounty Rome was at ransom; and Hadrian's visit of 128 was in a formative year in the imperial frontier's story.

First, however, the setting. In Arab terms we are now entering the Jazirat al Maghreb ('Island of the West'). These are also France's former North African possessions and the domain of French Roman frontier scholarship. A fundamental difference between northeast and northwest Africa is the dominance of mountain. Two long ranges, the Tellian and Saharan Atlas, run parallel to the coast with intermediate plateaux, all finally compressed into the High Atlas of today's Morocco. Between the southernmost ranges and the Sahara proper is a depression, beginning close to the Tunisian coast and running far toward the west. Into this the streams empty, are trapped and their waters subjected to intense evaporation, creating an almost continuous series of bitter lakes, known by the Berber name of *chott*.[21] The biggest, Djerid, is 80 miles long; though with its extension, the Chott el Fedjadj, it measures 120 miles from east to west. More typically they are 30 or 40 miles in length. Their ponded water dries to a condition more salty than fresh, more muddy than watery: immense, mirage-haunted marshes, sparkling like hoarfrost, squeezed into crystalline ridges or stretched into plains of white polygons. After occasional cloudbursts the chotts are flooded with shallow, brackish water; soon drying again to a creaking, crunching crust, firm or less firm, crossable with care but supporting no pasture and therefore an intermittent barrier to the desert herdfolk. For many miles the frontier faced these forlorn flats, reminiscent of the western outlook of Hadrian's Wall across the Solway at low tide.

The stretch between Libya and Tunisia, which the *Antonine Itinerary* calls the *Limes Tripolitanus*,[22] would, in its final form, swing north from the plateau behind Tripoli. There it picked up the Jebel Ksour, following its 2,000-foot ridge as far as Matmata, where it descended to join the line of the chotts, some 20 miles inland from

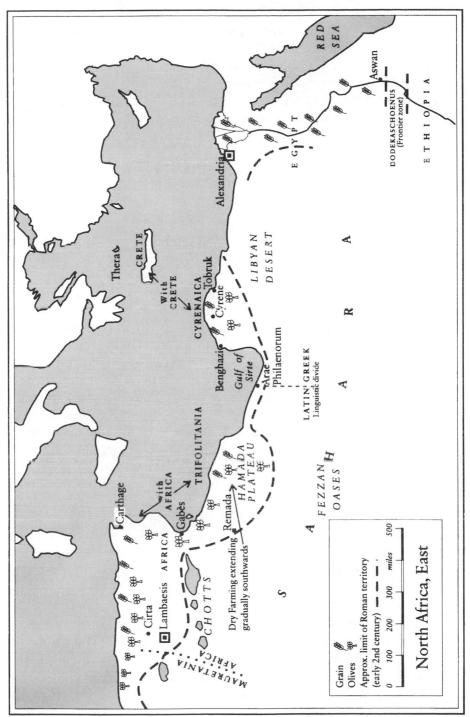

RED SEA

Aswan

EGYPT

DODEKASCHOENUS
(Frontier zone)

ETHIOPIA

Thera

CRETE

Alexandria

With
CRETE

CYRENAICA

Tobruk

Cyrene

LIBYAN   DESERT

A   R   A

Benghazi

Gulf of
Sirte

Arae
Philaenorum

LATIN: GREEK
Linguistic divide

A   R

TRIPOLITANIA

HAMADA
PLATEAU

FEZZAN

OASES H

Carthage

with
AFRICA

Gabès

Remada

A

Dry Farming extending
gradually southwards

S

Lambaesis

AFRICA

Cirta

CHOTTS

MAURETANIA

AFRICA

Grain

Olives

Approx. limit of Roman territory
(early 2nd century)

500

miles

100   200   300

0

North Africa, East

the port of Gabès. *Ksour* or *Gsur* (French and English translations of the same word) are Arabic for 'forts', their singular *kasr* o *gsar* are derived from the Latin *castrum*. Nevertheless the sector was lightly defended, for the Jebel Ksour faces inland onto the Great Eastern Erg,[23] a textbook Saharan region from whose sands no serious menace could be expected. But sand shifts and we cannot be sure of the Erg's extent or even existence in the Roman period. In any event, at Remada (Tillibari), 30 miles inside Tunisia, Hadrian established a large cohort fort, which might be seen as a marker for fuller defences to come. Like many of these desert-edge sites, it was discovered by a young French soldier; in this case one Lt. Lecoy de la March, in 1894, but not excavated till 1914, shortly before the entire site was levelled and its materials used to construct a military post and barracks, costing us fort remains without counterpart in southern Tunisia.[24] From the eastern extremity of the chotts the frontier turned inland, running due west along the Sahara's edge and deep into Algeria, always keeping the bitter lakes between itself and the desert. It took the form of a road with widely spaced forts at irregular intervals, following the spring line, where water issues from the feet of the Nementcha and Aurès massifs. Though incorporated into the African province this was formerly Numidia, the Berber kingdom of eastern Algeria. It may once have been Nomadia, derived from the Greek 'to pasture', for this was indeed a land of grass followers.

Though Trajan never visited Africa it was his initiative which brought the frontier to this part of the Saharan edge. On the whole it had been a sound step. But by the time of the imperial visit of 128, with Hadrian's oddities widely known, many must have wondered whether he would overturn Trajan's policy and abandon the Sahara line, or whether he would confirm it but seek to eclipse Trajan's achievement by adding some *tour de force* of his own.

Numidia was the station of *III Augusta*, the only legion on the African continent outside Egypt. It is difficult to grasp that a single legion should be responsible for all territory from Cyrenaica to the Atlantic. This was based on an appreciation that while 'vital Africa's' agricultural belt must be defended at all costs, other parts were of lesser consequence and could be lightly guarded. A balance must be struck, with a military establishment large enough to police the desert's edges but small enough to discourage an African *coup d'état* against Italy. In principle this was the suspicion-based formula applied to all frontier provinces though pitched, according to the supposed balance of internal and external dangers, between the extremes of three legions to one province in Britain and one legion to four provinces in North Africa. Surprisingly, the arrangement worked. Though the army of Africa was sorely stretched and in places nonexistent, *Legio III Augusta* and her auxiliaries were generally able to protect Roman territory, keep the peace and remain loyal. Here, however, we must forget such conventions as a one-to-one ratio between legionaries and auxiliaries, or frontier forts every seven miles. In North Africa the ratio may have been six auxiliaries to one legionary, rising during the next century to ten. Seventy miles between forts was not uncommon and, at the time of Hadrian's visit, extensive tracts of desert edge were not watched at all. Because of the larger numbers of *auxilia*, the manpower of the army of Africa roughly equalled that of Britain, though where Hadrian's Wall was 73½ miles long the legate of Africa was responsible for a front of 1,800 miles, between Tobruk in Libya and Rabat in Morocco.

Clearly a number of other question-marks hung over Hadrian's visit. Would he draft in a second legion? Or would he keep the same number of troops but devise some way of making the frontier more efficient? Only one sector really mattered: that part of the former Numidian kingdom on the Sahara's edge, southwestwards from 'vital Africa'. This is because topography lies on a slanting axis, with mountain chains and valley corridors running inland from Carthage (modern Tunis) for 300 miles in a southwesterly direction, toward the region of Biskra in today's eastern Algeria.

Due south of 'vital Africa', on the other hand, is today's southern Tunisia. This was a less vulnerable direction, thanks to the bitter lakes and the eastern erg. Trajan's frontier made use of a line of hills just north of the chotts, meaningfully called the Djebel Asker ('soldier's range') and Djebel Zitouna ('olive tree range'), though now treeless. Here a form of defence known as *claustrum* ('closure') was first applied to the boundaries of empire. Passes through the 1,500-foot ridge were sealed by closure walls (*clausurae*). In other words, mountains were left open, but gaps between them were plugged. Typically, such a barrier would begin on one side of a valley, where the gradient became less than 45°, cross the valley floor and end at the other side, where the slope again became steep or craggy. Being intermittent the obstacles could of course be circumvented. *Clausurae* offered large savings in construction time; and might easily have been applied to the central part of Hadrian's Wall, where gaps and cliffs alternate. However, in comparing different stretches we must not forget that there were different motives for entering imperial territory, as well as different types of entrant. Nimble individuals or small raiding parties are not the same as tribal groups with families, the elderly and flocks. *Clausurae* were especially suited to the control of migration by barring the passes through which families and animals might enter.

Among these stretches of closure wall the most spectacular is that of Bir Oum Ali (see map 9): in a setting of dry and deserted hills, preserved in parts to full height of about fifteen feet, though with some restoration. This blocks two valleys and the low crest between. Less than a mile long, its build is quite unlike Hadrian's Wall, being narrower and without a sentry walk. The facings are of natural stones built into two, mortared faces which slope gradually inwards to meet roof-like at the top. The upper part is hollow, the rest rubble-filled. In the valley was a gate with guardhouse, largely erased by the present dirt road, still used by nomads.

Control of the wells meant mastery of the desert, though it is not always certain how they were guarded. Watchtowers are strangely scarce in southern Tunisia, with only 30 identified over a front of two hundred miles, where 300 might be expected:[25] evidence of the smallness of Africa's garrison. There are names suggesting mirror signals: Ksar esh Shems (sunshine castle) and the fort of Speculum (mirror). These have been compared with one near the Danube's headwaters: Hohlspiegel ('concave mirror').[26]

The Djebel Asker and its *clausurae* peter out part way along the Chott Djerid. It is forty miles from here to the Algerian border, among the least studied parts of the African frontier across which, as we have said, Trajan's road continued westwards, including two or three forts, running between foothills and chotts. Well inside Algeria, beyond the Aurès massif, it turned north toward Mauretania, the next province. Rounding this corner, in the region of today's Biskra, we enter the most sensitive stretch in terms of potential invasion routes towards 'vital Africa'; though as yet even this was lightly guarded. But change was in the air. Even now the legionary masons and carpenters were putting the final touches to the fortress at Lambaesis (Lambèse), just north of the Aurès, with a view to controlling those mountains and the desert beyond.

The frontier's turn north towards Mauretania was in part because that province was understrength and had failed to push its limits further toward the south, in part because here the coastal ranges narrow, from a depth of 250 to only 60 miles, their retreat allowing the desert to advance. Mauretania was the land of the Maures, a Berber group, from which we have the word Moor. It included all North Africa from about longitude 6° E to the Atlantic. The entirety of Mauretania had passed into Roman hands in 33 BC, when its native ruler Bocchus willed his kingdom to the Senate. However Augustus, loath to look after so turbulent a territory, gave it to Selenê, daughter of Antony and Cleopatra, and her husband Juba. This colourful pair turned their capital, Caesarea (Cherchell), the former Punic colony of Iol, into a centre of culture, but did little to pacify the mountain hinterland. In due course their son, yet another Ptolemy, was invited by the malign and unstable Caligula to Rome, where he was murdered and his country subsequently annexed. This provoked a Moorish revolt, and Claudius, left to tidy up the mess, divided the ramshackle kingdom into two minor provinces with equestrian governors. Mauretania Caesariensis, named after its capital Caesarea, extended across three quarters of today's Algeria. Its border with the province of Africa lay not far west of Constantine. Mauretania Tingitana, named after its capital Tingis (Tangier), approximated to present-day northern Morocco.

Modern Algeria is the second biggest country in Africa, former jewel of the French empire, with a considerable agricultural output and large cities like Oran and Algiers. Given that most of this lay within the borders of Mauretania Caesariensis, we are surprised to find it 'A province poor in Romanity, without a legion, relegated to mere procuratorial rank, last on the list for defence spending; with concern for provincial improvement always weighed against other priorities and with geography generally dictating an unfavourable reply.'[27] Tillage was largely confined to the coastal strip, which was narrow and often marshy, and to valleys not far distant. The garrison may have been 8,000 or even as few as 5,000 auxiliaries guarding five hundred miles: the longest front of any province in the empire save Africa with Tripolitania. The plain around Sétif was almost unguarded. Further west, the river line of the Oued Chéllif was held by forts, twenty to thirty miles apart but sometimes further, passing only thirty-five miles south of today's Algiers and less than twenty south of Oran. This poor progress southwards suggests that the northern hillmen remained unsubdued and that the army was still looking over its shoulder, unable to advance beyond the coastal ranges onto the more amenable plateaux. In Mauretania Caesariensis we cannot yet speak of the nomad problem or the pre-desert, since the nomads had not been met nor the desert approached.

In a westerly direction, the last fort in this line was Numerus Syrorum at Maghnia, twenty-five miles west of today's Tlencem. Beyond this point no Roman road is known or milestone found. A wide and sterile plain separates Algeria and Morocco. To the north the Rif mountains, falling steeply to the sea, bar all connection along the coast. The *Antonine Itinerary* regards the sea passage from Caesarea to Tingis as the normal route, though in practice most would enter via Gibraltar. Thus between the two Mauretanias was another blank on the Roman map, a frontierless space comparable to that between Alexandria and Tobruk, or the halves of Libya, where the *barbaricum* was admitted to the Mediterranean because its coasts were not worth defending. However in Tingitana, today's Morocco, the tempo quickens. Though remote from Rome this small possession was closest to Baetica (Andalucia), Hadrian's birthplace, a rich and prestigious province, as tempting to the Moors as it would later be to the Arabs. Part of the Senate's share, Baetica was forbidden an army of her own. Accordingly Tingitana became Spain's *de facto* southern frontier, a role which redeemed her from what would otherwise have been obscurity.

Tingitana itself was a tricky province to defend. In the north-east the Rif remained an untangled knot, troublesome until the twentieth century. Even the limited expedient of sealing off this massif with a watchtower cordon was still many years away. South-east is the High Atlas: another Caucasus, at the opposite end of the ancient world but no less laden with grim legend. These memorable mountains rise from the warm plain to an icy 12,000 feet in one bold sweep. Beyond, with comparable abruptness, comes the Sahara. None of these wild zones would be tamed by Rome. Even the amenable coastal areas of central and southern Morocco, beyond today's Rabat, would remain outside the empire; though there was a commercial presence on the island of Mogador,[28] over 250 miles south, where a dye factory extracted the prized purple from the murex shell. Roman coins are found as far afield as the Ivory Coast.

During the disturbances provoked by Caligula's perfidy, the general who had defeated Boudicca, C. Suetonius Paulinus, crossed the High Atlas in pursuit of insurgents, but was obliged to retire in the

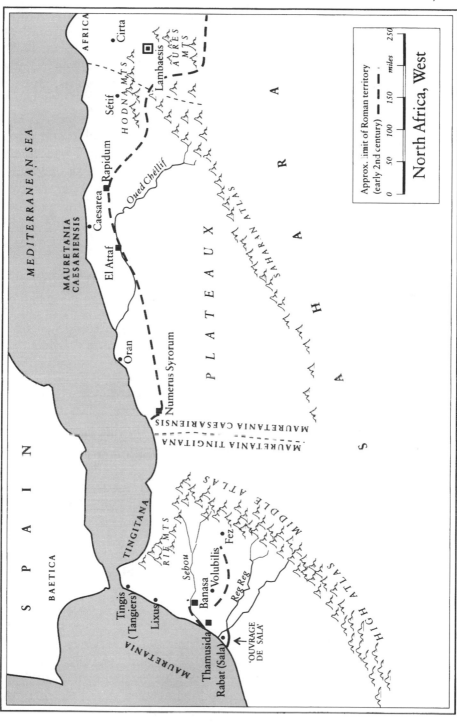

North Africa, West

Approx. limit of Roman territory
(early 2nd century)

MEDITERRANEAN SEA

SPAIN

BAETICA

MAURETANIA CAESARIENSIS

AFRICA

Cirta

Lambaesis

AURES MTS

Sétif

HODNA MTS

Rapidum

Caesarea

Oued Chellif

El Attaf

PLATEAUX

Oran

Numerus Syrorum

SAHARAN ATLAS

SAHARA

MAURETANIA CAESARIENSIS

MAURETANIA TINGITANA

TINGITANA

RIF MTS

MIDDLE ATLAS

Sebou

Fez

Volubilis

Banasa

Reg Reg

Tingis (Tangiers)

Lixus

MAURETANIA

Thamusida

Rabat (Sala)

'OUVRAGE DE SALA'

HIGH ATLAS

face of heat stroke and water shortage. We may also guess that morale was affected by a fear of the desert comparable to that of the German forest, the Sarmatian steppe or the outer ocean. Pliny gives us descriptions of both sides of the range. The west was friendly and fragrant with cedar forests; but once over the passes, sinister influences prevailed.

They say that by day its inhabitants become invisible and all is still, with the terrifying silence of the desert, so that a speechless awe creeps into the hearts of all who go there. The peak of Mount Atlas soars above the clouds and reaches the neighbourhood of the moon. At night its summit flashes fire and swarms with the wanton gambols of Pans and satyrs, the eerie music of flutes and pipes and the sound of drums and cymbals.[29]

The garrison of Tingitana has been estimated as 10,000 auxiliaries. Policy toward the province was minimalist: to protect the colonies of veterans put there by Augustus after the Spanish war, to shield the cities inherited from the pre-Roman period and to occupy only as much as was needed to find a good stopline. This was offered by the meandering Sububus (Oued Sebou) which takes its water from both the Rif and Middle Atlas, entering the Atlantic some 130 miles south of Gibraltar and twenty north of today's Rabat. Described by Pliny as 'a fine river and navigable',[30] its perennial flow is comparable to the Main at Frankfurt or the Tyne at Corbridge. South of here lay swamp and forest. The river was commanded by a fort at Thamusida, soon to be joined by another at Banasa, one of the Augustan colonies. Both ruins survive. Thamusida, enveloped by a *vicus* of six times its own area, in turn surrounded by a later city wall, was the Roman empire's most westerly fort.

The Sebou frontier had drawbacks. Two important cities, Volubilis and Sala (Rabat) lay outside it. Volubilis (near today's Meknès) is Morocco's only Roman ruin comparable to those urban sites for which North Africa is elsewhere famous. Since a strong wall already existed it was considered sufficient to establish a defensive box, twelve or fifteen miles across, containing five or six auxiliary forts, which covered the city. This places the frontier serving the inland side of the Moroccan plain at about the latitude of today's Fez. In Hadrian's time the Volubilis defensive zone existed only in outline, if at all. One of its forts, Tocolosida, has been dated to thirty or forty years later. Sala (Rabat) was near the mouth of the next river southwards, the Bou Regreg; and on the southern or exposed side of it. Pliny describes it as 'on the edge of nowhere, beset by herds of elephant and unruly tribes'.[31] This outlier, doubtless a headache for the Roman command, required special arrangements. It joins Bonn, Vienna, Budapest and Belgrade as a modern capital with imperial frontier connections.

On the eve of the First World War Louis Brunot, a young teacher at the Ecole Supérieure de Langue Arabe in Rabat noted, during walks close to the city, a long depression running between a loop of the river and the ocean. It was known to locals as the Seguia Faraoun ('canal of the Pharaohs'). Brunot claimed it as a Roman frontier work. Follow-up came in the 1920s when Henri Rouland-Mareschal, a civil servant of the French colonial administration, made the 'canal' his hobby, enlisting the advice of René Cagnat, renowned author of *L'Armée romaine d'Afrique* (1912). The result of their researches was published by the Académie des Inscriptions et Belles Lettres[32] in 1924.

The Ouvrage de Sala, seven miles long, runs through farmland, citrus groves and the southern suburbs of Rabat, clearly making for the coast and disappearing only two hundred yards before reaching it. It incorporates four fortlets and some fifteen towers or minor works. The main feature is a flat-bottomed ditch with a mound to its north, giving a combined height of twelve feet. The ditchslope is steep and usually revetted in stone, to prevent collapse. Dimensions differ considerably, reflecting varied soil conditions. There are also traces of a wall, fifteen feet to the ditch's south. A typical section of the work, described from the outside, might therefore have been: a wall perhaps seven feet high and three wide; a three-foot berm; then the ditch, six feet deep, with a stone-faced mound rising close behind to a further six feet. Opinion favours a Flavian dating, perhaps to Vespasian, with the wall added by Hadrian's successor, Antoninus.[33] Its effect was to cordon off an enclave of some 7 × 15 miles, enclosing the city, with the sea on one side, the river on two and the barrier completing the rectangle. At the roadside, heading out of Rabat towards Casablanca,[34] the westernmost piece of this work may be seen. The mound bright with wildflowers, the ditch acrid with excrement and urine; the bellicose traffic, the diesel haze and concrete glare of third-world industrial suburbia: such is our recollection of this last, unfragrant fragment of the imperial frontier as it nears the Atlantic and its southwestern extremity.

The Ouvrage de Sala was built from a fund of ingredients common to all Rome's linear barriers, arranged in a way peculiar to itself. Generally these consisted of mound, ditch, stone wall or turf wall and palisade; to these basics may be added differences of dimension, proportion and order, capable of considerable permutation. No two barriers were alike, and some were quite different. It is therefore fair to say that there was little attempt to co-ordinate frontier design and that this absence of standardisation held good throughout the imperial period. Evidently it was accepted that local circumstances invalidate central direction; materials, workforces, manning levels and the external threat were all allowed their say. So were the traditions of each regional command. In Africa, ditchwork seemed to have emerged as the central feature. Finally there were the inclinations, even whims, of the individuals in charge. In theory a deciding factor should have been knowledge of what had worked best on other frontiers. However, Rome's experience of man-made barriers was still short and distances between commands were long. It was imperial policy to keep provincial armies apart; and the price was ignorance of each other's practice.

It would appear that Hadrian did little of consequence for either of the Mauretanias, but through his fort of Rapidum, not far south of Algiers, and perhaps that of El Attaf, also in Algeria, we may again say that he laid down markers for later, improved defensive lines.

It is time to return to centre stage: Africa and Hadrian's visit of 128. To understand why this province was so important one must recall the turmoil preceding the Augustan peace, when an uprooted Italian peasantry flocked to the capital to be protected and fed, so starting a dangerous tradition that the world owed Rome a living. Here was a social time bomb which could only be defused by continuing to feed this large and idle underclass at government expense. Africa, today's Northern Tunisia, was the chief provider, stocking the Ostian granaries with a half million tons annually. Though there is no reason to suppose that the threat from the Sahara's edge was of the highest intensity or urgency, Africa's safeguarding could not be indefinitely postponed.

In early July Hadrian was approaching the southwestern extremity of the province; that part of the desert's edge where the provision for the protection of 'vital Africa' must be made. Ahead, across the glare of the dry plateau, towered the Aurès, dark with cloud and cedar. This is the final, 7,000-foot flourish of peaks before the Mediterranean capitulates to the Sahara at last. Procopius would write:

> There is a mountain in Numidia called Aurasius. It rises steeply to great heights and its bulk is such that it takes three days to travel round the base. It offers no easy path, but on climbing one finds deep soil, level terraces, meadows, trees and ploughland; springs bubbling from the rock and rippling rivers. Most remarkable of all are cornfields and trees which produce fruit double the size found elsewhere in Africa.[35]

Though centuries of spoliation have stripped these hills of leaf and lawn, the Aurès are tall enough to provoke rain and their winter snows release meltwater to thousands of streams over many weeks. This hanging garden in the midst of fruitlessness reveals the freakish nature of these desert margins, where high hills bring the north far south. Might garrisons be sustained by their run-off, far beyond the normal eight-inch rainfall limit for barley and ten-inch limit for wheat? Between Morocco and Egypt there is no navigable river and not one fort to which grain could be brought by water. This factor is crucial in understanding not only the African but also the imperial frontier as a whole. The cost of long-haul, overland transport for bulk goods was prohibitive in regions which lacked natural grazing, since it depended on draft animals who soon ate their own weight in fodder. This decreed that without sea or river access a sizeable or permanent military base would not normally be established unless self-support was assured.

Hence Lambaesis, the new fortress site in the well-watered valley to the immediate north of the Aurès.[36] Its intention was to control these mountains. A second intention must have been either to thicken Trajan's line along the desert's edge on the far side of this same massif, or to establish an alternative. In terms both of scenery and amount on view, Lambaesis is probably the most rewarding of all legionary bases. Its demerit is the prison, whose wall juts brutally into the site, obliterating most of its southwestern quarter: built in 1851 on a location whose choice, in a land of immense space, is incomprehensible. One consolation is that the fortress's 61 acres are otherwise well preserved and displayed. Another is its famous praetorium or legate's house. The legate at Lambaesis was effectively the military governor of all North Africa west of Egypt, and his

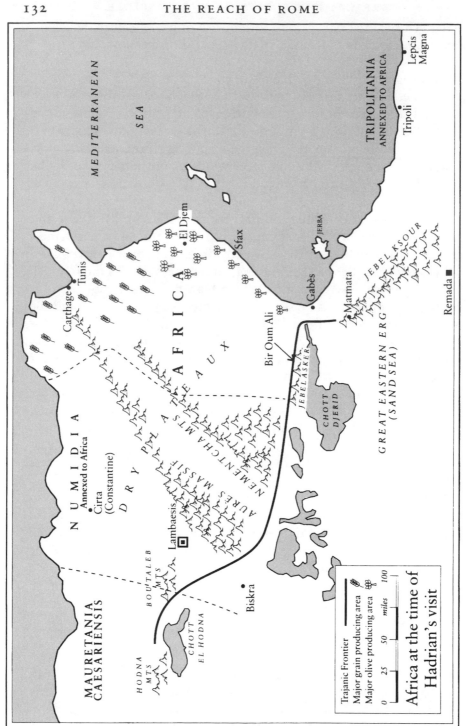

MEDITERRANEAN

SEA

TRIPOLITANIA
ANNEXED TO AFRICA

Lepcis
Magna

Tripoli

JERBA

JEBEL KSOUR

Remada ■

El Djem

Sfax

Tunis

Carthage

A F R I C A

Gabès

Matmata

GREAT EASTERN ERG
(SAND SEA)

Bir Oum Ali

JEBEL ASKER

CHOTT
DJERID

P L A T E A U X

NEMENTCHA MTS

N U M I D I A
Annexed to Africa

Cirta
(Constantine)

D R Y

AURES MASSIF

Lambaesis

BOU'TALEB MTS

Biskra

MAURETANIA
CAESARIENSIS

HODNA MTS

CHOTT
EL HODNA

Trajanic Frontier
Major grain producing area
Major olive producing area

0   25   50   miles   100

Africa at the time of
Hadrian's visit

residence no ordinary house, but a palace and headquarters combined. The shell stands intact to two storeys. Other than Diocletian's palace at Split, this is the most impressive of all Roman military building to survive. Rising to perhaps fifty feet over a foreground of barrack remains the usual two feet high, the praetorium has amazed all visitors from the time of Bruce, a nineteenth-century traveller who believed the Romans patrolled their African frontier on elephants and that this was their stable. The present remains are a late 3rd-century rebuild on the Hadrianic foundations.

A few miles east is the legion's retirement home of Timgad, another of Africa's most spectacular Roman sites, and the empire's best example of a veteran colony. It was laid out by the legion with wall and gates like a military base, though with full urban amenities. All around is rich farmland, watered from the Aurès, on which each old soldier had his plot. Timgad is a striking exercise in social security, demonstrating Rome's recompense for twenty years' loyal service; 'albeit with uncouth tribes still visible from the very doors'.[37] A mile and a half west of the Lambaesis fortress are the remnants of what was supposedly an auxiliary fort, 200 yards square, long known as the West Camp. In the early twentieth century clearance was begun under the direction of a French cleric, the Abbé Montagnon. Far from being an anticlimax to the fortress, this began to reveal an exciting discovery: the pedestal of a column, its tumbled shaft lying nearby. The latter had been 75 feet high and we may guess it originally held a statue of Hadrian. On the pedestal's front was a dedication to the emperor by the IIIrd Legion. At each corner was a pilaster, almost six feet high, with eight columns of carved text. These had shattered and were recovered over several decades. Louis Leschi, director of the Algiers Museum, painstakingly assembled the first batches and prepared to present his findings at the Berlin Archaeological Congress of 1940, a rendezvous which would not be kept. In the 1970s, 125 more fragments were unearthed and translated at the University of Paris. Substantial texts were at last published.[38] They proved to be the verbatim content of five addresses (plus fragments of others) given by Hadrian to units of the African Army in mid-July 128.[39]

The column had stood at the centre of an enclosure. What were thought to be fort ramparts turned out to be a thin wall with fourteen semicircular recesses. There were no internal buildings. It is thought that this was a parade-ground, created for the visit, and that here,

from the spot marked by the column, Hadrian addressed his soldiers.[40] From the text we know they had come from as far as today's
Libyan border, possibly a month's march away. We may guess that
fourteen regiments were represented; and that the embayments each
held a unit's standards and served as its mustering point. The inscriptions are part held at the Bardo Museum, Tunis, and part at the
Louvre. They are unique examples of Hadrian's *viva voce* expression.

   The speeches show a preoccupation with drills and manoeuvres,
an obsession with discipline and the punctilious observance of regu-
lations, and demonstrate considerable empathy with the life of the
soldier. Behind them one recognises the familiar scenario of Hadrianic pacifism: parade ground replacing battle ground, spit and
polish as an anodyne for action, a show of interest in the army as a
substitute for using it. A typical passage (to the Pannonians) reads:

> You have kept perfect dressing at all times. When at full gallop
> you used the space of the parade ground to excellent effect. Your
> throwing was done with maximum smartness, albeit using awk-
> ward, short-shafted spears. Many of you also showed skill in
> throwing the lance. Your jumping was sprightly and nimble and
> your bearing throughout the entire manoeuvre was first class. I
> can see how well your commander, Quintus Catullinus, looks after
> you. You will receive a bonus and take part in the end-of-visit
> parade.

In other passages one may detect apprehension that the soldiers might
become bored with their battleless role. He stresses the antidote,
'energy' (mentioned three times) and 'keenness' in drills and exer-
cises: 'You have avoided boredom by your keenness, discharging all
your duties with energy [. . .]'[41]
   As well as offering an insight into Hadrian's handling of an army
in abeyance, the Lambaesis texts give a hint of his other answer to
boredom: the creation of frontier works. Using materials to hand, a
Spanish cohort had been charged with building a specimen section
of wall and ditch as an exercise: 'You had to use big, rough rocks,
exceptionally difficult to fit flush. You had to dig the ditch straight,
through compacted gravel. And yet you managed to give everything
a smooth finish.' Were men like these soon to dig Hadrian a Saharan
frontier ditch? Owing to the smallness of Africa's workforce and the
length of its front, no one believed in the existence of such a barrier.

Ancient sources too are mute on the subject of an African frontier work, with a single exception, nearly three centuries later. On 29 April, AD 409, a window briefly opens before closing for ever.

The evidence takes the form of a letter, later included in the Theodosian Code, a compilation of imperial legislation covering the years 312 to 437. It was from the emperors of east and west to the Vicar of Africa. North of the Alps the empire was crumbling. A year later Honorius would cut Britain adrift. But *sauve-qui-peut* would not apply to Africa as long as the grain ships kept sailing.

> The Emperors Honorius and Theodosius to Gaudentius, Vicar of Africa: It has come to our notice that lands granted to certain outside peoples by our predecessors (who, with prudent care for the future, aimed to assure the upkeep of the *limes* and *fossatum*) have sometimes passed into the ownership of single individuals. If some are occupying, for personal gain, land whose purpose is to support the *limes* and *fossatum*, your obvious remedy must be to transfer these concessions to appropriate allies, or at least to veterans, so that danger to any part of the *limes* or *fossatum* may be averted.[42]

This appears to mean that (as was then common) frontier management had been contracted to adjacent treaty-tribes. However, the accompanying agricultural land, developed with the intention of feeding the garrisons, had apparently been sold off to individual speculators. Where this had occurred Gaudentius was instructed to restore it to corporate ownership. However, far more significant than any of this was one word which Honorius used: *fossatum* (ditchwork). Could there be a linear work, out on the Sahara's edge, comparable in importance to Hadrian's Wall but far longer; shrouded in sand and forgetfulness?

There *was* one feature, familiar to the local people and first noted by a Lt. Dinaux in the late nineteenth century. A groove or shallow undulation, puny but visible to the unaided eye, ran along the edge of sandy desert forty miles beyond the Aurès. It was known to folklore as the Seguia bent El Krass[43] (canal of the Princess Krass), thought to have been an irrigation canal (see map 10). The feature is aligned east–west and passes just south of the Ziban Oasis.[44] Stéphane Gsell, doyen of Roman North African scholars and author of the *Atlas Archéologique de l'Algérie* (1911), was the first to recognise the Seguia as Roman, calling it a *fosse frontière* (ditchwork frontier). Between the wars two forts were identified by aerial photography, lying behind it. In the 1930s Julien Guey of the French School in Rome excavated these, identified others and cut the first section across the linear feature, confirming it to be a ditch of Roman origin and finding it far bigger than appeared on the surface. His conclusion was that this is indeed the *fossatum* referred to in the Theodosian Code.[45] But the publication of Guey's results was something of a let-down. Where the Code appeared to refer to the African Diocese generally, the Seguia bent El Krass, 38 miles long, seemed to be protecting only an oasis. A little further north, where the whole grain of the land tilted toward 'vital Africa', large tracts of mountain and valley were apparently undefended. So the *fossatum* – if this were it – was a considerable disappointment. We now know that this was it, but by no means all of it.

It is time to introduce a man in whom the heroic age of Roman frontier discovery finds its finale: Jean Baradez (1895–1969), *colonel-aviateur*. A student of agriculture, he abandoned his studies during 1914 to enlist in the Chasseurs Alpins. When a serious accident left him unfit for infantry service, he volunteered as an artillery spotter. This involved perilous ascents in tethered balloons. Though his dream of becoming a pilot was unrealised, the end of hostilities left him, as it had Crawford, an experienced observer.[46] After the war he signed on in the regular air force, winning wings, the eventual rank of colonel, and specialising in photo interpretation. In the early months of the Second World War he achieved distinction through his sorties over the Siegfried Line, which he photographed in detail. Peace found him in Algiers, an out-of-work ex-airman, already in his fifties. The Algerian government employed him to advise on a feasibility study for a proposed dam in southeastern Algeria on the Oued Kantara, between El Kantara and Biskra; his job to interpret the results of an aerial survey already made. In examining the photographs Baradez found that the surveyors had exceeded their brief, taking the photocoverage well beyond the relevant catchment. It was there, across the bottom left-hand corner of the westernmost photo, that Baradez noticed the line which was to give direction to the remainder of his life. In the next three, crowded years he would explore extensively, discover abundantly, and attend the first Congress of Roman Frontier Studies, organised by Eric Birley at Newcastle in 1949. He passed through Paris to pick up copies of his book, hot from the press: *Fossatum Africae*,[47] an account of aerial and ground investigations in the Algerian south over vast zones. The congress was thrilled; Baradez lionised by a circle of scholars flattered by the spectacle of a man-of-action striding onto their neglected stage, ripping the dustsheets from a forgotten frontier and thrusting it into world attention.

However, discovery had excited him and his book was rushed. It offered glimpses which were startling but incomplete. His investigations would continue; but though life's lottery awarded him twenty more years, French Algeria would die first. This left rather less than half that time before the most savage of post-colonial conflicts put an end to gentle pursuits. Baradez introduces the discovery in his own words:

> Aerial photos in connection with a dam project revealed to me the existence of an important linear construction, continuous except where streams had effaced its course. The play of light and shade suggested the work was not of uniform build. At times it appeared as a scarcely visible groove; at others a groove edged by a low ridge on one or both of its sides, visible only in slanting light. However it showed more clearly in rocky and mountainous stretches, where it seemed to resemble a wall or raised line. The furrow rose and fell, clinging to the relief, its changes of direction seemingly dictated by the land forms. Punctuating its course, on either side or even on the line itself, small features[48] occurred at irregular intervals [...]
>
> The existence of this remarkable work was absolutely unsuspected in the area: missed by archaeologists, map-makers, local government officials, shepherds and nomads alike. Not a single one of its elements had been noted to date [...]
>
> I pored over the photos, millimetre by millimetre, without once having seen the region myself. Despite its location, a good one hundred kilometres north of the sole element of the *fosse frontière* already identified, only two interpretations were feasible. The pictures were unmistakable. We were either in the presence of a long and continuous *vallum* or of an unknown *clausura*.[49] Without doubt we had found a new stretch of the *fossatum Africae*.[50]

This was in Algiers, late in 1946. Baradez sought the help of Louis Leschi, now head of the Department of Antiquities, whose support was immediately promised. However, aerial reconnaissance would be crucial and cooperation of the general commanding the air forces of French Algeria must be sought. Baradez cooled his heels in Algiers and took a crash course in ancient history. It was during this time that he came upon an unpublished report, dated 1902, by one Lt. Soulé, in charge of a small post at the desert-edge settlement of Barika. This village lies in a dismal plain between the Djebel Mekrizan (the range of hills in which Baradez spotted the line across the survey photo) and a large bitter lake, the Chott el Hodna. In his report the young officer described finding a long ridge, extending southwards for 17 miles toward the Djebel. It was known locally as the Pharaoh's Dyke (see map 10). He had proposed it as yet another irrigational work, but a later discovery of milestones caused Gsell to record it in his *Atlas* as a Roman road. Both were wrong. As Baradez would soon find, the Pharaoh's Dyke was part of the *fossatum* and the milestones belonged to the military way running close behind it. It was already clear to Baradez, waiting in Algiers, that what he had spotted was the southern part of the feature reported by Soulé; though his was the longer part, the mountain part, the more impressive and interesting part; and the part which had dropped from the record of collective memory and folklore. It will not be difficult to see why.

In January 1947 Baradez made a brief ground visit with a local guide. Inexperienced in stony wilderness, he was taken aback by the difference between the aerial overview and the myopic vision vouchsafed the person on foot: 'In many places I was able to find the line only with the aerial photo in my hand and after measuring the distance between it and prominent features on the ground. In the midday glare all relief was ironed out and I often crossed and recrossed the obstacle without noticing it.'[51] Such is often the impression of the visitor today. However, parts of the line are better defined; and Baradez quickly learned to trace it by reference to the watchtower ruins: rubble heaps, crowning almost every knoll to the front and rear of the barrier itself. He describes first impressions:

The *fossatum*'s aspect changes considerably, depending on the ground it crosses and the degree of erosion to which it has been subjected. Where possible, however, it follows the counterslope.[52] Crossing the hills it was described by my Arab companion, on seeing it for the first time, as 'like the wake of a ship as it crosses the waves'. This metaphor was applied to a stretch of ditch silted almost to the brim, with a line of debris along both its edges, the whole having a shallow and weathered profile. In so far as I could judge its width was inconstant, ranging from twelve to thirty feet in varying terrain. However at one spot (south of Barika) the modern road crosses the *fossatum*, cutting a perfect cross-section. Including the mounds on either side, this measured 37 yards. Generally ditch spoil had been dumped on the side opposed to the enemy, though sometimes it was on both sides. In places the ditch was bordered to right or left (and occasionally on both sides) by the remains of a wide, drystone wall of 4–9-foot thickness. Where best preserved this stands to a height of three feet. Its construction was sometimes of natural rocks and sometimes of stream-bed stones. In places the lower level consists of huge unhewn blocks. On rocky ground there is sometimes no ditch at all, only traces of a wall, climbing, dipping and twisting. Watchtower remains are all around. Wherever there is a change either in the line's direction or its slope a watchtower may be found: either square or rectangular, with foundations between 9 × 9 and 12 × 18 feet. No single point on the line is outside their field of view. They lay on either side of the ditch and even astride it. Some are ranged far out to deepen the surveillance. Their frequency varied according to terrain and visibility. Without going into detail, I was looking at an obstacle of extreme suppleness, using very varied construction techniques, perfectly adapted to the changing landscape and the materials to hand.[53]

The word 'suppleness' immediately separates this work from Hadrian's Wall, whose design is rigid and whose role is less adaptation to the landscape than domination of it.

A wider grasp now awaited aerial investigation. In the next year the general came up trumps, enabling Baradez to add 65 stirring miles to the African frontier. The stretches discovered by him and by Lt. Soulé proved indeed to be two ends of the same piece of string. The *fossatum* crossed the rugged Mekrizan Range (3,200 feet), immediately west of the Aurès, running south–north, at right angles to the Seguia bent El Krass. This central sector, and the Seguia, or Saharan sector, are separated by a 30-mile gap. The change of axis is easy to explain: rounding the Aurès, the mountain front changes direction and with it the desert's edge. The gap is less easy. Despite five sorties no junction between the two stretches could be traced. It was the first setback to the hope of finding a fully coherent African frontier.

At the northern end of the central sector, another setback awaited. Some five miles south of Barika the *fossatum* 'exited from my photographic record' and repeated attempts to find it failed.[54] This time the line had petered out in the middle of a plain, for no apparent reason and with no natural feature to take over from it. Further north still Baradez now discovered a third *fossatum* stretch, again previously unknown, which may be called the northern sector. This was in the Hodna Mountains, part of the Saharan Atlas or pre-desert range, which crosses most of the Maghreb. The stretch was nearly fifty miles long, looping part of the range and almost encircling it. However it is not certain which way the defences faced: outwards, to bar desert from mountain; or inwards, to keep the mountaineers from raiding the plain. The discontinuity between the central and northern sectors was similar in length to that between the central and Saharan sectors.

Finally, having scrounged a day-trip in a Marauder bomber from Algiers to Gabès, Baradez claimed to have spotted a fourth *fossatum* stretch, athwart the Algerian–Tunisian border. This was similar in length to the other three, but with an even greater gap between it and the Saharan sector. His supporters could thus claim 250 miles of frontier revealed. But there were more gaps than works; though 'gaps' need not mean undefended spaces. Rather, as in Syria, these could be guarded roads; 'open' as distinct from 'closed' frontier sectors. Remembering Honorius' letter to the Vicar of Africa, with its threefold use of the phrase '*limes* and *fossatum*', might this have referred to their alternating character: *fossatum* where there was a barrier, *limes* where there was not?

Nonetheless *Fossatum Africae* devotes only five of its 400 pages to these two, last-discovered sectors. There is merely a brief description of their sitings, with no detail, no ground inspection, no analysis and no photographs. Nor is Baradez convincing about the discontinuities. His Chapter 9, on the gaps between the known elements of the *fossatum*, lacks an explanatory thesis. *Fossatum Africae* concentrates almost entirely on the central sector, especially its mountainous southern half whose discovery first inspired Baradez to devote his life to the African frontier. Here the results are impressive: fruits of many flights in a tiny Piper Cub, with untiring follow-up in an old Ford saloon; single-handed sallies with the spade; 275 published

photographs, mainly his own: a Herculean, solo effort. It was the
aerial pictures which thrilled contemporaries most. All are black and
white, the terrain resembling the hide of an aged elephant. Across
wrinkled ridges and the veined flanks of hills strides the clean, commanding line of Rome. It marches at a slant to the land, crossing
watersheds rather than running along them. It is this opposition
between work and setting which creates the rhythmic rise and fall,
reminding Baradez' guide of a ship butting into a cross-sea. The
photographic emulsion exudes information: roads; forts of different
periods; stretches where the *fossatum* forks into two strands; the
additions and modifications of three centuries, jumbled, superim-
posed and in sore need of the archaeological investigation for which
Baradez had neither time nor resources. He was, nevertheless, an
incomparable scrutineer. He examined photographs a square milli-
metre at a time, maintaining that an hour in flight meant a month
at the desk. Scholars were dazzled by the rush of data. The negative
factor – that the findings were raising more problems than they solved
– sunk in more slowly.

There was, moreover, a further discovery to fire frontier fanciers.
In 1947 Leschi offered Baradez the chance to excavate a fort on the
Saharan sector. This proved opportune, for he had so far found
no conclusive dating and the excavation, though doubtless more
enthusiastic than scientific, was to be blessed by luck. The fort was
Gemellae ('the twins'), a hundred miles south of Lambaesis and
central to the Seguia bent El Krass. It stands near the village of
Ourlala, which is part of the Ziban oasis; on the south bank of the
Oued Djedi. Like Thamusida it had been almost swamped by its
own *vicus*, which has traces of an outer wall over a mile long. The
sandy, sherd-strewn surface, littered with fineware fragments, suggests this was not the austere outpost it now seems. To the north is
the oasis (fed from the Aurès, 35 miles distant), a long, green slash
across the universal yellow. The Sahara begins at the fort's southern
rampart. Gemellae had in fact been dug, hastily and with little result,
in the late nineteenth century. Clearing the engulfed *principia* Baradez discovered a dedication to Hadrian by the IIIrd Legion, datable
to 132. Also a statue of the same emperor placed by the 3rd Cohort
of Chalcideans (from Syria) in 126. He then uncovered parts of the
fort wall, including an interval tower.[55] This proved almost identical
to a tower he had examined in a walled stretch of the central sector
and closely resembled the turrets on Hadrian's Wall. Baradez'

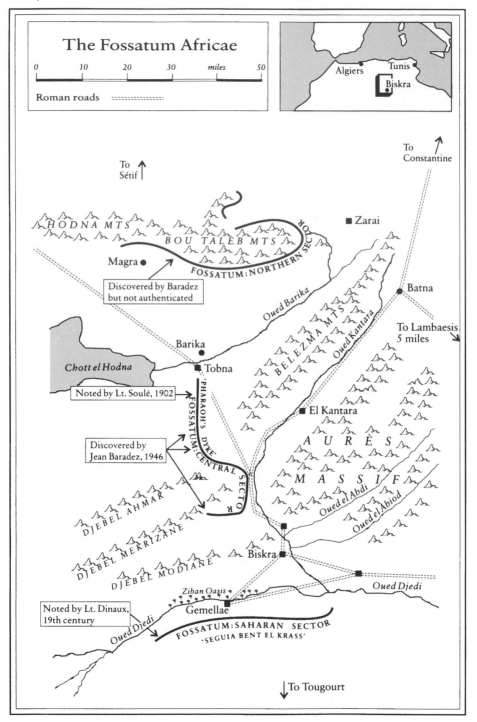

The Fossatum Africae

| 0 | 10 | 20 | 30 | *miles* | 50 |

Roman roads   ----------------

Algiers   Tunis

Biskra

To Sétif

To Constantine

HODNA MTS

BOU TALEB MTS

■ Zarai

FOSSATUM: NORTHERN SECTOR

Magra ●

Discovered by Baradez but not authenticated

Oued Barika

Batna ●

BELEZMA MTS

Oued Kantara

To Lambaesis 5 miles

Barika ●

Chott el Hodna

■ Tobna

Noted by Lt. Soulé, 1902

'PHARAOH'S DYKE'

FOSSATUM: CENTRAL SECTOR

■ El Kantara

AURÈS

Discovered by Jean Baradez, 1946

DJEBEL AHMAR

MASSIF

Oued el Abdi

Oued el Abiod

DJEBEL MERRIZANE

DJEBEL MODIANE

Biskra ■

Oued Djedi

Ziban Oasis

Noted by Lt. Dinaux, 19th century

Gemellae

Oued Djedi

FOSSATUM: SAHARAN SECTOR

'SEGUIA BENT EL KRASS'

↓ To Tougourt

opinion, based on these findings, was that the *fossatum* is Hadrianic: a preliminary conclusion, but one which has never been overturned. It therefore seems feasible that Hadrian had trumped his predecessor yet again: that Trajan's road along the Saharan fringe, a sort of Stanegate, had been superseded and outshone by the *fossatum*, a sort of Hadrian's Wall.

It is pleasing to see a pattern and to recognise a spectacular intelligence at work: in this case Hadrian in Romania, Germany, Britain and now in Algeria. By the same token it would be dispiriting to learn that frontier evolution was patternless and contradictory; a muddle, reflecting that of the Principate itself.[56] Baradez' findings at Gemellae were welcomed by adherents of the positive school, then in the ascendant. But *did* Hadrian mastermind a coherent series of frontiers? It is difficult to credit a long-term pattern to an intelligence so inconstant and perverse. The *fossatum* shares little with Hadrian's Wall except a desire to upstage Trajan's memory. We will again recall the biographer's comment that Hadrian was at the same time generous and stingy. This has been exemplified by the British extravagance contrasted with the thrift of the German palisade, which used only timber in the midst of a forest. The *fossatum* falls decisively into the latter category: 'I will specify that within a mile I have found a wall, or comparable obstacle, built in five different ways, but each time with material found on the spot and used in the best manner.'[57]

, *A propos* of the Ouvrage de Sala we said that all Rome's frontier barriers were variants on a small number of constructional themes. Here Baradez is describing such variations in the *same* barrier as it crosses changing terrain. On rocky ground digging is difficult and stone easy to find. Solution – no ditch, single or double stone walls. On soft ground digging is easy and finding stone difficult. Solution – no wall, extra wide ditch with marginal mounds. On intermediate ground, suitable variants.[58] It seems likely that the plan was sketchy, with Hadrian expressing his wishes in general terms and the detail left to those on the spot. Nowhere does construction approach legionary standards. There is no sign of prestige requirement or striving for effect. The *fossatum* was a cut-price project, a rule-of-thumb job and, given the manpower situation, doubtless a slow one.

At the sixth Roman Frontier Congress, held at Bonn in 1964, two years after the end of the Algerian War, a depressed Baradez, his efforts stymied, summed up his work in a paper entitled 'Unpublished Additions to "*Fossatum Africae*" ': 'Though I had long cherished the hope of publishing a second volume of *Fossatum Africae*, I was no longer able to pursue my investigations in the field nor to make the necessary excavations. Not knowing what the future may hold, I have decided to present key facts, not yet published [. . .]'[59] These consisted of precise detail concerning on-the-ground observations until hostilities forced abandonment of his quest. He described wall structures of rude blocks, even two-ton boulders, wedged and propped with splinters of dry stone. Regarding height, though presently standing nowhere to more than four feet, the amount of debris pointed to a minimum of 6–7½ feet. In addition the residual presence of clay fragments suggested that the stonework had been crowned by courses of mud brick.[60]

Even more interesting are his findings on the Saharan sector, to which he returned in the early 1950s. Here he discovered a method of sand deflection, by which low walls, placed to windward, created an artificial dune. This increased the ditch's value as an obstacle while preventing the sand from filling it:

> Near Gemellae, where violent winds and powdery sand erase the least relief and fill the smallest hollows, the *fossatum*'s visible trace is reduced to a double undulation, with mounds never higher than five feet and ditch a faint groove, two to twelve inches deep.
>
> But when a trench is cut one is in for a surprise. The thickness of sand is not great. It covers an underlying layer of chalk. It was into this rock, compacted but relatively soft, that the ditch was dug, often showing the marks of the tools with which it was cut. The southern or barbarian side is almost vertical, the northern side more gradual. The width is some 12½ feet across the top and over 4 at the bottom; the depth 8 foot 4 inches to 10 feet. Thus each linear yard dug supplied 8 cube yards of calcarious blocks. These were laid out as four low walls, parallel to each other and the ditch, and 3 or 4 yards from it. Their purpose was to deflect blown sand to form an artificial dune, perhaps 12 feet high, on the ditch's Roman side.[61]

On this sector there were three tower types. The first, a simple signal tower, was either in front of or some distance behind the *fossatum*. The second was a similar tower just behind the barrier. Both were common to the central sector also. The third, found on the Saharan sector only, was a gateway in the form of a double tower, always behind an undug causeway in the ditch and a gap in the artificial dune. Within was a passage which could be sealed by doors and on either side a guardroom. This passage was only six feet wide, suggesting the painstaking inspection of would-be entrants to the Roman province. (Tacitus[62] specified the conditions for Germans crossing the Rhine as unarmed, under guard, on payment of dues and in daylight; and similar restrictions may have applied here.) These double towers alternated with single at half-mile intervals, not unlike the third-of-a mile turret spacing on Hadrian's Wall; while their function is reminiscent of the milecastles, also gated. Hadrianic coins were found in some towers excavated. The Saharan sector was the more systematically built. The dating of Hadrian's statue at Gemellae to 126 could suggest it was the first constructed[63] and that techniques became increasingly haphazard as time passed.

Baradez' pupillage at the Institut National Agronomique was not wasted. That part of *Fossatum Africae* devoted to land use is a valuable contribution to our understanding of frontier support. Perhaps it is the best part of the book, helping us towards an interpretation of the *fossatum* which he himself was unable to reach.

Like others Baradez first felt constrained to enquire of North Africa's barometric record, in order to understand how Rome succeeded in farming the Saharan fringes, so far beyond the cultivated margins of our own day.

Why should once prosperous regions now be empty? So striking is the contrast that we assume profound climatic change. Yet here we must recall the Romans' own complaints about water supply. We have Sallust's verdict of 'a country rich in corn and cattle, poor in trees and rainfall'. We remember Hadrian's arrival, coinciding with the first rain for five years. We have St Augustine's rebuke to his diocesans, reminding them how lucky they were because 'the south is thirsty while the coast gets the rain'.[64]

He consulted Gsell, whose *Histoire ancienne de l'Afrique du Nord*[65] devotes fifty pages to this question, concluding that 'North Africa enjoyed a climate if not exactly the same then very similar to that of our own time, with summer drought normal, year-long drought common and rainfall erratic though at times torrential.'[66] Modern views of Roman rainfall agree in essentials with Gsell, sometimes for obvious reasons. For example the depth of ancient wells tells us that water tables were similar to today's. Another clue lies in Roman roads around the chotts, which have neither been inundated nor left high and dry, but follow the same edges still.

Baradez' survey of the central sector revealed 'astonishing areas of cultivation and colonisation, whose total appears to be in the region of 400,000 acres'.[67] He identified irrigation terraces and compartmented fields separated by grids of earthen mounds to aid water retention. Though seldom visible on the ground, he describes how his aged Ford would leave alternating deep and shallow tyre marks as it passed over the damper fields and drier dykes. There were many olive presses, mills and quernstones. On the hills, particularly beneath crests and ridges, he observed parallel 'walls' crossing the upper slopes, often less than thirty yards apart. These proved to be stones laid in lines about three feet wide. Baradez calls them 'protection cordons',[68] though they may better be described as drainage impeders, to check erosion and delay run-off, so that rainwater would be released to the streams more gradually. Altogether there were hundreds of miles of these ridges, striping the upper slopes of catchment areas. The modern answer would lie in tree planting. But forests are the outlaw's friend and there would have been no enthusiasm for them in Roman military zones.

At mid-level, between catchment and field, were abundant hydraulic works: feeder channels, dams, sluices, tunnels, wells and reservoirs; all with Middle Eastern pedigree, betraying the presence of Syrians, the largest overseas influence in the army of Africa. The pattern was of systematic techniques followed over long distances. This was not individual homesteading, American-style. It was subsidised farming in pursuance of official policy, depending on capital works built by the military or with their assistance. Only then would the land be turned over to civilians and veterans.

The Saharan sector was supplied by an oasis, the central sector depended on human ingenuity. Had Rome wished to base her frontier on oases these could have taken her deep into the Sahara. The result however would have been a scattering of outposts, like those of the French Foreign Legion. Her preference (at this time especially) was linear, with garrisons in touch by road and signal tower. She would use an oasis when suitably placed, but where there was none she would ask heroic efforts of her frontiersmen, encouraging them to create an agriculture from scant beginnings. *Fossatum Africae* helps to understand how this was done, in areas unploughed before or since. The answer lay in 'floodwater management', a modern term for a prehistoric principle. 'Floodwater' expresses the nature of desert rainfall, which runs uselessly away because the rock and gravel on which it falls are non-absorbent, 'management' being the regime for catching, storing and applying it. In principle a small field is established at the foot of a large slope. Suppose rain, falling on the field, provides only a quarter of requirement, then a catchment slope three times bigger than the plot will, in theory, augment the supply to the correct level. In practice evaporation and seepage mean an even larger catchment ratio. In this way, given suitable hills and a large investment in transmission and storage works, farming may be extended far beyond its normal limits. Baradez described the pre-Saharan massifs as 'water castles'.[69] A humbler parallel lies in roof and rosebed. With the aid of guttering, downpipe and waterbutt, the gardener can give June's flowers April's rain.

Following the 1949 conference Baradez invited Eric Birley to visit the Algerian south. Both may have hoped that parallels with the British Wall would support a unified view of Hadrian's policies. But Birley was quick to spot differences. The *fossatum* was a less formidable obstacle. The sparseness of its forts suggested it was too lightly manned to be considered a strictly military work.[70] This was the first hint that the road to understanding the *fossatum* might point in other directions. Two ideas then emerged to interpret the African frontier. The first was expressed by British scholars as 'the frontier of the sown' and by French colleagues as 'the separation of useful from useless Africa'. Though these are serviceable generalisations the *fossatum*, whose locations are far beyond the normal arable limit, fails to satisfy them. The second idea is the 'isohyet frontier': an attractive thesis because it is linear. It occurred to French savants that from Tripolitania to Numidia the Roman frontier coincided almost exactly with the 4-inch rainfall line. But further west the theory is dented by the frontier of Mauretania Caesariensis, its more northerly course coinciding with the 16-inch line. There the limiting factor was not rainfall but military strength. As Baradez insisted, rain cannot tell us everything.

A subsequent generation has sought to interpret the *fossatum* in terms of people rather than territory, for waterless land has no intrinsic worth. Could the *fossatum*'s design have been based on nomadism? It would be a new departure to find a frontier conditioned by the needs of outside tribes rather than the convenience of Rome. In transitional zones between farmland and desert the nomad problem is fundamental. Judaeo-Christian tradition almost begins with it: 'And Abel was a keeper of sheep but Cain was a tiller of the soil. . . And it came to pass when they were in the field that Cain rose up against his brother and slew him.'[71] On Rome's African frontier we must assume that the nomads were the enemy, because there was no other. Did the *fossatum* exclude them or accept them? Along the north Saharan fringe the supportive power of grass is said to drop between ten and twentyfold during early summer. To debar the nomads would be tantamount to their extinction. The summer end of their range lay within Roman territory. To be locked outside for a single hot season would destroy their livestock by a factor of ten or twenty to one. Exclusion would lead to desperate and interminable raids. We may therefore be almost certain that the object of the *fossatum* was not to prevent nomad entry. Roman frontiers existed to solve external problems, not to create or perpetuate them.

Hadrian's answer was to accept the inevitability of nomadism and to design a frontier which accommodated it. This, it has been said, meant that each summer farmer and shepherd would be in conflict.[72] Yet the clash, put so bluntly in Genesis, suggests its own solution. Cain and Abel are together 'in the field'. Why should practitioners of conflicting husbandries be so? Because at harvest time the farmer needs extra hands. Nevertheless tempers flared, with dire results. Hence the need for a referee. As an Israeli scholar writes:

> Comparison with other regions as well as present-day Israel prove that wherever transhumance is not under strict control, major damage is caused to crops [. . .] The arrangement is practical only when the farming population has the backing of sufficient forces of law enforcement[. . .] Since the tillers of the earth were easy prey to the agile, warlike nomad they were able to maintain themselves only against payments of regular protection money, *khuweh* in Arabic. The exaction of the *khuweh*, in addition to other forms of harassment resulted, if not checked, in complete impoverishment, causing abandonment of settlements or even the nomadisation of the farmers.[73]

In North Africa nomads help farmers to this day, trading meat for grain and pasturing their herds in the stubble fields, manuring them for the coming season. Now as then, the withering of grass in the region of the chotts precedes by a few weeks the wheat harvest on the plateaux; and olive gathering in the north is followed by the regreening of the south.[74] It is also likely that the nomads were the army's stockbreeders and meat suppliers. In short we may suppose that Hadrian replaced the pastoral-arable mismatch by a policy of supervised symbiosis. The Cain-and-Abel conflict was not beyond Rome's power to resolve, given the army's presence as peacekeeper.

It would be unfair to say that Baradez ignored the nomad factor, but he was unable to relate it to the *fossatum*'s design. He was a military man and heir to thinking which saw the frontier in adversarial terms, with the army 'rolling back the arid zone toward the limits of the possible and driving southwards both the desert and the habitual nomads who haunted it'.[75]

It was difficult for his generation to accept that the Sahara's edge is incompatible with strict definition and control; to see the *fossatum* as an easement, an accommodation by which peaceful nomadism could continue to function. We must however add that our knowledge of ancient nomadism is hazy. We have only the inferences of the Roman works and the uncertain parallel of migrational patterns in recent times. Some of these still pass between or over the *fossatum*'s sectors. All concur in common beginnings on the desert's edge and common endings in what were anciently zones of dry farming.[76] The *fossatum* lies toward the Saharan end of these ranges, so that if it were deflecting or filtering incoming migrational movements, this would be early in their courses. Guarding it were some eight Hadrianic forts, with dispositions becoming denser as time passed. An overview suggests two lines of forts: the first behind the *fossatum* and the second well back, at the beginning of cereal farming; in other words close to both ends of the migratory range. This second line is no surprise. Assuming nomad entries for half the year and wanderings of more than a hundred miles inside the province, it is unlikely the army would leave them unsupervised.

One second-line fort was Zarai, behind the gap between the *fossatum*'s central and northern sectors. Here, in 1858, was discovered a revealing frontier document: an inscription listing customs duties on some thirty items.[77] These included animals, clothing, skins, leather, glue, sponges, wine, dates, figs, nuts, resin, pitch, alum, iron ware and *garum* (fish sauce). The fort is Hadrianic, though the list dates to some 75 years later. A similar tariff was found at Lambaesis, though with only ten items legible. A third is known for Palmyra.

The empire was divided into at least five *portaria* (customs zones) with charges varying between 25% of value in Egypt, 12½% on the Danube and probably 2½% in Africa.[78] Duties may have been adjusted to restrain the outflow of gold, more serious in some provinces than others. Customs officers were normally civilians, though sometimes stationed at military posts. On the rivers collection seems to have been at bridges or ferry crossings; but on less precise frontiers, customs posts could be at rearward forts, road junctions or in convenient towns.[79]

The nomads still pass close to Zarai and Lambaesis; and we may guess their panniers still bear southern produce northwards in summer and northern produce southwards in winter. The commodities listed at Zarai divide along such lines, some being products of the south while others are of northern or coastal origin. It seems likely that Rome levied duty on all nomadic journeys which crossed her frontiers. Not unreasonably, for she offered entry and protection, paying several thousand soldiers to keep the peace throughout the zone between summer and winter grazing. While Zarai and Lambaesis appear to have been customs stations between *fossatum* stretches, the gateways in the Saharan sector suggest that payment was also levied for passage through the barrier. We do not know whether rates were adjusted to encourage migration through the gaps, or indeed the gaps' purpose.

What *was* the point of a discontinuous barrier? The likelihood seems to be that the *fossata* were nomad deflectors and migration guidelines, shielding the land designated for military settlement; influencing the nomads to use preselected corridors and reducing the danger of migrants merging into overlarge groups. None of this is easy to prove. It supposes, for example, that fields will lie within the shelter of continuous *fossatum* stretches, which they do not. Indeed some are on the 'unsafe' side of the obstacle. On the other hand the *fossatum* had a three-century history. We do not know the extent to which later developments contradict original intentions. We are not even sure that all sectors were contemporaneous. The information was largely gathered by one man over a few years and we are painfully close to the limit of what may be wrung from it. We may nevertheless venture a suggestion. Because migration moves both ways, according to season, might the *fossatum* too be seasonal and reversible? Did it face alternating directions: south and west in May, north and east in November? Agricultural works lie on both sides of the line; so do watchtowers. The barrier itself is often blind toward the Sahara. In some places the ditch has a wall on either rim. In others the line forks and duplicates. Were these double alignments guarding from both directions? The Saharan sector's orthodox progression of ditch, mound and towers suggests a desert-facing work. And yet this entire stretch is on the wrong side of the Oued Djedi, which runs parallel, five or six miles to the north. This major stream is a significant obstacle, wasted if control were only toward the south. More generally, it makes scant sense that the army of Africa should spend the long months of summer staring into a desert which the nomad had vacated.

Like Baradez we have concentrated on the central and Saharan sectors. Of the northern and the Algerian–Tunisian border stretches, less need be said. The latter's supposed sighting, from the window of a bomber, was an error. Between 1972 and 1974 the Institut d'Archéologie Mediterranéenne made a survey verifying what was long suspected. Baradez had seen part of Trajan's frontier road. Readers may wonder why such a gaffe was taken seriously by an entire generation of scholars and why, in a part of Tunisia by no means inaccessible, it should have required 25 years to rectify. The northern sector has not been debunked but neither, after 45 years, has it been verified. Should authentication follow it will be found to have been well placed to watch a main migration route via Zarai.

Baradez' work ended sadly, overtaken by the bitterness of the Franco–Algerian War. He was the last of a line of soldier-scholars whose view of the frontier was soon to be outmoded by more holistic thinking. He admired the Roman spirit, even equating it with that of imperial France. He describes the *fossatum* and its supporting work as 'This magnificently coherent ensemble ... as unified, thoughtful and ordered as it is possible to be ... Everywhere, behind the variations of local practice, one senses guidance, reason and wisdom.'[80] When faced with deficiencies in the Roman scheme he theorised upwards, believing that as future researchers swabbed the grime from this ancient canvas the grandeur and good sense of Rome's vision would show through. He even hoped his discoveries would help revive the pioneering ethic, quickening the development of the Algerian south:

In the agricultural, economic and social senses, our work could lead to new and enlarged conditions. My greatest reward would

be that something of the spirit which made human existence possible in places now desolate could be restored by human example.
In that event aerial archaeology would indeed have served the
civilising mission of France.[81]

Destiny, bolting the door on Romano-Algerian studies for a quarter
century and more, decided differently. Baradez' book would not run
to a second edition. It would never be translated. Nor would his
name even appear in *Larousse* or the Lafitte *Qui est qui en France*.
Was this a measure of French disenchantment, the too-lateness of
Baradez' imperialist sentiments, the out-of-dateness of his faith in
Rome, or all combined? The gauntlet he threw down in 1949 was
not picked up. In Britain and Germany excitement dwindled in the
absence of a theory which could account for the gaps between the
fossatum sectors. Though his reputation is still respected it has never
been convincingly tested either by spade or pen. Though the Eighth
Congress of Roman Frontier Studies (held at Cardiff in 1969) was
dedicated to his memory, no contribution relating to Africa appeared
in its proceedings. Even now Algerian researches lag far behind those
of other North African countries. Baradez remains a giant diminished
by faint response.

The *fossatum* itself is little known and seldom visited. We have
not questioned anyone in its neighbourhood without meeting blank
stares and shrugs of incomprehension. Aptly those who built it are
also in the ranks of the forgotten; without mention in a single text or
coin issue. Yet the *fossatum* is a rousing monument and a remarkable
achievement. Though crude compared with Hadrian's Wall it was
far more receptive to local conditions and needs. It was made and
manned under severe constraints of climate, distance, manpower and
budget. It was almost the only Roman frontier designed for controlled admission rather than controlled exclusion. In the realm of
husbandry it was a small victory over a big desert and its support
works are a landmark in conservation. Nevertheless, despite his legacy, there are still no Hadrian laundrettes or Hadrian hairdressing
salons in Algeria.

Baradez was amazed by the remnants of mills and oileries, the
vestiges of water storage and delivery systems, so far beyond the
cultivated land of his own day. Half a century later, facing population
increase and a drift to the coast, Algiers spends substantial oil income
to counteract the emptying of the south: drilling for water, implanting

villages, creating farms where none existed for fifteen centuries. Psychologically, too, the desert has become less remote. On the Tunisian side, the sparkling saltflats of the chotts, once watched by Roman towers, are now overlooked by the balconies of five-star hotels, to which French presidents and film stars fly in for winter breaks. The regions crossed by the *fossatum* are not yet tourist magnets, but man has been busier than Baradez could have dreamed. With every passing year, Rome's print grows fainter. Nothing has been done to relocate, photograph or consolidate Baradez' discoveries; and were this undertaken it would be found that some have been disfigured, even lost. Nor is there promise of protection. North Africans lack interest in a past not their own, except for major sites where the tourist nexus is clear.

Hadrian now left Africa for ever. In the afternoon of his reign, those influences which had soothed him – like walking, talking to the soldiers, and long absences from Rome – weakened, while moodiness and mistrust deepened. He had fought a long and fruitless duel with a dead man and was losing. He was dependent on an army to which Trajan was a legend. Isolation was growing. Despite all his gifts he lacked that of being liked. So Trajan leaves our story as the friendly warmaker, Hadrian as the friendless peacemaker.

The question of the succession now pressed. Hadrian naturally wished it to pass to someone who would continue his policies. His eye lighted on a youthful kinsman, Marcus Aurelius. However his health began to falter while Marcus was still too young. A stopgap was found in Lucius Verus, who promptly sickened and died. A second stopgap was needed and Antoninus became a candidate. His age and circumstances – already fifty and with no son – made him a sound interim choice. Renowned for goodness[82] and gentleness, Antoninus was the man least likely to revert to military adventurism. Lying on a couch in the palace, Hadrian recommended him to a group of senators. According to Dio he died a few days later, after a twenty-year reign, 'hated by the people'.[83] His surviving poem, '*Animula vagula blandula*', said to have been composed on his deathbed, is a small jewel of pathos:

> Where now, happy moth of a soul,
> So many years my body's guest?
> What cheerless gaol is your next goal?
> What joyless place will darken your bright jest?[84]

He was an artist of noble expression; a soldier with a minute grasp of the soldier's burden; a diplomat who dared give back conquered lands; a prophet claiming that greatness is compatible with peace. In character he was chameleonlike, with aspects of the best and worst of the caesars curiously combined. The perverse brilliance and restless vision were his own.

In what did that vision lie? Though Hadrian's measures for the defence of the empire were positive and long-lived, their quality and meaning were variable. Britain and Germany saw him separating Romans from barbarians; the Middle Danube and Africa allowing them to meet and mingle. What then *was* his policy? Evidently it was peace, guaranteed by military readiness and regulated by frontiers; several of which he made more effective by developing the continuous, man-made barrier as a key element in their defensive scheme. But faced with frontiers of such varied intention one can only plead that a plainer answer is clouded by contrariness of character.

Hadrian's interest in the army did not extend to revolutionising fighting techniques; especially in the cavalry arm, where the real scope for improvement lay. It is hard to grasp that Rome did not have horseshoes, without which horses were lamed by stone roads; that she had not invented stirrups, without which the lancer is unhorsed by the shock of contact; that she did not know the saddle, without which a mounted archer cannot swivel and shoot.

On the contrary, Hadrian's contributions were to static defence and efficient regulation, factors which would limit initiative and inhibit imaginative warfare. Despite exceptional mental powers he resembled other early emperors in conservatism and assumptions of invincibility. By confirming the empire's Maginot Line tendencies he contributed to the two-hundred-year eclipse in military inventiveness which is the notable failure of this generally successful era. The 2nd century was the least innovative in tactics and weaponry the western world has known.

Turnabout in foreign policy was not matched by reappraisal of strategy. Danger still lay on the Danube, particularly the deep re-entrants of both sides of Dacia, one of which had been created by Hadrian's own ineptitude. A strong, defensive line, closing the gap between Lower Danube and Carpathians, was the best bequest he could have left his successors. But that was Trajan's country. Instead he chose to leave his mark on Britain, with a wall both lavish and grandiose in relation to the problems it faced; enhancing Rome's protection in a place remotest from her vital interests.

Yet Hadrian's feud with his predecessor was not without advantage to our theme. By making war on one man's memory and peace with others he became imperial Rome's first and perhaps only advocate of non-aggression: her great defender, bringer of territorial definition and builder of boundaries. Aptly it is for his Wall, restored to him by Haverfield, Collingwood, Simpson, Richmond and Birley, that the world remembers him best.

CHAPTER 7

Antoninus and Marcus:
The Test of War

Antoninus, nicknamed Pius, the good and dutiful, gentle aristocrat, fifty years of age at the time of accession, chosen as the one most certain to continue Hadrian's policy of non-aggression, now issued the most startling order in the history of the Roman frontier: that preparations be put in hand for the reinvasion of Scotland and that Hadrian's Wall be abandoned. It is possible that this decision was taken within weeks of Hadrian's death. During the first year of the reign archaeology alerts us to a wind of change blowing through the supply bases of South Shields and Corbridge. Victualling and hammering at Corbridge has a specific meaning, for this storehouse and workshop stood close to where Dere Street bridged the Tyne and crossed the Wall. From here the favoured invasion route arcs like an arrow over brown moor and bleak pass, before falling into the green valley of the Tweed. Hadrian's Wall was not only a *pièce de résistance* among frontiers. It presented a powerful commitment to going no further. With it the century-long search for a British stop-line had ended. Fifteen years' fine tuning had brought it to perfection. Now Antoninus was about to revoke the irrevocable; to undo his predecessor's work and shoulder the burden put down by Julius Agricola fifty-four years earlier. It makes scant sense that a man of peace should begin his imperial career with so pointless an act of war.

Pausanias' *Descriptions of Greece*, a guidebook written soon after the death of Antoninus, breaks its narrative to offer this aside concerning the late emperor: 'Antoninus was never wilfully warlike. In Britain he confiscated most of the territory of the Brigantes only because they instigated an unprovoked attack on the Genounian district, whose people are subject to Rome.'[1] Lights have burned late at British universities over this passage, which makes it seem that the Brigantians lived outside the frontier when their homeland was the Pennines, apart from a small overspill north of the Solway Firth. Genounia continues to confound enquiry. We could be looking for a Nounia, since the letter g is frequently elided before n. The Nov antes of Galloway seem the likeliest candidates, as may be demonstrated by a tendentious spelling: NOVaNtIA. Nevertheless, when all is said and done, there is little likelihood that Antoninus would give up Hadrian's Wall because of a tribal squabble.

Professor A. R. Birley considers that the *démarche* may have been motivated by domestic politics.[2] He conjectures an expansionist party, loyal to Trajan's memory, which had lain low during Hadrian's lifetime but was now making itself heard. Few can doubt the unpopularity of Hadrian's pacifism and the shame that surrender of the Parthian provinces had inflicted. Centuries of glory could not be expunged by two decades of appeasement.

Hadrian had chosen thoughtfully. In Antoninus he found a man 'of conspicuous thrift; a careful landowner; gentle, generous and never covetous of what belonged to others';[3] a true dove. What might his response now be to a flock of hawks? Perhaps to throw them a morsel; and what tastier than Hadrian's Wall, that symbol of passivity? In any case the neck of land between Forth and Clyde is half as wide as that between Tyne and Solway. An advance of eighty miles to a shorter frontier was a small price to soothe ruffled feathers and add sparkle to the reign's commencement. Like Claudius, Antoninus was a civilian looking for laurels. He would find them in the same romantic and newsworthy setting. But, assuming Hadrian's Wall to have been the expression of a policy distasteful to the war party, why build another? Certainly the wall of Antoninus would be muted, functional, and of humbler materials. There would be no extravagances, like 160 stone turrets placed for rhythmic effect; no bridging of rivers at three times the necessary strength; no grandiose flanking system down the west coast; no *Vallum* sweeping from sea to sea like a motorway without traffic.

The advance into southern Scotland and the construction of a new line between Firth of Forth and River Clyde were entrusted to the first Antonine governor of Britain, Q. Lollius Urbicus: a North African, born around AD 100 in the pretty hilltop town of Castellum Tidditanorum, near Citra (Constantine). He had served on Hadrian's staff in the Jewish rebellion, commanded a legion on the Danube and governed Lower Germany. In Scotland he would prove cautious, perhaps believing himself understrength, with three legions instead of Agricola's four. Seemingly these proved ample, since there is no archaeological evidence for battles or sieges. We know that Antoninus received a salutation and in 142, two years after the campaign, a coin was issued showing the goddess Victory advancing, her shield inscribed *Britain*. His was the first acquisition made by Rome in twenty-five years, though it fails to impress the *Augustan History*, which gives the new wall even less space than the old: 'Lollius Urbicus, his legate, subdued the Britons and built another wall, of turf, after driving away the barbarians.'[4] Urbicus now stood on the isthmus reached by Agricola in AD 80 and described by Tacitus as that 'of Clyde and Forth, where the deep, tidal estuaries of opposing seas are separated by a short space only'. We will also recall the next phrase: 'This was secured during the second summer by garrisons [...]'[5] The same strip, in effect a wide valley between Southern Uplands and Highlands, had been Agricola's pausing place when he awaited instructions between the first and second parts of his Scottish war. To what extent had he secured central Scotland? Might Urbicus simply revive Agricola's forts and join them with a wall? Surely two distinguished Roman generals would see the problem with the same eyes and put their forts in the same place. Or were they different problems? Shielding the flank of an ongoing advance is not equivalent to blocking off an isthmus.

Confirmation of Flavian-under-Antonine would inevitably be sought beneath the forts of the Antonine Wall, and many an early excavator claimed to have found it. But the evidence tended to evaporate under scrutiny. Then a survey flown during the dry summer of 1977 confirmed a further Flavian fort at Drumquhassle,[6] near the south-east corner of Loch Lomond. Reminiscent of the forts of the 'glen-blocking' series, placed hard up against the Highland foothills to prevent egress (the method by which Agricola had protected his lifeline toward Aberdeen, or by which his successor protected Agricola's gains), Drumquhassle suggests that the same technique had been applied to central Scotland. By contrast the Antonine Wall would be sited quite differently: some ten miles back, on the crown of the isthmus.

We may guess that the Antonine Wall's inception was moreover very different from Hadrian's. The earlier wall was located within the province and preplanned. The later was built in what had till then been enemy territory. A preliminary survey had not been made. Accordingly it should not surprise us if the preparatory work was hasty. Seemingly, six large forts were built first, as a protective measure, then the wall was brought up to them; finally others were added *ex tempore*, with differences of shape and wide variations in size. Construction took four seasons; twice the time it might have taken if better preparations had been made.

The Wall was of turf, a common medium in Britain, especially for works built under campaign conditions. The alternative (more normal on the Continent) was to build walls of earth, retained by stakes. However this involved the labour of chopping, sawing and transportation of timber. The 1971 experiment at the Lunt, near Coventry, showed that a fort's ramparts could be built in twelve days when the ground is damp and the turf easy to lift. According to Vegetius, regulation size was $1^{1}/_{2} \times 1 \times ^{1}/_{2}$ feet.[7] Most turf cut in Britain was in fact square, though the squeezing of centuries makes dimensions difficult to determine. A scene on Trajan's Column depicts a grassy bank on which a large patch has been subdivided by spade cuts into squares, like a tray-cake. In a second operation a soldier undercuts them with a mattock. Compared with stone and mortar a turf wall offers major savings in quarrying, shaping, transporting, lime burning, sand procurement, water requirement and so on. Turfwork may be equated with a modern army's use of sandbags. These are no more resistant to shot and shell than loose sand, but they offer ease of handling, compactness and the means for creating vertical profiles and sharp corners. Likewise turf gives no more protection than soil *per se*, but it allows steeper faces, perhaps to an angle of 75°. The matted roots provide coherence, reducing mudflow and soil's tendency to creep, while the grass layers also arrest slippage. Turf's story does not end with the Antonine Wall. Soldiers continued to be trained in its use. The purpose of numerous fieldworks, sometimes no larger than a small room, long puzzled scholars. It is now accepted that they were practice camps. Llandrindod Common (Powys), a favourite place for summer manoeuvres, boasts eighteen miniature turf structures, the largest group in the empire.

Assuming Scots sod to be more meagre than that envisaged by Vegetius, it has been estimated that 1½ square miles of it were

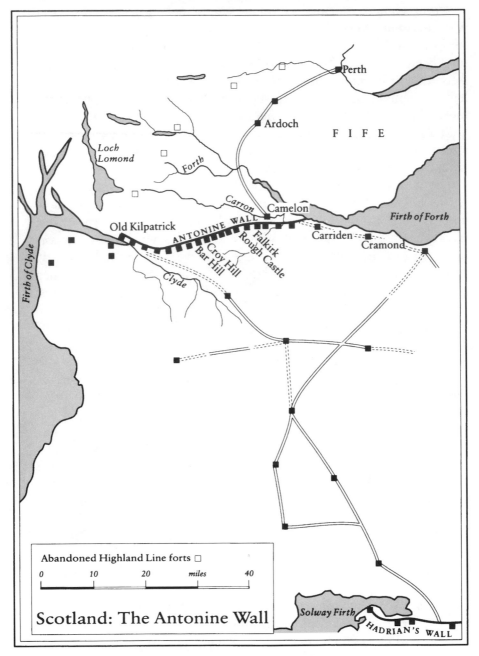

Scotland: The Antonine Wall

Abandoned Highland Line forts □

0   10   20   miles   40

required for the Antonine Wall, corresponding to a strip 63 yards wide across the isthmus. The Wall is believed to have been built westwards, from the south side of the Firth of Forth, eighteen miles above Edinburgh, to the north bank of the Clyde, five miles below Glasgow. For much of its 37-mile course (41 Roman miles, 60 km) it follows Carron and Kelvin, respective tributaries of Forth and Clyde, across north-facing slopes with fine views Highlandwards. Further west it passed round what are now the northern edges of Glasgow and Clydebank, joining the river near Old Kilpatrick, less than a mile below the Erskine Bridge. Its flanks were thus protected by broad, tidal estuaries at both ends. Construction differed from the turf sector of Hadrian's Wall in minor respects: it was narrower (14–16 compared with 18–20 feet) and had a cobblestone foundation to prevent slippage. The Antonine Wall was probably ten feet high, with a wooden breastwork giving a frontal elevation of fourteen feet. Along the top a six-foot-wide plank-walk is assumed. The remains survive to five or six feet just west of Rough Castle. Though many sections have been cut, twenty-two layers of turf are the most yet found. The more imposing feature may have been – and surely still is – the ditch, visible throughout much of its central course, even where the Wall's trace is slight. This varies greatly in dimensions and in distance from the Wall. At Watling Lodge, just west of Falkirk, is the most imposing stretch of frontier ditch in the empire: forty feet wide and twelve deep, but overzealously built, with a counterscarp so high that it is doubtful whether the Wall's sentries could have seen enemies close outside it.

From here the visitor may walk the 1½ miles westward along the Wall's best-preserved stretch. This includes Rough Castle,[8] microcosm of the monument,[9] where almost all its features are evident. Just in front of the fort is the ancient equivalent of a minefield: small pits, ranged in depth and originally concealed under vegetation. Caesar described similar traps as three feet deep, hiding stakes 'thigh-thick, with sharpened and fire hardened points'.[10] His soldiers called them 'lilies', after the stamens of that flower. Alas, this important site is shamed by a spectacular convergence of power pylons and high-tension cables. Other than this the Croy Hill–Bar Hill sector, three miles northwest of Cumbernauld, makes good walking, reminiscent of Hadrian's Wall. Behind ditch and Wall ran a service road joining forts and fortlets, of tamped gravel, seven feet wide. This may be traced at Seabeg's Wood, just west of Bonnybridge.

The six original forts were at normal frontier spacing of around seven miles. Twelve or more were added, probably soon after the Wall's completion, prompting the theory of an initial and a revised plan. As we have said, however, the exposed situation and irksome waiting time favoured premature fort construction, in the probable knowledge that more would be added. The additions are highly erratic, giving fort sizes from half an acre to six and a half acres. The so-called annexes – a peculiarity of Antonine Wall forts – consist of adjacent, walled enclosures, ranging from half as big to bigger than the forts themselves. They may have provided parking for wagons, space for workshops, or shelter for tented accommodation. There were also fortlets, not unlike the milecastles of Hadrian's Wall. Though these continue to be found there is as yet no certainty of a pattern, such as alternating fort and fortlet. Like the forts they may prove to have been thrown randomly into gaps. The outcome of so much gap-plugging is that there is seldom a space of more than two miles between installations. This may have rendered turrets or watchtowers superfluous, for none has been detected. Their absence is almost without precedent on imperial frontiers. It could suggest a reaction against Hadrian's towery wall, where hundreds of men had duplicated duty to fulfil a romantic fancy in a landscape often offering immense vistas even from ground level.

There are, however, unusual features known as 'expansions'. These consist of rearward bulges in the turf wall, about six yards square, occurring always in pairs, of which three are known. Traces of burnt material suggest they were beacon platforms. Perhaps one held a logpile (as on Trajan's Column) for night signals; the other leaves, grass, heather, etc., for smoke. Alternatively they could suggest two basic messages: a pair of fires meaning one thing, a single fire another. Their positions seem to favour north–south rather than lateral communication; and the intention may have been to transmit from the Wall or its outposts, eventually as far as York.

There were four outposts north of the Antonine Wall: all on Dere Street, Agricola's road from York, which crosses the southern wall near Corbridge and the northern near Falkirk, striking northwards to fade beyond Perth. These all made use of Agricolan forts. Occupation as far as Perth suggests a foot in the door of northeastern Scotland; but a more probable aim was to cordon Fife and make it a protectorate, so that the Wall's eastern flank would face a friendly shore. On the western side, only one fort and two fortlets guarded the Firth of Clyde, and there was no coastal system in Renfrew and Ayrshire comparable to the Cumbrian. Nevertheless southern Scotland was strongly held by forts along the two road axes from Corbridge and Carlisle.

The Wall was intensively manned. Though its forts were smaller than those of Hadrian's, there were more of them on a line of half the length. The concentration of defenders was therefore at least 1½ times greater, making this the most densely garrisoned of all Roman frontiers. One authority proposed that 'in Upper Germany there were some 47 men to the kilometre, on Hadrian's Wall 83 and on the Antonine Wall 300'[11] (though most would consider the latter figure high). The germ of these jitters was doubtless the fifty-year-old recollection of Mons Graupius. As dusk had fallen on that melancholy field, 20,000 men melted back into the hills. Despite the victory claimed by Tacitus, an enemy able to muster so memorable a host still held the dominant ground and the new frontier was under their noses. Given the number of men packed into the shortened line and those spread over the lengthened hinterland, it would be difficult to argue cost-effectiveness as the reason for discarding Hadrian's frontier.

The northern Wall was without pretensions. It had no message for army or people. All who knew the old Wall must have regarded the new as a cut-price version. Nonetheless, with its plenitude of forts and its siting on the downslope, the Antonine Wall was a serious obstacle, which made no attempt to hide its strength. Concealment is a recent military obsession. The ancient world had high regard for muscle and it was normal to display, indeed to exaggerate it. In the matter of decoration, however, the builders were allowed one indulgence. This took the form of ornamental stones marking the completion of various stretches by working parties from the three legions. Usually about four by two feet and originally painted, these appear to have been mounted on both front and rear faces of the Wall. Between the seventeenth century and 1969, eighteen or more have been ploughed up or stumbled upon, from a theoretical total of sixty: for the Wall is thought to have been built in fifteen sections, each with forward- and rearward-facing tablets at both ends. Of the distance slabs, as they are known, one (the best) is in the National Museum of Antiquities, Edinburgh, and fifteen are in the Hunterian Museum, Glasgow. Though of somewhat naïve execution, several are sophisticated in concept, sometimes framed in temple façades or triumphal arches. As well as the emperor's titles, legionary names and emblems, plus the distances built, content includes deities (especially *Victory*), religious ceremony, stylised combat or parade scenes, bearded and largely naked prisoners, scroll work, garlands and decorative framework. Two of the inscriptions mention Urbicus and two use the expression *opus valli*, which tells us that the army called the Wall '*vallum*'. (This was almost certainly the word used for Hadrian's Wall also, though no one knows what the Romans called the earthwork now known as the *Vallum*.) The slabs are a trove which may yet grow.

Two facts prompt us to ask whether the Scottish venture had been expected from the first to be short-lived. Turf was often considered temporary and there is no sign of its replacement in stone. Secondly, there was no attempt to advance the legionary bases. York was now some eleven days' march from the front and Chester two weeks'. To have moved them – for example to Newcastle and Carlisle – would have been the natural way to support the new frontier. But to do so would relax Rome's grip on the Pennines and Wales, a contradiction which demonstrates the weakness of Antonine strategy. On the other hand it is unlikely that any extension of empire would be taken lightly. We must accept that the army believed it was in Scotland to stay, at least for as long as the emperor lived.

We turn now to events in Germany, where Antoninus ordered major adjustments to the Rhine–Danube overland *limes*. These were in some respects comparable to the British advance. The difference was that they would be carried out without coin issue or other promotional device. We may therefore regard them as frontier rectification without political or propaganda motive. No doubt those in charge of the south German frontier had long been critical of its course, arising from the *ad hoc* measures of several reigns. Its object – to shorten and protect the inturned bend of the Rhine at Basle – was badly accomplished. The Upper Rhine and Danube form a right angle, to which the ideal complement would be a right-angled triangle of Roman territory, completed by a line between the two rivers of 45°. Temerity had made it otherwise. Clinging to the Taunus ridge, sheltering behind the Main and the Neckar, holding the crest of the Swabian Alb: these twists created a frontier twice as long as geometry required. However, prolonged peace along most of the front now favoured the prospect of correcting it; though the reappraisal could not be total since the Chattan nation, facing the Middle Rhine, was still untrustworthy. The northern part of the Upper German *limes* was therefore left unchanged; while the southern part, beyond the Main, plus the entire frontier of neighbouring Raetia, was advanced between ten and thirty-five miles to straighter alignments.

The Raetian forts moved first. Around AD 150 those in the province's west were brought down from the Alb ridge onto the Bavarian plateau. Further east the Upper Danube now ceased to be the frontier, since the new line ran across open country some thirty-five miles north of it, descending to the river fifteen miles above Regensburg, where it becomes wide and deep enough to offer good cover. The net gain for Raetia was a frontier reduction of some fifty miles, mainly at its western end. There the overlap of Raetian and Upper German forts was eliminated, the two provincial frontiers meeting cleanly near today's village of Lorch.[12] We may wonder why the two governors had not attempted remedy before. But it was surprisingly difficult for governors to confer. They were forbidden to meet for fear they might hatch a plot. There were also rivalries. Tacitus took it for granted that 'jealousy characterises the government of adjacent provinces'.[13] Only imperial intervention could settle questions such as this.

Nine years later matching moves were in hand in Upper Germany. This meant abandoning the Odenwald–Neckar position in favour of a revised siting ten miles (diverging to twenty-five miles) further east. From the Main, the new line stepped boldly across Baden-Württemberg to a point just north of the aforesaid Lorch, where it turned eastward to join the Raetian sector. The two frontiers were now fully closed for the first time. The advances were carefully planned, units from the earlier lines occupying corresponding forts on the later. The new works duplicated the old except that watchtower intervals were reduced from a 700- to a 400-yard average. The saving was even greater than Raetia's, for the upper Neckar twists back on itself and had been fortified as far as Rottweil.

A new feature of special interest is the Walldürn–Welzheim straight stretch, where the palisade ran unwaveringly for fifty miles. Measurements reveal that over this distance the line diverges one yard from the straight! It is intriguing to speculate how this might have been achieved, without telescope-aided theodolites or 100% precise, large-scale maps. The frontier crosses rolling country with views from ridge to ridge. The problem is to maintain a line across blind spots, where crests preclude sighting by the normal method of a line-up of poles. Special means were perhaps employed on rising ground, involving poles tall enough to be seen over the crown. What is the point of such precision? Absolutely none. A straight line brings economies, but this degree of straightness is of theoretical interest only. In several places divergences to take in hillcrests would in fact have increased the frontier's strength. These were ignored. All was ignored except the pursuit of linear perfection. Nevertheless, the straight stretch must have been a remarkable sight; its whitewashed turrets, four to the mile, gleaming by day; their long line of lights flickering by night.

The Upper German frontier now presents an exceptional range of response. North of Frankfurt it followed every twist of the Taunus, as if just crystallised out of Domitian's Chattan expedition, when the enemy was fierce and the forest dark. Seventy-five years later, in another part of the same province, the revised version sauntered across open ground, disdaining advantageous hilltops, its surveyors amusing themselves by seeing how straight they could make it. How times had changed. This was the midday of the *pax Romana* and the noontide of the imperial frontier's strength; the empire at peace with itself; two worlds, inside and outside the frontier, in balance; the entire defensive scheme in place and working smoothly.

So, in AD 159, the abandoned Odenwald–Neckar line began its long affair with oblivion, undisturbed till the 1890s when Mommsen's shovels began to redeem it for an excited nation. Today the Odenwald's northern half, between Wörth-am-Main and the village of Schlossau, is considered among the best, both for remains and setting. Of the twenty forsaken forts, several were given over to civilian use. One watchtower (near Schlossau) was even converted to a temple of Mars, or a local equivalent. In a canny piece of religious recycling a statue of Domitian, defaced and discarded when the Senate decreed his *damnatio*, had been retrieved from some scrap heap and tricked out like the war god for worship by the local worthies.[14]

The Rhine–Danube overland *limes* had reached its full length: in Upper Germany 240 miles, in Raetia 103 miles, in all 343 miles (548 km); nearly five times longer than Hadrian's and nine times longer than the Antonine Wall. It incorporated a hundred forts and fortlets, a thousand watchtowers and garrisons totalling 30,000 men. Apart from the single sentence in the *Augustan History* describing the inception of its palisade, the ensemble receives no mention in

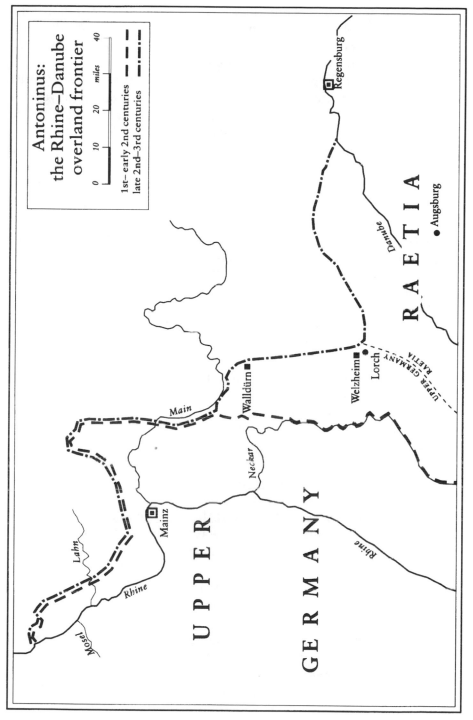

Antoninus:
the Rhine–Danube
overland frontier

1st– early 2nd centuries
late 2nd–3rd centuries

miles

0   10   20   40

Regensburg

RAETIA

• Augsburg

Danube

Walldürn

Welzheim

Lorch

UPPER GERMANY
RAETIA

Main

Neckar

UPPER

GERMANY

Mainz

Rhine

Lahn

Rhine

Mosel

surviving literature and our knowledge of it is the gift of archaeology.

It is archaeology which turns the next, sensational page: abandonment of the Forth–Clyde line and with it the relinquishing of the entire Antonine position in Scotland and a return to Hadrian's Wall. The withdrawal appears to have been orderly. Forts were dismantled and timbers burned. The distance slabs were carefully removed and buried. What provoked this recantation during Antoninus' lifetime, with its echo of Agricola and his wasted victory? Yet this time there was no crisis on the Danube to excuse retreat. The crisis must surely have been in Britain. In 1904 Haverfield invented the Brigantian revolt.[15] In this scenario, the powerful north of England tribe seized the Scottish distraction as a chance to slip the Roman leash. Support consists of an inscription recording reinforcement from Lower Germany to the Tyne and a coin with Britannia, chin on hand, in a posture suggesting grief or defeat. Since the issue does not exist which acknowledges a Roman defeat, this must have been suffered by dissident Britons. *Faute de mieux*, the Haverfield hypothesis still stands.[16]

Before long yet another surprise: Scotland was reinvaded and, according to the current rendition, the Antonine Wall reoccupied. Here is fiasco; so pure that it is hard to swallow, especially since the evidence, based on a few fort refurbishments, is sporadic and ambiguous.[17] This phase of occupation, if such there was, is known to the *cognoscenti* as Antonine II. It has the hallmarks of a face-saving operation and would not long outlast the reign. Whatever the precise course of events, it is clear that a tenth of the Roman army had not been enough. History's prescription: three legions to hold England and Wales; four to include southern Scotland and five to subdue the whole island, had been confirmed.

Antoninus died in March 161 at the ripe age of seventy-five, after a reign of twenty-three years. This was the man Hadrian had brought in as a stopgap, pending the maturity of his preferred candidate, Marcus Aurelius. In fact his reign was longer than that of either; and he was one of Rome's most successful rulers. Nevertheless, though the Antonine Age was the summit of imperial prosperity and prestige, in terms of weaponry, tactical initiative or strategic innovation no period better demonstrates the Principate's smugness and neglect. Within its proper limits of three thousand miles from east to west and two thousand from north to south, the empire was unchallenged. With peace on most fronts and no sign of collusion

SEVEN INSTRUMENTS OF ROMAN CONTROL

1. The Road

Blackstone Edge,
Lancashire

Wheeldale Moor,
North Yorkshire

2. The
Marching Camp

Rey Cross, Co. Durham.
East gateway

Fendoch, Perthshire. Site of Highland Line watchtower, within circular mound and ditch

Gunzenhausen, Germany. Timber tower within palisade (*in situ* reconstruction)

Zugmantel, Germany. Stone tower (reconstruction on original foundations)

The Lunt, near Coventry.
An auxiliary cavalry fort of
the Fosse Way system –
reconstructed timber
gateway

Kastell Saalburg, Germany.
An infantry cohort fort
(500 men) – reconstructed
stone gate and walls

Hardknott Castle,
Cumbria. A rearward
support fort for Hadrian's
Wall – corner tower

Tisavar (Ksar Ghillane) Tunisia. An auxiliary fort on Rome's Saharan frontier

5. THE FORTRESS

Lambaesis, Algeria. Home base of the *III Augusta* legion (6,000 men)

Lambaesis. The headquarters building

6. THE COLONY

Timgad, Algeria. Colonies, for legionary veterans, acted as backstops to the frontier proper

Hadrian's Wall, whose surviving works, combined with an incomparable mood and setting, . . .

Flawed formula: the tapering facing stones proved front-heavy and unstable

. . . make it the most famous monument of the Roman frontier

7. THE BARRIER
continued

Raetian Wall, Bavaria
(reconstruction on original
foundations)

Upper German palisade,
rear view
(*in situ* reconstruction)

Southern Tunisia.
Clausurum (blocking wall)
to control a pass giving
access to Roman territory

Portchester, Hampshire.
Forts begin at last to look
like castles

The Saxon shore. Land
and sea operations
co-ordinated

The Julian Alps (*Ad Pirum*,
Slovenia). The north-
eastern defences of Italy lie
half forgotten in pine forest

between enemies, there was little to prompt a reappraisal of the defences or a modernisation of the armed forces, or even to hint that they were needed. Tactics were frozen between an attacking past and a defending future. Military architecture drifted. The navy had seen no major action since the Battle of Actium (31 BC). It had received scant attention from Trajan or Hadrian and was now in decline. In the aftermath of Trajan's wars a sense of relaxation continued to grow. While Hadrian had striven to keep the army on its toes, Antoninus neither visited the frontier nor even set foot outside Italy. His long reign left few memorials. Its record was already missing from the Dio manuscript available to Xiphilinus in 11th-century Constantinople. The Column of Antoninus was devoured by architectural cannibals. It is sad that his Wall, built in a medium the Romans regarded as temporary, should have outlived marble monuments to remind posterity of a miscalculation; flouting the principle of a steady-state empire in the province where Hadrian had most forcefully expressed it, for no better reason than gesture politics and with the retardation of Roman Britain as its likeliest outcome.

The orthodox interpretation of Antonine North Britain, prevalent for most of the twentieth century, increasingly resembles a house of cards. The motive for the Scottish venture; the historicity of the Brigantian revolt and of Antonine II; the date of return to Hadrian's Wall; the links, if any, with continental events: all are little more than surmise. Here is a structure ripe to topple; and, had archaeology's hand been stronger, the push might already have come. Our only certainty, however, is that Britain had seen three contradictory boundary experiments in three reigns. Fortunately imperial interest now shifted elsewhere; for the frontier's story was about to take a very different turn.

The statue of the man who would face this crisis, sole equestrian bronze to survive intact from the ancient world, stands close to the home of the Caesars on Rome's Capitoline Hill:[18] Marcus Aurelius, lean of looks, serene yet grave, as if advancing at slow canter, right hand outstretched in famous gesture. Perhaps the extended arm symbolises the reach of Rome. Perhaps it is an expression of reconciliation toward her enemies. It has been said that the abiding memory of many visitors to the Eternal City is not of basilicas or other Christian monuments but this statue of a pagan prince; a man of peace, obliged by fate to be a soldier; a soldier at a critical juncture in Roman history. It is the resolution of these conflicts of character and destiny that make the statue great. The power in the horse's springing step, the rider's modesty, the majesty of the raised arm, the compassion in the face: all are reconciled, as Marcus reconciled them inwardly during a perplexing and exhausting reign. In the presence of high and haunting art it is churlish to add that the statue is strong in unintentional symbolism too. Through Marcus' stirrupless feet and saddleless horse, we are reminded that Roman backwardness in the technology of war continues to escape the imperial eye. After long grooming by his adoptive father and grandfather this exceptional man took office at the age of forty. Declaring the weight of empire too great for one man, he created as co-emperor Lucius Verus.[19] No previous *princeps* had dared trust half his power to another: a step whose benefit would become apparent if imperial attention were demanded in two parts of the empire at once. Within the year this happened. Vologeses IV of Parthia overran Armenia.

Though out on the sidelines Armenia was a perpetual source of apprehension, due to that rooftop kingdom's simultaneous views over the Black Sea, Asia Minor and Syria. Vologeses now moved in the last of these directions, his mounted archers annihilating a legion sent to intervene. It was an unexpected reverse. Internal weakness had hounded the Parthian dynasty for generations. This Vologeses seemed to have surmounted, for he had contrived a truce among his nobles. But the cracks had only been papered over and the governor of Syria, Avidius Cassius, a skilled soldier, needed only to mount a delaying action and wait for the enemy's unity to dissolve.

Meanwhile Marcus despatched his imperial colleague to the east, 'a younger man, better suited to military expeditions'.[20] But Verus, originally vigorous and of seemingly steady character, was proving a disappointment. Duty carried him no further than Antioch and its fun-loving suburb of Daphne, the Las Vegas of the empire. There he dawdled, gambled and fondled, sending Avidius Cassius to do the counter-attacking. The results were spectacular: Ctesiphon burned, Armenia pulled back into line, northern Mesopotamia seized, Singara transformed into a Roman bastion, the Chaboras[21] River occupied as a new defensive line and the Syrian frontier pushed 150 miles down the Euphrates to Dura Europus. It was an outcome Lucius Verus had been unwise to miss. He returned to Rome in triumph, though everyone knew his laurels were those of Daphne. Gaming, gluttony, drinking bouts, street brawling and nocturnal excursions now dominated his life. However, Verus was unable to stand his

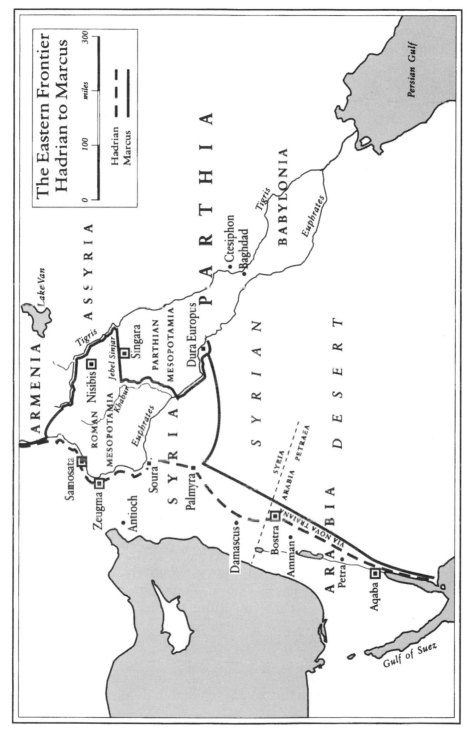

The Eastern Frontier
Hadrian to Marcus

miles

Hadrian
Marcus

0   100   300

Persian Gulf

P A R T H I A

A S S Y R I A

Lake Van

Tigris

Ctesiphon
Baghdad

BABYLONIA

Tigris

Euphrates

Dura Europus

PARTHIAN MESOPOTAMIA

Singara

Jebel Sinjar

Khabur

ARMENIA

Nisibis

ROMAN MESOPOTAMIA

Euphrates

S Y R I A N   D E S E R T

Samosata

Zeugma

Soura

Palmyra

Antioch

S Y R I A

SYRIA

ARABIA PETRAEA

Damascus

Bostra

Amman

VIA NOVA TRAIANA

A R A B I A

Petra

Aqaba

Gulf of Suez

own pace and died after only eight years in office, collapsing during a coach ride with his imperial partner. The Parthian victory had a double deficit. First, Avidius Cassius felt robbed of the fame. Secondly, his soldiers brought back plague. This would ravage Europe as far as the Pyrenees, returning during the next two decades and probably killing Marcus himself.

The catastrophic event of the reign was the Marcomannic War. This had two phases: the first, in which the empire suffered grievous reverses; the second, in which Marcus fought back and won. Its onset fell like a thunderclap and in no time Rome had lost control of events. The convulsion centred on what was till recently Czechoslovakia, where the Marcomannic tribe and their Quadan neighbours lived in Bohemia and Moravia respectively. This was the southeastern corner of Germany, the Slavic peoples having not yet arrived in central Europe. It was also the very region in which Trajan and Hadrian had applied the policy of peaceful penetration, with encouraging developments in Romano-German trade and every sign of goodwill. What had gone wrong?

The *Augustan History* offers the cryptic phrase: 'tribes driven on by more distant tribes would attack Italy unless peacefully received'.[22] Who were these distant tribes? Vandal and Langobard (Long Beards) are names which we now begin to hear for the first time. What is the meaning of 'peacefully received'? *Receptio* (reception) was the practice of allowing an outside group to settle within the empire. Typically, a harried or hungry tribe would appear on the frontier and ask for *receptio*, which would occasionally be granted; to relieve strain, fill empty land or provide recruits. Pressure from 'more distant tribes', and requests for *receptio* can thus be seen as normal cause and effect. The scale and urgency of the pressure on this occasion give grounds for supposing that the Gothic nation was on the move.

The Goths had originated in southern Sweden, where placenames like Göteborg and Gotland still survive. A century after the events of Marcus' reign they will enter history definitively, with their arrival on the north coast of the Black Sea. Their route in the meanwhile must be guessed. Deflected by the Rhine frontier and the bribery belt to its immediate east, it is probable that they travelled through today's eastern Germany and southern Poland. Indeed, the Visigoths may have taken their name from a sojourn on the upper Vistula, immediately north of today's Czech and Slovak lands. The transit of a large folk through this area is likely to have displaced Vandals,

Langobards and others who in turn squeezed the Marcomanns and Quadans against the Danube. Accordingly, in 166, two little-known clans, the Obii and Langobards, appeared out of nowhere at the junction of German and Sarmatian territory, forty miles above Budapest. Forcing their way across the Danube they entered a trap for the river bend allowed its defenders to intercept on shortened lines, and both the Budapest and *Brigetio* legions were close at hand. The invasion was repulsed. The Marcomannic king, Balomar, also hard pressed, demanded *receptio*. Marcus, encouraged by victory over the Langobards, refused him. It was a grave error. The Marcomanns and Quadans erupted. Bypassing Carnuntum and Vienna they trampled the rich lands of Upper Pannonia (western Hungary), poured across the low passes of the Julian Alps into north-eastern Italy, reached the head of the Adriatic and sacked Aquileia: the first violation of Italian soil for 260 years. A further thrust, higher up the Danube, took the Marcomanns into what we now call Austria. This was the Roman province of Noricum, considered, thanks to its harsh geography, the unlikeliest target for attack on the entire European frontier. It was therefore the most lightly guarded. The Danube was crossed below Linz, where the Enns gives quick access to the inner valleys. Further westwards a prong of this same attack penetrated Raetia (Bavaria), another legionless province, destroying forts at the eastern end of its newly realigned frontier.

The Rhine Germans now entered the conflict, though why is not known. Tribes from the Upper Main cut through new stretches of the Rhine–Danube *limes* and headed toward Basle. Ever game, the Chattans were then roused, breaking through the same frontier's Taunus section and devastating the region round today's Frankfurt-am-Main. The Lower Rhine remained at peace; but on the North Sea coast the Chauci, from modern Hamburg (inexplicably infected, though 250 miles from the nearest war zone and at least 500 from the epicentre) took to the sea. In a portentous manoeuvre they circumvented the Rhine mouths and fell on the unguarded coast of Gaul.

Shock waves spread down the Danube. From Moldova the free Dacians and their allies penetrated the Carpathian passes into the stronghold of Dacia Porolissensis, beat a path through Transylvania and crossed the Danube into what is now Bulgaria. Their southward march passed behind (west of) Hadrian's Olt line, whose garrisons could do little. The Iazyges of the Hungarian Plain were also heavily involved, though the timing and direction of their attack is unknown. Finally the Costoboccans of the Pontic Steppe, availing themselves of the corridor ceded by Hadrian to the Rhoxolan king, crossed into Lower Moesia. One branch headed into the southern Balkans, eventually to be discouraged by the mountainous terrain. The other swung southwards into Greece, violating the shrine at Eleusis. Here, in the heart of the unarmed provinces, they were stoutly resisted by local volunteers. In all there is little suggestion of plot or plan. With the exception of inroads into Italy and Greece, barbarian gains were neither deep nor deadly. The attackers had no common aim. More serious were the spread of the disturbances, their duration and the slowness of response. In the central theatre it was perhaps as much as three years before Marcus regained control. Plague, plus a treasury emptied to fight Parthia, were doubtless the reasons. The Pannonian army had been hardest hit and Marcus was obliged to fill the ranks with gladiators, slaves, criminals, urban cohorts and Germans.[23] He even auctioned the palace treasures.[24]

What was the meaning of the Marcomannic War for the frontier; not in terms of local damage, but of strategy? During the previous century and a half this question could not have been answered, simply because there had been no serious attack, and Rome's chosen method of defence had undergone no test. But in 166 it met its first serious challenge and it failed. The stretched membrane of Roman guardianship had been snapped almost, it seems, at will. What size of forces achieved this result? That of the Langobards is given as only six thousand. However, in view of the numbers of Roman prisoners later returned by the Marcomanns and Iazyges we must assume that these fielded bigger numbers by far, possibly in the region of a hundred thousand each. They had attacked between fortresses, even between forts, perhaps under cover of darkness, piercing the filament of watchtowers like an owl through cobwebs. Once inside, the imperial road system lay at their feet. The frontier could then be attacked from the rear. More often, however, the barbarians hastened inland, leaving the forts behind. The Costobocci pursued a slalom-like course, swerving round military obstacles as if intent on denying the archaeologist his evidence. The bigger bases especially were left untouched. Vienna, for example, either held out or was not attacked, though twelve miles upriver Zeiselmauer was burned by its own garrison and Traismauer, twelve miles further, was destroyed by enemy action.[25] The picture is varied and confused. It is nevertheless clear that the frontier had been broken not only many times, but under varied conditions. The enemy had prevailed against the long rivers, parts of the Rhine–Danube overland frontier and the Carpathians alike. He had even dared the North Sea. Another cause for disquiet was the conflagration's sideways spread, engulfing most of the European frontier within four years. Neither the intelligence networks painstakingly placed, nor the alliances expensively preserved, nor an encamped army with all its capital works had served to alert or avert. The received wisdom, that crisis at one point could be countered by reinforcement from another, had proved false. Troop withdrawals simply created points of weakness and emboldened the barbarians to attack.

If the genesis of the Marcomannic storm was, as we believe, far inside Germany, this gave grounds for the gravest concern of all. The transit of the Goths, like a ship in the night, had been beyond Roman control or even knowledge. Events had shown how background disturbance could create waves, drowning good intentions in the frontier's foreground. Who could anticipate the random workings of the deep *barbaricum*? The Marcomannic War expresses the fear of all central powers: war on two fronts. This Rome narrowly missed, for the Parthian conflict had already run its course. Meanwhile Avidius Cassius, smarting in Syria, chose the moment of crisis to raise his standard of revolt. Marcus was forced to disengage and rush to the east. Fortunately his journey proved unnecessary. Having failed to convince or bribe the Syrian legions, Avidius was murdered and on arrival the squeamish emperor was presented with his head.

With the war's commencement the sources go quiet. Dio and the *Augustan History* are at their most muddled and patchy for the years 166–72, perhaps reflecting a news blackout of the time. In few cases do we know how the invaders crossed the Danube: over ice, on rafts, or by capturing bridges. We have no account of the army's response. Most of our knowledge is archaeological: a rush to bury worldly goods and a charred stripe in the layercake of the soil. Doubtless it was a strange conflict, a non-match, a war of avoidance: the army in its fixed positions, reluctant to move; the enemy on the wing, afraid to be still.

The first step towards recovery was the safeguarding of Italy. A new command was established, known from an inscription[26] as the *Praetentura Italiae et Alpium* (Northern Italian and Alpine Command), whose purpose was to block entry via the eastern Alps.

Two legions were raised in the Italian north. Of these, *II Italica* was posted to Ločica,[27] guarding the Carnatic Alps. It was later advanced to its final station at Lauriacum (Lorch) on the Danube, thirteen miles below Linz. The other, *Legio III Italica concors*, was placed at Castra Regina (Regensburg). All three bases were built from scratch. At Regensburg, an auxiliary fort had been destroyed in the war. The new fortress, closer to the Danube and opposite the mouth of the Regen, now lies under the medieval centre and cathedral. Impressive remains of its north gate can still be seen on Unter den Schibbögen Strasse, built into the Bischofshof Hotel. Marcus also established a headquarters to deal with the Sarmatian problem: at Sirmium (Mitrovica) on the Sava, forty-five miles west of Belgrade. This was located to the rear of the Danube, opposite the deep re-entrant containing the Tisza river and the south Hungarian plain. His main command centre, however, was the legionary base at Carnuntum, below Vienna, perfectly placed to direct operations into Czechoslovakia. There Marcus lived for five years and there, or in Vienna, he died.

In all, the Marcomannic War lasted fourteen years and involved at least seventeen tribes. Many senior officers were lost. The *Augustan History* calls it 'a war of many nations . . . a war which surpassed any in man's memory'.[28] Though writing two centuries later, Ammian still speaks of 'calamitous losses . . . the horror of plundered cities . . . the corporate madness of many tribes'.[29] We are in the dark about how the war was won. If only we could read it, the age has left a doughty document on these very years when the conflict was being carried into enemy territory. This is the Column of Marcus Aurelius, whose ascending frieze recounts the war in detail. However, though the general concept is inspired by Trajan's Column, there are important differences and these have a bearing on comprehensibility. In essence the two Columns express their subject in opposite ways: Trajan's directly, the Aurelian symbolically. Where Trajan's is simple and soldierly, that of Marcus is complex and brooding. Where Trajan's draws on observation of an almost photographic accuracy, Marcus' deals in the realm of conscience; finding inspiration in the horror and pity, rather than in the events and techniques of war. The Aurelian Column demonstrates the problem of art as source material. Artists commonly prefer self-expression to reportage and metaphor to fact. In Trajan's Column, the historian is lucky that the frieze was based on observation rather than imagination. In the

Aurelian Column his luck runs out. Without captions neither is easy to follow; but the Aurelian especially has tended to frustrate its interpreters and is little studied. Today it stands in the Piazza Colonna in busiest Rome, its sooty shaft rising from a plinth of parked cars. Though a priceless, intact source, it remains wrapped in a cloudy imagery of its own. Much may yet be coaxed from it by thoughtful work coupled with archaeological advances in the Danubian lands.

By the war's end 20,000 Roman troops were on Marcomannic soil. At Trenčin, central Slovakia,[30] a detachment of *Legio II Adiutrix*, which wintered there in 181–2, left an inscription on a rockface above the river Váh:[31] the easternmost evidence of Roman arms in central Europe. Marcus' intention was to initiate two new provinces, Marcomannia and Sarmatia, so joining the Czechoslovak highlands and Carpathians in a near-continuous mountain line and removing pressure from the Danube almost entirely. Here was thinking in the Trajanic mould. Like Antoninus' foray into Scotland, it shows how far Hadrian's pacifism had diverged from the militant spirit which so obstinately remained the Roman norm. Expansion was, it seems, still instinctive, even to the gentlest emperors.

As if to requite us for his miserly account of the war, Dio gives generously regarding the peace. We see Marcus granting *receptio* to selected groups of the vanquished. Experience would show that, when barbarian immigrants were settled on Roman land, they swiftly developed a sense of ownership and defended their property vigorously, even resenting later arrivals of the same ethnic group. Naturally assimilation was not without problems:

The Quadans were refused the right to attend markets for fear other tribes might mingle with them and spy out the Roman positions. Some were drafted and sent to various battle fronts. Others were offered land in the provinces of Dacia, Pannonia, Moesia, the Germanies and even Italy. However, since some who had been settled round Ravenna made trouble and even looted the city, Marcus put an end to allowing barbarians into Italy and expelled those already there.[32]

The next excerpt again stresses the importance of markets, almost always an item on peace agendas:

Marcus restored to the Marcomanni half the neutral zone along their frontier, allowing them to settle up to five miles from the Danube. He established places and days for markets and exchanged hostages.[33]

A third passage startles us by the number of Roman prisoners said to have been taken by the Iazyges, for elsewhere Dio mentions only 30,000 repatriated by the Marcomanns. On this showing the conflict should have been called 'the Iazygian War'.

He imposed the same conditions on the Iazyges, except they could not live within ten miles of the river. Indeed Marcus had wanted them wiped out, for they had inflicted severe casualties, as proven by their return of 100,000 captives, to say nothing of the many who had already been sold, died or escaped. As their contribution to the reparations they furnished 8,000 cavalry of which more than 5,000 were posted to Britain.[34]

However, when the Iazyges kept promises and showed a cooperative spirit, the generous Marcus

released them from some restrictions, though not those affecting the right of assembly, or the prohibition against using boats of their own and against landing on any of the Danube's islands.[35]

Behind all questions concerning the war there loom the master-questions: what had Rome learnt from it and what remedies would she implement? Apart from putting two legions into provinces which should have had them already, we recognise no remedy and conclude that no lesson was learned. Essentially the old-type frontier will now be restored. There will be little change in style of fortification, no rethinking of deployments, no sign of defence in depth, no creation of rearward reserves or of a second line; in short nothing to reduce the danger of a single thin and brittle front, or to counter the consequences of its penetration.

Lauriacum and Ločica were fortresses of conventional design, with round corners and internal towers. Though Regensburg had thicker walls and projecting gate towers, these were grudging improvements to a traditional siting and plan. Remembering those craggy Rhenish and Danubian castles, dear to nineteenth-century painters and twentieth-century wine labels, it is not as if the rivers offer no sites to the military architect. Yet still we continue to see low-walled rectangles, often tamely placed on flat ground by the river. Indeed these are the sitings which lost many of the empire's riverine defences to inundation and river shift, while the donjons of later ages stand safely on the slopes above. As well as the three new fortresses, many forts had now to be rebuilt. Though tentative corner towers appear in a few there is nothing to suggest the revolution in castrametation so sorely needed. Most enervating of all was the fact that Rome won the war; for those who win final battles forget early defeats.

Marcus Aurelius must bear his share of blame for failure to read what the European frontier's sudden and almost total collapse had made clear. Nevertheless, it is difficult to judge too harshly a man who was a born civilian, yet made himself a soldier and won a brutal war. It is all the more remarkable that in the midst of mayhem he managed to produce that tranquil masterpiece known to posterity as the *Meditations*. It was partly composed in the governor's palace at Carnuntum, whose remains may still be seen on the Danube bank. Other passages were written on campaign. His Book One is subsigned 'among the Quadans, on the Gran' (the Slovakian river Hron). That solitary phrase is the book's only concession to geography. The frontier was hardly congenial to men of letters and little was written either on or about it. While the accident of Ovid's exile to the Black Sea in AD 9 provided a view of the empire's edge through the eyes of one of its greatest artists,[36] this quirk of literary history would never repeat itself. So Tacitus wrote about the frontier lands without visiting them; and the sculptors of Trajan's Column recreated Dacia in the studio. In the *Meditations*, on the contrary, we have a book written on the frontier – even beyond it – yet not about it! No part of Marcus' book is moored to the mundane; its view is inwards and it allows no inkling of the surroundings from which it was its author's refuge.

Marcus was gentle and pure-hearted, scholarly and frail. It is remarkable that such a man could act decisively on the battlefield. His limitations were those of all Romans. Marcus, Trajan and Hadrian: no three men could be more different; yet all were one in being heirs to the same, heroic history. All saw Rome as eternal, and the empire as indestructible. But time was now questioning the suppositions of centuries. In its first real encounter with war the imperial frontier had been set at nought. It was a time for change, for a young man to succeed to the throne and dedicate his energy to deep, remedial thinking.

Remedy would not be found in Commodus. This was Marcus' only surviving son, the first hereditary successor since Domitian. The years of the 'good emperors', when prudent rulers chose able successors, were over. With Commodus we turn from one sort of danger, frontier failure, to another, failure within. Dio regarded this moment as a watershed in the empire's history, for his description of Marcus' death[37] in March 180 ends with the famous but sombre words: 'Our history now descends from realms of gold to those of iron and rust, as did Rome's fortunes on that day.'[38] Marcus' two new provinces were not to be. On his death Commodus rejected the trans-Danubian involvement, made deals with the vanquished kings and returned to Rome. Though Dio arraigns him for indifference to duty, the treaties would endure for half a century and bring the Middle Danube its last, substantial peace. Nor was this reign wholly worthless in other respects for, as with all bad masters, good servants continued to do good work in their own corners. At the centre, however, the next thirteen years would give ample occasion for doubt regarding the genetic lottery, of which Commodus was so extreme a result. What quirk of fate sent a son like this to Rome's saintliest emperor? More broadly, a malign pattern is emerging. As a later chapter of the *Augustan History* reflects: 'Thinking back, it is evident that almost no great man left a son of merit or value. Most died childless, or had such children that it would have been better for mankind had they not.'[39] One might almost believe there was a curse on Rome: that her rulers should either have no sons or bad ones; a misfortune compounded by an army loyal to blue blood, which could always be relied on to reject a worthy adopted heir if an unworthy natural one were to hand:

Commodus was not born evil but his lack of intelligence left him prey to bad companions. I believe Marcus could see it all coming. Commodus was nineteen when his father died, but Marcus made sure his many guardians would include the best men in the Senate. These Commodus sent packing; and after making a truce with the barbarians he hurried to Rome, for he hated hard work and longed for the comforts of the city.[. . .][40] Here Commodus lived the life of Reilly: boozing and banqueting in the palace with three hundred concubines, chosen for their beauty from among Rome's whores and society women alike.[41]

As well as this, numerous kidnapped women were kept in confinement to be brought out in turn and debauched. Nor was it an unqualified pleasure to attend his banquets, for it amused Commodus to conceal excrement among the delicacies served. On one occasion the Praetorian colonel was forced to dance naked and clash cymbals to the applause of the imperial harem. All offices were for sale. When state papers were given him for perusal he simply wrote on them the word *vale* ('goodbye').

The barbarian attacks of Marcus' reign were now echoed on Hadrian's Wall where, in 184, we see yet another frontier failing the test: 'The British tribes, having crossed the Wall which separated them from the legions, wreaked havoc, killing soldiers and their general too. Commodus took fright and sent Ulpius Marcellus against them.'[42] Marcellus was a mean-minded man. Dio recounts his habit of writing orders on a dozen wooden tablets every evening, which he had messengers deliver hourly throughout the night, so promoting the legend that he never slept. Whatever the cause of this invasion he was seemingly able to repel it.

Time squandered in Rome was in part compensated for on the Rhine and Danube. The latter's southflowing stretch, facing the miscreant Iazyges, now becomes celebrated for the density of its forts and watchtowers: 'to guard places used for clandestine crossings by the *latrunculi*',[43] as an inscription of this date from Lower Moesia puts it. This is the diminutive of *latro* (thief), probably the actual term used by watchers to describe intruders. In specifying this daily duty it confirms the policing nature of the imperial frontier in time of peace. The beefing up of the African defences still proceeded, especially in the area of southern Tunisia's Ksour range. Beyond it, on the edge of the Great Eastern Erg (sand sea), a remarkably preserved installation merits mention. This is the small fort of Tisavar (Ksar Ghillane). Constructed soon after 184, discovered by Cdt. Lachouque in 1885 and excavated by Lt. Gombeaud in 1900, Tisavar is of orthodox, early empire shape, with exterior dimensions of only 30×40 yards. Smallness may be explained by situation: on an isolated, limestone knoll above rolling dunes. To save space accommodation consisted of cells built against the inside of the rampart on all four sides. Their roofs provided a continuous wall-walk, allowing a larger-than-normal number of defenders to muster at any point. The fort's centre is almost filled by a *principia* or redoubt, of massive masonry. Steps point to a second or third floor, even a central tower. There is one gate only, double and again of large masonry, with a deep passage and murder holes let into the wall from the adjoining chambers. Room walls survive to full height, ramparts (despite collapse at one corner) to parapet level with crenellations intact and gateway with arch complete. The fort, which may have housed fifty, is a marvel of compactness. In some respects (hilltop siting, small size, rooms against ramparts and solitary gate) it foreshadows the later empire, though these advances were perhaps a product of circumstance rather than design.

In 1943 General Leclerc's column passed close by on its northward trek from Chad, and there are signs of subsequent calls by the French army. But generally the fort's remoteness has shielded it from stone-robber and vandal. The encroachment of the desert is plain to see for the fort, doubtless once on the edge, is now entirely surrounded by a vast sea of dunes. Nor is there sign of the fields which the garrison required for its support. Here and there yellow sand, soft and fine as flour, sidles up the hill, drifts over the ten-foot rampart and spills into the inner rooms. A well, still used by nomads, lies in a hollow perhaps a thousand yards distant. For outlook, atmosphere and sense of ultimate outpost, Tisavar surpasses even its other-side-of-the-coin experience, Hadrian's Wall in the snow.

Ksar Ghillane can be reached from Gabès, where desertworthy vehicle and driver may be had from tour operators. During high summer, the Erg is best left to its *djinns* and mirages.

At thirty-one years old and after thirteen years' misrule, Commodus was strangled in the bath, following a plot between the cymbal-clashing colonel and an out-of-favour mistress. With their usual display of *post-facto* courage, the senators reviled the late emperor as 'foe of the fatherland, enemy of the gods, scourge of the state, slaughterer of the Senate, more brutal than Domitian, fouler than Nero!'[44] Their *damnatio* debate includes forty lines of Latin text devoted to oaths, expletives and exhortations that the corpse be dragged by a meat hook and thrown into the Tiber.

Though one man's excesses do not destroy empires, danger lies in the weeks which follow; especially when a clear-cut and clean-handed heir is not readily apparent. 'No wrong troubles righteous rule,'[45] had been the Senate's verdict on Marcus. It was largely true of the

early empire that only bad rulers came to bad ends. Sound government and the general acceptance of a respected successor had long
proved a sure formula for calm, both on the streets and in the camps.
With Commodus' murder, army and state were once more in uproar
and the stage was set for a rerun of the Year of the Four Emperors.

CHAPTER 8

Septimius:
A Prophetic Principate

IN THE GRAB FOR THE PURPLE which followed the strangling of Commodus, legitimacy gave way to bribery. Pertinax, who failed to pay the guardsmen the 12,000 sesterces per man which he had promised, lasted six months. Then, in a disgraceful auction held in the Praetorian camp, the empire was knocked down to one Julianus, who beggared his rival with a wild bid of 25,000. Power had fled from politicians to Praetorians. But ultimate power lay elsewhere. As the news reached the frontiers the real army stirred. Its sentiments were not, however, unified. Rome's sundered soldiers rarely spoke as one. By deploying them in mutual isolation the caesars had ensured that in time of crisis each would champion its own man. It was thus the Principate's peculiar weakness that murder in Rome could end by army slaughtering army, with the frontiers left unguarded; and it was purest luck that the barbarians did not rouse themselves during the four years which followed. The legions of the East declared for C. Pescennius Niger, of Britain for D. Clodius Albinus and of the Danube for L. Septimius Severus, governor of Pannonia. The last was closest to the centre, with three legions of his own and call on a further nine. He marched on Rome, took it without a fight, dismissed the Praetorians and replaced them with his own men. Meanwhile, throughout its length, the Danube was guarded by scarecrow cohorts.

These events of June 193 remind us of another remarkable fact: Rome had never seen her own soldiers. Suddenly the streets were full of them and the Romans did not like what they saw. The crudity of the frontiersmen was frightening: 'Septimius flooded the city with the men of many regiments: wild to look at, terrifyingly noisy, coarse and boorish of speech. [...]¹ They billeted themselves in temples, porticoes and even on the Palatine, taking anything they wanted without paying and threatening to wreck the city if refused.'²

Septimius' struggle for power continued. After a damaging conflict in western Asia Minor, Niger was defeated. Albinus crossed with his three legions from Britain to be beaten near Lyons, where Septimius commanded in person. Albinus committed suicide. Hadrian's Wall was without defenders.

Dio, a senator and in Rome, witnessed these disagreeable days. At last, after quoting this indispensable source over a two-century span, we have reached his own lifetime. Dio Cassius Cocceianus, from Nicaea in Asia Minor, was a descendant of the orator Dio Chrysostom (the golden-mouthed). He had held proconsulships in Asia Minor, Africa and Dalmatia and the governorship of Pannonia. In the mid 190s he set himself the task of writing a *History of Rome*, beginning with Aeneas and ending in his own lifetime. He corresponded with the emperor and claims to have been inspired to write his *History* when Septimius encouraged him in a dream. The work continues to 229, eighteen years after Septimius' death when, at a time of growing menace and instability, Dio gratefully retires to his native Bithynia. As a contemporary his comments on the Severan period are of special value. Even here, however, we still read him through Xiphilinus. Even (since Trajan) through Zonaras, a Byzantine editor of the 12th century, epitomising the 11th-century epitome of Xiphilinus! Though perhaps not golden-mouthed, he is one of the great tellers of Rome's story and many a tapestry would be threadbare without him.

L. Septimius Severus, Rome's first African emperor, had been born at Leptis³ Magna some fifty years earlier. His second wife Julia Domna, mother of their two sons Geta and Caracalla, was from Emesa in Syria. Intelligent and influential, she would be a lifelong spokeswoman for the Roman east. Given the backgrounds of these two, this would be a reign of less than usual European bias.

Though Severus was a family name, the term 'severe' suits Septimius well. He was a no-nonsense emperor. He believed in swatting opposition and in scratching the frontier wherever it might itch. He was a shrewd ruler, an able soldier and the last expansionist emperor.

Nonetheless, comparison with Mussolini is difficult to resist. Indeed it is one which the Italian himself encouraged, for as he strode into the Fascist Grand Council the shout would ring out: 'Salute the *Duce*, *propagatore d'imperio*!' 'Enlarger of empire' is a title borrowed from Septimius. In both cases there was much fuss about modest enlargement; and each was a century late for imperialism's heyday.

The best of Septimius' achievements was Mesopotamia. Rome's convulsion had allowed Vologeses to retake what he had lost to Avidius Cassius. Septimius replied with the breathtaking campaign of 197–8, inflicting a defeat so stunning that it would hasten the death of the Parthian kingdom itself. But Septimius remained realistic, confining annexation to a portion of what is now Kurdish Iraq, north-west from Mosul, fringing into north-eastern Syria. Like Trajan, he failed to take Hatra, key to the south. His two attempts 'cost much money and many siege machines, to say nothing of men in large numbers'.[4] True to the tradition of war between these empires, all depended on supply lines and water points and hence on the ability of a few citadels, commanding these elements, to hold out. In western sieges, time was against those inside. In the desert, if a city could enclose the available wells within its walls, time was against those outside.

Despite this setback, Trajan's short-lived province of Mesopotamia was now reconstituted and given two, newly recruited legions: *I Parthica* at Singara (Blat Sinjar) and *II Parthica* at Nisibis (Nusaybin). To join the territory to Syria a second province was established in the former borderland of Osrhoëne,[5] straddling the modern Turco-Syrian frontier. Finally, Syria was divided into two, Syria Coele and Syria Phoenice, so that each governor would have no more than two legions. Accordingly Syria Coele, Osrhoëne and Mesopotamia now formed a bridge running west–east across the northern segment of the fertile crescent, consisting of North Syria from the Mediterranean to the Euphrates, Osrhoëne from the Euphrates to the Khabur and Mesopotamia from the Khabur to the Tigris. Two legions were now advanced from Vespasian's former frontier on the middle Euphrates: *XVI Flavia* from Samosata (Samsat, Turkey) to Sura (Souriya, Syria) 125 miles downstream; and *IV Scythica* from Zeugma (Bireçik, Turkey) eastwards to Oriza, capital of Osrhoëne.

The Mesopotamian province blocked Parthian access to Armenia and stopped the seesaw of Roman–Parthian rivalry over that country; freezing it, so to speak, with Rome in the commanding position. But despite strategic gains there would be little benefit from this outpost, over 400 miles from the Mediterranean. Dio, writing after Septimius' death, already deprecates his eastern policy, with its danger of being out on a limb among old enemies: 'He was fond of boasting what a portion he had added to the empire and how he had made a shield for Syria. But in truth it has been nothing but a nuisance, yielding little and costing much. For having paddled into the Parthian pond we now find ourselves muddied by ancient quarrels.'[6] Nevertheless, Roman Mesopotamia would survive into the early Byzantine period.

Frontiers had now to be found to protect Mesopotamia from Parthia to its east and south. In the former direction the Tigris provided a clear line. In the latter an east–west range of hills, the Jebel Sinjar, was well situated and of suitable ruggedness to interdict cavalry, the main Parthian arm. Its ridge is more than seventy miles long, 4,800 feet high and attracts eight inches of annual rain; ample to provide springs or act as catchment for installations at its feet. Unfortunately it peters out some thirty miles from the Tigris to its east and a similar distance from the Khabur to its west, so that an assailant could turn either end. In front of the Jebel Sinjar was the town of Singara which Septimius now reinforced as the line's centrepiece. Behind (to its north) was Nisibis, the provincial capital, which would act as backstop.

Today's Iraq–Syria border crosses the western end of the Sinjar range and bisects Roman Mesopotamia, except for the northern part, in present-day Turkey. Tensions arising from the Kurdish problem have made the entire area politically sensitive, and the Sinjar line remains the least accessible and least known of imperial frontier stretches. Reading his paper *The Roman Frontiers in Mesopotamia* at the first Congress of Roman Frontier Studies in Newcastle upon Tyne, 1949, Sir Mortimer Wheeler concluded:

I am assured that at the present time conditions in Iraq are favourable for exploration. Let us now find an enterprising young scholar for work in northern Mesopotamia. If he has already had preliminary training on our own, complex frontier system, so much the better. Thereafter, with jeep and proper sense of adventure, he can sally forth into the desert with the complete assurance of immortal fame.

These 'favourable conditions' ended in 1958 with the assassination of Feisal II. Fortunately the attention of exceptional men had already been engaged. In May 1925 Père Poidebard's aerial sorties covered the western end of the Sinjar frontier, within the confines of France's Syrian mandate. Accordingly he was able to point the way for Aurel Stein to study the remainder. As we will remember Britain held the mandate for Iraq as well as Jordan. Stein's survey included both; he himself describing it as 'from the foot of the Kurdestan Hills to the Gulf of Aqaba, in a straight line of over 700 miles'.[7] This two-year task began on the Sinjar frontier, with Stein pitching his tents at Singara in March 1938. The immense ramparts were still largely visible, with their facing of large, limestone blocks and U-shaped towers of late Roman date. The walled area was about 1,000×400 yards and the high part, an ancient citadel, was still inhabited. Singara was a fortified city lying forward of the main Roman position and protruding into unfriendly territory. No legionary fortress has been found, but it was common eastern practice for units to occupy a portion of the town.

Regarding the line itself, this appears to have been a guarded road along the southern base of the Jebel Sinjar, perhaps with periodic forts. Stein discovered few; but with total desert barring the approach from the south, the mountains behind and a reserve legion behind *them*, many forts would not have been needed. Most of the available units were deployed to plug the gaps at either end of the Jebel. There were also outposts down the Tigris road toward Hatra. On the western flank, between the hills and the Khabur (Habour, Roman Chaboras) river, Poidebard reported stretches of ditch, about fifteen miles in all. In addition, running between two forts was a decayed wall of large boulders and rubble, with a ditch on either side of it. These were evidently intended as cavalry obstacles. Several watch-tower bases lay close behind. From here for almost a hundred miles the Khabur runs south by south-west to its confluence with the Euphrates. This too was now imperial frontier. Much of its course is fronted, on the Parthian side, by chotts (Arabic *sebkhat*) and attack across these almost waterless plains is in any case unlikely. Along the Khabur Poidebard reported several forts and there are periodic tels suggesting towns or villages in which Roman units may have been stationed.

On the eastern flank, between the hills and the Tigris, Stein discovered no barrier works but identified eight forts, including Ain

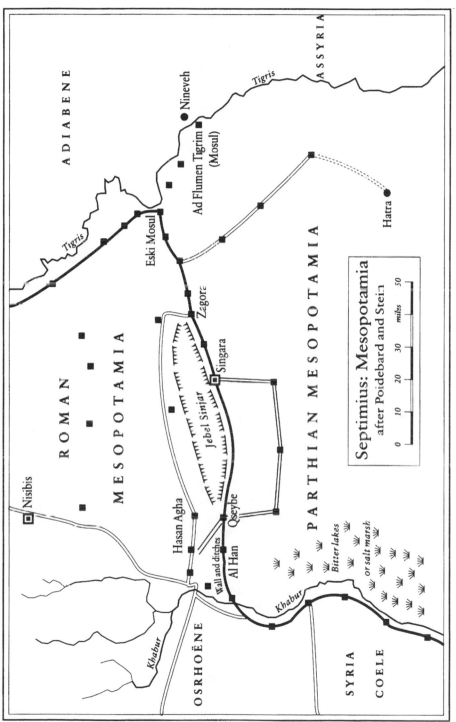

Septimius: Mesopotamia
after Poidebard and Stein

Sinu in the foothills and Eski Mosul (Old Mosul) on the riverbank.
Ain Sinu (Zagorra) is an interesting site, for outside the Severan fort
are the remains of large barracks. This may have been a recruiting
centre, as Mesopotamia became a gathering ground for the mailed
cavalry and mounted archers increasingly employed on other Roman
frontiers. Eski Mosul, where a bend in the Tigris brings it closest to
the Jebel Sinjar, was the *limes'* eastern terminus. Here Stein sketched
a walled city nearly three miles in circumference, with a small village
amid its ruins and the outline of a Roman fort outside its gates.
Downriver was the fort of Ad Pontem, then that of Ad Flumen
Tigrim (Mosul), across from the site of ancient Nineveh.

Beyond the Tigris lay the Parthian province of Assyria, briefly held
by Trajan. The river frontier north of Eski Mosul seems to have
taken the form of patrolled roads some fifteen miles to the rear.
Though fort sites could be lost under mud or to river movement,
enemies more pestilential than Parthians may have prevented a
tighter hold on the bank; as Ammian found when visiting the area
a century and a half later:

> During winter lions in their hundreds roam the reed forests. But
> with the onset of summer and its heat they are tortured both by
> the sun and by the millions of mosquitoes for which the region is
> notorious. These make for the moisture of the eyes, stinging the
> lions' eyelids till either they plunge into the river and are drowned
> or they blind themselves by constant scratching.[8]

Such was the eastern extremity of the classical West. Such too is our
limited knowledge of Septimius' long salient. We are little better
informed than when Sir Mortimer spoke so hopefully in 1949; and
no paper on Kurdish Iraq has been read to the fifteen congresses
since.

The scene brightens when we turn to the Hellenistic city of Dura
Europus on the Euphrates, a Syrian site and source of fascinating
finds. As described in the previous chapter, it was captured by Avidius
Cassius when his push down the Euphrates advanced the limit of
Roman territory by 150 miles. Septimius now retook Dura and
placed there two auxiliary regiments, later reinforced by legionary
detachments. The northern quarter was walled off as a military district, illustrating what may have happened in other Syrian cities. But
unlike Antioch and the rest, Dura is a fly in amber, untouched

between its destruction by the Persians in 256 and the evening in 1918 when British soldiers, encamped over its ruins, chanced to dig a latrine trench. This remarkable border city, founded by Alexander, was a Seleucid stronghold for a century, a Parthian for three and a Roman for one more; after which it would be destroyed by Shapur I and abandoned forever. It contained a mixed Greek, Syrian, Jewish, Iranian and Roman population. Excavations in the military area revealed a palace and headquarters of the commander of the Roman Euphrates frontier; and in the civilian area a synagogue, church and *mithraeum* cheek by jowl. This was a cultural *mélange* whose peaceful coexistence in so limited a space was made feasible only by the military presence.

In the 1930s American excavators found an exceptional cache of written evidence, best of which was the papyrus archive of *cohors XX Palmyrenorum*, covering a fifty-year period, most important vestige of Rome's military paperwork to survive.[9] It includes duty rosters, stores manifests, leave and transfer records, pay lists, details of pay days and discharge dates, plus an entire military calendar (the *feriale duranum*) giving religious holidays, imperial birthdays and other festivals observed by the army with appropriate ceremonial and parades. Another interesting discovery was the Dura Europus shield map. Ovid's mention[10] of soldiers decorating their shields with maps relating to the theatres in which they served, received dramatic confirmation in 1922 when a piece of painted leather, measuring about 14×6 inches, from a shield's outer skin, was unearthed. It appears to have belonged to a Palmyrene auxiliary soldier in garrison during the 230s. We may assume his previous postings included the Pontic Region. Sea covers the shield's centre and includes scenes of warships. Land, representing the Pontic coast, rings the shield's edge and contains the names of Black Sea stations of which several are legible.[11] However, like the Peutinger Table, there is little representation of real scale or topographic detail. The result is as much decorative as practical, though not without general value. Whether soldiers campaigning in *enemy* territory were so equipped is less certain.

Dura was not Rome's last outpost on the Euphrates. At a colloquium held by Sheffield University in 1986, Professor A. Invernizzi reported on excavations at Kifrin on the left bank of the Euphrates, below Anah (Anath). As part of the archaeological salvage operation prior to a new dam at Haditha, the Turin Excavations Centre for the Middle East was invited by the Iraqi authorities to dig during

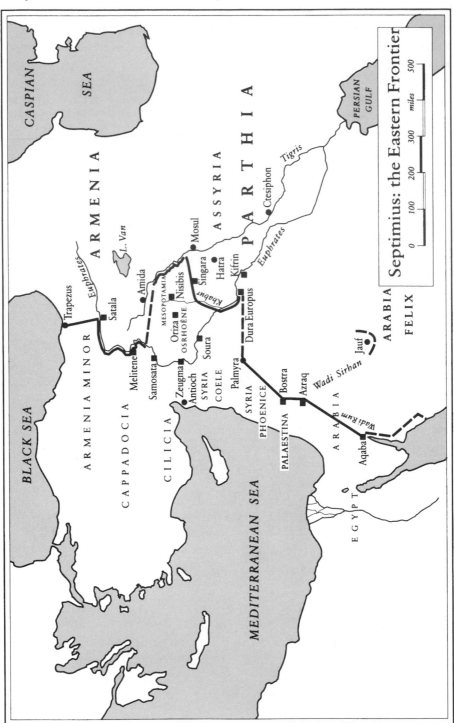

Septimius: the Eastern Frontier

the 1981–3 seasons. Kifrin was a pre-existing town and citadel, a hundred miles below Dura Europus. Within it the Italians discovered a Roman military establishment of probable Severan date.[12] A few miles downriver again, on the island of Bijan, a Roman outstation was identified: the furthest known frontier post in this direction. Here we are 1,900 miles east of Rome and only 125 from modern Baghdad or nearby Ctesiphon, Parthia's capital.

Activities in the province of Arabia (Jordan), though less dramatic, typify Septimius' style. Where there was trouble he extended Roman control to envelop it. Trouble was evidently emerging from the Wadi Sirhan. This depression runs southeastwards from the Jordanian oasis at el Azraq. It is two hundred miles long and twenty wide, ending in the Nafud sandy desert, well within today's Saudi Arabia. Because it holds some water the Wadi Sirhan is an escape route from Arabia's centre in time of drought. An altar from Jauf, dedicated by a centurion of *Legio III Cyrenaica*, suggests the corridor was now being patrolled, with an army post at its southern end. Again this is a farthest point for the imperial frontier. New forts were built at the Jordanian end of the wadi. Aerial investigation reveals a probable Severan installation under the impressive 4th-century fort remains at Azraq; and others (Hallabat, Uweinid and Usaikin) were now added. All this had the effect of advancing the frontier in northern Jordan some fifty miles eastwards from Trajan's axial road, the Via Nova. Further south this highway was kept as the frontier, probably because of Antoninus' investment in forts along it. By now these numbered eight, increased by Septimius to nine, mostly between the Dead Sea and Aqaba. The *limes Arabicus* is exceptional in that no major campaign had been fought there. Accordingly it attracted few imperial visits and inspired few mentions. Its interest lies in individual sites and particularly the standard of preservation of its forts.

Developments in Africa were comparable, though with more ground gained. Again, the principle was to smother trouble by stepping out to points of tactical vantage like oases and scarp edges. Hadrian saw frontiers as linear; Septimius in terms of outposts and spot advances. In Africa, this showy but relatively inexpensive technique could be applied to advantage. Activity was largely guided by Q. Anicius Faustus, legate in Africa from 197 to 201, at a time when Septimius was preoccupied in the East. There can be little doubt, however, that Faustus, a fellow African, was given a very positive brief: to express, in frontier terms, that Africa's security was close to the emperor's heart. Knowing that 'every man has a lurking wish to appear considerable in his native place',[13] it is not surprising that Faustus should scatter inscriptions of Septimius as *propagator imperii* unstintingly, or that of eighteen known examples of this title seventeen should be from North Africa.[14]

Numidia was now separated from Africa and created an armed province whose purpose was to jacket the agricultural region. In Tripolitania, the emperor's birthplace, three forts were placed 300 miles from the coast. If a line were drawn to link them it would run from the Gulf of Sirte across the pre-Saharan plateau to a point where the modern boundaries of Libya, Tunisia and Algeria meet. It is, however, difficult to stretch the term *limes* to fit Severan Libya, for the three new forts are but dots on a notional front of four hundred miles. Rather they were lonely outposts placed to guard routes from the Sahara, just under half-way between the coastal cities and the Fezzan oases; sufficiently far out to cover dry farming on the plateau. The propaganda splash made by these daring locations may have been considerable, but their value was diminished by isolation and circumventability, and they were kept for only sixty years. The three forts are, from east to west: Bu Njem,[15] 85 miles south-west of Sirte; Gheria el Garbia, 170 miles almost due south of Tripoli; and Ghadames, at the convergence of the three countries. Of these the first two were excavated by the Institut d'Archéologie Mediterranéenne en Libye from the late 1960s. Bu Njem (Talalati) is especially interesting. An engraving of 1819 by Capt. G. F. Lyon showed it as one of the empire's best preserved, with arched north gate complete with building inscription and gatetowers surviving to the second storey. A quarter of a century later these were robbed by the Turkish army for its own fort, about a mile distant. Besides a harvest of *ostraca*,[16] clearance of the sand-smothered interior revealed an almost intact bathroom, on a wall of which is a *grafitto* drawing of the fort. This unique sketch shows gate and corner towers as three storeyed, standing high over a wall of perhaps fourteen or fifteen feet. It also shows two spires of unknown purpose rising from within the fort. They are slimmer than the towers and a little shorter. Each is surmounted by what seems to be a cupola: in effect minarets, several centuries before Islam; raising the question of whether the minaret was a pre-Islamic device, perhaps connected with pagan worship within the fort. The army arrived at Bu Njem on 24 January AD 201 and left sometime between 259 and 263.[17] Its garrison, like that of the other two forts, was a detachment of the *III Augusta* legion.

In Chapter 6 we considered floodwater management and how its use had allowed farming to support the African *fossatum* in regions which had never known the plough. Thanks to the growing oil market and to confidence given by the new forts, Tripolitanian agriculture now continued to expand from the four-inch rainfall zone to a southern limit of as little as one inch. This was due less to the techniques used on the *fossatum* (concentrating run-off from large catchments) than to cross-terracing the actual streams and cultivating humid patches in their beds. Prior to the advent of deep boreholes and electric-powered pumping, Roman Tripolitania probably held the all-time record for dry farming achievement. The farms continued to be civilian in character and would remain so until the withdrawal of the three Severan forts obliged these sub-Saharan pioneers to seek some form of self-protection.

Some 500 miles to the west is an even more extreme example of Septimius' forward policy. South-west of Lambaesis, 110 miles beyond the farthest element of the *fossatum Africae*, lie the remains of Castellum Dimmidi (Messad): a hilltop fort of irregular shape and few pretensions, housing perhaps a hundred men. It was built by Anicius Faustus in 198 and evacuated in 235, when expensive gestures were less affordable. It was supported by a lone road with three staging-posts, which may have terminated seventy miles further on at Laghouat. Why were these forts placed so deeply into the Sahara? Perhaps to counter some tribal misdemeanour, or as a demonstration of how far the arm of Rome could stretch. By contrast, along the whole width of Mauretania Caesariensis, the frontier now advances in breadth, from a valley line between coastal range and plateau to a road-and-fort line along the plateau's southern rim. Here, on a 500-mile front across most of today's Algeria, the auxiliary army moved forward some fifty miles to seize the belvedere overlooking the Sahara. This was not a sporadic or short-lived advance, but one which was rational and overdue. Its long postponement reflected the low priority of this cut-price province. Since over twenty forts in the new line now replaced perhaps twelve in the old, we may assume a cash injection on the part of the African emperor. Here, as elsewhere on that continent, Roman tenure now reached its high tide.

Along continental Europe's borders, at this time largely quiet, one development is of interest. We will recall Hadrian's line behind the

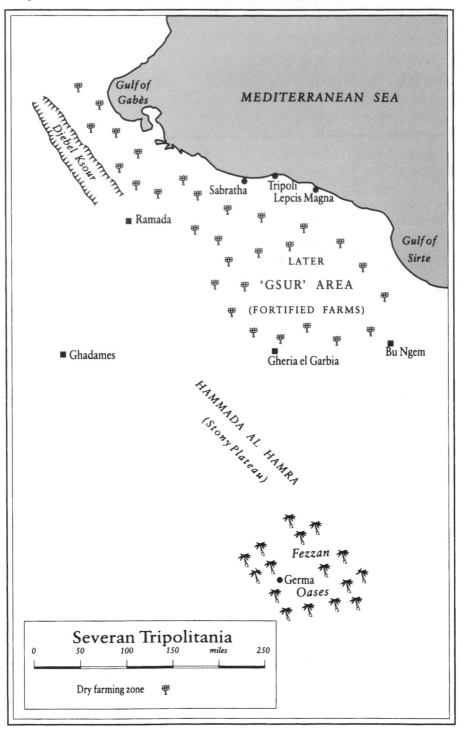

Gulf of Gabès

MEDITERRANEAN SEA

Djebel Ksour

Sabratha

Tripoli
Lepcis Magna

■ Ramada

Gulf of Sirte

LATER

'GSUR' AREA

(FORTIFIED FARMS)

■ Ghadames

Gheria el Garbia

■ Bu Ngem

HAMMADA AL HAMRA
(Stony Plateau)

Fezzan

●Germa
Oases

Severan Tripolitania

0	50	100	150	*miles*	250

Dry farming zone

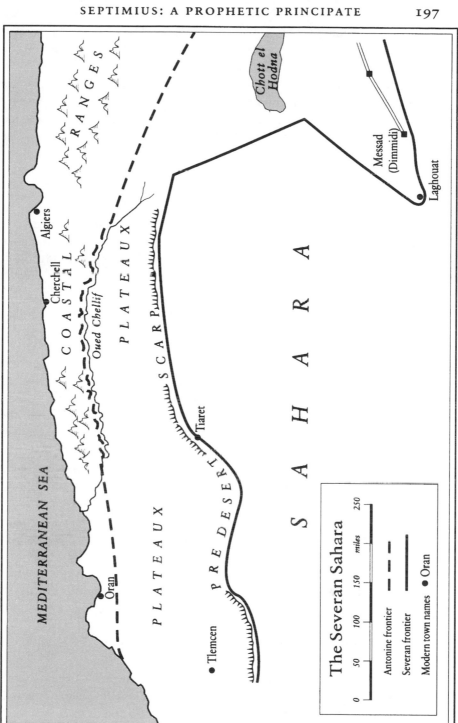

The Severan Sahara

Antonine frontier
Severan frontier
Oran   Modern town names

MEDITERRANEAN SEA

COASTAL RANGES

Algiers
Cherchell
Oued Chellif

PLATEAUX

SCARP

PLATEAUX   PREDESERT

Oran

Tlemcen

Tiaret

SAHARA

Chott el Hodna

Messad (Dimmidi)

Laghouat

miles
0   50   100   150   250

Olt river, which protected the road linking Dacia with the rest of Roman territory. This faced eastwards against Muntenia, the tongue of land between the Lower Danube and the southern Carpathians, rashly ceded to the Rhoxolans. We may also remember the Olt's imperfections. Though the line was shielded by the river, the enemy bank was higher than the Roman, denying the defender a forward view and presenting the attacker with favourable ground. Towns had since developed along this important road, increasing the need for protection. Accordingly, a second line was now built in front of the first. It begins on the Danube at Flamînda, ten miles below the Olt's mouth. For thirty miles it heads north across plain till it picks up the Vedea, the next river east of the Olt. Here the two lines are fifteen miles apart; subsequently they diverge to forty, in obedience to Carpathian landforms. They are known as *limes alutanus* (the Olt frontier) and *limes transalutanus* (the trans-Olt frontier), terms coined by twentieth-century Romanian scholars.

With a total length of 145 miles the new line was a third longer than the old and defended by some eighteen forts to the other's fifteen, of which only three have been thoroughly investigated. The line was surveyed from the air in 1954. Conclusive proof of inception has not been presented, but V. Christescu's pre-war excavation of the Sapata de Jos fort uncovered a hoard in which the earliest coin was Severan. Most now accept this dating. It is probable that the second frontier did not replace the first but that the two acted in unison, an idea supported by the tendency of the stronger parts of the trans-Olt to coincide with the weaker parts of the Olt line.[18] Also the absence of *vici* behind the new forts, or of any trace of civilian occupation between the lines, points to an evacuated zone and to military activity inside it. In sectors unprotected by river or slope, the new line took the form of a mound with palisade. This crosses the Wallachian plain and foothills until reaching the River Vedea. Further north three other short stretches cover vulnerable points. The mound is still visible, standing to 2½ feet. In the last century it was mistaken for the base of a Roman road. Where it is absent the line consisted simply of a road with watchtowers and forts.

The mound is of unusual construction. It could be described as an earth *vallum* with post reinforcement. Early sections revealed two rows of posts about six feet apart buried at the centre of the mound. However a section cut at Rosiorii de Vede in 1981 produced a refinement: two similar rows of posts only two feet apart, but with planks nailed across them to create solid fences. Red soil had been packed into the space between. Black soil had then been dressed on top. Traces of wickerwork led G. Tocilescu to propose that the mound was crowned by a fence.[19] Cataniciu suggests that the red and black earth represent two building phases.[20] Since the red soil is almost certainly a product of bonfires, we may guess at large-scale woodland clearance, intended to create a forward field of view and a treeless zone between the two lines. Presumably this produced substantial amounts of soil which could be used for the mound without need to dig a ditch (the normal way of providing earth). But burnt soil is powdery. It was therefore found necessary to contain it between two fences. Later the work was strengthened and enlarged, using topsoil raked from the surrounding ground. The Trans-Olt Line was never a formidable obstacle. Often on open ground, always without defensive ditch, its forts small and built only of clay and wood, it has the hallmarks of a cheap job. Its lifespan would only be forty years. Both lines collapsed under Carpian attack in 245 and a decision was taken to abandon the trans-Olt position, ploughing all resources into an upgraded version of the original Olt line.

Hadrian's Wall was also rebuilt around this time (AD 205). Eight years earlier the army of Britain had backed the wrong champion and lost at Lyons. It needed time to make good the losses and restore morale. Work was then begun on damaged forts in the Pennines. It was not until the arrival of Alfenus Senecio, Septimius' third governor, that rebuilding inscriptions started to appear on the Wall. This would be a project so radical that Septimius' biographer, writing in the 4th century, attributed the original construction to him, raising a hare which would run for fifteen centuries: 'He fortified Britain with a Wall, which crossed the island from sea to sea. This was counted his greatest achievement and it was for this he accepted the title *Britannicus*.'[21] Measures included the narrowing or closure of milecastle doors, plus turret demolition where field of view made them superfluous. Today the Wall's hilly stretches are so bereft of turrets that many a visitor walks all day without knowing they existed. Under Antoninus, when southern Scotland had been reoccupied, the *Vallum* had been slighted by digging gaps every 45 yards through both mounds, the earth being used to make causeways across the ditch. No attempt at restoration was now made, suggesting that this questionable work was now discarded entirely.

Most important was the rebuilding of the Wall itself, sometimes

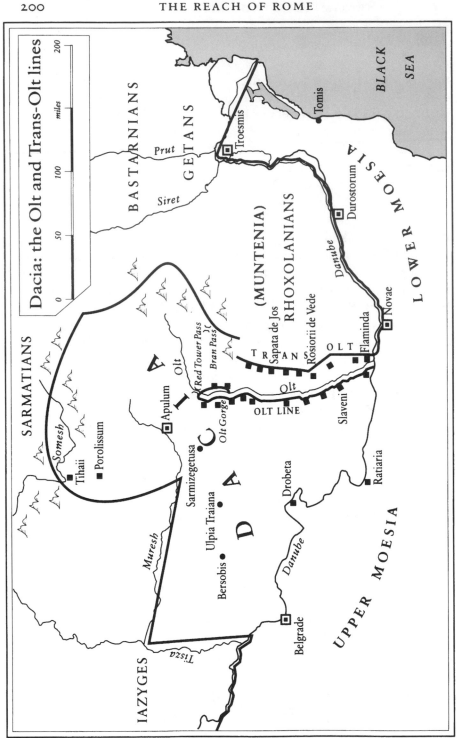

Dacia: the Olt and Trans-Olt lines

miles

0   50   100   200

BLACK SEA

BASTARNIANS

GETANS

Prut

Siret

Tomis

Troesmis

LOWER MOESIA

Durostorum

Danube

(MUNTENIA)

RHOXOLANIANS

Novae

Sapata de Jos

Rosiorii de Vede

Flaminda

TRANS   OLT

Red Tower Pass

Bran Pass

SARMATIANS

DACIA

Olt

Olt

OLT LINE

Slaveni

Apulum

Olt Gorge

Somesh

Porolissum

Sarmizegetusa

Ratiaria

Tihaii

Ulpia Traiana

Drobeta

Muresh

Bersobis

Danube

UPPER MOESIA

Tisza

Belgrade

IAZYGES

in toto. Was this because of destruction by the Britons, when Albinus stripped the Wall of its defenders to make his bid for the throne? Or was it because of defects in the original building, eighty years earlier? It is unlikely that a tribal revolt would have the discipline for a systematic demolition requiring weeks of hard work, when there were empty forts to be ransacked and defenceless towns beyond. The front-heavy specification of the facing stones, the over-reliance on a mortar-bonded core and the use of poor-quality lime may already have revealed themselves as underlying culprits. Nevertheless, though the rebuilders made every effort to improve the binding-power of their mortar by seeking the best available limestone, they made no attempt to recut the stones or restructure the fabric. This would doubtless have been beyond Senecio's means. The scale of effort already made guaranteed that in essentials Hadrian's works would stand. His *Vallum* was too big to flatten, and thirty million facing stones dictated their own terms. It was in any case soon apparent that Senecio was working in an atmosphere of growing menace. Before long he was forced to call on the centre for help, 'because of a barbarian rising, accompanied by much looting and destruction'.[22] With the emperor's decision to intervene in person, Britain returns to the forefront of events.

The peaks of Septimius' imperial effort were two external wars. Both involved expeditions and both were among Rome's last attempts to extend the frontiers. The first had been Mesopotamia; the second, at the very end of his reign, was Britain. It is surprising that the emperor, sixty-two and with severe gout, should decide to take command of a campaign into Europe's most inclement corner; and also that he should wish to be accompanied by the empress Julia and their two teenage sons. It is not as if the old warhorse intended to await events in London. On the contrary, he would be carried by litter far into Scotland, possibly as far as Agricola had penetrated 125 years earlier, and on a campaign of comparable privation. Nor is it known why he should intend (as Dio makes clear) to enlarge the empire northwards, while his governor was restoring Hadrian's Wall. Was Dio mistaken on this score? The legionary base now set up at Carpow on the Tay does not suggest a short stay. Excavation has revealed the massive masonry of its central buildings, where the imperial family was presumably housed. Coin issues of 208 and 209 show bridges, one of boats the other permanent. At this point the Tay estuary is a thousand yards wide.[23] The fortress, of which little is visible, lay on the south bank about twelve miles below Perth. It was first recognised in 1783 but not seriously excavated until 1961.

The party must also have been accompanied by at least a four-legion equivalent army, probably composed of Danubian and Rhenish detachments. The enemy consisted of two formidable confederacies. The Maeatae, whose name survives in placenames like Dumyat and Myot Hill (Stirlingshire),[24] appear to have been from the south-central Highlands; the Caledonii from further north. The appearance of new tribal names, increasingly common, may be explained by the formation of coalitions rather than the arrival of peoples:

> In (north) Britain there are two main ethnic groups: the Caledonians and the Maeatae, into both of which many tribal names have been submerged. The Maeatae are near the (Antonine) wall which cuts Britain in half, the Caledonians beyond them. Both live among wild, dry hills and dreary, wet valleys. They know neither towns, (permanent) dwellings, nor agriculture; but tend flocks, hunt and pick berries. They live in light or temporary huts, go naked and unshod, and are polygamous. They are formidable raiders and choose the boldest men to be their chieftains. They are hardy and can hide indefinitely in swamps or forests.
>
> Such is the general character of this people, at least in the hostile part of the island, which measures overall 951 miles in length, 308 in greatest width and whose narrowest neck is 40 miles. Just under half is in Roman hands.
>
> Septimius, wishing to conquer it all, invaded Caledonia, but met great setbacks in the shape of mountain, swamp and stream. He could never bring the enemy to battle. His soldiers were lured off course and were picked off if they lagged behind. The wounded were slain by our own men rather than be taken alive. At least 50,000 died. Yet Septimius persisted till he approached the very end of the island, forcing the Britons to surrender and cede much territory. Having been carried most of the way by litter, he then returned to the friendly portion.[25]

Severan marching camps can usually be distinguished from Flavian in shape and size. They suggest two seasons' march and the trail goes cold within a few miles of the Moray Firth. The advance seems tamely similar to that of Agricola; and so was the reason for its

outcome. Complete conquest would not be achieved without a fortress in the Inverness region and the boldness to overwinter there.
Restarting each spring from Forth or Tay meant summer would never
be long enough. Nonetheless we may guess that all of southern,
central and north-eastern Scotland was now in Roman hands: not
quite the target Septimius had set, but a compromise which a first-
hand view of the terrain had made acceptable.

The imperial family now retired south of Hadrian's Wall where,
winterbound in York, the emperor watched helplessly as treaties were
scrapped and conquests collapsed behind him. He swore revenge,
haranguing his soldiers to prepare for a third season and a general
massacre. But this was the pit of the year and the emperor weakening
daily. He died in the fortress at York on 4 February 211. On his
deathbed he asked to see the urn which would bear his ashes back
to Rome, saying to it, 'You will hold a man the world could not
hold.'[26] Then he called for his sons, to whom he gave advice almost
as portentous as Augustus' posthumous *consilium* of two centuries
earlier:

Be good brothers; grease the army's palm; and to hell with the
rest.[27]

Like Commodus, Caracalla and Geta would abandon their father's
struggle and return to Rome. It seems rulers now reversed their
predecessors' policies automatically. But the start-stop game was
almost over. Roman weakness would henceforward forbid expansion. With small exceptions Septimius had produced Rome's last
frontiers of advance. Other lines will be drawn, but these will largely
be frontiers of retreat, marks left by a withdrawing tide.

Hadrian's Wall, though again triumphant, still would not function
as Hadrian had imagined. Fingertip control, with all eyes straining
toward the skyline, with hundreds of hands ready to light the signal
torches and thousands of men and horses eager to burst forth from the
front gates: these were Hadrianic fancies which had probably never
materialised. Rather the Wall continues as a peacetime frontier against
infiltrators, but with its wartime functions modified. It is now seen
as a startline for the forward patrolling of southern Scotland. This is
supported by the fact that two of Hadrian's three western outposts and
two Antonine forts on Dere Street were kept open. There is also the
evidence of the *loci* (meeting places). Describing the terms imposed on

the Marcomanns, Dio told us that 'he (Commodus) ordered them not
to assemble in a random or spontaneous manner, but monthly, at a
stipulated place and in the presence of a Roman officer [. . .]'[28] The
Antonine Itinerary gives eight *loci* north of Hadrian's Wall: supposedly moots, where Roman officials powwowed with the tribes. With
some ingenuity Ian Richmond deciphered five, for example proposing
the *locus Maponi* as Lochmaben (Dumfriesshire) and the *locus Manavi*
as Clackmannan. The theory envisages southern Scotland as a protectorate, undisturbed till the appearance of another dangerous confederacy, the Picts, in about AD 300.

With Septimius, the Principate deserts the toga-clad image of the
man of culture and moves towards that of the military strongman.
Though only three or four decades removed from Antoninus and
Marcus this is a transformation, more than fad or fashion, that points
towards profound changes in Roman civilisation. In this it resembles
the twentieth century which, within the same span, saw a shift from
heads-of-state in top hats and wing collars to men in fatigue caps
and battledress.

Like Mussolini, Septimius marched on Rome. He packed the
Guard with his own men. He doubled its size to 10,000. He recruited
a new legion, *II Parthica*, and placed it meaningfully at Albanum,
only fourteen miles from the Tiber. This gave him the equivalent of
three legions, centrally stationed: unknown for two centuries since
Augustus had dismissed the army from the Italian scene. He cowed
the Senate. He put down *coups d'état* cruelly, though he himself had
led one. He made numerous and harsh confiscations. He increased
the soldiers' pay by 40% and debased the silver currency by 50%.
He regularised the corn levy, creating in effect an empire-wide tax
for the army's support. He was the first to allow soldiers to marry
during their period of service. Even so his measures made little contribution to their family life, for he uprooted armies for his wars on a
scale not seen since Trajan. Forts became smaller. Projecting towers
and gateways began to appear at last. Many of his measures and
characteristics (sternness, fiscal severity, military dictatorship, the
increased status of the soldier, the diminution of the civilian, the
creation of a central reserve, mobility, smaller and stronger forts)
are pointers to the future. Septimius is prophetic of a less civilian,
less civilised age. Only in its confidence does his reign recall the past.
But it was late to be an expander of empire; a Trajan, when Trajan
himself had been too late.

The brothers returned to Rome, where Caracalla arranged for Geta's murder. His name was then erased from every monument in the empire, as if the chisel undid the deed. In character Caracalla[29] resembled his father, though with instability and megalomania thrown in. He established a reign of terror, toadied to the army and fraternised with the rank and file. Soldiers were now treated to a further 50% pay rise and the coinage again debased. To find money he devised the *Constitutio Antoniana* of 212, under which all free subjects of the empire were granted citizenship. Though a genuine step in social evolution, its object was to broaden the tax base. It also removed an incentive to enlist in the auxiliary army, where service had been rewarded by citizenship, encouraging the recruitment of barbarians and even criminals instead. Caracalla is said to have bribed the barbarians with handouts equal to the salary of the entire army. Henceforward the 'fix' of buying peace would deepen into addiction; for as Kipling reminds us, 'once you have paid him the Danegeld/You will never get rid of the Dane'. Dio sourly notes: 'He gave gold to the Germans and plated coin to the Romans; for the so-called silver coins were now lead, washed with silver; and the gold were gilded copper.'[30]

The Rhine front now began to rumble. The south German tribes were merging into the Alamannic coalition. In 213 Caracalla was obliged to sally from the Raetian frontier and march north to the upper Main, where he defeated them. Near the village of Dalkingen, at the western end of the Raetian *limes*, are the remains of a ceremonial gateway. It was excavated in 1885 but its significance was not then understood. Re-examined in 1973, it was found to be a normal frontier gate consisting of an entrance passage flanked by guard chambers, giving access to and from barbarian Germany. Fifty fragments of a huge, bronze statue, believed to be of Caracalla, lay around. It is assumed that this is where his expedition left or re-entered imperial territory. The gate is now part of the Raetian Limes Open Air Museum, Rainau, which includes the nearby fort of Buch, plus a *Limes Lehrpad* (educational footpath) leading to a reconstructed watchtower and short frontier stretch at Mahdholz. This is forty miles east of Stuttgart and five north of Aalen, a town which takes its name from the *ala* (cavalry wing) once stationed there. The headquarters building of Aalen fort is on display and there is an excellent museum in St Johann Strasse, with local finds shown in a wide context.

The Alamannic disturbances led to a further strengthening of the Rhine–Danube overland frontier. In its Raetian or eastern half the palisade was removed and replaced by a stone wall, linking the watchtowers and abutted to them. This may have been inspired by Hadrian's Wall, but if so it was rather less imposing: perhaps nine or ten feet tall and scarcely more than two wide, built of undressed stone, mortared, with flat capping stones. There is no question of its being broad enough for a sentry walk. Its proportions resembled what we might now call a park wall, surrounding an estate. A rebuilt section is on display at the above-mentioned Mahdholz. In English, it is called the Raetian Wall, locally known in the Middle Ages as the *Teufelsmauer* (Devil's Wall), a name still sometimes used. As Gibbon drolly summarised: 'The scattered ruins, universally ascribed to the power of the daemon, now serve only to excite the wonder of the Swabian peasant.'[31] The wall's remains can be traced across the Bavarian countryside as a line of tumbled masonry, sometimes overgrown with a hedge. It is generally better preserved in its eastern half, for example in the Raitenbuch area, southeast of Weissenburg and northwest of Eichstätt. It descends to the Danube some twenty miles west of Regensburg, near the village of Hienheim, where traces of wall are visible on both sides of the road and a reconstructed watchtower stands.

Like Hadrian's and the Antonine Wall, the Raetian was probably built from east to west,[32] ending at Lorch, where Upper Germany began. There, a short time later, corresponding improvements were put in hand. Throughout the frontier's entire length, between Lorch and the Rhine, palisade and watchtowers were left intact but a linear feature, consisting of ditch with mound, was inserted between them. The ditch, about eight feet deep, was dug immediately behind the palisade and the soil thrown up to make a ridge of similar height. The German name is *Pfahlgraben* (palisade ditch), a term which seems to include both ditch and mound. In most stretches it is the main surviving feature. A reconstructed section with palisade, ditch, mound and stone watchtower is located near the remains of Zugmantel fort, about ten miles north-north-west of Wiesbaden.[33]

Lorch is the only place in the empire where an overland frontier of barrier type crossed from one province to another; and it is interesting that the governors of Raetia and Upper Germany should have chosen different ways to reinforce it. We must remember, however, that the two frontiers had spent most of their history unjoined, with

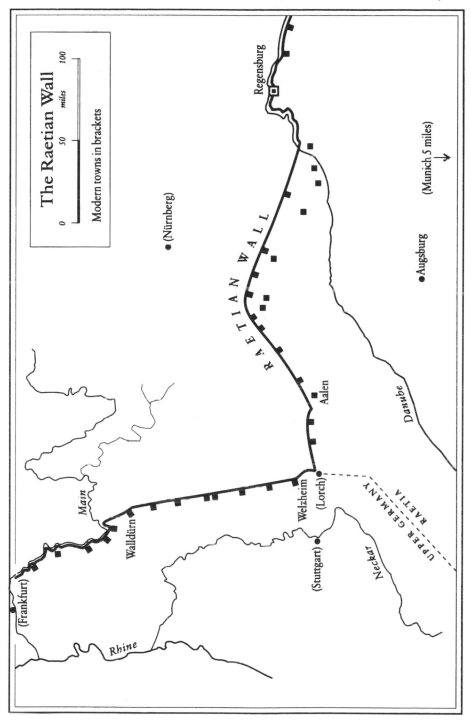

The Raetian Wall

Modern towns in brackets

0   50   100
    miles

Regensburg

(Nürnberg)

(Munich 5 miles)
→

Augsburg

RAETIAN WALL

Danube

Aalen

Welzheim
(Lorch)

Walldürn

UPPER GERMANY
RAETIA

(Stuttgart)

Neckar

Main

(Frankfurt)

Rhine

ample time for differences to develop. Frontier building began at Upper Germany's northern end, where the universality of trees and the need to clear them created a distinct tradition into which Hadrian's idea of a palisade more naturally fitted. Nevertheless, the contrast between wall and *Pfahlgraben* suggests how much was left to provincial discretion. Here it seems that frontier strengthening was ordered by Rome, but the details were worked out in Regensburg and Mainz. The Rhine–Danube overland frontier had now reached its final form.

Like Trajan, though less stable, Caracalla began to see himself as Alexander the Great. As ever the Parthian path promised greatest glory. Here the father had won the title *Parthicus Maximus*, and the son wanted nothing less. In 214 Caracalla crossed the Tigris but was stalemated by the Parthians; though not before he had reached Arbela, opened the tombs of their kings and scattered the bones. Two contradictory obsessions were growing in his mind: to be a great general and conqueror of the orient; and to be a common soldier and march with the men. He became increasingly hallucinatory, with visions of his father and brother hounding him with swords. He was assassinated in April 217 in an officers' plot. Caracalla was succeeded by a Syrian youth, Elagebalus or Heliogabalus, a nephew of Julia Domna, who worshipped the sun, was a sex maniac and who, after a three-year reign, was murdered by the Praetorians and thrown into the Tiber. Another nephew followed: Severus Alexander, fourteen years old and dominated by his remarkable mother, Julia Mamaea. A stable decade ensued, but fateful events were emerging in the east. Mortifying defeats, at the hands of Avidius Cassius and Septimius Severus, had fatally weakened the standing of the Parthian kings. Now they were tottering toward collapse. In 224 Ardashir, first of a new dynasty, grabbed the helm.

The Parthian state had endured for almost five centuries. A border people like the Manchu in China, the Parthians had learned mounted warfare from the steppe and seized power on the heels of Alexander's disintegrating dominions. But as outsiders they seldom commanded the loyalty of the Persians in the south and centre. These looked back wistfully to the age of the Achaemenids: great kings, whose mastery of the world between Indus and Aegean almost led to the extinguishing of 5th-century Athens. Rome had long profited from Parthian disunity. It would now be replaced by Persian resolve. In 230 Ardashir attacked Roman Mesopotamia. Either the Sinjar line was breached, the Tigris crossed or both. Roman forces contracted to the centre, where Nisibis held. Severus Alexander, now twenty and with his mother still in tow, assembled an army, hurried east and relieved the siege. Ardashir had acted prematurely, without allowing time to consolidate his strength. It was the last feather in the cap of the Severan dynasty and the last victory of the early Roman empire.

While the army was preoccupied in Mesopotamia, the Alamanni made a surprise attack near the eastern end of the Raetian Wall and obliterated the fort at modern-day Pfünz, probably in a single night. Dramatic evidence was found at the south gate. Shield bosses, in one of its guard rooms, suggested by their position that the sentries did not have time to arm themselves. Their skeletons lay in the adjacent room among charred debris. Coins were scattered where someone was cut down before being able to hide them. It would not be many years before the Alamanni would be back in greater strength.

Three years after his victory at Nisibis the young emperor was in Mainz facing another Alamannic crisis, when a mutiny was sparked by his use of the war chest to bribe Germans rather than pay Romans. In the ensuing riots he and his mother were murdered. Worse was imminent; so much worse that the death of Severus Alexander is generally accepted as the end of the early empire and the beginning of the late. Not because of the murder itself – few have even heard of it – but because there now followed Rome's descent into a different kind of empire, with a different sort of army and a different quality of life. 'After Septimius' death his sons brought no good to the state; and after them, when invaders swept in from all directions, the empire became a battered barque for any pirate to plunder.'[34] However, a buffeting from the barbarians will not alone explain the plight of 3rd-century Rome, whose ills were, in the language of modern medicine, as much systemic as traumatic.

CHAPTER 9

Frontiers of Retreat

In Paris, on 16 May 1940, a British delegation was being briefed on the ominous German breakthrough at Sedan. The commander-in-chief spoke for some minutes.

> When he stopped there was a considerable silence. I then asked: 'Where is the strategic reserve?' and breaking into French, which I used indifferently: 'Où est la masse de manoeuvre?' General Gamelin turned to me and, with a shake of his head and a shrug, said 'Aucune' (there is none).[1]

Late antiquity is a formative and fascinating era. And yet (if a theatrical image may be forgiven) the later empire has seldom played to packed houses. Its plot is dispiriting and the curtain falls on a thousand-year setback. Even the friendliest historian finds the transformation from early to late a curiously dislocating, almost surreal experience. It has been compared to a train journey in which we enter a long tunnel. When we emerge we are in a different country.[2] The simile is apt, for the tunnel not only expresses the bewilderment of egress, but also the loss of touch due to the absence of written sources during transit. It is an absence which reminds us of the early years of the Marcomannic War. This time, however, the informational blackout is longer and the change springs upon us unexplained, after a knowledge gap of fifty years.

What is the nature of the land beyond the tunnel, into which we blinkingly emerge? An inkling of the extent of change may be had from late Roman art, for example the sculptural group built into the front of St Mark's Cathedral, Venice, consisting of four men in military dress, carved in porphyry. For centuries no one believed it Roman. The scowling, dumpy figures are so 'medieval' they were taken for crusaders. Coin portraits are comparable. Fluency and charm are gone. Emperors have become men in battledress, with set jaw and fixed intensity of stare.

What happened, while we were in the tunnel, to transform ways of seeing so abruptly that artworks seem the product of a different age; especially in a state which we have shown as conservative and exceptionally slow to change? Modern analogies, like the difference between Czarist and Bolshevik art, point to exceptional events such as revolutionary trauma and wartime defeat. In Rome's case defeat was not in pitched battles. The nature of imperial defence makes it likelier to have taken the form of at least partial frontier collapse, accompanied by internal convulsion.

The most revealing record is numismatic: new coins for new emperors following one another with gruesome rapidity; not to mention reigns too short even to complete the minting arrangements. The lynching of Severus Alexander at Mainz in 235 inaugurated fifty years of military anarchy and high-level butchery during which emperors, pretenders and usurpers averaged one a year. The tally of those who actually seized the prize is twenty-one, giving an average reign of under three years. The period's characteristics were an army out of control, *coup d'état*, civil war, barbarian invasion and frontier disintegration: a convergence of ills between the years 235 and 285 known as the Third-century Crisis.

Though living sedately on, the city of Rome now lost her ancient sway. It mattered little what the Senate said or who the mob might favour. Emperors were made and unmade on the frontiers. Of an army now numbering thirty-three legions, fourteen were on the Danube. So the Danubian soldiery became the arbiters of empire. The emperors they chose were of their own kind: tough, rough and professional. Largely from the Balkan provinces they became known as the *Illyriciani*. In reaction to these ugliest of times the new strongmen surrounded themselves with big bodyguards, so instigating a profound change in army composition. Two centuries of emperors banishing their soldiers from the centre gave way to a reverse process, in which warlords gathered their men about them like a cloak.

What happened to the frontier during these desperate days? Archaeology tells of massive break-ins and we may take it that garrisons were wiped out or brushed aside. Not all frontiers buckled. Britain and North Africa were almost untouched by the crisis. But in general we must assume failures so grave that they led to the demotion of the armed perimeter from an exclusive shield to one component among several in the empire's defensive system. The mid- to late 3rd century therefore marks an end of the imperial frontier in its fullest meaning: as Rome's sole protection and her only sphere of military deployment. This does not however mean that the fortified frontier will disappear. Nor should it imply that a more rational approach to military matters will dominate the later Roman scene. On the contrary, frontier policy will be more than ever subject to the inconstancies of the caesars, for the idea of a strategic reserve introduces a new set of variables into the defensive equation.

At last the tide of war was turning in the barbarians' favour. By the end of the previous century some tribes had achieved confederacy. Now confederacies were beginning to work together and all had learned to recognise where Roman weakness lay. In the orient the accession of Shapur I quickened Persian confidence. Danger flared at both ends of the Danube. But the deadliest damage was to Gaul. While Illyrican eyes were on their native Danube, the Rhine, almost three centuries quiescent, detonated along its entire front. Fortunes touched bottom around 260. In that year an emperor was captured in Persia and the overland frontier was abandoned in Germany, neither to be redeemed. Then, like bees at the first sign of summer, two large groups of provinces hived off and sought separate destinies: simultaneous disasters at opposite ends of an empire requiring weeks to cross.

Shapur I, known to the Romans as Sapor or Saansaan (a soldiers' version of *shah 'n shah*), succeeded Ardashir in AD 241. His thirty-year reign would coincide with those of sixteen Roman emperors. At his coronation he adopted the menacing title 'King of Kings, King of Iran and Beyond Iran'. In attempting to contain his three attacks Gordian III was killed, Valerian taken prisoner and Philip the Arab forced to sign a demeaning treaty. The second, in 256, cost Rome thirty-seven cities, including Dura Europus, whose survivors were deported and enslaved. A Roman army came upon the site some ninety years later.[3] It was totally desolate and would remain so. As ever these were wars of siege whose outcome depended on a few strongholds. Such cities, into which refugees and reinforcements invariably flowed, served as foci for Persian anger and so proved deathtraps. Singara and Nisibis fell and with them most of Roman Mesopotamia. In the last of three campaigns Valerian was captured while attempting to relieve Edessa (Urfa, Turkey). Shapur used him as a mounting block. At Bishapur ('the place of Shapur'), near Shiraz, are two cliff-carved reliefs. In one, Gordian's body lies beneath the hooves of the king's horse. The other shows Philip the Arab kneeling in supplication while an exultant Shapur holds Valerian by the wrist. Gallienus, Valerian's son and heir, made no attempt at ransom. Tradition has it that, when all propaganda value had been wrung from the incident, Valerian was sent to labour with other prisoners on a barrage, whose remains are still called Band-i-Qaysar ('Caesar's Dam').[4] He died in captivity.

Finally Shapur took the war 500 miles westward by invading Asia Minor and Syria. Antioch, 'a city known the world over and without rival',[5] was twice sacked. Nevertheless Shapur's booty-burdened army was defeated on its return journey by a Roman–Palmyran combination, assisted by the garrison of Hatra, which had managed to hold out. His final treaty (with Probus) involved the partition of Armenia, with Rome receiving the smaller share. Rome was also obliged to accept a partitioned Mesopotamia. The Jebel Sinjar frontier together with its pivot, Singara, and the capital, Nisibis, were abandoned and the front line became the Khabur for the entirety of its course.

In Europe the Goths were pressing against Dacia. We have noted that their allies or subjects, the Carpians, severed the two Olt lines in 245. Roman Transylvania, its tendon now cut, limped on for another twenty-five years. Junta politics then drew the Pannonian army to Italy, provoking a Gothic invasion under King Kniva and a Roman defeat at Abrittus (Bulgaria). This – and the inability to maintain the road link into Transylvania – led to a decision to abandon the Dacian province without a fight. It had been 165 years since Trajan's conquest. In 260 the Rhine–Danube overland *limes*, its garrison emaciated by calls from other quarters, fell to attack by the Alamannic king, Chrocus.

Though it is sometimes prudent to give ground and buy time, these retreats created bigger problems than they solved. Loss of Dacia meant a 350-mile frontage of the Serbian–Bulgarian Danube was exposed anew, with its four rundown fortresses and dozens of lesser installations neglected almost beyond redemption. It was not just a matter of clearing weeds. Ingrowing civilian settlements had engulfed their mother forts. The Oescus and Novae bases had become fifteen-acre cities. All were now defenceless. The population of the lost province required resettlement; and to maintain the fiction of a Dacia still Roman a new province, Riverbank Dacia (Dacia Ripensis), was created out of Moesia. Rome would never return to the Carpathians.

Loss of the Rhine–Danube overland *limes* had consequences even more grievous. It exposed an L-shaped salient of 500-mile length, from Coblenz southwards to Basle and from Basle eastwards to Regensburg. The Upper Rhine defences had lapsed totally, opening a wide door into southeastern Gaul. The Alpine front was equally bereft and the passes to Italy lay open. A new line was urgently needed to keep the Germans out of what is now Switzerland. It would be based on Lake Constance. The lake is a sizeable barrier, ten miles wide. However it covers only a small part of the gap. Most of the protection would be from rivers of only medium width, though with strong currents. More explicitly, the new frontier would follow the Upper Rhine eastwards to Constance; the lake's southern shore to Bregenz (Brigantium); then twenty-five miles across open country to the Iller; and finally northwards to the Iller's junction with the Danube (at today's Ulm). This is a total of 250 miles of which the eastern half was entirely new as an imperial boundary. Proximity to Italy (barely seventy-five miles) would at any other time have guaranteed priority. However, archaeology tells of no fort construction for twenty years, throughout which time only scratch units and makeshift barricades stood between wildest Germany and the empire's heart. Luckily for Italy, Gaul was a tempting target too – and even closer. Chrocus lunged westwards across the Rhine into the Saarland and Lorraine. Whole communities were now expunged, like Schwarzenacher[6] ('black acre'), named for the charred soil of town and fields.

Seizing the moment, the Frankish confederation rolled across the river into Lower Germany whose governor, M. C. Latinius Postumus, surprised them with a rebuke so sharp that his delighted legions declared him emperor. Lent wings by the knowledge that the *Illyriciani* – who had done nothing to help him – could now do nothing to stop him, Postumus gathered Gaul, Spain and Britain to his cause and proclaimed the Gallic empire. At his capital, Trier (Augusta Treverorum) on the Moselle, he set up his own civil service, mint, Praetorian guard and senate. Though over two thousand miles away, this was a signal Queen Zenobia could understand. Rome owed

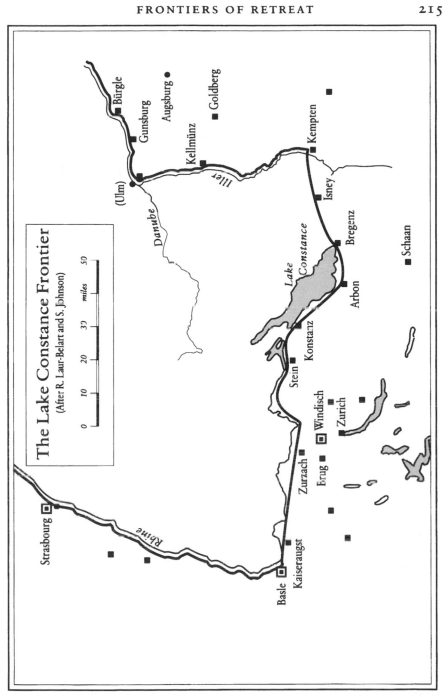

The Lake Constance Frontier
(After R. Laur-Belart and S. Johnson)

miles
0 10 20 30 50

much to Palmyra, antiquity's leading exponent of desert warfare and lynchpin of the Syrian *limes*. But Zenobia had fought enough of Rome's battles and considered Palmyra's puppetry demeaning. She is said to have been as beautiful as her ancestress Cleopatra and events would show her twice as bold. With the Illyricans enmeshed in Europe, her Lilliputian army annexed Syria. She then switched southwards, demolishing *Legio III Cyrenaica* at Bostra and not stopping till she had seized the cornfields of Lower Egypt. An empire-wide disintegration was at hand. And yet professionalism would prevail. The *Illyriciani*, their minds concentrated by assassination as the almost certain price of failure, began to win battles. In 269 the Goths came back, crossing into the disorganised province of Dacia Ripensis. Claudius II, thereafter named *Gothicus*, in a series of swift marches through the central Balkans, gave them at Naissus (Nish), 'such a lesson in the art of war as Scipio or Caesar might have inflicted'.[7]

His successor, Aurelian (270–75), a Balkan officer of humble background, succeeded him at fifty years of age. Known as *manu ad ferrum* ('hand on hilt') he would earn the title *restitutor orbis* ('restorer of the world'). He defeated a Vandalic invasion of Pannonia then, turning to the east, snatched back Syria, bribed the bedouin to help his army across eighty miles of desert, took Palmyra and deposed Zenobia. Half-way home, news of a second rebellion overtook him. Retracing his steps, he destroyed Palmyra so completely that (until its rediscovery in 1678 by two English merchants trading in Aleppo) it was thought a place of legend or fancy. Nevertheless, in terms of Rome's desert frontier, this was a Pyrrhic victory. A substitute for in-depth surveillance by camel-mounted Palmyrans would in due course have to be found; and inevitably it would be costly. Aurelian returned to square accounts with the Gallic empire, defeating Postumus' successor Tetricus near Châlons-sur-Marne. Tetricus and Zenobia walked in his Triumph after which, with a magnanimity rare in that ungracious century, both were pensioned off. Aurelian's achievements, amazing in five years, were repaid by murder. Probus (276–82) repulsed the Vandals yet again and redeemed Gaul from a second Alamannic attack. This is thought to be the time when *allemand*, meaning 'German', entered the French vocabulary.

So within a few years Rome, though battered, was answering to a single helm. A decade later Britain would again cut loose when Carausius, a renegade naval officer, seized power in the final gamble of 3rd-century separatism. But this would prove less damaging than events in Gaul, where the general improvement came too late to prevent further and almost fatal Frankish and Alamannic attacks. The century's last decades saw the Gallic interior gutted from end to end. According to the *Augustan History* Probus was obliged to retake seventy cities.[8] More coin hoards and buried treasures are now found than in any previous period. The trowel tells us that a third of villages in northeastern Gaul ceased to exist.[9] A new word enters Latin, *bacaudae* or *bagaudae*: deserters, bands of refugees, victims of destruction or of crime; the ruined, desperate and destitute; roaming the countryside and living by banditry.

In tandem with this grim spectacle, inflation pressed at the empire's windpipe. While pretenders fought each other they bought off the barbarian with gold. This, together with the loss of Dacia's mines and a doubling of military commitments, led to progressive coin debasement, the use of metallic washes over copper, the disappearance of gold and the collapse of the so-called silver currency. By 301 prices had risen, relative to the 2nd century, at least two hundredfold. Soldiers' wages were becoming worthless when their loyalty was most crucial. There was no alternative but to pay them in rations, weapons and clothing. When armies came to assist the devastated areas food, fodder, horses, wagons, billets and clothing had all to be requisitioned, further ruining the ruined.

The *raison d'être* of the *limes* had been to make the empire so generally safe that no part required defences of its own. But from the moment of frontier breakdown, all else was found wanting. Roads and bridges were at the enemy's disposal, grain awaited him in the granaries, country folk had no hiding place, farms and estates were helpless and towns defenceless. In particular there was an almost total absence of city walls. As Herodian said of Aquileia: 'The ancient walls had been demolished. Since Roman rule began the Italian cities had no need of them. They enjoyed lasting peace and the benefits of citizenship. Now there was no choice but to restore the wall, to rebuild its towers and battlements from their former foundations.'[10] Some seventy cities in Gaul, a similar number in Italy, possibly as many on the Danube and in Thrace, forty in Spain, perhaps 300 in all, had now to be walled as a consequence of one wall's failure: the wall of forts and men which for two and a half centuries had shielded, lulled and finally failed the Roman people.

The effort was immense and its effects lasting, shaping defensive thinking for a thousand years and setting the pattern of Europe's cities until the invasion of the motor vehicle. True to form, the building wave is almost unrecorded. Urgency is implied by the re-used masonry. Column drums, capitals, bases and cornices; fragments of friezes, architraves, mouldings and scrollwork; sculptural details and parts of wellheads and fountains; milestones, millstones, tombstones, and altars: all manner of functional and decorative stonework, torn from temples, baths, *fora*, cemeteries, roads and thrown into foundations and walls in a fit of uncaring. The rush to build city walls and the universal disregard for past monuments suggest a deep psychological change, an adieu to a nobler era of which shattered, frightened cities no longer felt part. The walls are more advanced in terms of tower, gate and structural design than their military counterparts, and were probably built by civilian contractors. It seems that civilians, less hidebound by tradition, now led and the army followed. Nonetheless, advances on Hellenistic practice were few. With the exception of concrete techniques (notably construction by means of successive levels poured within wooden shuttering), nothing was now done in the western provinces that had not been on display in the eastern for five centuries.

The Germans still sought booty rather than vantage. Their strategy was raid and return rather than stay and settle. Their trump card was mobility and they were loath to throw it away by carrying ladders or battering-rams. Similarly, they seldom encumbered themselves with reserves of food and fodder. It followed that, if livestock and farm produce could be withheld by bringing it into walled towns, the invaders would in due course face starvation and withdraw. They must also be denied the road system. All key facilities must be defended. It was a time of fortified farms and even walled estates. In Pannonia these, plus walled towns and defended enclosures for peasants and animals, constituted a strong defensive zone based on Lake Balaton, which Hungarian scholars have called a second frontier. About a dozen of its sites survive, of which Fenekpuszta is best known.

Of all developments none has more pathos than the rural refuges. Three centuries earlier, in the process called *deductio in plana*, the army was bringing Celts and others down from their hilltops and onto the plain, out of prehistory and into history. Now, heavy with symbolism, the hillforts began to be reopened and reoccupied. The *pax Romana* was ebbing; the iron age, with its fear and pessimism, flowing back.

Between Rhine and France proper a tangle of hill and forest is variously known as the Ardennes, Eifel, Hunsrück, Saarland, Pfalz and Vosges. It is ambiguous country, where geography and history hesitate. Only at the Meuse does an unmistakably French character prevail. In the late 3rd century, though clearly a danger area, this wild region offered consolations of concealment denied to the open country beyond. Here, as in all Europe's uplands, from the bronze age onwards, nameless thousands had been busy with their basket-loads of soil, shaping countless summits to protective purpose. Some of these had been spurs or saddles, approached via a causeway or neck of land. It was this type, above all in places well concealed from the invasion corridors, that was now redeemed from the nettles and brambles of the peaceful centuries. Such sites could be strength-ened at modest cost by the insertion of a blocking wall with gateway. This is a hallmark of the late Roman refuge, though interior build-ings, usually of rough and ready character, are also found. Some have traces of a troop detachment or even a military cemetery.

Such were the hiding places where country people, with their live-stock, produce and provender, could await the passing of the German storm. About a hundred are known in the French–Belgian–Luxembourg–German borderlands, of which perhaps 10% have been dug. They are mentioned in the letters of a 5th-century Gallo-Roman senator, Sidonius Apollinaris, who calls them *montana castella* (mountain forts),[11] later known as *Heidenburgen* (heathen castles) or more recently *Fliehburgen* (refuges). They are frequent along the Alpine rim, from the Franco-Swiss Jura, through today's Zurich–Lucerne area, then eastwards to Liechtenstein, the Vorarlberg and Carnatic Alps. In the Tirol and other areas entire towns and villages were evacuated to hilltops, where their chapels are still objects of pilgrimage. Above the river Drau (Drava) near today's Villach and Klagenfurt, many sites with military buildings have led Austrian colleagues to propose a late Roman Drau *limes*, in effect an outer screen for the defence of north-eastern Italy.[12] Spain too is rich in refuges, particularly near the upper Douro and its tributaries. None exists in Britain, or is yet proven.

Though the *Fliehburgen* may have been reopened under army supervision, some have yielded purely civilian remains. It is therefore possible that assistance was given by local landowners; but self-help, a concept previously unknown in the empire, is likely too. The peasantry, unarmed, untrained and passive in the face of attack had, for two and a half centuries, let all defensive thinking be done for them. Now in desperation, they were stirring: some towards brigandage, some towards self-protection. Denied other means of defence they began to draw on the limitless stock of earthworks bequeathed by their prehistoric ancestors.

The symbol *par excellence* of the 3rd century is the city wall of Rome. Besides his achievement in snatching back the initiative from barbarians and separatists, Aurelian's feats included two sombre provisions: abandonment of Dacia; and construction of that mural circuit which rings the Eternal City yet. So, though 150 years separate their actions, Aurelian shares with Hadrian the curious double of abandoning one of Trajan's conquests and being remembered for a wall. Yet how different a wall: Hadrian's 1,150 miles from the Capitol, Aurelian's 800 yards from it. Aurelian's Wall thinks the unthinkable: the recoil of empire; the return of the Romans, salmon-like to their birthplace; ideas unimaginable sixty years earlier when Septimius bequeathed an expanded empire to his sons. Since the Wall of Servius,[13] 600 years earlier, Rome's armies and frontiers had been thought sufficient for her protection. Now Aurelian's Wall would include an area slightly over twice as large. It would be over 11 miles long, 12 feet thick and 30 feet high including parapet; with 18 gates (of which half remain) and 381 towers at approximate 30-yard intervals. Towers project and are rectangular; gate bastions are round or square, with gates recessed and doubled across internal courtyards, designed as deathtraps. These were the most sophisticated defences which the western provinces had seen and were quite beyond the reach of barbarians without siege equipment. The work was begun in 271 and completed under Probus. Forty years later its height was doubled by Maxentius, who added an upper section of half-thickness. Such is the wall as we now see it: sixty feet tall, its towers approaching double that height, with parapet and merlons still intact. In fact, central Italy was to be unmolested by the 3rd-century invasions, and the wall remained untested for a century and a half.

As to the general question of manpower, the problem lay in recruiting soldiers of the number and quality needed to secure all fronts. The history of enlistment had been centrifugal, from central Italy outwards to the less sophisticated provinces, reaching even the nearer barbarians. The latter had proved excellent material, providing they were Roman officered and diluted. However, with the traditional sources fully stretched, a different solution was now tried.

From the later 3rd century the word *laeti* is increasingly used. It signified those barbarians admitted *en bloc*, armed and with their own leaders, to whom the defence of a portion of the empire was subcontracted. This meant using Germans against Germans. Who were the *laeti*? Is there a connection with modern Latvia and Lithuania? It is not impossible that some originated in the Baltic, or subsequently moved there. In the 4th century, however, they were known simply as the Germans from across the Rhine, who had been settled on the Roman side for some time, yet still maintained a barbarian identity: 'I will add to your infantry some youthful *laeti*, descendants of the barbarians living on this side of the Rhine, or at any rate of those who had come over to us freely.'[14] A. H. M. Jones considered them a system rather than a nation: outsiders of any extraction, invited to take imperial land in exchange for military service. The word *laetus* may simply derive from the German *loicht* (light), referring to armament.

Recalling the barbarian settlements of Marcus' reign, the *receptio*, with an obligation to defend, was by no means new. It is the scale which now increases, implying that the centuries of Romanising the Germans were over and those of Germanising the Romans had begun. However, the *laeti*, though retaining their own organisation and styles of combat, remained loyal; and there is no recorded instance of defection from the Roman cause. They were supervised by officials based in nearby cities, the *praefecti laetorum*; while the farmer-warriors themselves were kept out of harm's way in the countryside. They were probably settled in devastated areas, some distance back from the frontiers, as part of the new strategy of defence in depth. It is they who are most associated with garrison duty in the rural refuges. *Terrae Laeticae* are known in northern Italy, northern Spain, Germany and above all in today's northeastern France, Luxembourg and the Ardennes, where their presence is identified by Germanic motifs on belt buckles and weapons found in graves.

Main settlement areas, then, lay midway between the Rhine and interior Gaul. However, they were equally well placed to face northwards towards the Low Countries, where a considerable natural disaster was now at hand. This consisted of a fall in land level which was gradually making the entire coast between Bruges and

The Hague untenable. In geological terms the southern North Sea is unstable. During the Holocene it had risen and fallen five times, as is shown by alternating deposits of peat and marine sediments. The effect was the invasion of land by sea, known to science as 'marine transgression', of which this was the 'Dunkirk 2 transgression'. Its duration is usually put as the 1st to the 5th or 6th centuries of our era, peaking in the 4th, by which time a rise in water level of some eighty feet is thought to have occurred.[15] We are presently in the middle of a comparable transgression, though centuries of defensive works invalidate modern comparison. The point is that coastal change, initially slight, was, by the mid-3rd century, having a pronounced effect. Occupation of what is today the Belgian coast and the Dutch province of Zeeland (indeed the entire deltaic region) ceased around AD 270. It was a populous area, whose people had now to be evacuated and resettled. Military consequences were no less severe. The rising sea was outflanking the Lower Rhine, creating a landscape of mudbanks and tidal creeks, perfect for stealthy entry and incompatible with systematic defence. The same transgression was also unsettling the Germans next along the coast in Friesland and Holstein; prompting tribes unable to retreat because of other tribes, to seek a living elsewhere.

It was probably the renegade Postumus who took the bold decision to give up the Lower Rhine and form a new frontier, parallel with the drowned coast. This involved abandoning some five forts on the Old Rhine below Nijmegen, seventy miles from the mouth. The new line would be based on a road, Cologne–Bavay–Boulogne. It is known as the *limes Belgicus*, a term coined by Belgian scholars during the inter-war years. Though inundation had pushed the coast some twelve miles southwards from its present position, the road chosen was more like forty miles inland. It was nevertheless the nearest, pre-existing trunk route, with towns and villages already walled or capable of fortification. Gaps would be plugged with forts, hastily built but upgraded later. Garrisons are known at Tongres, Liberchies, Bavay, Tournai, Kortrijk (Courtrai) and Cassel. Though strongly anchored by a legion at one end and a naval base at the other, the line itself was a mixed bag, including three walled cities but with some of its stations little more than villages or *burgi*. Raising it to frontier standards would require six or seven new forts and several fortlets. South of the Cologne–Bavay stretch, the Laetic settlement provided a zone of secondary defence. Parts of the line are still

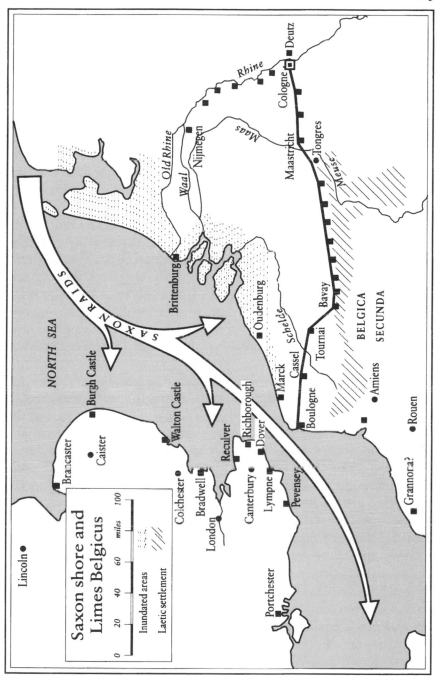

Saxon shore and
Limes Belgicus

Inundated areas

Laetic settlement

0   20   40   60   80   100
miles

traceable in the modern road pattern. From Cologne it ran west to today's Maastricht in the Netherlands. Passing into Belgium at Tongres, it first parallels the Meuse, as far as Namur, then the Sambre, running some 8–10 miles north of these rivers and 23 south of Brussels. Here its former strongpoints are today small villages or less: Braives, Taviers, Pentevilles, Liberchies, Moranwelz, Givry and so on. For the last 25 miles into Bavay the modern and Roman roads coincide. From here the frontier turned north-west, crossing First World War battlefields to Tournai and Kortrijk; passing eventually into France and reaching the Channel at Boulogne. The total distance from Cologne is a little under 260 miles and includes four present-day countries.

Two or three outposts continued to be held, including Oudenburg, a small fort near Ostend, of which only foundations survive; and the Brittenburg at Katwijk (Lugdunum) near the mouth of the Old Rhine, where the Lower German frontier originally ended. A third is suspected at Marck, four miles east of Calais. Long forgotten, the Brittenburg miraculously emerged from beneath coastal dunes on a windy day in 1520, vanishing and reappearing three times during the next sixty years, before its final return to oblivion. It is now beneath the sea some hundreds of yards off Katwijk. An engraving, from a bird's eye viewpoint, was executed by the illustrator Abraham Ortelius for a sixteenth-century guide book.[16] It shows a fort of late character, enclosing a large grainstore, hard pressed by the sea in front and the dunes behind. Gentlefolk have come to stare and higher up the beach a coachload of them is bogged down in sand to the axle. Less gentle folk toil with crowbar and chisel at three of the four walls, while another trundles away stones in a wheelbarrow. This fort, and the connection with Britain implied by its name, is a pointer towards another, very different late Roman frontier, more extensive and colourful than the *limes Belgicus*: the Saxon Shore.

The Saxon Shore was not Rome's only maritime frontier, for we recall the Black Sea, Red Sea and Cumbrian coasts. It was nevertheless her only system based on a sea–land strategy. The Flemish outposts were but one corner of an amphibious network based in southeastern England, where the remains are still largely visible. The Saxon Shore is the sixth[17] and last of the frontier experiments played out, over a two-and-a-half-century timespan, on the British stage. Its supplanting of Hadrian's Wall as Britain's principal shield signals the first of a series of ironies in which famous frontiers of the early empire will be found to face the wrong way, or to stand at the wrong end of their provinces. The Roman term *litus Saxonicum* described a chain of coastal forts whose presumed purpose was to counter Saxon raids, which had been growing in extent and severity throughout the century. Though Saxons were already in Britain as mercenary soldiers, the term describes shores fortified against them rather than those upon which they had settled; as the Danubian sectors *ripa Suebica*, *ripa Sarmatica* and *ripa Gothica* were now known by the names of the opposing peoples.

The Saxons combined piracy with violent coastal swoops and inland penetration by the skilful use of estuaries. Ammian speaks of

> [. . .] the Gallic coasts attacked by Franks and their Saxon neighbours with piracy, burning and the slaughter of all prisoners.[18]

And (in relation to Syrian bandits):

> . . . their arrival was always unexpected; for they were totally unmethodical, striking randomly, wherever the wind led; like the Saxons, feared above all enemies for this kind of attack.[19]

What was 'this kind of attack'? By taking to the sea England's ancestors had rewritten the rules, waging war in the army's rear at a time when the navy was in dangerous decline. Their unorthodoxy was well rewarded for, as everywhere in the ancient world, wealth was seldom far from coasts and rivers. Accordingly the underside of provinces, in areas long civilianised and made vulnerable by peace, must now be armoured. Since resources were scarce and a high density of defensive works unattainable, it was a time to answer inventive attack with imaginative defence.

The Saxon Shore was a thoughtful frontier. It included not just the twin elements of sea and land, but also a unified command in four provinces on two sides of the Channel. Its stations were forts with harbours housing both army and navy units, patrolling endangered sea areas and sensitive shorelines, covering some 350 miles of coast in Britain alone, with an average interval between bases of 35 miles. As well as protecting ports its strongpoints were sited on estuaries with a view to the defence of upriver cities like London, Colchester, Caister-by-Norwich, Canterbury, Amiens and Rouen. Admiration for the plan must nevertheless be modified by its slow implementation, suggesting the gradual extension of a successful formula rather than a single vision. It began with a random fort or two, followed, perhaps in the 270s, by a wider recognition of the need. This is implied by the evolution in styles, which begins late in the early and ends early in the late period of Roman military architecture. It had probably been the final wave of Gallic devastation that shook the system into coherence, for in its main spurt of fort building the walls closely resemble those of Gaul's cities. Probus seems its most vigorous exponent, though most of the individual projects fall outside his short reign. The line, with seven forts between Kent and the Wash, seems first to have faced east; the emphasis later shifting southwards. Here the Channel beckoned the intruder while Boulogne and Dover, bases of a demoralised and underfunded navy, did little to deter him. In fact the Dover station had been shut down for some decades and with it perhaps the entire British fleet. Soon thieving hands were on the Solent and the Cotentin peninsula, then round Finisterre to the Loire and Gironde. The potential of the Strait of Dover to block this villainy, or to intercept its return journey, is plain.

Though building inscriptions are virtually unknown, the forts have been dated circumstantially to AD 230–345, suggesting more than a century's lapse between the first, isolated need at Brancaster, near the Wash, and the afterthought of Pevensey, on the Sussex coast. A later document, the *Notitia Dignitatum*,[20] lists nine forts under the command of the *comes litoris Saxonici* ('count of the Saxon Shore'),[21] though remains exist of a probable twelve. Little is known of town garrisons, the use of the road network, or the number and location of road stations. The forts had few stone buildings and their archaeological yield is disappointing. Entering through impressive walls the visitor is faced with empty interiors, some ploughed for centuries, whose grass was once thought to cover the streets of Roman cities, as is suggested in one case by the name Walton (walled town). All harbour works have been drowned or washed away. Vegetius gives a description of the British ships; fast, light and camouflaged: 'Fifty-oared scouting boats, used for surveillance and the interception of enemy flotillas. Ships, sails, rigging and uniforms all dyed and painted blue [. . .]'[22] Apart from this and a list of names in the *Notitia*, little remains but walls; with the names not always easy to put to them. Fieldwork is frustrated by erosion and sedimentation, which have destroyed forts, removed them inland or totally altered their relationship to coast or riverbank. Vexation is, however, mitigated by the excellence of much which survives. This is among the richest of late Roman patrimonies and its better forts are romantic and evocative.

Brancaster, on the Norfolk coast, is not one of them. This earliest and most northerly of the forts was demolished by its landowner in 1770. Burgh Castle, close to Great Yarmouth, is the empire's most transitional fort: its new-style (projecting) towers stuck onto old-style (rounded) corners. Walton Castle, near Felixstowe, was lost to the sea in the eighteenth century and survives only in drawings. Bradwell (Essex) is half-eroded, with most of its surviving masonry built into the Saxon chapel which dominates the lonely spot. Reculver, on the North Kent coast, guarded the sea approach to London. Nearly half the fort platform has been washed away.

London was forty miles distant. Built as early as AD 200, its city wall had been designed to meet landward attack. The addition of the riverside wall, a hundred or more years later, illustrates Britain's turnabout from a north-facing to a south-facing strategy. In the early 1970s the foundations of a 3rd-century signal tower were discovered at Shadwell, a mile east of the Tower of London. This is doubtless one of many which joined upriver towns to Shore forts in networks yet unproven. By linking London to the Saxon Shore, Shadwell associates Britain's capital with a Roman frontier system, adding it to a sizeable list of national capitals so related.

Richborough (Rutupiae) is one of England's most interesting Roman locations. It stands on the east-facing coast of Kent, only five miles north of Deal. A favourable landfall, missed by Caesar, this is probably where the main part of Claudius' army disembarked; for J. P. Bushe-Fox, excavating between the wars, uncovered the remains of a huge, temporary camp, underlapping all later constructions. Until its eclipse by Dover in the early 3rd century, Richborough would be Britain's main point of entry; and at this symbolic gate was built the arch thought to have commemorated Agricola's 'conquest' of the entire island. Visitors soon detect the unEnglish glint of purest white as light catches chips of marble among the later masonry. In a less sentimental era this monument was converted to a lookout tower and surrounded by triple ditches, now recut. Finally in the mid- to late 3rd century, a Shore fort was built, largely of recycled materials. Sixty per cent of its walls survive, mostly to near full height: of free-standing concrete, 22 feet tall and faced in small blockwork, decoratively applied. It was occupied by the *II Augusta* legion whose fortress (at Caerleon, on the Welsh border) had by now been abandoned and the unit demoted in quality and size to cohort level. Richborough's situation, at the hinge between North Sea and Channel, gives it a strong claim as headquarters of the system. A unique surge of coins dated 402–10 suggests a buzz of activity during the final years of Roman Britain, whose story seems to end at the spot where 332 years earlier it had begun.

Investigations prior to road development in the 1970s revealed, beneath modern Dover, a Saxon Shore fort overlying the earlier station of the *classis Britannica* (British fleet). The latter's walls, preserved under blown sand, lay just seven feet from the position predicted by Mortimer Wheeler in 1929: a guess based on a shoreline shift, known to have been 1,220 yards seawards from the Roman. At that time the harbour was not on the seafront, but inside the estuary of the Dour, now flowing underground. Two lighthouses flanked the approaches, of which the western was destroyed by the building of Napoleonic defences, while the eastern still stands in the grounds of Dover Castle.

Lympne[23] (Portus Lemanis), seven miles west of Folkestone, is sometimes known as Stutfall Castle, to distinguish it from the medieval Lympne Castle on the crest above. It is a romantic ruin, tumbled and contorted by slippage. In Stukeley's words: 'Where not standing it lies sideways, in prodigious parcels; or where standing cracked through the whole solid thickness, as if Time were in a merry humour and ruined it in sport.'[24] This is a capricious coast. Stutfall is now some two and a half miles from the sea and the estuary of the Rother, which it controlled, is lost to view.

Pevensey (Sussex), the Roman Anderitum, was seemingly the last fort built. It dates to about 345 and its highest walls, tallest towers and deepest gate make it the most advanced of the series. A circuit, corresponding closely to its site (originally oval and an island) also suggests 'modernity'. With twenty-three-foot walls, eleven bastions, an extremely strong western gateway and patterned facings displaying the accomplishments of several gangs, it is a *tour de force* among late Roman defensive works.

Portchester (Hampshire) is no less spectacular. This fine survival at the inner end of Portsmouth harbour is the only Shore fort to maintain its relationship to the shore. With the sea still lapping the outer wall, a thirteenth-century church in one corner and a Norman keep in the other, Portchester is a place of unusual continuity and interest. It is a large fort of almost eight-and-a-half acres, with walls and towers (though much reclad during the Middle Ages) almost complete. Like Pevensey, it stands to original height, with twenty projecting bastions at ninety-foot intervals. It is, however, some seventy-five years earlier than Pevensey, being built in the 270s or 80s. Professor B. Cunliffe's excavations of 1961–79, covering an eighth of the interior, revealed traces of timber buildings, none of which was recognisably military. Infant burials, women's shoes, jewellery, weaving and spinning equipment, skeletons of cats and dogs, all heighten the impression of discipline in decline, fort blurring into town, merging military and civilian lifestyles, flowing on without noticeable break past the end of Roman Britain into the uncertain years beyond. In summary, despite Walton lost and Reculver half-lost to the sea, Brancaster, Bradwell and Dover largely lost to man, five forts (Burgh, Richborough, Lympne, Pevensey and Portchester) are well worth seeing, with the last two among the best of late antiquity.

Time and tide have been less kind on the continental side. Besides forts already mentioned, a chain of coastal or estuarine cities, from today's Belgium as far as Bordeaux, was apparently co-opted to the system and placed under the Shore commander or his Breton and Aquitanian counterparts. Stiffening these garrison towns were several forts of Saxon Shore type, but these have been elusive: submerged by sea, later settlement, or just lost; their whereabouts guessed with reference to spacing and placenames. There remains, however, a fortlet of some atmosphere, at Longy Bay on the northeastern tip of the island of Alderney, known locally as the Nunnery. Though mute and anonymous it is stylistically comparable, with walls standing to seventeen feet. This extremity of the remotest, perhaps least spoilt of the larger Channel Islands, offers another place to savour the world's-end atmosphere of the Roman frontier and reflect on its extent and variety.

The 4th century will see Britain yet more widely molested. On clifftops north from Flamborough Head, the Yorkshire and Durham coasts were watched by towers whose strong bases suggest four floors. These were probably controlled from York, where *Legio VI Victrix* still hung on. The most easily visited is on Castle Hill, Scarborough. Southwards, bold cliffs give way to the soft sediments of Holderness and Lincolnshire, so gnawed by the rodent sea that all links with the distant past are lost. The limits of northbound Saxon and southbound Pictish piracy are therefore unknown. Westwards lay the Irish Shore.[25] Here these troubled years provoked knavery sufficient to give us another imperial frontier, though of less weight than the Saxon. Cardiff Castle, its octagonal bastions and gatetowers reconstructed around 1900 by the Marquis of Bute, is its most prominent memorial. The same raids bequeathed the walls of Caerwent (Gwent), one of Britain's best civilian sites. At Holyhead (Anglesey), above the quay where the Dublin packet docks, is Caer Gybi, a three-sided, beachhead fort of unmistakably late Roman character. Caernarvon, Chester and Lancaster are other likely locations. Ravenglass and Maryport, leftovers from the coastal system of Hadrian's Wall, were still functioning as coastal stations.

Hadrian's Wall was now under separate management. Its commander, the *dux Britanniarum* (Duke of Britain), because he faced the less dangerous enemy found his budget falling, his forts ageing and his soldiers ill equipped. A well-known inscription from Birdoswald, discovered in 1930, records repairs to 'the commander's house, which was covered in soil and in a state of collapse. Likewise the HQ building and bathhouse'.[26] Comparable decay is attested at two other forts. Shortage of officers as well as the southward drafting of men seems a reasonable recipe for this neglect.

Henceforward there were two armies of Britain and the gap would widen. In the north and inland the early empire lingered on. Even new forts like Piercebridge (Durham) and 3rd-century Vindolanda followed the traditional plan. Garrisons kept their old names and units, though skeletal, their old styles. On the Wall more turrets were shut down, gateways blocked and guard houses converted to outhouses. By contrast on the shore, above all the Saxon Shore, ideas flowed. Hadrian's Wall was now the lumber room; the Saxon Shore, with its advanced buildings, its sea–land operations and its supraprovincial command, the laboratory.

Let us round out our account of the 3rd-century frontier with a *resumé* of events in the Northern Alps, Northern Spain, Morocco and Libya.

Thanks to Aurelian's staunching of the imperial haemorrhage, Probus could begin work on the Lake Constance or Pre-Alp Line (see map 20) whose neglect, but for the diversion of German attention towards Gaul, could already have proved fatal. It was the western or Swiss Sector, sixty-five miles of the Upper Rhine between Basle and Lake Constance, which was in most urgent need of watchtowers and forts. East of the lake, where the valleys lead less obviously southwards, the main effort could be left to the next generation. Isny, Goldberg and Kellmünz, strongholds on the River Iller comparable to Portchester and Pevensey, were in fact the work of Diocletian. The last, Celio Monte,[27] discovered in 1952, has been dated by coins to about 308, some twenty-six years later than Probus. In all, the new frontier would have seventy-five towers, known or supposed, with at least seventeen new forts, backed by four defended towns and numerous rural refuges. Most forts were small in ground area, but strongly walled and shrewdly sited; as exemplified by the Bürgle, on a hilltop overlooking the Danube.[28] At last *castella* were beginning to look like castles. Their role here was to cover fords in front and valley entrances to the rear. The frontier was thus conventional in its use of river and lake but advanced in its emphasis on strongpoint strategy. It relied on siege-proof forts commanding key points; quite different from the old-style line, chosen for the defender's convenience, with forts sited on grounds of spacing. The Lake Constance frontier was a considerable achievement, given the critical times and the necessity to start from scratch. Its active life was about 120 years, ample to justify the labour. Its deathknell would be the renewed Alamannic attack of 384, coupled with troop withdrawals to defend Italy. The front would then fall back to the southern Alpine passes. In modern terms the Lake Constance line ran from Switzerland, through the western extremity of Austria and into Bavaria. Since there was also a backup fort at Schaan, Liechtenstein, it rivals the *limes Belgicus* as a four-country frontier. Though poor in standing remains it is strong in scenery, with settings to stir the imagination.

The late frontier across Spain is richer in remains, but of less certain purpose. A north-facing line based on the Ebro and Douro rivers would debar one quarter of Portugal and Spain and retain three quarters. In this way the Cantabrian Mountains and the Pyrenees could be excluded at less cost than it needed to police them; while the Meseta and the south would be well rid of their light-fingered cousins the Asturians, Cantabrians and Basques. There is however a school of thought which considers that the north was the truly profitable part and the purpose of the Ebro–Douro garrisons was not to exclude but to secure it. This refers of course to Galician gold. Defending it would mean not only the mines, in Spain's northwest corner, but also the export routes by which the gold was transported down the Ebro to Barcelona, or round the Atlantic end of the Pyrenees. A third proposal, perhaps most attractive, is that the military dispositions were originally gold-related, but when the gold ran out the army posts were adapted to separating the now useless north from the still useful centre and south. Any theory must however include the military and paramilitary sites spread right across the north and east, as well as 4th-century evidence of belt buckles and weapons suggesting Laetic mercenaries, who appear to have occupied a support zone similar to that behind the Rhine.

Spain had experienced a long period of prosperity, her economy balanced by an animal centre, a vegetable south and a mineral north. The 3rd century saw the focus of wealth moving from Baetica (Andalucia) onto the Meseta or central plateau. Unrest, responding to the times, then began to return, spreading down from the northern mountains. The rich ranches and large Castilian villas were especially vulnerable to banditry and appear to have hired German protection. The estate at Olmeda (one of several in the upper Douro and Valladolid regions) was found to contain enough graves to indicate a private army.

Meanwhile the gold was running out. J. M. Blazquez considers production effectively ceased with the 2nd century.[29] Together with the loss of the Dacian mines this may well have been a calamity such as the 21st century's oil producers may expect to see. The legionary base at León (Legio), now given 3rd-century walls, had guarded the goldfields, with the urban centres of Lugo (Lucus Augusti) and Astorga (Asturica Augusta) in support. All three have fine circuits, bristling with closely spaced towers. From here to Barcelona and Gerona was a west to east line of defended cities, garrison towns and late period forts, about sixteen in all. At the halfway point, this chain of strongpoints branched via Iruña[30] into Gaul, where there were forts at Bayonne and Dax. As we have noted, both routes were probably bullion outlets. Having protected the gold trains against mountain bandits, their garrisons and guardposts would be equally qualified to shield citizen and farmer from the same quarter. Though it may stretch philology to propose Basques as the origin of *Bacaudae*, we may be sure the northern peoples had contributed to the turbulence of the times. Small wonder if the governors of Tarraconensis and the other Spanish provinces were glad to see the last of them.

The Ebro–Douro frontier, if such it was, consisted of *Legio VII Gemina* and five infantry cohorts deployed between the Douro and the Cantabrian range, from Lugo in the north-west to Pamplona in the north-east, plus garrisons in towns like Zaragoza (Caesaraugusta) and Laeti or federates, mainly south of the rivers at locations implying the protection of rearward roads and major estates. Its purpose was to answer the problem of late Roman Spain which was, in the language of the board room, how to sell off the loss-making subsidiaries yet retain the profitable core sector. However, it should not be imagined as a riparian frontier matching those of Rhine and Danube. The Ebro–Douro remains shadowy and incompletely proven.

Vital also to Spanish strategy were decisions soon to affect the fate of Roman Morocco (Tingitana). Towards the century's end, with a callousness typical of the times, three-quarters of the province was lopped off; and though the sea link with Sala would be retained, the frontier system was otherwise scrapped and defence left in the hands of local leaders. The perimeter was now withdrawn to the northern cape on which Tangier stands. Tingitana had always been distant, difficult of access and marginal to Roman interests. Doubtless it would now have been abandoned entirely but for the advantage of controlling the Strait of Gibraltar from both sides and of shielding Spain from raids across it. Tangier therefore became a last-ditch position, buffered round by fortified farms and an inner watchtower cordon. To assist the control of piracy the Atlantic coast was held to Frigidae, near the lagoon at today's Moulay Bousselham, seventy-five miles south of Tangier. On the Mediterranean, Tetouan (Tamuda), only thirty miles from Tangier, became the final outpost, with an outer screen of towers watching the Rif foothills.

In Libya the time of the *gsur*[31] was arriving. These were the fortified farms, proposed by R. Goodchild (1918–68) as the building blocks of an imperial frontier refreshingly different from any known elsewhere. First reported by nineteenth-century travellers, the *gsur* were found by Goodchild to extend to some 95 miles behind the Tripolitanian Shore, over a width of 125 miles. During the 1950s and 60s he and a colleague, Lady Olwen Brogan, proposed that the *gsur* were manned by soldier-farmers as a defensive shield for the coastal zone. They practised 'streambed farming', in which water courses were divided by crosswalls to assist moisture and silt retention. A variety of crops was then planted into the actual bed. Despite the risk of flash flooding, a useful harvest could be taken from zones of almost total sterility.

Despite the lapse of forty years, vagaries remain. Were the *gsur* a product of central direction or self-help? Was the frontier guarded by a formal militia or vigilante groups, Romans or federated tribesmen? What is the difference between fortified farm and fortlet? Certainly we must avoid the 'archaeological militarism' of the nineteenth and early twentieth centuries, when the enthusiasm of scholarly soldiers tended to endow any rectangular foundations with a martial meaning.[32] The parameters are nevertheless clear. On the one hand the demand for oil and grain was still expanding with enough vigour to tempt the farmer towards the Sahara. It would not be till the 4th century that the economy contracted sufficiently to begin a retreat towards the coast. On the other, Septimius' three outposts had been shut down around 260 and the pre-desert farmers were without regular protection. Though North Africa escaped the Third-century Crisis this was generally a time of droughts, tribal tension and nomad nuisance.

The problems of interpreting the Libyan *gsur* must not conceal their interest, numbers and state of preservation. In the area covered by a more recent survey (a minority part of the pre-desert zone), roughly 300 were identified. The Wadi Umm el Kharab, 130 miles south of Tripoli, contains a classic group of eight within two miles, on spurs above a stream bed.[33] These stand to two floors and are well built of limestone blocks with ornamental doorways, single gates and inner courtyards, to a maximum size of ninety square feet. In a few cases there are indications of internal towers. All have a strength suggesting a military function, yet a relationship to water management works points equally to an agricultural function. Many are built onto or near farms of civilian type. The latter are about twice as numerous as the *gsur* and appear to have coexisted with them.

Where Goodchild, with little excavational evidence, assumed the fortified farms to be an aspect of Septimius' southward push, it is now thought that they came later. His assumption that they were constructed (at any rate initially) under official guidance has given way to the idea that they were privately commissioned[34] and built by civilian gangs for civilian clients. His belief that they were garrisoned by *limitanei*, in the sense of an officially sponsored militia, has been overtaken by the theory that their occupiers were simply the owners of the former civilian farms, which the *gsur* now partially displaced.[35] This is based on inscriptions in Punic, indicating that the occupants were native Libyans. In short, the pendulum has swung from the views of soldier-scholars towards private initiative, self-help and a civilian, in-depth frontier which appears to have something in common with the Anglo-Scottish border at the end of the Middle Ages.

Tripolitania, Tingitana, Hispania, Dacia: we are witnessing Rome's progressive reneging on her commitments, dumping provinces or parts of them and leaving frontier folk to fend for themselves. The reason was manpower; a shortfall of soldiers in time of crisis. The evacuation of marginal territory brought a quick gain in units now available for other fronts.

The political centre was faced with the consequences of the Third-century Crisis, greatest of which was the need for army reform. The blank in 3rd century written sources conceals the extent to which the army had forfeited the trust of the state. It would now be made anew: mounted, mobile, attacking, without attachment to forts and fortresses and having no loyalty to linear works. Yet this was not a time of deep reflection. Far-reaching changes began as panic measures. Fear of murder by their own troops, suspicion of their own inner circles, the imminence of enemies, the need to meet the barbarian's fighting skills and match his speed: such were the currents on which the Illyrican emperors were tossed.

In 261 Gallienus published his edict banning senators from army command. Though this helped block challenge to the throne from that direction, its other consequence was more memorable. The aristocratic monopoly of officership was ended, and the problem of military incompetence squarely faced at last. Henceforward 'none would lead save those hardened in the dust of war'.[36] Rome, too, was now dismissed from the direction of Roman affairs. Gallienus moved the capital to Milan (Mediolanum), closer to Germany and the breakaway Gallic empire. The Eternal City, far from the fighting fronts and steeped in irrelevant traditions, now became an archaism and an *objet d'art*. It had taken a thousand years to make these decisions and the next would be even more momentous. Gallienus gathered about him the empire's first, true, central reserve. Since the early 1st century, offensive war had been made by borrowing units from defensive frontiers. Here at last was an army conceived as a *force de frappe*: Balkaners, Anatolians, Syrians and Moors, the emperor's toughest and loyalest, which he called his *comites* (retinue). These would be shock troops: the best paid, best mounted, best trained and best armed in the empire. New coinage flooded from the mint carrying slogans like 'Speed', 'Spirit of the Illyricans', 'Bravery of the Horse,' 'Loyalty of the Cavalry'. Unhappily the coinage did not always prove sound or the cavalry loyal. A single reserve was cumbersome, a single command inflexible and a single capital must sooner or later be in the wrong place. Gallienus had broken old moulds without making successful new ones. Nevertheless lessons were now learned quickly; and though we lack firm evidence it is probable that within twenty years sufficient field armies had been created to place one behind each major front.

Surprisingly, no field army base has been found. This must surely mean that none existed, at least in the familiar sense. It was policy for the reformed army to avoid putting down roots. It is therefore likely that the Syrian device of stationing soldiers in towns was now widely applied, which gives extra meaning to the drive to build city walls. A mobile army, with scores of impregnable bases and the road system at its disposal, had a flying start. The cities would act simultaneously as strongpoints, military depots and food safes, allowing a supply-and-deny strategy, with well-fed Romans facing starving barbarians.

What of the frontier army? It remained, but with its strength and role reduced. Its best men and equipment were drawn off to form the cadres of the new, mobile armies. The residue would continue normal frontier duties, but on the understanding that they could not deal with large-scale attack. In that event they would either try to hold out until the arrival of reserves or to channel the enemy in a favourable direction. In terms of pay and prestige the frontier soldiers would henceforward be regarded as an inferior force. Legions which had not been caught in the German shredder were now reduced to ten per cent of original establishment. Many of their bases were closed or converted to towns; many of their men posted on detachment, never to reassemble. The rump was relegated to auxiliary duties. The imperial frontier had been mended or at least its bleeding staunched. Most of all it had been given a realistic place in a balanced scheme which included walled cities, defence in depth and a roving, counterstrike army.

Henceforward it would be rare for an emperor to visit Rome. The capital was now the place best suited to controlling the battlefronts. Milan gave way to Sirmium (Mitrovica, Serbia) first used by Marcus. The southern Balkans and adjacent Asia Minor were well placed between eastern and western fronts; and in the coming century would produce seven capitals, with Serdica (Sofia) and Naissus (Nish) already in use during the 3rd. Though capital-hopping was more realistic than hiding in Rome, it was a tortuous way to respond to invasion. Division of the empire into independent commands was now inevitable and only postponed by the old suspicions.

Recalling the metaphor of a long, dark tunnel, the Illyricans were the engine which pulled Rome through. What of the barely recognisable country into which she emerged? The muted monarchy of Augustus was gone, replaced by stern autocracy, which will dominate Western Europe till the eighteenth century and Eastern till the twentieth. Civilisation was sick, cities had shrunk, theatres become rubbish dumps, circuses and hippodromes refugee camps. The countryside was devastated and depopulated. Death rate had overtaken birth rate. The walling of cities and the stationing within them of crack troops favoured town survival at the expense of country. Villages and smallholdings were being abandoned, marginal farmland returning to woodland, with whole frontier regions dismissed as war zones. Brigandage and piracy were ubiquitous. Inflation was eroding resolve. The empire was reverting to barter. The bribery of the barbarians and their payment to defend imperial territory had become ways of life.

Roman diplomacy, backed by the reputation of an unmatchable army, had won more than the army itself. Now its only bargaining counters were gold and *receptio*, the admission of the barbarian. The army, commanded at last by professionals, had begun to win battles, but its composition was transformed. Rome's traditions were in infantry and the spiral of need for more horses to counter more horses was drawing her ever deeper into dependence on barbarian cavalry. By now the army had doubled in size. Survival depended on it and it must be rewarded. In material terms the soldier's prospects were at least twice as bright as the peasant's. Taxation, which had changed little between Augustus and Septimius, was now crushing, with the main burden falling on agriculture. Taxes in kind, chaotic and wasteful, required a vast machinery of counting, checking, haulage and storage. The sudden and arbitrary demands of marching armies were devastating. Fodder must be gathered from ten miles on either side of the route. The increased cost of campaigning, the growing number of campaigns, the support of an army now perhaps 650,000 strong, the gruelling taxation to pay for it, the coercion to enforce it and the military dictatorship to command it; these are the differences between the Principate and the Late Empire.

In the midst of storm, large sections of society were rowing in contrary directions or not at all. The Mediterranean provinces sat tight, pretending they were in the Antonine age. A hundred and twenty thousand citizens of Rome (and before long 80,000 of Constantinople) were still living on handouts of free, imported grain. Italians were still excused taxes and military service. The army too was tax-exempt, with many bonuses and grants of tax-free land. Commanding the fiscal Frankenstein was a booming civil service. Enterprise wilted. Manufacturing ceased. Towns became yet another burden on the land.

Most revealing was the response of the gentry, who dispersed as crisis gathered, leaving the cities and taking to their estates. They paid large taxes, but these were small compared to their income. Land was now the abiding reality and perhaps a thousand landlords were the economic controllers of empire. Theirs were the pampered acres, seldom close to frontiers. We are of course referring to the senators, whose once august assembly had shrunk to being 'the town council of Rome'.[37] Gone was their control over the unarmed provinces and their dominance of army command. The empire was ruled by upstarts from the Balkan *vici*. The Senate's military function now consisted in sending congratulatory messages to the battlefronts. Small wonder that members ceased to attend sessions or that patricians, in whom so much patriotism had been anciently invested, should now be lost to all but selfish causes.

The 3rd century had reached its nadir with a Persian king mounting his horse on a crouching emperor's back. Only a hundred years earlier the eulogist Aelius Aristedes had been telling complacent Romans that 'the empire's greatness lies in controlling its frontiers rather than in frontiers themselves; like a neatly tended and well-fenced garden [...]' Frankish frost and Alamannic storm had changed that for ever. The frontier had failed. In fact the instances when it had worked in the way popular imagination supposes, with gallant defenders repelling mighty attackers, are surprisingly few. The Third-century Crisis had revealed its bankruptcy and perhaps more: the fragility of the vision that a largely civilian empire could be created outside the Mediterranean and held indefinitely against a big and barbarous world.

Such is the debit side. Yet clouds were parting. Twenty years after Valerian's capture the Roman empire was reformed and revived; admittedly a reduced Rome and an empire less worth saving, but saveable nonetheless. The Illyricans had weathered the storm and the helm could now be taken by leaders of wider vision. Surprisingly the story of the imperial *limes* is not over, for two of these leaders – Diocletian and Valentinian – would yet believe that the frontier could be made to work.

CHAPTER 10

False Dawn

JUST AS FATAL ILLNESS sometimes follows a distressful progression from bad to worse, from worse to revival and from revival to relapse and death, so the course followed by Rome was from the depth of sickness to apparent recovery, then collapse. A more favourable outcome awaited the eastern provinces, whose rally was real and whose survival long. It was the western half that failed, a comfortless fact for the Westerner, who has usually been persuaded that the part of the empire to which he feels himself heir was the dynamic part; the base, in fact, from which the Roman world had been won. This is because the century upon which our education concentrates is heavily weighted with western achievement. But as time passed the tide of wealth and creativity ran eastwards. Literature and historical writing are now dominantly from the eastern provinces, and the exceptions are largely African.

The 4th century, then, is one of reprieve, won by the Illyricans and built on by Diocletian and Constantine, though at continuing cost. Rome had found a new strategy consisting of two layers: a moderate-quality army of defence in front, with a high-quality army of attack behind. The invading barbarian, without logistical or siege ability, was at sea among walled cities offering no landfall. Here was a formula which could work, though at twice the cost in manpower. Was this a late hour to apply it, when resources were shrinking and the outside menace growing? And would it be thoroughly applied; or would the old suspicions and contradictions prevail?

Diocletian has been called an Augustus in an unaugust age. But he could easily be overrated by our own time; obsessed, as he was, by restructuring and a belief in organisational reform as a cure for fundamental ills. Despite valiant steps in that direction he aged rather than rejuvenated the Roman state by intensifying its despotism and bureaucracy. Moreover his arrangements for the succession were unrealistic and their failure provoked another round of self-slaughter. Lastly he undid military improvements inherited from the Illyricans, disbanding their field forces and returning to a strategy based on frontiers. So began another century of cross-purposes: faith in frontiers alternating with faith in mobile armies; much as, under the early empire, consolidation had alternated with expansion.

Diocletian too was a Balkaner, though a longer and more stable reign (284–305) separates him from the run-of-the-mill *Illyriciani*. Nonetheless he had lived through those grim years and they shaped him. Son of freed slaves, he rose through the ranks until the murder of Probus sucked him into the savage politics of the day. Ousting three rivals, he owed his survival to a powerful reaction of disgust against junta politics, felt even by the Danubian soldiery. His mission would be to examine the post-crisis empire, diagnose its ills and equip it for survival in a harsher world. The result would be a grey regime, brightened by a show of building and the splendour with which he would surround the throne. He believed the army to be dangerous, and that the emperor should be kept remote from it. Accordingly he would protect himself behind a screen of ritual. The army, after the practice of Augustus and Tiberius, would be banished to the frontiers and war zones. So we move from identification with the army to separation from it; and from emperors in the eye of the storm to one who sought solitude and time to think. Surprisingly it worked. The *mystique* protected the man. Regicide, so long an everyday matter, was made to seem a sacrilege. He lived to seventy-three and died naturally. In an age when none dared dismount the tiger, he was even able to retire. Charismatic kingship was evidently what the Romans needed.

Taxation did not relent with the return of stability. The state required gold and fighting-men. The two were interchangeable since gold would buy soldiers from the *barbaricum*. Centuries of conquest and mining had brought huge amounts of precious metal into the empire, if only it could be elicited. Diocletian now instituted conscription on a quota system which could be commuted for cash. It did draw gold from the wealthy; but many bribed criminals and vagabonds to take their place, lending strength to the idea that it was better to recruit money from inside and men from outside the empire. Nevertheless, a majority of Diocletian's half-million-strong army was still Roman and, to maintain their numbers, he resorted to the equally Draconian measure of caste creation, by which all sons of soldiers were forced to serve. This would be applied to other essential professions and eventually to husbandry, so foreshadowing medieval serfdom. The number of provinces was doubled by subdivision to over a hundred. Civil servants were organised in cohorts, uniformed and presented as fighters in the patriotic cause. Their number, estimated as 30,000 for the late empire, is unprecedented before modern times and equal to five full-size legions. In practice civil service energies were largely dedicated to dragging the tax juggernaut.

The involvement of Gallienus' central reserve army – and subsequently of the various field armies – in murder and *putsch*, led Diocletian to regard them all with deep suspicion.[1] In his view they had simply taken over the Praetorians' role as umpires of empire. By contrast, newly recruited barbarians were politically innocent. He therefore created a German guard known as the *scholae palatina* ('palace scholars'), referring not to their learning but the fact that the soldiers chanced to be housed in a former school building. The frontier army had interfered little in politics. Accordingly it would be preserved and strengthened, while the field armies would be abolished or reduced. This meant a return to the tortuous method of reinforcement by moving troops from one frontier to another.

In AD 301, the ninth year of his reign, Diocletian launched his most dramatic reform: creation of the Tetrarchy or rule of four. This involved a fourfold division of empire, with separate armies and freedom of action in each. The tetrarchs are the rulers represented in the sculptural group in Venice: fellow-Danubians and brother officers. The idea was for two senior rulers (*augusti*) and two junior (*caesari*). In due course both *augusti* would abdicate, nominating two new caesars as they did so. The two existing caesars would replace them as *augusti*. In this scheme Diocletian appointed himself *augustus* of the east, with his capital at Nicomedia (Izmit), on the Sea of Marmara. It is significant that this should already be seen as the senior part of the empire. His deputy or caesar, Galerius, based in Thessalonika, ruled Greece and the Middle Danube. The western *augustus*, Maximian, with his capital in Milan, had charge of the Upper Danube, Italy and Africa; while his deputy, Constantius, residing at Trier, was responsible for Gaul, Britain and Spain. This may seem a recipe for dismemberment; but in fact it was Diocletian's most realistic measure, for the command had been so wide that orders sent across it were almost always obsolete on arrival. On the other hand, how realistic were his plans for the succession? What if the army should revert to its hereditary preferences? For centuries sons were never there when they were needed. But now that Diocletian had thought up a system which dispensed with sons, both caesars were blessed with them!

On 1 May 305, after twelve years' tetrarchic rule, Diocletian abdicated in Nicomedia, having persuaded Maximian to resign simultaneously in Milan. Lactantius, a 4th-century Christian historian, left a description of the ceremony, at which Constantine, son of the Gallic tetrarch, was unceremoniously passed over. Diocletian retired to Split, where his remarkable palace survives. It was built in imitation of a legionary base, perhaps symbolising the empire as a fortress. There the only Roman emperor to have taken voluntary redundancy lived out his last eleven years. Like another Balkaner, Tito, he had held together an artificial structure through strength of personality. But the Tetrarchy was unbuttressed by precedent and six pretenders were soon fighting in its ruins.

In 298, Galerius had been given command of a Persian expedition, though this was strictly speaking his senior partner's territory. One of Rome's best Danubian generals, disposing of heavy cavalry to match the enemy's and profiting from a moment of weakness between the reigns of Shapur I and II, Galerius won a resounding victory which included capture of the entire harem of Narses I. Diocletian was now in a position to dictate almost any frontier settlement. However, he was circumspect about extending Roman territory southwards. Apart from redeeming the lost part of Mesopotamia, he confined annexation to five south Armenian satrapies, formerly under Persian rule. These lay north of the upper Tigris, between that river and Lake Van. Extension into so remote a corner is puzzling and presumably means there was yet life in the old Armenian game. Its immediate effect however was the creation of a new frontier of a hundred miles across Corduene (Kurdistan), running north from the Tigris to the lake. The transtigritan acquisition would be held for sixty-five years. Ammian tells us it was then rescinded, together with fifteen forts,[2] which we may assume were built or begun by Diocletian to defend the new possessions.

In the earliest years of the twentieth century, Canon Wigram, a Church of England missionary crossing Turkish Kurdistan and escorted by the consul in Van, Captain B. Dickson, spent a night in a ruined fort as guest of the local *agha*, whose house was within the walls. The *agha* embarrassed his guests by offering one of his wives in exchange for a rifle, a proposal which His Majesty's consul properly rejected. Dickson later wrote that they had found, 'in the picturesque valley of Khizan what I believe to be a Roman fortress in a wonderful state of preservation' (though marred by 'Kurdish hovels').[3] At the same 1986 *colloquium*[4] as Professor Invernizzi revealed his findings on the Euphrates, T. B. Mitford and C. S. Lightfoot described intriguing forays into southeastern Turkey, each to investigate one of the supposed Diocletianic forts. Dr Lightfoot visited the ruin of Tilli on the Tigris some sixty miles southwest of Lake Van; and Dr Mitford that of Gayda, near Hizan, about twenty-five miles from the lake. The two seem of comparable date. Both scholars commented on similarities to the later Saxon Shore forts, which approximate to the same period.[5] Gayda, the more striking, with fifteen towers recognisable and wall fragments surviving to over thirty-five feet, is clearly the fort visited by Wigram and Dickson.

In Jordan the heyday of the *limes Arabicus* had arrived. The 3rd century, a time of warming and drying, had generated restlessness on all Rome's desert edges, with the bedouin's bite made sharper by the invention of the camel saddle. In 290 Diocletian was obliged to undertake a Saracen expedition. Few details are known but the fact of an emperor's visit was enough to start things moving. Fort numbers increase from fourteen to thirty.[6] Azraq, northern Jordan's principal oasis, has an extant fort of this date. The two fortresses now appear, at El Lejjun and Udruh, plugging the long gap between Bostra, on the Syrian border, and Aqaba. All these, plus new watchtowers, deepened the frontier zone to 15–20 miles, leaving it 'studded with strong forts and fortresses to repel the attacks of Arab tribes'.[7] Though we may censure Diocletian for his faith in frontiers, work on them was thorough. His architects grasped the fort improvements of recent decades and took them further, favouring a small, tall, square pattern known as the *quadriburgium* (four-tower fort). This had large, projecting angle towers, usually also square, a single gate and round-the-wall barracks. Qasr B'shir, ten miles north-east of Lejjun, is the best preserved in the Roman world. Its garrison was roughly 200 and that of Lejjun 2,000, less than half early empire

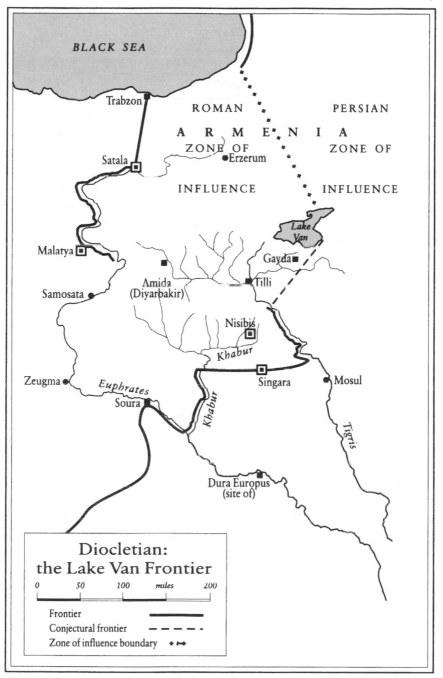

BLACK SEA

Trabzon

ROMAN   PERSIAN

A R M E N I A
ZONE OF   ZONE OF

Satala

INFLUENCE   INFLUENCE

Lake
Van

Malatya

Gayda

Amida
(Diyarbakir)   Tilli

Samosata

Nisibis

Khabur

Zeugma   Euphrates   Singara   Mosul

Soura   Khabur

Tigris

Dura Europus
(site of)

Diocletian:
the Lake Van Frontier

0   50   100   miles   200

Frontier
Conjectural frontier
Zone of influence boundary

numbers. Both remain as the 4th century left them, in the sense of being free from later occupation or alteration.

The El Lejjun fortress is sixty miles south of Amman and less than two miles north of the branch of the Desert Highway to Kerak. Built around AD 300 on a site occupied neither before nor since, it is a time-capsule of the later imperial army, as was Inchtuthil of the early. Moreover it is of stone in a dry climate, while its Scots counterpart was of timber in a wet one. In 1876 Charles Doughty, explorer of Arabia, passed this way. Recognising that Lejjun (like León in Spain and Caerleon in Wales) is simply the word legion, he asked, in his quaint prose: 'Is Lejjun perchance *legio*? See we here a Roman military station?' The fortress was surveyed by Brünnow and Domaszewski in 1897, since which time the facing stones of its ramparts have been lifted; doubtless recently, for in remote places it is the advent of the lorry which makes these larcenies feasible.

Lejjun has been excavated by the North Carolina State University as part of the *limes Arabicus* project. Excellence of preservation plus the use of modern techniques bring new insights, for example on food. In describing soldiers' diet, ancient authors relished trotting out spartan, northern menus like the '*lerido, caseo et posca*'[8] which Hadrian shared with his soldiers. The finding at Lejjun is that they were varied and good. Not only were wheat, barley and lentils detected but olives, dates, grapes and peaches, as well as most meats including chicken and game. There would also be eggs, milk and cheese.[9] Soldiers are seldom backward in arranging such matters. The dig produced interesting information on religion. The fortress contained both a church and a pagan shrine, implying that conversion had been gradual and the atmosphere tolerant. The church was rough and ready, which suggests it was privately funded and built by the soldiers themselves. The 4th century was a religious watershed. At its beginning Diocletian banned Christianity from the army and at its end Theodosius closed all pagan temples. Matters appear to have been more relaxed at Lejjun, where the cult of the standards continued into the early 6th century, albeit only sixty miles from Bethlehem.

Biggest change of all was the 300-mile-long *strata Diocletiana*, whose construction in 293–305 remade the south Syrian frontier. This *limes* road was a *piste aménagée* of cleared stones, linking a dozen and a half forts of the frontier army, interspersed with and backed by heavy cavalry. It ran northwards from Azraq, paralleling

Early and late fort designs

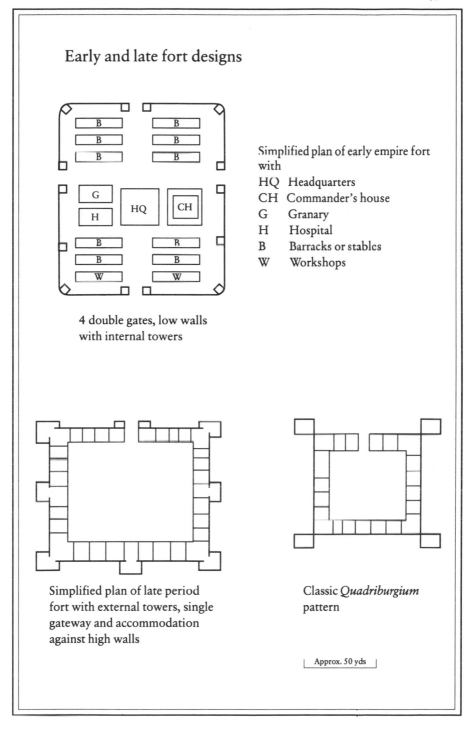

Simplified plan of early empire fort with

HQ   Headquarters
CH   Commander's house
G   Granary
H   Hospital
B   Barracks or stables
W   Workshops

4 double gates, low walls with internal towers

Simplified plan of late period fort with external towers, single gateway and accommodation against high walls

Classic *Quadriburgium* pattern

Approx. 50 yds

Trajan's highway at about twenty miles to its east. Beyond Damascus it swung northeastwards to Palmyra and finally north again to the Euphrates at Sura. Though known from milestones since at least the early twentieth century, Poidebard observed road stretches in 1927, identifying watchtowers and photographing a number of its many-towered *castella*, spaced at approximate twenty-mile intervals. The new road included the Palmyran oasis, but its main alignment was below the Jebel Rawag, last range of hills before the gravelly monotony of the Syrian Desert prevails. It was able therefore to utilise run-off from the slope and the various wells and springs at its foot. Installations in this type of country were given reservoirs or underground cisterns, whose excavation often provided building stone for the fort. The substitution of regular garrisons for Palmyrene patrols makes this the final instance of the replacement of informal, client-run frontiers with firm, linear, Roman versions. But the hour was late for costly reappraisals in lonely corners. The future tendency would in fact be the opposite: to save on the deserts' edges and spend on the protection of Europe. The *strata Diocletiana*, expensive in men and works at a time when regular soldiers were at a premium on all fronts, was the bill footed by Diocletian for Aurelian's destruction of Palmyra, two decades earlier. In Arabia and Syria Rome's boundaries were now much as they would be when taken over by the Byzantine empire.

The *limes Palaestinae* also approaches maturity. This had been the fortified line along the Negev's northern edge, running from the Dead Sea through Beersheba to the coast below Gaza. Its true origins may have predated its Roman revival by a thousand years, for it probably protected Judah against the Amalekites. However, with annexation of the whole area by Trajan it became an interior frontier, though arguably a valid one since the nomads, though nominally Rome's subjects, continued to live beyond the tax collector's reach. Nevertheless Hadrian, having reinforced Judaea internally after the Bar Kokba rebellion, allowed the external defences to lapse.[10]

In the 4th century, with Sinai scorched by drought, Diocletian decided that a resuscitation of the Negev line could not be postponed. It was therefore reoccupied and braced with extra watchtowers and *quadriburgia*, plus a screen of fortified farms in a buffer zone extending ten to twenty miles southwards. For security these were organised in groups. Farmhouses had strong walls, interior wells and could often be entered only by ladder at upper floor level. Professor

Gichon notes how closely arrangements resembled those of Saul and Solomon's time; and also how the use of farmer-soldiers long pre-dated Rome's arrival, providing further examples of lack of original-ity in Roman defensive thinking.[11] Like the Arabian *limes*, that of Palaestina will continue to serve the eastern empire till the Muslim conquest.

Comparable to the *limes Palaestinae*, in fact the other side of the Negev bad penny, was the defence of Lower Egypt. Previously the Nile had been guarded only against Ethiopia and, more lightly, from the Red Sea. In the 4th century, given the restlessness of all deserts, protection was needed from Sinai. There was however another cause for concern. It is no surprise that Diocletian, who, like Augustus, had raised Rome from the depths of civil strife, had comparable suspicions of Egypt as a base for insurgency and a target for anyone thinking to choke off the corn supply. Accordingly garrisons were deployed to counter threats from within the empire, even from within Egypt herself. Pelusium (Tel el Farma), twenty miles east of today's Port Said, was now the key frontier post. The delta's roads were guarded, especially the crosswise highway to Alexandria and the riverside route to Memphis (Cairo). Lower Egypt had thirty auxiliary regiments, Upper Egypt forty. A new legion was placed centrally at Luxor;[12] its fortress adapted from the great temple of Ammon where puny remains, unnoticed by the thousands of daily visitors, are still to be seen in the form of a north gate and the foundations of a U-shaped tower, close under the pylon of Rameses II. Though not directly related to frontiers, Luxor is noteworthy for the picture it presents of legionaries camping in the abodes of Egypt's gods, already fifteen centuries old; as other races will before long be squatting among Roman ruins.

History repeated itself, for as Augustus' fears for Egypt proved groundless, so no 4th- or 5th-century invasion materialised, and in practice the garrison's main concerns were with internal order, grain guarding and tax collection. There was, however, a revolt in Alexan-dria which brought Diocletian to Egypt in 297. He inspected the southern frontier and decided to abandon the Dodekaschœnus, con-centrating his forces at the cascade. The Eastern Desert saw a con-tinuation of the roadholding and guardpost strategy in defence of the mines and Red Sea caravans, while there is also evidence for strengthening the coast against piracy. In 1990 excavations at the Roman-Byzantine fort of Abu Sha'ar (Myos Hormos), where the Red

Sea narrows to the Gulf of Suez, uncovered part of an early 4th-century inscription including the words *limitibus litorum*[13] ('from the coastal frontiers'), apparently suggesting an 'Arabian Shore' system. Egypt will continue to serve Roman or East Roman masters till succumbing to Islam in the 640s.

Till now the Western Desert had been without frontier. This was because the eastern Sahara is one of the world's driest places. In fact there are oases opposite the Middle Nile, of which the most important is Kharga, which lies 130 miles west of Luxor and was known to the Romans as Oasis Maior ('the larger oasis'). Strabo considered 'there were three oases belonging to Egypt' and he describes Kharga as 'abounding in water, with wine and other produce, seven days' journey through wilderness'.[14] Beyond here, the desert is total. No trans-Saharan route passes this way and nomadism is unknown. Accordingly there is no record of outside threat.

Despite this the 4th century has left imposing ruins at Kharga, including tall, strong forts with walls of thirty feet and more. They have survived well; being of sun-dried brick, which tempts few robbers and – in these rainless conditions – is little harmed by weather. Placenames include the words for fort or fortlet (*ksar* and *borj*)[15] while plentiful *ostraca* attest the presence of Roman soldiers. The sites are spread on a north–south axis across the entire eighty-five miles of the Kharga waterholes and may include as many as two dozen military establishments. Military purpose is not always clear and the true total could be half. At least six, including the fort of Ed Deir, east of Kharga, seem decisively military, being on hillocks, high-walled and in some cases impressively bastioned. Dush is a re-used Egyptian temple to which a galleried outer wall was added. Excavations are few, but that at Dush between 1976 and 1982, is of special interest, uncovering a military commissariat with 700 Greek *ostraca* and papyrus fragments, the majority dealing with food supplied by the civil authorities. Was this for on-the-spot consumption, was the aim to collect produce for despatch to Egypt, or had the forts some other purpose? We may ask why the fruits of small oases should be hauled 130 miles to the superabundant Nile and why hundreds of soldiers should be tied to the task. If, on the other hand, it was to feed local garrisons, what was their purpose if no substantial enemy could have sprung from that almost oceanic emptiness beyond?[16] The Kharga forts remain a mystery.

In Numidia the *fossatum* operated still. Baradez' photographs

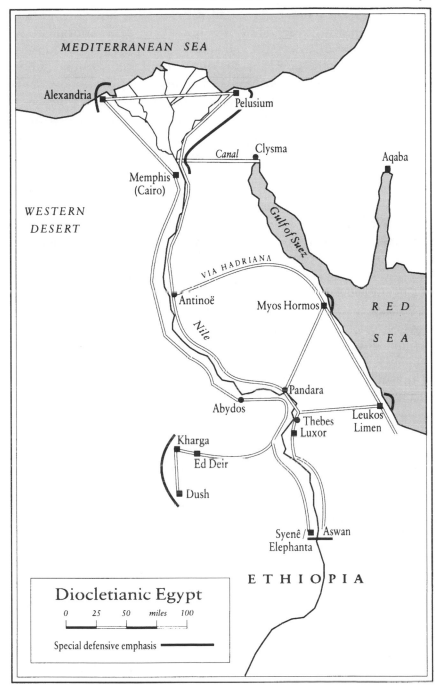

MEDITERRANEAN SEA

Alexandria

Pelusium

Canal Clysma

Aqaba

Memphis
(Cairo)

WESTERN
DESERT

Gulf of Suez

VIA HADRIANA

Antinoë

Myos Hormos

RED

Nile

SEA

Pandara

Abydos

Thebes
Luxor

Leukos
Limen

Kharga

Ed Deir

Dush

Syenê /
Elephanta

Aswan

ETHIOPIA

Diocletianic Egypt

0   25   50   *miles*   100

Special defensive emphasis

show 4th-century *quadriburgia* added behind the line. Some fifteen have been identified near the frontier and in the Aurès foothills. This was also a time of increase in smaller works (towers, blockhouses and fortlets) and the development of the *limitanei* (frontier militia) toward their soldier-farmer role. Some small forts were now called *centenaria*, though sizes varied widely. Inscriptions imply they were built with private funds. In Libya, Goodchild found references to donations by a local lady, Macrina, and a couple, Flavius and Flavia. In Algeria the Kasr el Kaoua near Ammi Moussa is still well preserved. Its building inscription reads '*Spes in Deo Ferini amen*'[17] ('Hope in God, Ferinus, amen'). Another was erected by a landlord 'with his own labour, for his sons' and grandsons' protection'.[18] This is an echo of the self-help movement which sees landowners fortifying villas and civilians re-opening hillforts in provinces elsewhere.

Numidia sprouts towers. These go hand-in-hand with the kind of do-it-yourself, farmer frontier, towards which North Africa is now moving. In some instances towers cluster among fields, their densities suggesting one for each smallholding. Baradez interpreted them in terms of fear:[19] peasant soldiers, increasingly nervous in the face of declining government support, each building a tower for himself and his family. In Algeria a group can be seen near Highway 3, at about 36 km south of Biskra and a few miles beyond the Oued Djedi. Here road and railway cross the *fossatum*'s Saharan sector. Just over the railway line are many stone mounds which formed the tower bases, some near or almost on the faintly visible *fossatum*. There is no sign of system, and spacing is too close to warrant signalling. More probably they were individual dwellings. We are seeing a time when towers were becoming privately owned and for safety, rather than army owned and for surveillance; recalling the 16th-century Italian states, also with insecure borders, which had a comparable craze for family towers, as seen for example in San Gimignano.

Turning to the Tetrarchy in Europe: the reversion from a mobile army to fixed fortifications led to a major rebuilding rush, in which new features were at last emerging. In 1934, I. Paulovics found the first of a fortlet type till then unknown on the Danube, though two had been identified on the Rhine during the nineteenth century. It had corner towers and three walls, the fourth side being open to the river.[20] Oak piles were embedded in the mud. A second was recognised by a Hungarian, F. Halácz, one of several village schoolmasters to enrich Danubian frontier studies. At first assumed to be forts with one wall washed away, these are now accepted as fortified landing places, arranged in pairs on opposite banks to provide protection during shuttling operations. They are especially common on the *ripa Sarmatica* (the Hungarian–Serbian stretch). Counterforts also increase in frequency. Sited on the enemy bank, these powerful bases gave notice of rapid retribution. On the Middle Danube, ten forts were restored and eight new ones built, four being counterforts. Hinterland cities were strongly walled, including Scarbantia (Sopron, northwestern Hungary), whose circuit survives.

Not unconnected with such measures, singular travail was now afoot in the *barbaricum*: the creation of earthen dykes, whose size and extent are beyond anything seen on the imperial frontiers. They run roughly parallel with the Danube, reaching even beyond its mouth: from the mountains of Slovakia to the river Dniestr in the Ukraine. Earthworks are notoriously enigmatic. In this case they seldom touch existing settlements or cross other works which can be dated archaeologically. It is thus by no means certain that they *are* Diocletianic. On the contrary, arguments must be considered before we can even accept a 4th-century attribution.

The dykes' siting suggests they would be pointless during the Roman occupation of Transylvania, since some appear to defend from that direction. If we accept this view it eliminates a 2nd- or 3rd-century dating. Nor does such expenditure of labour (in effect doubling the line of the Danube) seem appropriate to the 1st century, when Rome was preoccupied with the consolidation of the nearside provinces. Nor again do they seem within the capacity of the weakened empire of the 5th century. That they were a barbarian concept is denied by the instability of the regions and their changing ownership, and they do not correspond with the boundaries of any known state before or since. That they were post-Roman is also contradicted by their tendency to shadow the imperial frontier, implying one as an outwork of the other. Such arguments point to the 4th century of our era. What can be deduced from these mounds and ditches? Though their sweep suggests a grasp of geography beyond the merely tribal, the work itself is labour-intensive and unskilled. In other words it is an enterprise compatible with barbarian exertion under Roman direction. As usual there is nothing in ancient literature or epigraphy to guide us toward a closer definition or provenance.

In later ages these mighty earthworks produced a substantial mythology, to which the following legend is central. Satan made a pact with God by which he might have half the world providing that, within a single day, he could dig a ditch separating the two shares. Failing to complete in the specified time he received nothing, leaving only vast ditches and mounds across portions of the earth to commemorate his labours. This is a big legend and big works inspired it. Of course all manner of smaller ditches, mounds and walls would then be drawn in; so that scores, even hundreds of linear features, in many countries and languages, would be labelled devil's ditches, devil's causeways, grim's dykes, black dykes, heathen walls and so on, with occasional deference to more local demons.

From Slovakia to the Hungarian border an earthwall follows the west banks of the Gran (Hron) and Eipel (Ipoly) rivers. First brought to attention in 1876 but still undated, it is probably part of a barrier between the Danube and the Middle Slovakian range, intended to funnel barbarian attack toward the strongly held Brigetio sector, west of the great bend. This is, however, the smallest of the works. Near the same bend there begins, just upstream from Budapest, a dyke complex whose scale has few rivals. From here it travels east by northeast for 110 miles across the plain. Near the town of Nyíregyháza it turns south past Debrecen for another 200 miles, entering Romanian territory and fringing the western foothills of the Carpathians before rejoining the Danube some 20 miles east of Belgrade. This great loop of earthworks enclosed 37,500 square miles, three quarters the size of England. But its length of 310 miles is misleading. For 40% of its course the line is double and for 20% triple or quadruple. On the other hand there are many breaks, corresponding (we assume) to ancient marsh or forest. Allowing for these but adding the extra distance which doubling entails, we arrive at about 500 miles of line. This is again deceptive, since each 'line' consists of fivefold ditches with intermediate mounds. Placing these end to end would give us 2,500 miles of single ditch with mound, the combined length of the Rhine and Danube frontiers!

Other dimensions are also impressive. A section cut through the inner line near the village of Covasint[21] by K. Horedt, B. Boroneant and E. Dörner revealed a composite of five ditches each averaging 18 feet wide and 7 deep, with five intermediate mounds and an overall width of 56 yards. The outer ditch had traces of a palisade along its bottom. This suggests an extensive timber supply and indeed the name Transylvania (across the woods) implies that the Carpathian foothills were forested. Today the Hungarian plain is populous

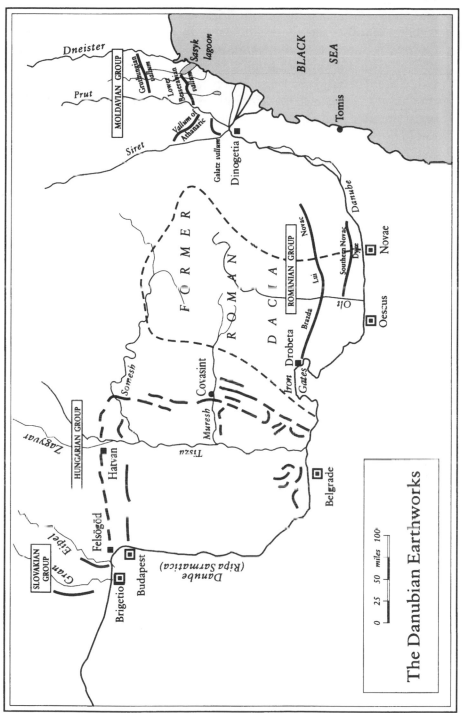

The Danubian Earthworks

and cultivated. This, plus centuries of flood and silt, has largely levelled or obscured the earthworks. In one case, also in the Arad district, the cutting of an irrigation canal revealed a complete profile of the fivefold ditchwork in its side walls. The area enclosed – effectively the Theiss (Tisza) basin – corresponded with the territory of the Iazygian tribe (a name seldom heard in the late period, when they were simply called Sarmatians). Though fitful friends the Sarmatians could be increasingly relied upon now the Goths were milling around outside, for these later arrivals were a menace to all. It was a long-standing Roman policy to support smaller tribes against larger; and to do so in this case had the advantage of reinforcing the Danube at a crucial point, opposite the Drava and Sava corridors. Such arguments have led to a tentative acceptance that this earthwork group, known in Magyar as Ördögárok ('devil's dyke'), was planned by Rome and built with Sarmatian assistance, probably against the Goths.

How was the barrier intended to function? Again we can only infer from the remains by arguments of common sense. Here is a multiple ditch system, made with prodigious labour, yet too long to be strongly manned and with little sign of forts to suggest that it was. An obvious answer is that the intention was not exclusion but hindrance. If so, it suggests a new kind of invasion with a new kind of goal. As long as the frontier had been a kind of orchard wall, tempting the outsider to scramble over, stuff his pockets and scramble back, break-in was not catastrophic. But suppose these pranks were over. Suppose barbarians in significant numbers had now begun to think of flight from the violence and uncertainty of the world outside the Roman provinces, or even to aspire to owning a piece of them. Is the Ördögárok telling us that the Age of the Migrations had begun; and may we therefore consider the dyke system as a hindrance to migratory movement? Raiding parties are not long delayed by ditches; but the approach of a nation, with its herds and wagons, would entail stoppages of perhaps two days at each line while gaps and causeways were dug. The earthworks would thus act both as a stalling device and an early-warning system. In this sense they give meaning to the counterforts and landing places. Of the latter, nine pairs have now been found on the Hungarian Danube's 150-mile, south-flowing reach.[22] However none of this carries conviction without proof of a signals network, for an enemy approaching the outer dyke could be over a hundred miles from the nearest Roman posts on the Danube bank.

In 1875 three tiles stamped with the insignium of the Budapest legion's brickworks were found at Hatvan-Gombospuszta, forty miles inside former barbarian territory. For ninety years these gathered dust in the Hungarian National Museum. In 1966 an attempt was made to trace their origin and two years later a watchtower with two-roomed guardhouse was unearthed. The site is close to the outer dyke complex and overlooks a ford in the nearby river Zagyvar. In the late 1960s, near Felsögöd, a 4th-century fort was discovered close to the same line. Though only a few miles from the Danube, this was possibly a support station for a series of signal towers.[23] There the case for an early-warning system presently rests. Heavy reinforcement to the Middle Danube two generations later suggests that by then the Hungarian dyke complex had failed, perhaps because the Sarmatians proved untrustworthy. Its useful life may only have been fifty years.

Below Belgrade, at the Iron Gates, the Danube penetrates hill country, uninviting to the attacker. Out on the plain again, in Oltenia (southern Romania) the earthworks recommence on an approximately matching alignment, which could support the idea of a grand design.[24] On the other hand the Romanian continuation takes the more modest form of a single large ditch with mound. It is known as *Brazda lui Novac* (Novac's Dyke) after a legendary Romanian giant. Starting from the village of Hinova, just below the Iron Gates, it travels east at about 40 miles north of the Danube, diverging to 60. It is 300 miles long and peters out somewhere beyond Ploieshti. At best it now stands to only three feet, being much degraded by plough and rain. It defended from the Carpathian direction, for its ditch is on the north side. There is a second dyke, also with its ditch to the north: 90 miles long and only 15 from the river. This is the Southern Novac Dyke, covering the frontier stretch containing the Oescus and Novae legionary bases. Here at last was an opportunity for dating, as the dyke intersects with the *vallum* of the Trans-Olt line. On investigation dyke was found to underlie *vallum*, proving it to be earlier than AD 200, when Septimius established the Trans-Olt frontier. The Southern Novac dyke seems therefore to be a 1st-century work, from the unsettled years before Trajan's conquest; while the main *Brazda lui Novac* is thought to be from the 4th century, probably a Roman outwork against Gothic migration.

A third group lies beyond the Danube's final bend and outside the delta,[25] a direction against which Rome should have made more timely provision. Here are four works: shorter than those further west but still adding up to some 225 miles of ditch and mound. As in the other instances, all appear to have been without forts and therefore unmanned. Nearest and shortest is the Galatz *vallum*, 15 miles long, which covered the bend and runs north-west of the Romanian town of that name. The bend constituted a salient into a perennially troubled zone, which the ford at Dinogetia (Garvan) made especially vulnerable. The dyke is well constructed and believed to be Roman of the 4th century.

Parallel with the Danube's last reach and 20 miles outside it is an 80-mile-long, west–east earthwork called the Lower Bessarabian *vallum*. It runs from the Prut to the Sasyk lagoon on the Black Sea coast. The dyke is crossed by two lesser rivers, which divide its course into three lengths, different in design and workmanship. The western third, with mound, berm and north-facing ditch, is carefully built and well preserved. Even today it stands 15 feet high from ditch bottom to mound top. The middle third is of hastier construction, with the ditch spoil piled onto the southern lip in a way inviting slippage. The eastern third is similar but even more erratic. This points to the three sections being separately built, probably at different times during the 4th century. Either each was constructed in more haste than the last, or what began with the army ended with hired labour. Such is Rome's mark on the soil of the former Soviet Union, other than in the Crimea and the enclaves round the Black Sea ports. The two remaining earthworks are considered barbarian in imitation of Roman: the *vallum* of Athanaric, between Siret and Prut (53 miles) and the Gruthungian *vallum* between Prut and Dniestr (75 miles). Both are some distance beyond the imperial frontier and of hurried workmanship. They are believed to be Gothic, built against the Huns during the later 4th century. That of Athanaric faces south. It is mentioned in a Roman source[26] and may be dated to 376. In summary the earthworks believed of Roman origin, despite varying design and quality, all share the ability to hinder migration and buy time for counter-measures. The *limes* had been devised to repel able-bodied intruders, travelling light. The dykes may be seen as an add-on device, whose intention was to adapt the frontier to a new kind of danger: from migrating families, the land-hungry, home-seekers and refugees.

Let us review Diocletian's achievement. He reformed – or attempted to reform – the army, the civil service, the currency, prices and the constitution. He strengthened the frontiers and continued the work of defending cities. On his coinage he calls himself *renovator*, *recuperator* and *reparator*. He or his colleagues defeated the Persians and the Alamanns. He assessed the empire's resources and matched them to its needs. He founded and integrated an empire-wide system of state weapons, armour, uniform and footwear factories. He terminated Italy's privileged status regarding military service and tax exemption. He ended the distinction between senatorial and imperial provinces. He steadied inflation and moderated agricultural decline. But, on the debit side, administration quadrupled, while taxation and compulsion grew. So did caste creation and the tying of people to professions. Cities continued to wither and small farmers and businessmen to be ruined. In strategic thinking the advances of the previous thirty years were rejected.

Around 296 Constantius, caesar in the west, invaded Britain, ending the separatist regime of Carausius and Allectus, which had defied Diocletian for a decade. After Diocletian's abdication he returned, campaigning in Scotland with his son Constantine. As if this were not sufficient to remind us of Septimius he wintered in York, died there, and his son was proclaimed emperor by the soldiers. This was in 306, though it was only after prolonged civil war that Constantine would emerge as sole ruler. Like Diocletian's his reign was lengthy (306–37), his achievement sizeable and the empire reverted to chaos on his death. Two great events, however, were peculiarly his own: conversion to Christianity and the founding of Constantinople. These would have incalculable consequences; indeed some have seen in them the commencement of the Middle Ages. The new capital, between Europe and Asia, strategically incomparable and incomparably defensible, would prove a heart transplant for the eastern empire. As an answer to the downslide of the western provinces Christianity would prove a false dawn. In the shorter term, however, it offered a timely weapon against insolvency. The problem of shaking out the precious metals concealed in the empire's undergarments was dramatically assisted by the sequestration of the temple treasures. This thousand-year accumulation of gifts to the gods of Rome was a windfall equalling the war booties of the heroic age, bringing the currency rapidly to its feet and returning taxation to a cash basis.

Foremost in Constantine's defence policy was a return to the heavy-cavalry-based strategies of Aurelian and Probus, though without neglecting the European frontiers and without forgetting Diocletian's idea of buildings designed for counter-attack. Accordingly he endorsed the use of the counterfort, as in the case of his castle of Divitia (Köln-Deutz). This great, square fort, with eighteen round towers, jutted into the land of the Franks, the self-styled 'free men'. Its garrison of 900 was linked to urban Cologne by a bridge on the site of today's Deutzer Brücke; while the remains of its east gate, which led into the *barbaricum*, are preserved, near the Lufthansa Building. Germans were increasingly employed to counter Germans. They would dominate the 4th century as Danubians had the 3rd, at all levels from trooper to general. Germans continued to show no interest in Roman politics and employing them had some advantage over the internecine Illyricans. Constantine now dissolved the Praetorian Guard, ending three centuries of mischief.

The reign saw no slackening of taxation's screw or coercion's rack. Despite adopting Christianity there are few signs of charity in Constantine's execution of his wife and son; nor of humility in the continuing cult of the purple. Though canonised by the Orthodox Church, to some he is more aptly symbolised by the nine-ton head, preserved in the Palazzo dei Conservatori; surviving component of a seven-times-lifesize likeness which sat in one of Rome's basilicas. The empire which he passed to his surviving sons and nephews was over-regulated, over-taxed, over-Germanised, slipping towards servitude and with its future in the east. But it was solvent and strongly defended at last.

Regarding sources, the first half of the 4th century finds us in clover, the second half knee-deep in it. There are the Christian fathers, legal codes and itineraries; plus the Greek historians Priscus, Zosimus and Procopius, of later date but useful in retrospect. St Jerome, originally a Dalmatian, engaged in translating the Bible into Latin, watched the first tottering of the ancient world from his cell in Bethlehem and wrote of it, in his correspondence, with concern and compassion. In complete contrast are two pagan writers; Vegetius, author of *Epitoma Rei Militaris* ('A digest of military matters'); and the anonymous author of a late 4th-century military tract known as *de Rebus Bellicis* ('on warfare'). However, Vegetius commented little on his own time and his interest is mainly in the light he sheds on warfare in the earlier period. The Anonymous, on the other hand, is passionately concerned with the late empire's troubles, but his solutions are unrealistic. He is a would-be inventor, with a Hitlerian belief in V-weapons, such as warships with paddles turned by yoked bulls. His fantasies serve to emphasise Rome's backwardness, both in invention and application, and the improbability of her ever achieving technological breakthrough of a quality likely to confound her enemies. For the frontier he suggests that 'Among measures for the public benefit it would be opportune to guard our frontiers with permanent forts, a mile apart, equipped with strong walls and towers. The cost of building need not be borne by the state but would be shared by the landholders through which it passed.'[27] Here is an echo of the initiatives already being privately sponsored in Africa and elsewhere. However, his suggestion, in matter-of-fact tones, of building a belated Hadrianic cordon round several thousand miles of imperial perimeter would be difficult to take seriously.

All fade beside Ammian, chronicler of late antiquity and close runner as the best historian the ancient world produced. He has been called 'the greatest literary genius between Tacitus and Dante',[28] and we are aware of few challenges to this claim. Ammian was a Syrian Greek who spent formative years with the colours. This was a period so laden with exceptional experiences that it prompted him to write an account which would place his own adventures in the perspective of history. Accordingly he took AD 96, where Tacitus left off, as his starting point; writing thirty-one books (in Latin), whose scope expands as they reach contemporaneity. Almost half is lost, but by good fortune it is the part describing his military career, plus that covering a further fifteen years of his lifetime, which survive. Heavy with information the text covers the years 353–78 in some 150,000 words. Books 14–25 reveal him as a staff officer on both eastern and western fronts and 26–31 as a traveller, researcher and author. The upshot is an empire-wide canvas which combines the fine brush-strokes of an eyewitness with the broad sweep of an interpreter of historical processes. Ammian is the equal of Tacitus except in literary skills, though as a supplier of fact far surpassing him. And yet he is an artist neglected, victim of the classicist's bias against late Latin and the historian's against the post-Antonine. His reputation begins at last to be redeemed.[29]

Constantine was buried at Constantinople in 337. The army then mutinied, murdering nephews and half-brothers and leaving three sons at daggers drawn. One was killed in civil war, another in a palace revolution and the youngest became Constantius II. Ammian now lifts the curtain. In 353 he was attached to Ursicinus, the general commanding the eastern armies, joining his staff at Nisibis

(Nusaybin) where Constantius was involved in a losing war with Shapur II over Mesopotamia. He later accompanied the general on missions, including one to Cologne. On the Rhine he saw Julian, the emperor's surviving cousin, in action against the Franks and Alamanns. In Mesopotamia he witnessed the siege of Nisibis from the outside and that of Amida (Diyarbakir, on the upper Tigris) from within, escaping by night from the final débâcle. His account of this siege, which cost Shapur 73 days and 30,000 men, is a high point of ancient historical writing. Diyarbakir's black walls, restored by Justinian, still stand. Equally awesome is the occasion when Ammian spied out the advancing Persian army, watching from a hillside as its glittering column wound over the dusty plain toward Roman territory. He then served under Julian in Gaul and describes his rout of the Alamanni at the battle of Strasbourg. Finally he accompanied Julian's fateful expedition to Persia.

This young prince, later emperor, is the tragic hero of Ammian's history. A secluded upbringing in the eastern provinces had shielded him from early murder. Now Constantius, his cousin, unable to douse two flaring fronts at once, called him to Germany: 'Julian, who not long ago had been sent for from Athens and arrived still wearing a student's gown[30][. . .] was a seeker after truth and harmony, like Marcus Aurelius, on whom he modelled himself.'[31]

The battle against the Alamannic confederation was fought in a part of the Upper Rhine which the Germans had come to see as their rightful doorway into Gaul. The armies met near Strasbourg 'on a gentle hill, covered with ripe wheat, not far from the Rhine bank'.[32] Julian's was a hastily assembled force, greatly inferior in numbers. On the German side we note the weakness of confederational politics, for two kings shared the command 'followed by five others, next in power, ten princes and a long line of nobles, with 35,000 soldiers from various tribes. The Germans gnashed their teeth repulsively, with hair flowing wildly and a mad light in their eyes.'[33] It is probable that Alamannic unity buckled under strain. Though they had several times combined to force a way through the imperial frontier, the trick of coordination in a set-piece battle was less easy to acquire. At any rate the youthful philosopher outgeneralled them all: 'Two hundred and forty-three Roman soldiers fell in this battle and four high officers. Of the Alamanni there were counted on the field six thousand slain, while numbers beyond counting floated down the Rhine.'[34] It was like the good old days.

Nevertheless, as Constantius had feared, Julian became too popular and conflict ensued, with final confrontation only averted by the
emperor's death. Julian's short reign of 361–3 now followed. It is
principally remembered for his reversion to paganism and Christendom's dismissal of him as Julian the Apostate. Posterity's neglect of
Ammian's work has also served to enhance his oblivion, though none
of Rome's Christian emperors matches his magnetism or patriotism.
Unfortunately Julian soon succumbed to the orient's lure. Though
inspired by the great deeds of the past he claimed most to be compelled 'by the sorry plight of captured cities, the unavenged ghosts
of defeated armies and the destruction of numberless forts. We must
expunge a dangerous nation whose swords are still wet with our
brothers' blood!'[35]

An army of 65,000 now descended the Euphrates. This was accompanied by 'a thousand cargo carriers, fifty warships and fifty bridge
pontoons, for which the wide Euphrates was almost too narrow'.[36]
Shapur avoided battle. With the Persian host intact, Julian dared not
turn his back or lay siege to Ctesiphon. Scorched earth and failing
food supply obliged him to burn the fleet and retire toward Mesopotamia. At this juncture, a skirmish occurred near the Roman command post. Julian rushed to take charge and, neglecting to don body
armour, was killed by a random spear. So the house of Constantine
was extinguished and the army left in a retreat-from-Moscow situation. A Danubian officer, Jovian, was elected emperor in the field.
But he was ill-suited to the sudden responsibility and in a rash treaty
ceded all Mesopotamia, plus Diocletian's five pocket provinces
beyond the Tigris. Ammian survived the long march back to Antioch,
where his military service ended and the years of preparation for his
History began.

It is worth mentioning a few of his views. Like Julian, Ammian
was a pagan and (like a surprising number of upper-class Greeks) a
committed Roman. Though his narrative concludes with the grave
setback of Hadrianople (378) he cannot imagine a Rome which is
other than invulnerable, as expressed in phrases like, 'by the divine
will which nurtured Rome from the cradle and promised her eternity'.[37] Though an able commentator on war, he is not a deep, strategic thinker. Furthermore his experience is dominantly eastern at a
time when Rome's destiny was beginning to be shaped by events
between Black Sea and North Sea. His view of the frontier is traditional. For example, of Valentinian, last to pursue a policy of

frontier reliance, he writes: 'Not even his sternest critics can say he was backward in defending the empire, especially remembering how much more valuable it is to halt the barbarian at the frontier than to defeat him in battle.'[38]

Regarding the barbarians, opinions have changed little since Tacitus, when admiration for courage was qualified by deprecation of other capabilities. Ammian calls the Germans 'Our persistent and ferocious foe[39] [. . .] cringing one moment, crowing the next.'[40] But the ominous character of their cohesion is dawning. Most alliances disintegrate in the face of defeat, but the Alamann never give up. Seven years after Strasbourg they will be back in Gaul. 'This savage nation, though afflicted by disasters from its very birth, recovers so readily that it seems always to have been unharmed.'[41]

His close experience of sieges and artillery duels made Ammian a keen advocate of technology and he describes in some detail the *ballista* and *scorpio* (catapults), the *aries* (battering ram), ram on wheels, fire darts and so on.[42] Again this shows the eastern bias of his viewpoint, for siege will prove peripheral during the century to come, when the decisive factor would be mobility. Foreign policy shines darkly from the page. Frequently it means Roman perfidy. Of the Alamannic king Vithicabius, for example: 'He who had kindled the flame of war against us [. . .] no effort would be spared to dispose of him, by whatever means [. . .] And when war and treachery did not suffice he was murdered by bribing his servants.'[43] King Papa of Armenia was invited to lunch by Valens and run through by a contract killer.[44] The emperor's nephew Marcellianus made a similar end of the Quadan king, causing uproar on the Danube.[45] On the last page of Ammian's final book an entire Gothic army is duped into attending a pay parade and butchered.[46] Roman treachery, the variable calibre of her leadership, the greed and callousness of her soldiers, plus many instances of cruelty, torture, deceit, flattery and paranoia: all have a place in Ammian's work. Such was his record of the dealings of Christian Rome.

There remains another 4th-century source, the *Notitia Dignitatum* ('Register of Officials'), a curious product of historical chance, oceans apart from Ammian, difficult to read without nodding off, never (as far as we are aware) translated into a modern language or published in a manner accessible to the general reader. And yet it forms the basis of our knowledge of the army and administration of the late Roman world. It appears to originate from the archive of a government department and is a register of every civil and military post in the empire, listing all commanding officers with the names of their units and stations; so giving a paper picture of almost the entire army. Preceding each section is an illustrated title page, sometimes informative, sometimes symbolic or heraldic. Gibbon placed the *Notitia* between AD 395 and 407. A century later Bury advanced it to about 423. We now consider both were in a sense correct. In the 1930s K. Polaschek and H. Nesselhauf noticed that some regiments seemed to be recorded at different posts simultaneously. They explained this in terms of a running record, carelessly kept over a number of decades, with new information not always added and obsolete information not always discarded. Thus, when a unit was moved, its new location might be entered without the old being deleted. This is substantially the view held today. It is also supposed that two copies existed, one in Ravenna and the other in Constantinople. The version which has come down to us was the one held in the western capital. Naturally greater care was taken with the western information, which was updated more assiduously than the eastern. What therefore remains is a record of the western army's state to about 423 and the eastern to about 395. In a frontier sense the *Notitia* is the most important document we have, though it reflects a frontier well past its prime. It affords an overview which centuries of archaeological effort might never provide.

The *Notitia* suggests an army strength of over half a million, with 350,000 frontier-based and 150,000 mobile troops. *Laeti* and other affiliates are also listed, giving a grand total nearly double that of the early empire's. The ratio of frontier to mobile is roughly 7 to 3, though this varies from one diocese to another. A remarkable total of 188 legions is given, compared with 32 in the last days of the Principate. Of these, 48 had been promoted into the mobile armies and 140 remained on the frontier. Zosimus tells us the legions were now only 1,200 strong[47] (from an original 6,000). Doubtless they had been downgraded in armament and quality as well. Auxiliary cohorts were reduced from 500 men to a probable 160 or 170. Some legions may have been ghost units for which corrupt officials drew pay or rations. It is both noticeable and significant that the frontier (or second-class) regiments have predominantly Roman names, while the mobile (or first-class) units are German.

The *Notitia* shows us an army still concentrated in the Middle and Lower Danube, with the Rhine relatively lightly guarded. Clearly the Middle Danube was Italy's shield from the direction of eastern Europe and the Lower Danube Constantinople's. The proportion of frontier troops is higher than average: on the Middle Danube about 3½ to 1. The Balkan terrain is generally less favourable to an army of manoeuvre. In Gaul, by contrast, the field army was bigger because a more open style of warfare was feasible. Even so overall numbers in Gaul, Spain and Tingitana (Morocco) are less than a third of those in the mid-to-lower Danube zone. To the strategist this might suggest that the line of least resistance toward the empire's heart was now Rhine–Pyrenees–Strait of Gibraltar–Africa.

But we must not allow the *Notitia* to entice us into the 5th century. With Julian's death, Rome lost another part of herself; a cultural milestone, not unlike the time builders began to throw inscriptions and decorative stonework into the foundations of town walls. Julian was almost the last pagan emperor, the last inspired by classical learning, the last Roman dreamer. His forlorn death, in Alexander's footsteps, ends the classical past on an oddly romantic note.

This is also the place to take leave of Persia, except to add that Gothic presence in the Crimea and south Ukraine would soon influence Valens to relinquish the Roman outposts at the eastern end of the Black Sea, which passed under the sway of Shapur II. How might we summarise the long and futile feud between those empires? In three centuries positions had changed little, either in territory or attitudes. Here were two states whose vital interests posed no mutual threat and which were perfectly placed to be trading partners. Instead, emperors gambling for glory had mounted extravagant expeditions, lost as often as they won and involved themselves in costly defence for modest gain. The preponderance of aggression had been Rome's. Augustus and Hadrian had been wise to have no part of it.

Jovian died in 364 after an eighteen-month reign. At a gathering of the powerful in Nicaea, Valentinian, another Danubian officer and son of a peasant, was elected. He is memorable in two ways. First for his reversion to the frontier policy of Diocletian, which in turn had been a reversion to that of the early empire. Like André Maginot, he saw construction as the antidote to invasion and applied it in a manner suited to his reputation as last of the frontier emperors. 'Valentinian, in pursuit of a carefully considered plan, strengthened the entire Rhine from Raetia to the Ocean, with major earthworks, forts and towers, closely spaced at key points along the whole length of Gaul; and forts in some instances placed on the far side of the river.'[48]

Ideas in castrametation, often attributed to the Middle Ages, continued to be developed: hilltop siting, small circuits, high walls, projecting towers, recessed gates, sallyports, inner citadels, encircling walkways, double guardrooms and the rest. Special emphasis was given to the closure of the Rhine between Mainz and Basle, where Altrip (Alta Ripa), Boppard (Bodbriga), Alzey and Speyer (Noviomagus), are Valentinianic foundations. The Upper Rhine forts received new garrisons. The *Notitia* contains only barbaric-sounding names and *Legio XXII Primigenia* is heard of no more. Fortified crossings at Rheinbrohl, Engers, Niederlahnstein and Zullestein are probably also from this reign. Roadforts were built at Bitburg, Junkerath, Neumagen and other key points, 35–60 miles behind the river. With the choice of many way-stations and walled towns in which to shelter, marching camp construction had long lapsed. When obliged to bivouac soldiers simply protected themselves with stakes or rows of shields.[49]

In Czechoslovakia, Valentinian returned to Hadrian's policy of discreet penetration. Cifer-Pac, twenty-five miles north of the Danube at Bratislava, with its mixed Roman and German buildings, is a late-4th-century site. Ammian tells us Valentinian built forward posts 'actually in Quadanland'.[50] But the Quadans were misbehaving again. He calls them 'Expert thieves, kidnappers and rustlers, who delight in killing and burning; who appear without warning and murder without mercy.'[51]

It was such annoyances which led to the emperor's death on the Danube bank. Ammian describes how Quadan envoys begged that the emperor might hear their people's pleas. At the time appointed the tribal notables crossed the river and approached the throne, humbly suing for peace and forgiveness. But as the audience progressed they became bolder, complaining at the building of fortifications against them.

At this the emperor boiled over in a fit of rage, yelling abuse at the whole nation and cursing them for their ingratitude at his many acts of kindness. He appeared to calm down somewhat but then in a trice was struck dumb. Fighting for breath he turned bright red and broke into a deadly sweat. His servants rushed to prop him up and help him under cover. There he still tried to speak, heaving his chest, grinding his teeth and flailing his arms. After a protracted fight for life he breathed his last, in his 55th year and the 12th of his reign.[52]

Valentinian is also memorable for his partition of the empire. Spending most of his reign at Trier, he accepted that simultaneous control of east and west was now impossible. Accordingly, an amicable separation was arranged, by which his brother Valens ruled the empire's eastern half from Constantinople. No one saw this as a division for all time, but in fact the halves would recombine only once, and at that for just three years. Rather they would begin a cultural floating apart; the eastern empire back toward its Hellenistic home, though with Roman law and the Bible now in tow.

Valens, too, would be killed by the barbarians, under circumstances no less spectacular. With his death the 4th century recovery was over, and Ammian's account closes. The last great historian of antiquity points inexorably downwards. Yet, a few years earlier, the empire had seemed strong, the rivers reinforced, the German threat contained, world order restored and Rome put to rights. They had called the era of Diocletian and Constantine *reparatio saeculi*, the age of restoration. The disaster now impending had been centuries in the making. It had been approaching at the pace of grazing animals along the almost limitless, grassy way of the Asian steppe. Through the long years of Rome's rise, ascendancy and decline the danger had been advancing stealthily, over a lingering timespan, to arrive with fearsome suddenness at last. It was a nation new to the European scene, a fresh player in the imperial end-game; an enemy not unlike the Sarmatians, but more numerous, more dangerous and more vile.

CHAPTER 11

The Wrath of Mars

... the wall is down that parted their fathers'
A Midsummer Night's Dream, V.i.350

THE HUNS, perhaps originally the Hiung-Nu,[1] against whom the Great Wall of China[2] had first been built,[3] approached Europe via the Black Sea's northern shore, entering the Roman view in 373. They were wagon-dwellers and inveterate pastoralists. 'Nowhere, between Volga and Danube has a ploughshare, corn grinder or sickle been found which might be connected with the Huns or Alans.'[4] All describe them as repellently ugly, their looks not improved by the custom of deforming the infant skull, binding it to make the crown of the head conical; and scarring chin and jowl to inhibit beard growth. They were the most audacious and acrobatic of all horsemen and the most skilled of mounted archers. Their approach froze the blood. The events of the 370s fall within the scope of Ammian's *History*, though his knowledge of them was not first-hand:

> The source of all destruction wrought by the wrath of Mars is the Hun, that most savage and ugly of all races. They have short, strong limbs, bull necks and bodies so stumpy and malformed one might take them for the Janus[5] figures which we put on bridges. So tough are they that they dispense with cooking, but eat roots and raw meat; the latter being warmed and tenderised by placing it between rider and horse. They dress in cloth or garments of mouse skin.[6] Once they put their heads into a shirt it is not taken off until it disintegrates. They are glued as it were to their mounts,

269

sitting on them to perform daily tasks: eating, drinking, bartering, even sleeping draped around the horse's neck. In war they excel in the extreme rapidity of their attack, whirling about in scattered bands, spreading havoc, fighting from a distance with bone-pointed arrows, then suddenly closing to use lasso and sabre. They are brave in war, faithless in truce, deceitful in speech, quick to anger and insatiably hungry for gold.[7]

The Huns' first impact upon Rome was indirect and concerns their effect upon the Goths who lay directly in their path. As in billiard-like games, when the cue ball is played with exceptional wildness, striking the object ball which in turn cannons into others, producing second-ary consequences unforeseen in the original stroke; so the Hunnic onslaught caused perturbations unimagined in the German world: 'News ran through the Gothic peoples of a race of men, previously unknown, arisen as if from beneath the earth, which was now destroying all in its path.'[8]

The Huns first fell upon the Ostrogoths or Gruthungi, beating them so roundly that their king Ermanaric[9] committed suicide. The Visigoths, on the Dniestr, were next. Athanaric's hastily built *vallum* was in vain. His people broke and fled toward the Lower Danube. Alarming rumours reached the Roman bank: 'Scare stories were spreading of a huge commotion among the Goths. From the Black Sea to Marcomannia their savage hordes, uprooted by some sudden storm, were milling around the Danube region with their families.'[10] Tacitus had long ago said that inter-barbarian conflicts played into Rome's hands. But did they? Two huge, human waves were now moving (in the eternal direction of refugees) westwards. A clamour for entry to the empire on an unprecedented scale was about to begin. Its outcome would be the *receptio* of 375; and though this involved the eastern empire only, it was the first in a chain of events which would end in the fall of western Rome.

The eastern emperor was delighted. He showed no understanding of steppe events and failed to grasp their scale.

Valens was overjoyed at the prospect of so many recruits. He reasoned that if the Goths were integrated into his army it would give him an overwhelming force. Accordingly he sent officers to direct the transport of this savage host across the Danube and to supervise their settlement in parts of Thrace. Crowded into boats, onto rafts, even in hollowed tree trunks they were ferried across over a period of several days and nights. The river was swollen with rain and many who tried to swim were drowned. Thus eagerly was the ruin of Rome ushered in and our frontiers unbarred. Those who supervised the operation tried to estimate the number but abandoned the attempt. On their arrival the emperor ordered that they be given provisions for their present needs and land to farm.[11]

The Visigoths were to find Roman hospitality wanting. Winter was near, and they were forced to buy food at prices fixed by the Count of Thrace, whose agents sold them dead dogs. Soon uprisings began to sweep the squatter camps. Many rallied to Fritigern, their king, who led them in an attempt to take Hadrianople (Edirne), only 150 miles from Constantinople. But his ragged regiments were routed by its wall-mounted artillery, which was something they had never seen. Fritigern took this philosophically. By now it was summer and the countryside promised spoils enough. 'Seeing what the siege was costing due to his people's inexperience, Fritigern ordered them to make peace with walls and make war on fields, whose riches were there for the taking.'[12]

In early August 378 Valens, having mustered the eastern army, decided to take back the initiative. Marching from Constantinople in exceptionally hot weather, he came suddenly upon the Visigoths, camped among wagons near Hadrianople. Though his soldiers were tired, thirsty and still in column of march, he ordered an immediate attack. Gothic resistance was unexpectedly sharp. The Roman van reeled back, colliding with the main infantry in mid-deployment. Fritigern counter-attacked. Valens was pinned in the middle of his own soldiers and could see almost nothing. As the battle neared its climax a large party of mounted Goths chanced to return from a foraging mission. Charging into the Roman rear they tipped the scales. 'Certainly' (says Ammian) 'barely a third of our men left the field.'[13] One story is that Valens was killed by a Gothic arrow, another that he was blockaded in a cottage and there burned to death. Such was the welcome of the first eastern emperor to his throne. The shock was profound. A hundred-year run of victories had ended in Julian's retreat from Persia and Valens' defeat in Thrace, both within a decade and both costing an emperor's life. The implications were even grimmer. The Goths were now at liberty to rampage through the Balkan provinces. The enemy was within and the Danube's defences faced outwards.

Fritigern's first instinct was to go for Constantinople; but the walls saved the city and the city the eastern provinces. His options were narrowing. The Ostrogoths, deflected further northwards by the Huns towards the Middle Danube, had been partially admitted as federates. It was probably their presence in the eastern Balkans which caused the Visigoths to keep to the Adriatic side, contributing to the fateful decision by Fritigern's successor, Alaric, to lead his people into Italy.

Meanwhile the Huns, whose dominion still stretched along the northern Black Sea, attacked the eastern provinces by way of Georgia, Armenia and Syria. Their goal was rumoured to be Jerusalem, a city which had never known the northern barbarian. Jerome, writing from Bethlehem, describes the panic and dismay, ending with a famous comment on the horsebound Hun:

> The Roman world is falling. We thought the east immune but last year [AD 395] the northern wolves descended on us. How many monasteries fell to them, how many rivers ran red? It is our vices which bring defeat to Rome's armies. Fighting among ourselves has cost us more than fighting our enemies. The Roman army which conquered the world now runs from men who know not how to walk, who once they are unhorsed count themselves as dead.[14]

The threat to Jerusalem, however, did not materialise. The Huns had overreached and withdrew. The main body of their nation was moving westwards, absorbing Transylvania, then descending into Hungary, whose name still bears the stigma of their stay. Here on the wide plain, outside the Danube but within the great arc of the Ördögárok or Devil's Dyke, they made their capital and founded an empire under Mundiuch and Rua, father and uncle of Attila.

Despite this the Gothic danger was the more pressing. During the 5th century's first decade the Visigoths invaded Italy three times and the Ostrogoths once. Honorius moved the capital from Milan – a city without natural defence – to Ravenna, taking court, bodyguard and the bureaucratic battalions with him. The west's hope lay in a Vandal named Stilicho (commander of the field armies and *de facto* ruler during much of the reign of the ineffectual Honorius), who defeated Alaric's first foray and also that of the Ostrogoths. However, envious Roman officers, in a last effort to regain influence, led an anti-German coup in which Stilicho was murdered. The likelihood of defeating Alaric diminished. He soon returned, reaching central Italy and besieging Rome. He was bribed to retire, but within two years was again camped outside the city. On 24 August 410, traitorous citizens who had experienced starvation in the earlier siege and feared it more than Alaric, opened a gate. For the first time in eight centuries a barbarian army was inside the city. Jerome wrote: 'A dreadful whisper has reached us from the west. The city which had taken the whole world is herself taken. Oh God, the heathen has come into Thine inheritance.'[15]

Capitur urbs quae totum cepit orbem: 'The city taken, by which the world was taken'! It had been only thirty-four years since the Hunnic hammer whacked the Gothic wedge into the empire's side. And yet Rome still seemed eternal, even to Alaric. His eyes were on Africa as a Gothic national home. His column must not be overburdened and there was a fleet to build. Restraint was therefore exercised, and the sack lasted only three days. Alaric left for the south, taking the emperor's sister Galla Placidia as hostage. But his improvised armada was caught by a storm in the Strait of Messina and he died soon after. His heirs hesitated then withdrew from Italy altogether, setting up home in Aquitania, south-west Gaul. Rome had been let off lightly and would endure fifty more years.

Ravenna now burgeons briefly: city of haunting mosaics, cultural codicil of the ancient world. Here, between the Po marshes and the Adriatic lagoons, was a refuge such as would later be found in Venice; closed to the land except by narrow causeway but open to the sea and Constantinople. The Middle Danube was less secure. With the Goths inside and the Huns outside, its worth was in doubt and its men at risk. Though evacuation would mean the abandonment of Pannonia, at least nature had given Italy defences of her own. It was time to look to them. The Julian Alps, behind today's Trieste, are the setting for the second last of Rome's many efforts at frontier creation. Like most Roman *limites*, its scenery and atmosphere are of high order; though, as we might expect from a time of near collapse, the effort was less than the danger deserved.

The Julian Alpine frontier includes no continuous barrier or even fort chain. It is a *clausura* system, whose mainstay was the closure wall, used to seal passes or block valleys, with the intermediate hills and forests left to look after themselves. We have seen this method in southern Tunisia.[16] Ammian calls it *claustra alpium Iuliarum* (the Julian Alpine barricades). Typically these defensive plugs take the form of an isolated fort or fortlet, placed in a natural gap or on a mountain road, with wing walls running out as far as a steep slope or crags on either side. The walls are usually short – perhaps half a mile – though one is as long as seven. A local historian writes of thirteen lengths identified positively and eleven tentatively.[17] In short, the frontier was highly discontinuous, with perhaps two dozen posts spread unevenly over an area about fifty miles by twenty-five; arranged to cover road, track or even footpath approaches.

The Julian Alps, northeastern limit of Italy and border with Illyricum, were named after Octavian's family at the time of his campaign to subdue the Adriatic.[18] At the junction of the Italian and Balkan peninsulas, this is an eternal borderland, as is later suggested by its changing status: Austrian till Versailles, Italian till 1945, Jugoslavian till 1990 and now part Slovenian and part Croatian. It is also the extremity of the Alpine arc, joining the Dinaric Alps at the lowest part of both. Octavian carried the first road, from Aquileia at the head of the Adriatic to Emona (Ljubljana), using a pass later known as *ad pirum* (by the pear tree) probably from an inn of that name on the summit. This was part of the *via Gemina*, highway to Pannonia and conversely, in the late period, an invasion route from the Balkans. As the Danubian position worsened it was natural to develop the Julian Alps with *ad pirum* as its pivot. Accordingly this was strongest held, with a fort and blocking walls at the summit, three more *clausurae* on the approach road and a fort in the valley at either end.

Peartree Pass – in Slovene Hrušica[19] – lies between Aidovščina and Vrhnika on a motorable gravel road. At 2,900 feet it is the second lowest in the Alps and anciently negotiable by wagon. The fort ruins, totally lost in pine forest, were cleared and restored by Italian archaeologists in 1938, when the bimillennium of Augustus' birth was celebrated with a variety of projects; but investigated more thoroughly in the Slovenian–German excavations of 1971–3.[20] The ruins lie crosswise on the summit of the pass, probably of Valentinianic date: a large fort, with wing walls added perhaps in the early 5th century.

The next *clausura* eastwards is also worth seeing. This is Lanišče,[21] a fortlet only a stone's throw from the track but half-hidden among

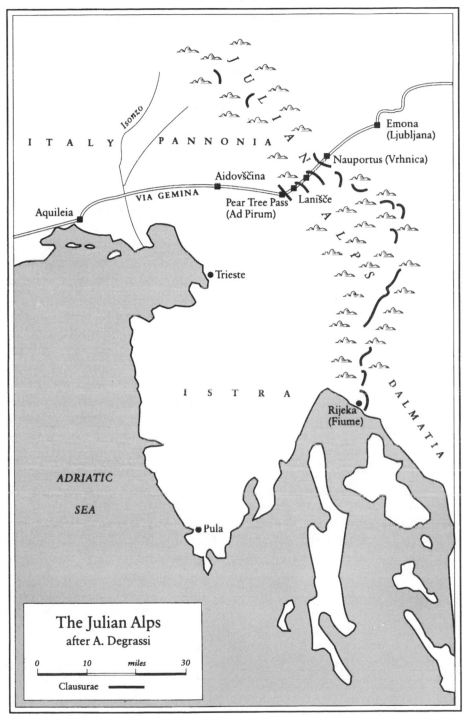

The Julian Alps
after A. Degrassi

| 0 | 10 | miles | 30 |

Clausurae ━━━━━

trees. Its walls, restored to full height and whitewashed in imitation of their original state, have a short stretch of closure wall attached. Excavation has dated it to the end of the 4th century.[22] At least two other short *clausurae* have been located some twenty miles north-west of Peartree Pass, but most lay eastwards and southwards, in a rough arc ending at Rijeka (formerly Fiume) on the Dalmatian coast. The remains are scanty and the likely outcome of a long hike over forest paths might at best be a few mossy mounds and some crumbs of mortar disturbed by tree roots.

This was a low-cost *limes*, fragmentary and lightly guarded, its scattered outposts unlinked by road. It probably fell between two policies: Valentinian devoting his resources to the Rhine and Danube and his successors giving theirs to the field armies. Its strategic intentions are unclear and the theory that the main danger was now migratory offers only partial answers. It is true that since migration involves wagons, defence could concentrate on the passes, avoiding the expense of a cross-country barrier. But by no means all the Julian Alpine closures were on roads. Speculation is weakened by lack of knowledge of the Gothic invasions. However, we do know that Alaric was seeking a homeland and it is unlikely he would leave the women, children and elderly unprotected in the Balkans. It therefore seems probable that Peartree Pass, the obvious route for a national trek into Italy, witnessed invasions during the 5th century. It is unlikely that its defences did much to stop them. Delaying tactics, including the felling of trees across the road, were doubtless the intention, allowing time to alert the Count of Italy, who was waiting at Aquileia with large forces. Peartree Pass has an even more painful memory. Partition of the empire made it feasible for each half to establish frontiers of its own; feasible even that Roman might one day fight Roman across them. This now occurred. In the valley below, east met west in a conflict so deadly that casualties exceeded those of Hadrianople. The battle of Fluvius Frigidus ('cold river')[23] was fought in 394 between the eastern emperor Theodosius I and a western pretender Eugenius. So a frontier intended to rebut the common foe of east and west is remembered for their mutual slaughter.

Not surprisingly, the decade between Alaric's decision to march against the west and his sack of Rome in 410 was one of such alarm that reserves were sucked in towards Italy from all directions. This exposed the Rhine as never before. Meanwhile the Huns, having first established themselves in Hungary, encroached northwards into present-day Slovakian and Polish lands, founding there an empire of sorts. No doubt there were battles and deep disturbance, hidden from the Roman view by the veil of forest and distance. The effect was that background Germans began to push their way into the foreground: tribes previously unknown on the Rhine, such as the Burgundians, Langobards and Vandals. The Burgundians will of course end in Burgundy and the Langobards in Lombardy. The Vandals have further to travel. They exemplify this period, not least in their name, from the German *wandern*, to wander. It seems in the light of what happened that these folk had hazy geographic goals, but were fairly clear what sort of life they were seeking. They aspired not to the destruction of the empire but to inclusion within it. In short they were refugees, albeit armed refugees, ready to take their country of refuge by force. But like most 5th-century Germans they would use minimum force, for there is little point in destroying one's future country.

The Vandalic confederation appeared on the Rhine during the bitter winter of 405–6; a horde totalling possibly 300,000. We can hardly doubt their distress. These were uprooted people who now faced the choice of starving on the German bank or of crossing and starving in Gaul. The invasion of Roman territory made sense only in summer, when fields were full and cupboards bare. Now the opposite was true: bare fields and food locked inside walled cities. There were nevertheless temptations to cross. Stilicho had drafted Gaul's entire field army for the defence of Italy. Then there was the freezing of the Rhine, unusually hard and exceptionally early. Accordingly, near Mainz, on New Year's Eve 405, there began a flow of fighting men, families, horses and wagons across the glassy pavement. Here was a haemorrhage which would be fatal to Rome. Germany was emptying her tribes and this time they would not return.

The almost continuous strip of Rhenish towns from Mainz to Cologne were bypassed and would survive. So, thanks to their walls, would many interior cities. With gates barred and fields empty there was little to detain the invaders and they fanned out across Gaul, some toward the Channel. Alarm-bells rang in Britain where the soldiers, seeking a strong leader, found one in a Constantine, who styled himself Constantine III. In his view, with Italy helpless to assist, the situation demanded a restored Gallic empire. Gathering all forces still in the island he crossed to Gaul, but became so embroiled that neither he nor his army returned. Control of Britain therefore lapsed and Roman coin issues cease for ever in 407. Zosimus tells us the Britons took the law into their own hands, throwing out the remaining officials and arming themselves.[24] We hear of Honorius writing from Ravenna in 410, advising the British cities to look to their own defence.[25] So, almost casually, snap threads first spun by Caesar four and a half centuries earlier. After thirty years' silence a message-in-a-bottle floats out of the post-Roman darkness, part of an appeal for help to Aetius, commander of the Italian field army: 'To Aetius came the groans of the Britons. The barbarians drive us into the sea, the sea drives us into the barbarians and between them we are being killed or drowned.'[26]

By 409 the Vandals were over the Pyrenees, with the Visigoths not far behind. Soon 200,000 Germans were settling Spanish land and Roman rule was confined to Catalonia. In the south Baetica – once as Roman as Italy – became Vandalucia. Spain, like Britain, was now cut loose from the Mediterranean world and drifted into isolation.

The Vandals were not destined for obscurity. They would stay in southern Spain for twenty years, during which time Carthage fell out with Ravenna. Turning the tiff to advantage the new Vandalic king, Gaiseric, crossed the Strait of Gibraltar. With him went a mere 80,000 people, from which we may infer some 20,000 fighting men, compared with a population of Roman North Africa of at least eight million. Nevertheless it took only ten years for his mailed cavalry to cut its way across the Mauretanias and Numidia. Carthage fell to him in 439. In a treaty with Valentinian III, Gaiseric kept Africa and Tripolitania, handing back Mauretania and Numidia in exchange for the betrothal of his son to the emperor's daughter. Africans, relieved of a bread-hungry Rome and a tax-hungry Ravenna, found themselves better off. By contrast, the residual provinces of Roman North Africa, with an army still to be supported and little good land to pay for it, remained poor. In practice frontiers now lapsed. As support dwindled and pay ceased, their guardians drifted away.

Though we have not yet seen the end of the Vandalic meteor, its flight has already put this tribe among military history's immortals. The left hook, from Germany via Gibraltar to Carthage, must rank with warfare's most breathtaking ploys, implying boundless strategic vision. In fact these unlettered Vandals were merely following a fault line in the imperial defences; entering by whichever door yielded to their touch. Reminiscing (in their African villas) about that freezing night only thirty-five years earlier when they had crossed the Rhine as vagabonds, the Vandalic elders had cause for satisfaction. For Romans, with the granary of the western empire lost and the enemy in the central Mediterranean, it was a preview of the end.

How had Gaul fared following the Vandalic breakthrough of 405? Remarkably, some sixty years would elapse between the end of Roman Britain and that of Roman Gaul. Though full of Germans, crisis management by Aetius and others would keep it nominally Roman and the immigrants as federates, signed up to defend imperial land. Real Romanity was nonetheless fading: cities going, villas gone, industry moribund, mints closing, half the countryside abandoned, the *bacaudae* ubiquitous and public life expiring.

Other provinces were on the same slope. The 5th century is a time of compulsion and flight from compulsion; of taxes irrespective of war damage or crop failure. It is a time of vagrancy and *agri deserti* (abandoned fields). From the corn-growing regions of what is now northern Tunisia, on the eve of the Vandalic invasion, we have the sombre statistic of a third of wheatgrowing land lying empty and in the olive zone a half. Farming everywhere returns to its core areas, with poorer or drier terrain falling fallow. The coin hoards which signal the 3rd century's troubles are almost absent in the 5th, when few have money to hide. More Roman gold coins are found in Germany than in the Roman provinces. Crime, the revenge of the ruined, reaches a new crescendo, combined now with separatist intent. Armorica (Brittany), for example, becomes virtually a criminal state.

In the face of coercion, public-spiritedness withers. Long gone are the do-gooders and status seekers, vying in benefactions and public works. Cities decay, *fora* sprout weeds and private money goes into private spending. Most toxic of all is the eclipse of patriotism. The populace is passive in the face of invasion. The empire had rarely touched hearts or evoked deep loyalty in the mass of its subjects. It was, after all, largely an association of the conquered. Now they would resign themselves to other conquerors. Civilisation's losses would be bearable because so much had been lost already. A decayed literature and philosophy, a Germanised army, a sick economy, a governmental structure not worth keeping and a frontier hardly worth defending: this was the legacy now at risk.

The rich continued to turn their energies toward tillage and tax evasion. Their estates became islands of prosperity in the decremental sea. Most famous had been those of Africa, which Ammian described as walled and citylike.[27] Whatever their shortcomings these squire-senators preserved something of the classical past, shored up a collapsing rural life and gave refuge and employment to many. The villa remains near Enna, central Sicily, and the floor mosaics in the Bardo Museum, Tunis, are among their autumnal monuments.

What of 'our soldiers, for whose pay the whole wealth of empire is becoming insufficient'?[28] Taxes doubled in the 4th century and may have done so again in the 5th. Soldiers still enjoyed the mighty perquisite of exemption and their living standards were twice those of the labouring classes. Military service, with all its risks, was the main avenue of escape from rural poverty. Even so, recruits were difficult to find, especially from the inner provinces whose citizens had for centuries bought protection with their taxes and were now oblivious of arms. We hear of the newly inducted locked every night in local gaols during transit to their units.[29] The self-mutilated were obliged to serve whatever their condition, with two counted as one in the local quotas. As morale sank, desertion rose. Some fled to the big estates. Others joined the robber bands. On the subject of discipline Vegetius writes that many soldiers had come to consider armour and helmets irksome and threw them away.[30] Zosimus, on the mood two years after Hadrianople, tells us: 'There was no discipline. Romans and barbarians mucked in together. No record was kept of who had enlisted. Some were allowed to go home and send others in their places.'[31]

In the sphere of central events we have seen Rome sacked, provinces lost, *receptiones* gone wrong and power passing into the hands of foreign mercenaries. The inflow of barbarians was matched only by the outflow of precious metals: 'From full coffers the Roman state has been brought to beggary by those who taught emperors to purchase peace from barbarians with gold.'[32] Stilicho paid Alaric 4,000 lbs of it and the Senate bought him off with 5,000 plus 30,000 of silver, 3,000 of pepper and a vast wardrobe of silk shirts. The west also paid 700 lbs of gold a year to the Huns and 8 *solidi* per head for the return of prisoners. The loot from the Roman world did not of course end in some Aladdin's cave deep in the *barbaricum*. Much returned in exchange for products the barbarians needed, before being paid out yet again.

We will see *receptio* as fatal. Invaders, refugees, economic opportunists, migrant workers, treaty tribes, mercenary soldiers and ambitious individuals: the empire played host to them all. In a process known to chemistry as deliquescence, certain types of crystal attract moisture until, eventually, they become solutions themselves. In a comparable process barbarians and Romans were merging. Rome was drawing in outsiders to the extent that her frontiers were ceasing to have meaning. Her high command was already melting and in the end would actually drown in the Germanity it was attracting.

The east fared better. With Anatolian recruiting grounds intact, it could defend itself without barbarian help. Asia Minor, Syria and Egypt were fully productive and unharmed. The eastern empire was not only wealthier but had a healthier distribution of wealth and a more vigorous economy. It contained 900 cities and two-thirds of the imperial population. Constantinople reaped 65% of total revenue, while Ravenna bore 65% of military costs. Of the Rhine and Danube, jointly the most dangerous and expensive frontiers, three-quarters was Ravenna's responsibility.[33] The Gothic decision to turn west, followed by eruption on the Rhine, were the east's reprieve. Even when the Lower Danube was overrun, no enemy succeeded in forcing the Bosphorus. The walls of Constantinople, aided by diplomacy and bribery, would continue to deflect invaders westwards.

Constantinople, today's Istanbul, is roughly triangular, with sea on two sides. On the third or western side, to a length of some five and a half miles, are the Land Walls. They were built in 430–440, replacing defences of lesser strength, by the regent Anthemius for the infant Theodosius II. This was soon after the sack of Rome and the shock spurred the project to greatness, for these double and sometimes triple walls are the climax of Roman fortification and among the finest defences of any age. They have 300 towers. Fronted by a huge moat, their total width is 70 yards and their height, from moat bottom to wall top, 105 feet. They will defend the city for a thousand years, defying Goth, Hun, Slav and Arab. They are a vivid demonstration of a wall's effectiveness, provided that strength, length and manning are in balance. They are largely intact and walking them is a stirring experience still. These were supplemented by an outer wall, where Europe narrows toward the Bosphorus, forty miles west of the city. It is twenty-seven miles long, from Evçik on the Black Sea to near Silivri on the Sea of Marmara, and still standing in parts to ten feet high or more, with ditch, turrets and forts.[34] It is probably of mid-5th-century date and offers an instructive contrast with the Land Walls, showing how the manpower strain of defending ramparts becomes interdictive beyond a modest length. As Procopius puts it: 'Anastasius built long walls forty miles from Byzantium, uniting the two coasts. But it proved impossible to give adequate protection to a structure of such length. When attacked its defenders were easily overpowered and those within were taken unawares.'[35] So, at Istanbul, we have history's most successful wall, of five miles length, in proximity to a forgotten and abandoned one of twenty-seven.

We left the Hunnic kingdom consolidating itself on the east Hungarian plain. Attila, born about 383, became king at the age of fifty. During his twenty-one-year reign Hunnia will balloon into the world's most powerful state, though based more on threat than substance. In the face of terror Ravenna will surrender the Middle Danube, reoccupying it briefly after Attila's death. Similarly, Constantinople will lose control of some of the Lower Danube, but will regain it more permanently. However these events did not spell doom, for initially the Huns could be contained by bribery. Attila's early strategy was to take land from the Germans and gold from the Romans. Accordingly, for the first fifteen years of his reign he lived by blackmailing Constantinople, making his point by raids of appalling brutality. At the treaty of Margus,[36] the eastern empire was forced to pay 2,000 pounds of gold annually and void a three-hundred-mile stretch of Danube frontage to a depth of a hundred miles. Again Constantinople survived by its wits and its walls. Yet the eastern empire was stronger and the Hunnic weaker than they seemed. Constantinople had resources, such as control of Egypt, far beyond the Huns' reach. Her annual revenue has been estimated at 270,000 pounds of gold a year. Attila had failed to grasp what his victim was worth. On the other hand, his own people produced nothing. They were without skills other than those of the nomad. They continued to be herders and their fodder requirement obliged them to scatter widely. At the centre, kingship and a status rivalling that of Roman emperors produced a rush of expenses. Here was a dispersed, ramshackle and unproductive empire caught up in accelerating extravagance and the quest for prestige.

During this time the historian Priscus accompanied a legation from Constantinople to the Hunnic court. His *History* survives only in fragments, but one of them – the famous *Excerpt 46* – is a 4,000-word account of this mission. It is rich in detail, with the darting observation one would today expect from a skilled journalist, opening a window into the very heart of Hunnia at a critical moment in its story. Of particular interest to the frontier historian is the state of the Lower-to-Middle Danube. As the small party enters the region devastated by Hunnic raids, the diplomats are sickened by what they see. Though it is six years since Attila's visitation, they find themselves in a realm of ruin and starvation. Nish, a former imperial capital, is empty of all but the sick and wounded, sheltering in its blitzed churches. There is no intact roof under which to lodge. Thinking to camp on the banks of the Morava the travellers find it so covered with skeletons and *disiecta membra* that they can scarcely pitch their tents. A barbarian ferries them across the Danube in a hollowed tree trunk. They begin the second part of their journey, of perhaps ten days in all, northwards into the Hungarian plain. At length they reach the Hunnic capital and attend a banquet in Attila's wooden palace. The great khan sits on a couch with two of his sons, surrounded by many chieftains. The guests take chairs round the walls. Wine is served and lengthy toasts follow, drunk in an elaborate order of precedence. Side tables are brought and the legation seated close to the royal bench. A meal is served on silver plates, with goblets of silver and gold. But Attila, who eats only meat, uses a wooden platter and drinks from a plain cup. His clothing too is the simplest of all present. Priscus and others describe him as squat, powerful, dark-eyed, flat-nosed, silent, unsmiling and inscrutable.

Attila's happy years of terror and extortion were about to be ended by the arrival of a *billet-doux* from a Roman princess. This was the wayward Honoria, daughter of Galla Placidia and sister of Valentinian III. Having been promised in marriage to someone she did not fancy, this spirited girl changed the course of history by writing to Attila, asking him to help her and provocatively enclosing a ring. It turned his head. He demanded her hand and half the western empire as dowry. The conundrum of his spiralling costs seemed about to be solved. Now he had only to give the west a taste of his power, as he had done to the east by cataclysmic raids. He marched to collect the Hunnic forces in eastern Germany, then swung toward the Rhine, crossing probably by raft at Neuwied. It is unlikely that the garrisons dared intervene.

Meanwhile, Aetius had brought the Italian field army to add to that of Gaul. These were doubled by contingents from the Gothic and other German settlers who, with the well-known dislike of new arrivals for the even newer, would fight lustily on Rome's side. Attila, having crossed much of northern Gaul and met many barred gates, was probably close to starvation. The armies clashed near Châlons-sur-Marne. The battle, sometimes known as the Catalaunian Plains (AD 451), was, in military terms, a draw. Nevertheless it is rated by retired generals[37] as one of history's most decisive, for Attila, deep in hostile territory and dogged by logistical problems, was obliged to withdraw. Aetius had performed a near-miracle. His reward for winning the last great Roman victory in the west was to be murdered by the jealous Valentinian III, for whom he had fought.

Attila, by no means spent, invaded Italy the next summer, almost certainly via Peartree Pass. His destruction of Aquileia was so total that the silence of this once great base would next be broken by the pick and shovel of its modern excavators. Attila prepared to march on Rome. The Italian field army was incapable of holding him. But now a second near-miracle occurred. Pope Leo I, persuaded by a hapless Ravenna and a desperate Rome, amazed the world with his intercession. Leo and Attila met on the river Mincio, near Mantua, and no one knows what was said. And yet, after a conversation with Christ's Vicar, God's Scourge returned to Hungary. Italy was however in the grip of plague; and it may be that a substantial offer of gold gave a welcome excuse to call off the campaign. Now seventy, Attila retired to his Hungarian palace. Before long he took to wife a strapping German girl named Hilda, a quarter of his age. The morning after the wedding he was found lying dead across the bed, the bride sobbing. Germany had succeeded where Rome failed. Unity now dissolved. Eighty years after that first thunderclap from the steppe, the word Hun disappears from meaningful history.

As for Rome's final frontier, it is not known when the decision was taken to defend Italy by blocking the Alpine approaches and sealing the passes, though the Vandalic breakthrough must have raised the spectre of Italy's standing alone. The works themselves were evidently feeble, due to manpower shortage and shoestring budgets. Nor has there been great effort by the learned of five Alpine countries to correlate observations. Nevertheless, indirect evidence makes it fairly certain that a line of some sort was now created.

The *Notitia Dignitatum* gives a *tractus Italiae circa Alpes* under the Count of Italy, which may be translated as the Alpine Circuit Command. An illustrated title page for this chapter shows the northern plain backed by the Alps, with towers and two short wall sections in the foothills. There is also the parallel with the Julian Alps, which were part of the same command. On the other hand the Julian Alpine *clausurae* were of stone and have left remains whereas, despite the picture in the *Notitia*, no stretches of wall have survived or are known in the central or western Alps. Fortunately there is the evidence of placenames: words derived from *claustrum* or *clausura* are common on the Alpine approaches or in the interior valleys. French examples include Cluses, La Clusaz and Vaucluse; Italian Chiasso, Chiusa and Chiusaforte; German Klausen and Kluze. More frequent still are names suggesting roadblocks, guardposts or fortlets, from the Latin *burgus*. At the foot of the Italian lakes, for example, are two towns called Borgo. On the French side, toward the west and southwest we have Bourg and Lanslebourg on the approach to the Mont Cenis, Bourg-St-Maurice on the Little St Bernard and Bourg-St-Pierre on the Great St Bernard; while in Switzerland there is Brig. All suggest light fortification and makeshift structures, with improvised barriers across valleys and passes, perhaps of wooden hurdling. There were also rural refuges, existing forts and walled towns, in all of which garrisons could be stationed. Of this last, rather pathetic attempt to make a defensive line there is presently not much more to be said, except that the Alps themselves were a formidable barrier, uncrossed since Hannibal. But neither *clausurae*, *burgi*, nor mountains would concern Italy's next caller.

When Gaiseric took Carthage he found the grain fleet in harbour and the shipyards operational. These became the basis of a powerful navy. At first it was used randomly and for piracy. Before long however this imaginative fighter had seized the Balearic Islands, Sicily, Sardinia and Corsica. In 457 he set sail for Rome. Unusually for this period – and unluckily – the emperor Petronius chanced to be visiting the former capital. When the Vandals were sighted he attempted to flee, but was lynched by the mob. With all forces in the north, Rome's city walls were hopelessly undermanned. The redoubtable Leo I was again produced and his pleas persuaded Gaiseric to refrain from murder or arson. This time however the sack was thorough and lasted fourteen days. Innumerable treasures and art works vanished for ever. Carthage had returned to plunder Rome and the term 'vandalism' was born.

Now ancient Rome begins to be medieval Rome, with seedy streets, derelict temples and ever more churches. At sea the navy disappears. Nothing more is heard of the once great bases at Misenum, near

Naples, and Classis, near Ravenna. Nor is the fate of the Rhine and Danube flotillas known. With priority given to the inland armies we may assume their demise.

After the Vandalic sack of Rome in 457, the wrath of Mars subsides. The western empire has taken all the knocks the barbarians will send. Henceforward it just fades away. Britain, Spain and Africa are already gone. In Gaul and Pannonia barbarian settlement has become universal and Roman control nominal. Italy, Raetia and Noricum are virtually all that remain. Of the last few emperors there is little worth saying. They are flimsy figures and power is in the hands of German generalissimos. At first they had felt obliged to work behind a screen of emperors and a show of Romanity, but before long they would cease to bother; and when this happened, Rome ended. So it was when the Ostrogothic warlord Odoacer took over Ravenna in 476 and casually deposed the youthful and harmless Romulus Augustulus, who was pensioned off to live in a villa on the Bay of Naples.

Odoacer styled himself *rex*. He was soon overthrown by Theodoric. These were kings of Italy and the northern Balkans only. Raetia and Noricum were abandoned to the Alamann, while the flickerings of Roman influence in Provence, Dalmatia and Catalonia were left quietly to gutter.

A quiet fading also typifies the frontiers. They had never been the target of invasion. The invader sought to overleap boundaries and sidestep obstacles. His mind was not on frontiers but on what they guarded. Nor had there been advantage in leaving suicide garrisons when soldiers were needed to defend the inner provinces. We must not expect the average frontier to end in a fight to the death or look for the destruction of its works. Stealthy troop withdrawal, abandonment and quiet decay would be their frequent fate. The barbarian takeover was on the whole peaceful. People were generally not oppressed and escape from the tax trap offered the successor-states a flying start. Rather than means of enslavement the new kingdoms tended to be accommodations between victors and vanquished. Formulas for coexistence were evolved. In western Gaul, for example, Romans kept a third of acreage and gave two thirds to the Visigoths, while in most of Gaul and Italy it was the Romans who kept two thirds.

Pay had driven the frontier. It had influenced how it worked and now its cessation influenced how it stopped. What happens to an army when the pay ceases? On the west's surviving frontiers – and we must remember that some outlasted the centre – the soldiers' impression would not be of defeat and disaster, but of silence and loss of contact. No money arrived, no orders, no news. What then did soldiers do? Some reverted to the land. But in military zones pay was the prime mover and when it stopped the entire economy would sag. There must therefore have been at least a partial withdrawal from the frontier regions, inland and toward the towns, or toward islands of Romanity which still persisted among the barbarian settlements.

Victorious armies are usually discharged, the defeated discharge themselves. Whether on the frontiers or elsewhere, soldiers looked to their own demobilisation, much as in Germany during May 1945. Civilians moved into forts and forts became walled villages. Soldiers became farmers and farmers prepared to defend themselves. Officials ceased to be paid and they too melted away. Power passed to barbarian chiefs, or where the barbarians had not arrived local leaders took over responsibility for defence. Whatever defence might mean it no longer had to do with fortified frontiers or standing armies. Such things were largely consigned to oblivion. In Italy Theodoric paid off the imperial bodyguard, plus whatever other Roman forces remained, and they went home.

Following the great ingress of New Year's Eve 405, the Rhine frontier died quietly: not of wounds but of anaemia, brought on by lack of defenders. It is probable that the understrength garrisons had grouped at vital points like fortresses and bridges, only to be sidestepped by the invaders, crossing by raft or over ice. In any case, with the extensive settlement in Gaul of German federates and *laeti*, not to mention a Visigothic kingdom behind the lines, there was no longer much point in defending the river.

The Salian Franks, already spreading into Belgic Gaul after the abandonment of the flooded lands, would, under Clovis, in the immediate Roman aftermath, advance to the Loire, pointing the way toward the future France. Removal of the C from his name reminds us of eighteen kings called Louis and their thousand-year kingdom which was to follow. Constantine's fort at Coblenz becomes one of the seats of the Frankish court and the palace of the governor of Lower Germany at Cologne another.

Valens' massive *receptio* of the asylum-seeking Goths and their subsequent win at Hadrianople, had meant that one deadly enemy was at large inside the Danube with another close outside. The northern Balkans were evacuated to the Huns during the 430s and only partially restored after Attila's death. Influence was finally confined to the Pannonian interior (western Hungary) with its fortified towns, villas and walled refuges, where Roman life continued for a generation after the Ostrogothic takeover in Ravenna. The legionary base at Carnuntum was already in ruins. A fortlet inside it and another against its wall tell of small-scale reoccupations during the 4th century.

Aquincum (Budapest), the greatest of all Danubian bases, was probably the first abandoned. Most of its garrison had been withdrawn to defend Italy against Alaric. With the Hunnic capital close by, it would in any case be untenable. The old fortress of II Adiutrix was partially converted to a civilian refuge. Across the river, linked by wooden bridge, was the counterfort of Trans Aquincum; with the third, smaller fort of Contra Aquincum, also on the barbarian bank, now under the modern city. On the Roman side the fortress had been flanked by two forts. Another covered the governor's palace, on an island in the river, making six installations in total. All were relinquished without a fight, as was the huge investment of forts and towers added by Constantine and Valentinian to the Middle Danube generally. A Hungarian chronicle of the medieval period tells how, in the early 450s, Attila had for a time held court at 'a place called by the Germans Ecilburg'. This is believed to be Aquincum. It is thus entirely feasible that the unsmiling Hun ate from his plain trencher and drank from his wooden cup in the gutted grandeur of the palace built by Hadrian as a statement to the steppe.

At the Danube mouth Lower Moesia had been renamed Scythia Minor and its capital Tomis changed to Constantia, in honour of Constantine's sister, giving us the modern Constantza. On the river's last 200 miles were now three dozen fortresses or forts and half-a-dozen fortified towns. They are listed by Procopius in de Aedificiis ('On buildings') where he describes Justinian's repairs, though only half have been identified with certainty. Riches await the archaeologist in this busy corner, and it must be hoped that dam projects do not overtake him. This fortress-province was to be much reinforced by the eastern emperors and shielded Constantinople on several occasions before its final loss in the 10th century.

At the other end of the Danube Noricum is of special interest, for here we have evidence in the form of a biography, written during the final years of Roman rule. This is the *Life of St Severinus*,[38] bishop of Noricum, who died in 482, by Eugippius, a priest and disciple. Severinus, of probable Syrian origin, spent his last twenty-two years in what we now call Western Austria, a region under the deepening shadow of Alamannic attack from the north, but sheltered by mountain from the main winds of war to its south and west. As no coins have been found postdating 400, we may assume garrisons ceased to receive outside financial support from that time. We know however from the biography that some soldiers were still at their posts around 460, either because local loyalties still held units together, or because the region was safer than its surroundings. Some frontier installations had, it seems, already been abandoned, since Severinus lived in a fortlet, and some soldiers were pursuing other occupations. Eugippius tells of two officers being ordained, one later becoming a bishop. As the Alamannic noose tightened, Severinus helped organise the evacuation of frontier towns. In 488, six years after his death, Noricum's entire Roman population including what was left of its army walked across the passes into Italy, with the saint's remains drawn on a wagon. The soldiers were now ex-soldiers, for this was twelve years after the abdication of the last Roman emperor and the Italy to which they were fleeing was an Ostrogothic kingdom. But there are barbarians and barbarians. Those attacking Noricum were rapacious as ever, but those who had won Italy were by now relatively relaxed. Besides, the Goths were already Christians; though the Romans were of the Nicene and the Goths of the Arian kind. This evacuation of Noricum's Romano-Celtic population helps explain why Austria is one of only three regions of German language gain; the others being the German-speaking areas west of the Rhine and the larger part of Britain. By contrast, the much wider survival of Romance languages suggests areas with a smaller German-to-Roman ratio and the likelihood of peaceful accommodation between them. In the Balkan area linguistic evidence will be submerged beneath Slavic and Magyar at a later time.

The year 476, which sees the end of Roman rule in Ravenna, is an entirely arbitrary date in relation to the eastern empire's frontiers, most of which continued for two centuries. Let us nevertheless record how things stood at the time of the west's collapse. In Asia Minor the *Notitia* gives twenty-six frontier-type regiments under the Duke of Armenia, and it is generally assumed these were holding the northern half of the old Upper Euphrates line, from Trabzon on the

Black Sea to about as far downriver as Malatya (Melitene). South of here the Euphrates did not need to be held due to the Roman position further east. The ditch across Armenia, marking the boundary agreed between Probus and Shapur I, seems to have signified zones of interest and was probably unguarded. From the vicinity of Malatya the frontier ran east to the Tigris headwaters and downriver to a point below Diyarbakir (Amida) near the source of the Khabur, then down the Khabur to the Euphrates again. The southern section, facing the Syrian Desert, continued to be Diocletian's Road as far as Azraq, then based on Trajan's to the Gulf of Aqaba.

Stalemate with Persia during the 5th century would lead to neglect of the Syrian and Arabian defences, which passed into the care of *limitanei* (soldier-farmers). The garrison of the El Lejjun fortress is believed to have been demobilised about 532. However Justinian's expensive programme of Italian reconquest led him to the even cheaper solution of placing control in the hands of the Saracen *phylarchs* (sheikhs). These had little interest in frontier installations; and the Arab conquest of the 7th century emphasised their irrelevance. In due course the empty forts along the *Via Nova Traiana* became camp sites for Mecca-bound pilgrims. When European travellers arrived in the nineteenth century, they found these desert margins much as East Rome had left them. Apart from a few stones removed to make animal pens and minor damage by earth tremor or the clambering goat, little had changed.

On the *limes Palaestinae* emphasis continued to shift from formal fortification to fortified farmstead. Excavators of En Boqeq, on the Dead Sea, deduced that the fort was acting as a kind of local militia headquarters or territorial army drill hall, with the men living out.[39] From the southern borders of Egypt in the 6th century there is papyrological evidence that frontiersmen were by then part-timers on half pay, supplementing their wages as farmers or Nile boatmen. It was stipulated that they should attend a daily drill and the forts should be kept in good order. The *fossatum Africae* had reverted to soldier-farming long before the end. However, with the Vandal conquest any residual meaning evaporated. The Vandals ignored their southern frontiers and Berber raids fostered neglect, soil erosion and desert spread. Vandal Africa lasted slightly less than a century and left almost no trace. It was toppled by Count Belisarius, who led an invasion fleet from Constantinople in 533 as part of Justinian's plan to retake vital areas of the former west. Byzantine Africa would last a further 165 years. It is possible that there was now some restoration of Numidia's defences, for Justinian ordered Solomon, his first governor, to revive the *limitanei*. Again, this arrangement was later replaced by the paying of borderland tribes to keep the peace. In fact the main Byzantine reliance was on internal strongpoints, consisting of massively walled citadels built of refused Roman masonry.

The interjacency of Vandal Africa meant an end to the Roman Mauretanias. Caesariensis (Algeria) and what remained of Tingitana (Morocco), their sea links severed by the Vandalic navy, now atrophied and succumbed to Berber invasion.

Carthage fell to the Arabs in 698. North Africa, ever a cultural chameleon, now took the colours of the Orient and would remain Arab or Turkish until a French army disembarked at Algiers in 1830. Christian communities, a direct legacy of Rome, survived in Tunisia till the 12th century and in Egypt till the present day. By the early 7th century, with the loss of Egypt, Syria and Africa, the Byzantine empire would be thrown back upon its core areas of Asia Minor and the southern Balkans, yet still survived. In essence its frontier policy remained Roman. Procopius says of Justinian: 'He restored the empire, which lay open to the barbarians in all directions, so staffing it with soldiers and strengthening it by fort building that he created as it were a wall round its edges.'[40] This could have been written three centuries earlier. More precisely the east was basing its security on the same elements as the late Roman west: mobile armies in combination with fortified cities and defended borders; the latter heavily guarded near the capital, with increasing use of part-timers further afield. The story of the Byzantine frontiers is not an academic postscript to the Roman. They were critical in shielding Europe against a militant Islam, which would otherwise have smothered the infant West.

The combined protection of Hadrian's Wall and the Saxon Shore had given Britain a quiet 4th century. When it came, the end was sudden and the break total. After four hundred years' docility the Britons were obliged to arm themselves against what would prove the most remorseless of all the barbarian invaders. The Anglo-Saxons sought not accommodation but ownership, and within two centuries the Roman inheritance in terms of placenames, language, religion – and indeed the British nation itself – all but disappears from the south, east and centre of the island. The Britons will now be squeezed toward Wales, Cornwall and the north-west. The Romance vocabulary of the English language will not be added till the Middle Ages, mainly via France. If Rome lives, lexically, in the British Isles it is in Welsh, where some six hundred Latin words survive.

In Mediterranean memory Britain reverted to her macabre role as an abode of the departed; and Hadrian's Wall began to sink into legend as a frontier between good and ill. In the version transmitted by Procopius and quoted by Gibbon its alignment has turned through ninety degrees:

> One hundred and fifty years after Honorius, the gravest historian of the times describes the wonders of a remote isle whose eastern and western parts are divided by an antique wall, the boundary of life and death or, more properly, of truth and fiction. The east is a fair country, inhabited by civilised people: the air is healthy, earth yields her regular and fruitful increase. In the west, beyond the wall, the air is infectious and mortal; the ground is covered with serpents; and in this dreary solitude is the region of departed spirits.[41]

The end of occupation of Hadrian's Wall seems to have coincided with that of Roman Britain. Only two forts, Birdoswald and Vindolanda are known to have ended violently and there is no evidence for widespread destruction of the Wall itself. The century preceding had seen its progressive winding down: abandonment of outpost forts, closure of turrets and blocking of gates. By the early 4th century only four turrets (one fortieth of Hadrian's original number) are known to have been in use, plus perhaps ten milecastles.[42] The *vici* too were being abandoned, and civilians were moving into forts. In due course headquarters buildings and granaries would be converted to living accommodation and gates blocked, with squatters even occupying guard chambers. Jewellery and infant burials tell their story. Professor J. Wilkes' 1961 excavations at Housesteads revealed barrack blocks subdivided in a way suggesting married quarters, later corroborated at other sites.[43] Fifth-century Housesteads, surrounded by its terraced fields, was now a limitanean walled village. Birdoswald boasts even longer continuity. First built over an iron age promontory fort, there may be a thousand-year timespan between this and the converted granary, where post-Roman chieftains caroused; plus a thousand more to the border farmhouse, whose tower echoes the gatetowers of the fort in which it stands. Equally evocative is the outpost fort of Bewcastle, some twenty miles north of Carlisle, with farm, castle, church and famous dark-age cross, all within the Hadrianic site.

In its later stages Hadrian's Wall has been called a military backwater. Perhaps 'irrelevancy' would be more apt, for this strongest of Roman frontier works had proved valueless against the Saxons, Roman Britain's final enemy. It was at the wrong end of the province and faced the wrong way. Let us apply this test to other frontiers. The Danube will hardly pass with flying colours, for the *receptio* of 375 had allowed the Goths behind it. What of the Rhine? Again the Visigoths, retreating from Italy to found their kingdom in Aquitania, entered Gaul from the south-east, 400 miles from the nearest forts of the Rhine frontier. Spain expected invasion from the south and her shield was northern Morocco. The enemy came over the Pyrenees. North Africa's defences faced the Sahara. The enemy came via the Strait of Gibraltar. The Alps were fortified against attack from the north and the city of Rome fell to a seaborne invasion from the south. Fixed defences, based on other threats at other times, had cost Rome dearly. They ended as a jest of history; bulwarks against no one, defending that which had already fallen; frontiers which found themselves at the back.

CHAPTER 12

Fallible Friend

> Time, which antiquates antiquities, and hath an art to make
> dust of all things, hath yet spared these minor monuments.
>   Thomas Browne, *Urn Burial*, 1658

WITH OUR OWN CENTURY'S Iron Curtain, its Berlin Wall, its dividing line across Cyprus, its 'bamboo curtain' between China and Hong Kong, its 37th parallel in Korea and its 17th parallel in Vietnam, we are uniquely placed to appreciate ways in which people may be kept apart. And yet, during the writing of this book, profound changes in Eastern Europe brought at least part of this mischief to an end. Through TV's Argus-eyes, audiences could watch Hungarian guards chopping the wire of their borderlines into saleable lengths, or fragments of graffiti-enriched concrete being traded for western currency in the Potsdamer Platz. Few lamented the fall of these spiteful obstacles.

Though such barriers are inseparable from dogmas that did not perplex the ancient world, they remind us of the irksomeness of restraints and help explain the sadness of abandoned frontiers. No one wanted them in the first place. Though boundaries are as inevitable as our sense of property, only landlords like them. Though they are a natural response to danger, we forget them when danger has passed. Nothing is less relevant to a people than the boundary of a former people across its land. Frontiers are history's orphans.

Those of Rome are especially touching because they are failed frontiers, which let the enemy in; misplaced frontiers, which he circumvented; unnecessary frontiers, before which he never appeared.

They are a memorial to an army which had won a world and whose reward was to be given the long, thankless and finally hopeless task of guarding it.

Most sorts of structure can be converted or re-used. Of the thirty million facing stones cut for Hadrian's Wall, perhaps 5% remain *in situ* and the rest are serving someone in some way, even by sheltering sheep. More generally, however, frontiers were seldom convertible. They could be made to serve no useful purpose and had little meaning for those through whose hands they passed. Even in military thinking, Roman linear barriers and the early fort types that went with them would leave no mark upon the future. Perimeter defence and the omnipotence of the front line enlisted almost no exponents between King Offa of Mercia and Foch, Haig and Hindenburg. So the Roman frontier, born absentmindedly and imposed peremptorily, died unmourned and was swiftly forgotten. It was not until two or three centuries ago, when everything which survived from the distant past came at last to seem precious, that sad monuments began to be prized along with the noble and successful.

Nevertheless, there are two ways in which Roman defensive methods in particular, and the imperial frontier in general, affected future ages. First is the legacy of late Roman military architecture. The second, broader and more important, lies in the frontier's influence on nations and on national boundaries yet to be, as well as on the shape and character of future Europe. Concerning the first one may, for example, ask why English church towers are battlemented and have narrow, louvred windows, high from the ground. Why indeed do churches need towers at all? During the 5th century there was a tendency to use abandoned Roman signal towers as refuges. In England, where Saxon and Danish raids extended the terror for centuries, the habit continued and the blueprint was adapted to each village. Tower merged with church, for the one would defend the other. The signalling function was remembered in the use of bells.

The medieval castle has comparable lineage. In its simplest form of keep within walls we see the idea of combining watchtower and fort into a single concept by building a tower inside a Roman *castellum*, hundreds of which were still standing. At Europe's other end, in Andalucia, it is difficult to see the 9th-century Alhambra's brick ramparts and square towers without being reminded of the great, late Roman urban circuits. The Arabs brought ancient fortification back to Europe by a clockwise route from the Roman east; and with it words like *alcazar* and *qasba* (kasbah); today coexisting in Spanish with terms of the same origin and meaning, which had already arrived clockwise from the Roman west, like *castro*, Castilla and Cataluña. Ideas deriving from late antiquity's forts and town walls would slosh back and forward across Christendom and the Crusader lands for centuries, echoing into Islamic territory, where they are remembered in words like *qasr* and *borj* (Turkish *burç*) from Latin *burgus*, a strongpoint.

A failed frontier is an equivocal memorial to one of history's most successful armies. There persists however a military monument of happier outcome which serves mankind in remarkable measure still: the imperial road system, which in its developed state has been calculated as 53,250 miles, not counting uncountable by-roads; comparable to twice the earth's circumference and substantially greater than the US interstate system. 85,000 inscribed and many uninscribed milestones have survived. It was of course typical of Rome's eccentric development that the traffic should be unworthy of the roads. Reluctance to convert to cavalry meant that for most of our period reinforcement was at walking speed; giving a 'modern' infrastructure with a prehistoric flow rate. Nevertheless, the scale and quality of the achievement, as well as its value to succeeding ages, makes this Rome's greatest practical legacy. Though roads would have been required whatever the strategy, the frontier, with its scattered armies, ensured that the network would be centrifugal rather than centripetal.

The number of today's countries reached by Rome never ceases to amaze us. The total has been augmented by the break-up of the Soviet Union, Jugoslavia and Czechoslovakia. Without counting the smallest, like Malta and Liechtenstein, and rating Britain as one, our present reckoning is forty-two; and there was frontier defence, in some form or at some time, in over half of them. The recognition of Rome's impress across so many since-sundered lands, over what is today so wide a linguistic and religious spectrum with the broadest political and developmental range, surprises the most *blasé* traveller. In a short poem Thomas Hardy describes how it struck him when, wandering in a ruin near Florence, a peasant girl offered him a coin identical to one he had unearthed in his own garden in Dorchester:

> [...] her act flashed home
> In that mute moment to my opened mind
> The power, the pride, the reach of perished Rome.[1]

Although Rome's greatest bequests are cultural and derived from central energies, far-reaching consequences have arisen from her borderlands. Nations have been formed by the frontier's presence or the accident of where the line chanced to fall. Romania is a clear example. It could be argued that Scotland's beginnings lay in Hadrian's Wall, for it was he who established the precedent for dividing Britain at the Solway Firth. Ireland's conviction of uniqueness and apartness may originate from her survival as a free entity, close outside Rome's grasp. Another near-miss, of greater magnitude, was the failure of imperial boundaries to include the Arabian heartland. Had the Hejaz come within the empire it would have been Christianised and neither the rise of Islam nor the Arab invasions might have followed. Less speculative is the role of Byzantium, whose investment in city walls and whose management of Rome's eastern frontiers greatly lengthened her life, averting Arab and delaying Turkish attacks on Europe until a time when they could be more vigorously resisted.

Clearest of all is the influence of the Roman Rhine. It began the twofold division of Europe whose healing is the mission of the European Community. France and Germany's bickering over Alsace and the Saar were but twinges of a wound opened by Augustus' German War. Rome was the first to formalise a Rhenish frontier and her four-century tenure made the division permanent. History offers no more fearful partition than the Franco-German, across which millions were at length to die. Europe remains linguistically divided, her tongue still forked between Romance and Teutonic; a two-thousand-year estrangement, felt as far away as Quebec. Were it not for later invasions and ethnic overlays the Danube's former Roman and barbarian banks might have been a setting for rivalries every bit as deadly as those of the Rhine.

The frontier's sterner legacies are brightened by cultural gain. The Roman Peace was mankind's greatest creation until that time and among the greatest of all time. Its guarantor was the Roman army and its guarantee the imperial frontier. This fortified chain, linking Irish Sea, North Sea, Black Sea, Red Sea and Atlantic, enclosed a quadrilateral of some 1,600×2,800 miles, whose sides were three continents and an ocean. China apart, no comparable defensive scheme had been or would be seen again. More meaningful than the circuit was what it encircled. It protected forty provinces and eighty million people. It guarded much that the ancient world had accomplished and the medieval world would inherit. This it helped preserve for over four centuries, by which time acorns from the classical oak had sprouted and would survive Rome's fall. The frontier had the West's future in its keeping.

It remains to summarise and venture final views. The imperial *limes* resembled modern cold-war frontiers in length, cross-country character, arbitrariness of imposition and the mutual suspicion of those divided. It differed from them in not being inspired by political or religious ideology. Its basis lay in more primitive emotions: Rome's fear of the *ferae gentes*,[2] or wild peoples; as well as a deep-seated determination to hold what was hers. Its intentions were to defend and differentiate: the subjugated from the unsubdued, the governable from the unruly, the promising from the profitless.

Regarding ancestry, we will not easily find precedent for a mode of protection unique in western history. Rome arrived at her perimeter system gropingly and of her own volition, the starting point having been an embarrassment of serving units left over from the civil wars and Augustus' eagerness to disperse them in a way which minimised danger to the throne. Precedent for the actual works consisted of Rome's own experience plus a ragbag of Celtic, Hellenistic, Jewish and Nabataean practice, loosely adapted to a grand design. Nor does Western history offer a precise counterpart in tactical terms. Almost no modern states, including Iron Curtain countries, see their frontiers as intensively held lines intended to repel all-out attack. By contrast the Roman perimeter was where the army would make its stand. It was policed, but garrisoned as well; openable, but capable of total closure; a peacetime frontier designed for the possibility of war.

War on the frontier was nevertheless rare. The norm approximated to what one may call cold war. We suppose this to be a recent invention, arising from a twentieth-century acceptance that nuclear exchange would be unwinnable. In fact it corresponds quite closely with Augustus' acceptance that the world was unwinnable. Though without the political dimension, the balance between Rome and the outside nations was not dissimilar to that between eastern and western blocs in the later twentieth century. Having reached military or climatic stalemate in all directions, Rome accepted a *de facto* accommodation with her neighbours which amounted to a settling into armed camps, divided by that interdictive or at least restrictive curtain which is seemingly a hallmark of cold war.

What is the difference between 'friendly' and 'unfriendly' frontiers?

In part it lies in the degree of surveillance and hindrance; but we may also note that today's borders between amicable nations are usually double, with entries and customs posts facing each other across a gap, where the actual boundary lies. A barrier of Iron Curtain character is usually single and imposed by one side only: the side with something to lose or to hide. The principal difference between twentieth- and first-century examples is that while modern Iron Curtain countries have something to hide from those inside, Rome had something to lose to those outside.

Where the frontier fell was broadly determined by what, within a thousand miles of Rome, was amenable to settled agriculture based on cereal crops. This resolved into core areas, well suited; and fringe areas, partially suited; with frontiers drawn round the latter, so that heartlands would not also be borderlands. With a few exceptions the inner provinces were Hellenistic or Punic takeovers, the outer provinces won by force.

As time passed, the frontier acquired an economic dimension. It separated two worlds at different levels of material development, in some ways comparable to the rich and poor nations today. The barbarians, initially passive, moved gradually through a raiding to a migrational mentality, responding to a variety of opportunist or refugee motives. The difference between immigrants then and now is that in the ancient world they were armed and ready to fight for their place in the sun. Frontiers between economic unequals seldom achieve equilibrium.

Roman ebb and barbarian flow combine to suggest the frontier as a knowledge barrier, with Rome as the long-term loser. Despite overseas contacts in commerce and diplomacy it is difficult not to see her frontier fixation as a form of isolationism. We think of Rome as outward-looking because she faced the world across her borders; but was not the reality more like a porcupine, whose bristles point outwards because the animal has turned inwards? Locking out the barbarians meant locking in the Romans: a cultural quarantine which reduced Rome's ability to learn from the outside peoples or influence them favourably.

The components of frontier policy may now be restated. The *limes* embodied three principles: a halt to expansion, an empire enclosed by perimeter barriers and an army dedicated to their defence. That these were endorsed by most emperors in most theatres implies consistency. On the other hand the variety of actual works implies improvisation, reflecting two influences in frontier creation: the emperor's and the army's. We have seen how it produced a patch-work of central initiatives and local interpretations. More widely one is reminded that an army has a continuous life and its soldiers are creatures of habit, while an emperor's life is finite and he is a creature of circumstance. Temperamental differences melt in the pot of military service, but those of the autocrat are heightened by ego and the urge to make an individual mark. So terms of service, tactics, weaponry and fort building tended to be left to the army and changed slowly. Policy (in matters like peace or war, frontier creation or abandonment) was the monopoly of the emperor and could change at will. In sum frontier management tended toward a policy, but a policy seldom immune from the turbulence of politics and rarely re-examined in the light of long-term benefit.

We learn – almost with the first Latin verbs – to admire the early empire and censure the late. In the crucial matter of defence, however, it seems clear that the 1st century handed on a flawed formula to the 2nd and 3rd; conceptual errors planted by Augustus and nurtured by all whose policies were based on suspicion. Such was the fear of generals who might be popular, officers who might conspire and legions which might combine, that the armed forces were bereft of brainpower above sergeant-major level. There was no general staff, no war office, no admiralty, no military academies, no institute of strategic studies and no professional officer corps. Military expertise and planning were the emperor's preserve. The empire remained an advanced power with rudimentary institutions and primitive instincts. We cannot of course attribute all ills to imperial paranoia. Rome was unproductive of ideas in many fields. The six-century-long marriage between thinking Greeks and doing Romans, which might have given the world thinking and doing Graeco-Romans, seems instead to have produced non-doing Greeks and non-thinking Romans. Meanwhile, on the barbarian side, we recognise slow but ominous advances in combative and combinative skills. By the mid-2nd century it was already time to match them: by improving weaponry, by increasing army size, by augmenting the cavalry arm, by ending amateurism in the senior ranks, by rethinking military architecture, by forming counterstrike forces and by adopting in-depth strategies. The road to improvement was slow and the throne its bottleneck. Such was the habit of self-satisfaction generated by the frontier's protection that only a profound crisis could break it.

The 3rd century produced the crisis, providing new ideas but releasing yet another surge of fear and suspicion, which would warp the late empire much as civil war had distorted the early.

With the faltering of Roman expansion there emerged the question of how a wearying superpower might preserve the harem of provinces procured in its youth. Rome had evolved only one answer, the fortified perimeter; and continued to apply it in the teeth of contrary signals. She was now locked into frontier dependence in proportion to her need to hold provinces. Here the empire's response differed fundamentally from that of the sixteenth-to-twentieth-century maritime powers. When it suited the European motherlands to detach their overseas colonies they did so; but Rome, with her contiguous provinces and their intertwined destinies, could less easily repudiate youthful liaisons and was obliged to spend her autumnal years preserving them. The truth was that Italy could no longer do without the provinces. By the mid-1st century she could neither pay her way, feed, nor defend herself. The empire had grown onion-like, jacketed by juicy rings but without substantial core.

It is easy to blame Augustus for taking steps which would lead towards a perimetric strategy; but at so precarious a moment it was natural that he should wish to disperse the excessive and not always reliable forces assembled for the civil war. No one could have dreamed how binding this centrifugal deployment would prove to be, or that insecurity and mistrust would become *idées fixes* of imperial polity. It would nevertheless be overstating the case against the frontier to judge it as decisive in the fall of Rome. By the late period the frontier was in any case no longer paramount in the defensive scheme. The western empire's collapse seems rather to have lain in a combination of weaknesses of which military stagnation was only one. More telling was the intensity of the barbarian onslaught, without which the Roman edifice might have stood indefinitely. The urge of the outside peoples to migrate in the face of danger or hunger had been frustrated too long. By the 4th century these primordial, westward-tending forces awaited catalysis. Once the Hunnic fat was in the Gothic fire, a flare-up was at hand which would melt the constraints of all central and eastern Europe. Whether the flames then bent toward Constantinople or Rome was in some measure accidental.

In summary, the frontier was a circuit of interceptive and preventive character which long maintained a condition of peace;

but a wary kind of peace, made uneasy by mistrust and disparity. Its faults were those of all linear defences. Foremost they are absorbers of defenders. Since the attacker will improve his chances by concentrating at one or few points, the defenders guarding other sectors will be wasted. Should he break through they will be stranded, facing the wrong way. Defensive works are against dangers at the time of building, not against future threats of unknown direction and extent. The fixed frontier was an incitement to immobility, a source of comfort in which the defender placed his faith, the means by which tens of thousands of Roman soldiers became attached to objects of stone or timber whose failure left them bewildered.

Such were its weaknesses from the standpoint of the empire's rim. Seen from the centre they were no less serious. Since the frontier was the most far-flung line Rome could defend, it was certain from the outset that effective control would be stymied by distance. And yet, despite an eight-week return journey by courier between edge and centre, almost all emperors from Augustus to Diocletian clung to exclusivity of command. Furthermore the busy rulers of an overcentralised state seldom had time to visit their armies or to acquire a real understanding of warfare. Complacency, induced by centuries of victory, masked the obsolescence of military thinking and often led to no thinking at all.

Gaps would widen and wounds weep. Old suspicions would continue to poison unity. The death of an emperor would still, in Gibbon's phrase, be 'a moment big with danger and mischief'.[3] Differences between those inside and outside the imperial boundaries would continue to grow. Faith in frontiers would continue to keep civilians innocent of arms and the inner provinces ignorant of war. Perimeterism would continue to cloud the official vision until such time as the army was too arthritic to cope with change. A mode of defence which began as alien to Roman tradition would become first a comfort and then a fatal dependence.

In the first century of our era the elder Pliny had used, perhaps invented, the famous phrase *'immensa Romanae pacis maiestate*'[4] ('the boundless majesty of the Roman peace'). Though the presiding deity of this condition was ostensibly the goddess Pax, more truthfully its creation had been the work of Mars. The dereliction of the Roman war machine, which even Hannibal had failed to achieve, was quietly accomplished by four centuries of guard duty. Blunted by boredom and the listless years, a 1st-century army was unable to respond to a 5th-century call. Rome's response was to employ a German army. This worked well enough, but as the business continued to fail it was almost automatic that the employees would want to try their hand at the management role. These Germans were unconcerned with static defence. They had learned many things from Rome but immobility was not one of them. So the frontier receded as a principle of warfare; and the idea of a world mightily encircled, which the Principate had spent so much of its lifetime perfecting, dropped quietly from view. As Tacitus once warned: '*Non enim ignavia magna imperia contineri; virorum armorumque faciendum certamen*'[5] ('Passivity does not preserve great empires. These are things to be fought for').

It is a commonplace that the fascination of Rome's story lies in the length and completeness of its span, demonstrating the emergence, ascent and decline of an entire civilisation. In this far-ranging sense, history allows us to see the armed frontier not as a short-term experiment or the victim of an abrupt accident, like the Maginot Line; but as an extended event, running the gamut of its nine lives; and to judge it in a five-century context of statecraft and psychology. The frontier sufficed to steady the empire and restrain its spread, to bind its edges and salve their irritations, to remove the soldiers from political temptation and occupy them with daily duty, to comfort the provinces and give all subjects a sense of benign protection: advantages irresistible to the Roman state. The wider view is less positive. In it we see the frontier as an ambiguous beacon, not only beaming a message of strength outwards toward the *barbaricum*, but also inwards, where its effect was to spread a warm glow of self-deception and misplaced confidence. It would prove a fallible friend, sedating Rome's spirit, inviting her to doze while the never-pausing pen of war moved on, writing a new chapter which would be better understood beyond the frontier than inside it.

List of Abbreviations

Agr.	Tacitus, *Agricola*
A.H.	*Augustan History*
A.H. (A)	id., *Life of Antoninus*
A.H. (C)	id., *Life of Caracalla*
A.H. (Co)	id., *Life of Commodus*
A.H. (H)	id., *Life of Hadrian*
A.H. (M)	id., *Life of Marcus*
A.H. (S)	id., *Life of Septimius*
AI	Académie des Inscriptions et Belles Lettres: comptes rendues des séances
Ammian	Ammianus Marcellinus
An.	Tacitus, *Annales*
ANRW	*Aufstieg und Niedergang der römischen Welt*
AS	*International Journal of African Studies*
BAR	*British Archaeological Reports*
Bldgs.	Procopius, *de Aedificiis* (*Buildings*)
CIL	*Corpus Inscriptionum Latinarum*
Compléments	'Complements Inédits au Fossatum Africae', *RFS*, vi (1964)
dBA	Caesar, *de Bello Africano* (*The African War*)
dBG	Caesar, *de Bello Gallico* (*The Gallic War*)
D & N Trans	*The Durham and Northumberland Transactions*
Dio	*Dio Cassius, History of Rome*
dRB	Anonymous, *de Rebus Bellicis* (*On Warfare*)

F.A.	J. Baradez, *Fossatum Africae: recherches aériennes sur l'organisation des confins sahariens à l'époque romaine* (Paris, 1949)
Fronto	*Correspondence*
Geog.	Strabo, *Geographica*
Ger.	Tacitus, *Germania*
Gibbon	Edward Gibbon, *The Decline and Fall of the Roman Empire*
Hist.	Tacitus, *Historiae*
ILS	*Jugoslav Latin Inscriptions*
Itin. Ant.	*Antonine Itinerary*
JRS	*Journal of Roman Studies*
JW	Josephus, *The Jewish War*
LS	*Journal of Libyan Studies*
N.D.	*Notitia Dignitatum*
N.H.	Pliny, *Natural History*
Pan.	Younger Pliny, *Panegyricus*
PSAS	Proceedings of the Society of Antiquaries for Scotland
RFS	Congresses of Roman Frontier Studies
RFS, ii	'*Carnuntia*'. *Ergebnisse der Forschung über die Grenzprovinzen des römischen Reiches Vorträge beim internationalen Kongress der Altumforscher* (Carnuntum, Lower Austria, 1955)
RFS, v	*Quintus Congressus Internationalis Limitis Romani Studiosorum* (Zagreb, Jugoslavia, 1963)
RFS, vi	*Studien zu den Militärgrenzen Roms I* (Bonn, 1964; pub. 1967)
RFS, viii	*Eighth International Congress of Limesforschung*, (Cardiff, 1969; pub. 1974)
RFS, ix	*Actes du IXe Congrès International d'Etudes sur les Frontières Romaines* (Mamaia, Romania, 1972)
RFS, x	*Studien zu den Militärgrenzen Roms II, Vorträge des 10 internationalen Limeskongress in der Germania Inferior* (Bonn, 1976)
RFS, xi	*Limes, Akten des XI internationalen Limes*

	Kongresses (Székesfehérvár, Hungary, 1976; pub. 1978)
RFS, xii	*Roman Frontier Studies. Papers presented to the 12th International Congress of Roman Frontier Studies* (Univ. of Stirling, 1979; *BAR Int. Series 71, 1980*)
RFS, xiii	*Studien zu den Militärgrenzen Roms III. Internationaler Limeskongress* (Aalen, 1983; pub. 1986)
RFS, xiv	*Akten des 14 internationalen Limeskongresses,* (Carnuntum, 1986; pub. 1990)
RFS, xv	*Roman Frontier Studies. Proceedings of the 15th International Congress of Roman Frontier Studies* (Canterbury, 1989; pub. 1991)
RG	*Res Gestae Divi Augusti*
RIB	*Roman Inscriptions of Britain*
Strat.	Frontinus, *Strategematon*
Suetonius	Suetonius, *The Twelve Caesars*
TCWAA	*Transactions of the Cumberland and Westmorland Antiquarian and Archaeological Society*
Vegetius	Vegetius, *Epitoma Rei Militaris (On Military Matters)*
Vitruvius	Vitruvius, *de Architectura (Ten Books on Architecture)*
ZNH	Zosimus, *New History*

Notes

CHAPTER 1 Augustus: The Advice (pp. 1–12)

1. '*Res gestae divi augusti*' ('The accomplishments of the deified Augustus'), temple inscription, Ankara, Turkey, 32, etc.
2. Dio Cassius, *History of Rome*, 51.3.2.
3. Dio, 53.12, 3–4.
4. Tacitus, *Historiae*, 1.89.
5. Suetonius, *The Twelve Caesars* (Augustus), 18 and 31.
6. Virgil, *Aeneid*, 1.278–9 and 6.851; Vitruvius, *de Architectura*, (*Ten Books on Architecture*), 6.1.12; Ovid, *Fasti*, 2.667–84, etc.
7. Dio, 56.30, 3–5.
8. Tacitus, *Annales*, 1. 11.
9. Dio, 56.33.5.
10. i.e. 'barbarian lands', a term generally applied to central and eastern Europe, though not to the older civilisations of the east.
11. *An.*, 1.67.
12. *An.*, 2.26.
13. 'The *scandza* Peninsula (Scandinavia) a man-manufactury, a womb of nations' (Jordanes, *Getica*, 4.25); from which Goth and Viking would be born.
14. *An.*, 2.26.
15. id.
16. The Rubicon's identity is lost.
17. 1,400 miles, 2,240 km.
18. Herodotus, 4.48.1.

19. The word's first syllable reminds us of the volume of what we eat.
20. A. H. M. Jones, *The Later Roman Empire* (Oxford, 1964), ii, 1048.
21. *An.*, 6.32.1.
22. *Hist.*, 4.27.
23. Tacitus, *Agricola*, 12.
24. Tacitus, *Germania*, 33.

CHAPTER 2 Vespasian: A Frontier Emerging (pp. 13–39)

1. i.e. torsion catapults hurling stones, bolts or firebrands.
2. North Dorset downs, Mendip, Chiltern, Northampton uplands.
3. Generously aided by Lord Iliffe of Yattendon.
4. Suetonius, *The Twelve Caesars* (Vespasian), 4.
5. According to context this word henceforward has one of three meanings: Julius Caesar (spelt with capital), any emperor, or the heir to the throne.
6. Judges 20:1.
7. id., 6:3–5.
8. M. Gichon, 'Towers on the Limes Palaestinae', Congress of Roman Frontier Studies (*RFS*), ix (1972), 513.
9. For cross-country frontiers (other than on rivers) 7 miles was more usual for auxiliary units.
10. The Danube's whole course is presently within the 0–5°C January isotherm, as is the Rhine down to Strasbourg, where the Atlantic influence begins. Both would freeze more frequently today were it not for warming caused by industrial development.
11. Ger. *Mauer* = wall.
12. From the German Quadans in today's Slovakia and the Sarmatian Iazyges on the Hungarian Plain.
13. lit. 'frontier field'.
14. A. Aricescu, 'The Roman Army in the Dobrudja', *BAR*, 86 (1980), 76, 166.
15. *Année Epigraphique*, no. 633 (1951): attributed to second half of Domitian's reign.
16. Sebastopolis is so far the only one where 1st-century occupation has been proved.
17. i.e. Gk. *a-Suria* = 'not Syria'.
18. Cornelius Fronto to Lucius Verus (AD 165), *Correspondence*, 7.

19. Four wars between Rome and Parthia in the first two centuries AD.
20. *An.*, 2.56.
21. Annexed by Tiberius in 17, restored by Caligula in 38, retaken by Vespasian in 72.
22. *Britannia* (1600): 'The Wall goeth near to Busie Gappe, a place infamous for thieving and robbing, where stood some castels (*chesters* they called them) but I could not with safetie take the full survey of it, for the rank robbers thereabouts.'
23. J. Crow in 'The Defence of the Roman and Byzantine East', *BAR*, 297, i (1986), 87.
24. Study of land surface and visible remains, usually by walking the ground and as a preliminary to further investigation. In the West this stage is largely over.
25. T. B. Mitford, 'The Euphrates Frontier in Cappadocia', *RFS*, x (1974), 501.
26. Completed by Rome's annexation of Nabataea (Jordan) in AD 106.
27. A mood evoked in Rose Macaulay's novel, *The Towers of Trebizond* (London, 1956).
28. Combining the earlier Mysia, Lydia, Caria and Phrygia.
29. Alexander the Great's eastern conquests, named after his successor Seleucus.
30. Fronto to Marcus, 19.
31. *An.*, 15.3.
32. e.g. in his seminal book: O. G. S. Crawford and A. Keiller, *Wessex from the Air* (Oxford, 1928).
33. Assuming a correspondence between rainfall then and now. Discussed pp. 145–6 *infra*.
34. Librarie Orientaliste, ed. Paul Geuthner.
35. Pliny, *Natural History*, 5.21.
36. *Augustan History* (Hadrian), 12.
37. *Dizionario Epigraphico di Antichità Romana*, 4.34: 'Elementi e Carrateristiche Generali del Limes', 1080, 1083.
38. In Britain, depending on the prejudices of one's Classics teacher, either lee-maze or lime-ease.
39. *An.*, 1.9.
40. With the probable exception of Tiberius, all had ended under violent or suspicious circumstances.

CHAPTER 3 Domitian: Sour Prizes (pp. 40–53)

1. In Suetonius, *The Twelve Caesars* (Domitian), 10.
2. Used for convenience. The Scots did not arrive (from Ireland) until the post-Roman period.
3. Probably Bennachie, 6 miles northwest of Inverurie and 23 northwest of Aberdeen. Its misspelling produced the word Grampian.
4. Near Edzell (10 miles northwest of Montrose), the empire's most northerly fort, invisible on the ground.
5. 14 miles north by northwest of Perth or 5 north by northeast of Crieff, junction A822/B8063. Fort site ½ mile west of the junction, near stream; tower site by main road, on the second ridge north of the junction.
6. Fort names were usually vernacular.
7. *pinna* = merlon. It is unclear why plurals were used.
8. Near Spittalfield, on the A984, 6 miles east of Dunkeld.
9. Near Melrose, Roxburghshire.
10. 'The Helpful'.
11. Adapted from Celtic anti-cavalry defences, e.g. in Belgic Gaul (Caesar, *de Bello Gallico*, 2.17 and Strabo, *Geog.*, 4.3.5) also described by Tacitus in the Crimea (*An.*, 12.16).
12. Described below, pp. 166–68.
13. E. Fabricius, F. Hettner and O. von Sarwey, *Der obergermanisch–raetische Limes des Römerreichs* (Berlin, 1894–1937).
14. Just east of Milecastle 39, Castle Nick.
15. Dietwulf Baatz, *Der römische Limes* (Berlin, 1974), 71.
16. The word can mean most types of barrier.
17. E. Condurachi and C. Daicoviciu, *Romania* (Geneva, 1971), 205.
18. C. Schuchardt, *Die sogenannten Trajanswälle in der Dobrudscha* (Prussian Academy, Berlin, 1918).
19. Of dry stonework braced by wooden beams.
20. *An.*, 15.9.
21. Agricola was his father-in-law.

CHAPTER 4 Trajan: Triumph and Trouble (pp. 54–83)

1. Dio Cassius, *History of Rome*, 68.6.1.
2. S. Soproni in *The Archaeology of Roman Pannonia* (Kentucky and Budapest, 1980), 236.

3. A. Mócsy, *Pannonia and Upper Moesia* (London, 1974), 47.

4. Dio, 68.9.6.

5. Though the presence of engineers and artillery experts means they were ex-legionaries too.

6. For a few miles only, in the upper valley of the Crishul Alb river: an earthen mound with a ditch to its west.

7. N. Gudea, 'The Defensive System of Roman Dacia', *Britannia*, 10 (1979), 75.

8. 'Die Nordstrecke des dakischen Limes vom Crisul Repede bis zu den Ostkarpaten', *RFS*, ix (1972), 201–5.

9. Lit. 'units'.

10. Ovid, *Tristia*, 4.1. 79–85, etc.

11. A. G. Poulter, 'Rural Communities and their Role in the Organisation of the *Limes* of *Moesia Inferior*', *RFS*, xii (1980), 735–6.

12. During the later period expressed as the *Ripa Suebica* and the *Ripa Sarmatica*.

13. F. Fülep in *The Archaeology of Roman Pannonia*. (Kentucky and Budapest, 1980), 38.

14. *Geog.*, 2.5.32.

15. Gk. = white village. Arab. *haura* also = white.

16. A coastal guide to Arabia, possibly by a Greek skipper, *c*.AD 65.

17. id., trans. W. H. Schoff (New York, 1912), 101.

18. T. Bowsher, 'The Frontier Post of Medain Saleh', *BAR*, 297(i) (1986), 23–7.

19. *Pace* C. G. Starr, *The Roman Imperial Navy* (Cornell, 1941), 175.

20. Numbers 20:17: 'We will go by the king's high way and turn not to the right nor to the left.'

21. H. C. Butler, *Publications of an American Archaeological Expedition to Syria (1899–1900)*, 3A, 10–11.

22. Arab. *sharq'ein* = 'easterners'.

23. Ammian, 14.4.

24. *N.H.*, 12.84.

25. S. Gregory and D. L. Kennedy, 'Sir Aurel Stein's *Limes* Report', *BAR*, 272 (1985).

26. Regarding China's use of silk to buy off the barbarians, who then filtered westwards informally rather than via an organised trade route, see M. G. Raschke, 'Roman Commerce with the East', *ANRW* (1987); also Ammian, 23.6.8.

27. See pp. 189–190 *infra*.
28. V. S. Clark and S. T. Parker in 'The Roman Frontier in Central Jordan', *BAR*, 340, i (1987), 177–81.
29. Vegetius, Epitoma Rei Militaris 3.5. Also Frontinus, *Strategematon*, 2.5.16 (that the Arabs used these methods), while Exodus 13 gives a bronze age precedent.
30. See *infra* pp. 124.
31. S. T. Parker in 'The Roman Frontier in Central Jordan', *BAR*, 340, i, (1987), 1.
32. *qasr* (with guttural Q) variously *ksar*, *gsur*, *alcazar*, etc., from the Latin *castrum*, though applied to forts and castles of all periods.
33. Arab. *khirbet* = ruin.
34. Arab. *rum* or *room* = Roman.
35. R. G. Collingwood and J. N. L. Myres, *Roman Britain and the English Settlements* (Oxford, 1936), 126–7.
36. A. K. Bowman and J. D. Thomas, *Vindolanda: The Latin Writing Tablets* (London).
37. Location unidentified.
38. *Britannia*, 18 (1987), 125; *RFS*, xv (1989), 16; *JRS*, 81 (1991), 62.
39. A. R. Birley, 'Vindolanda; New Writing Tablets 1986–9', *RFS*, xv (1989), 18.
40. Today's Tongres, Belgium.
41. Presumably the guard commander.
42. Bowman and Thomas, 'New Texts from Vindolanda', *Britannia*, 18 (1987), 138.
43. i.e. the 10th.
44. The *Lex Oppia*, repealed 195 BC.
45. *An.*, 3.34.
46. For further discussion on *vicus*, see p. 105 *infra*.
47. Dio, 68.17.1.
48. Parthia's winter capital, near Baghdad.
49. Dio, 68.26.4, 28.2 and 30.1.
50. Dacia, Arabia, Armenia, Mesopotamia, Assyria and Babylonia.
51. Dio, 68.29.4.
52. id., 68.30.1.
53. In today's northern Iraq.
54. Capital of Roman Cyrenaica. Modern Shahhat, near Al Bayda, Libya.

CHAPTER 5 Hadrian: 'Britain will be a monument for us' (pp. 84– 114)

1. *Historia Augusta* or *Scriptores Historiae Augustae*, noted as *A.H.* with the subject's initial in brackets; e.g. (*H*) = Hadrian.
2. Edward Gibbon, *Decline and Fall of the Roman Empire*, 3.122.
3. *A.H. (H)*, 20.12.
4. Dio, 69.3.2.
5. *A.H. (H)*, 16.1.
6. Dio, 69.3.3.
7. A.H. (H), 14.11–18.
8. Followed by Palladio and later by English Palladianism.
9. *A.H. (H)*, 5.3.
10. Eutropius, *Breviarium Historiae Romanae*, 8.6.2.
11. *A.H. (H)* 9.2–3.
12. Procopius, *Buildings*, 1.6.11.
13. *A.H. (H)*, 5.8. and 7.3.
14. E. Birley, *Alae and Cohortes Milliaria* (Graz, 1966), 54.
15. In Britain, France, Germany and U.S.A., *Economist*, 16 January 1993, 53.
16. Fronto to Lucius Verus, 10 and 12.
17. *A.H. (H)*, 6.6.
18. L. F. Marsigli, *Description du Danube* (Amsterdam, 1744).
19. I. B. Cataniciu, 'Evolution of the System of Defence Works in Roman Dacia', *BAR*, 116 (1981), 48–9.
20. I. Ferenczi,' Zur Verteidigung der Nordgrenze der Provinz Dazien RFS, viii (1969), 210.
21. Gudea, op. cit.
22. E. Condurachi and D. Daicoviciu, *The Ancient Civilization of Romania* (Bucharest, 1971), 135.
23. T. Kolnik, 'Cifer Pác: eine spätrömische Station in Quadenland?' *RFS*, xi (1967), 181–93.
24. F. Krížek, 'Die römischen Stationen im Vorland des norisch-pannonischen Limes bis zu den Marcomannkrieg,' *RFS*, vi (1967), 131–7.
25. *A.H. (H)*, 12.6.
26. D. Baatz, *Der römische Limes* (Berlin, 1974), 36–7.
27. e.g. Pfahldorf, Pfahlheim, Pfahlbronn, etc.
28. Ger. *Pfahl* from Lat. *palus* = stake.

29. Condurachi and Daicoviciu, op.cit., 157.
30. *A.H. (H)*, 4.10.2.
31. Fronto to Antoninus (AD 62), 2.
32. *A.H. (H)*, 11.12.
33. '*qui barbaros Romanosque divideret*'.
34. '*separavit*'.
35. *An.*, 2.26.
36. J. G. Crow, 'The Functioning of Hadrian's Wall and the Comparative Evidence of Late Roman Long Walls', *RFS*, xiii (1983), 725.
37. D. Divine, *The North-west Frontier of Rome* (London, 1969) 129–30.
38. H. Ubl, 'Der österreichische Abschnitt des Donaulimes', *RFS*, xii (1980), 598–9.
39. J. Bennett, 'Temporary Camps along Hadrian's Wall', *RFS*, xii (1979), 169–70.
40. S. S. Frere, *Britannia* (London, 1967), 163.
41. M. E. Snape, '*Vici* on the North British Frontier', *RFS*, xv (1989), 470.
42. G. D. B. Jones in 'Invasion and Response in Roman Britain', *BAR*, 73 (1979), 62–5.
43. Collingwood and Myres, op. cit., 135.
44. R. Chevalier, *Roman Roads* (London, 1976), 158.
45. D. Williams, 'The Vallum's Original Intention', *TCWAA* (1983), 33–9.
46. Counting milecastle, fort and road exits.
47. A practice known also from the Middle Ages, giving its name to the White Tower of London.
48. J. G. Crow, 'Construction and Reconstruction in the Central Portion of Hadrian's Wall', *RFS*, xv (1989), 46.
49. Vitruvius (preface), 2–3.
50. Pliny the Younger, *Letters*, 41.
51. Dio, 62.11.5.
52. S. Perowne, *Hadrian* (London, 1960), 171–2.
53. In bricklaying parlance, stretchers are bricks laid to show the long side, headers the same brick end-on.
54. Longer-lived Portland Cement, discovered 1824, made by firing chalk mixed with clay at higher temperatures.
55. A composite of quotations from a longer argument, *Vitruvius.*, 7.2, 7.7 and 7.8.

56. J. G. Crow, op. cit., (1989), 44–5.
57. *Vitruvius.*, 1.5.3 and 1.5.7.
58. 'Had you seen these roads before they were made,
    You'd lift up your hands and bless General Wade.'
59. M. Browning, 'Archaeology Historicized', *RFS*, xv (1989),355.
60. *A.H. (H)*, 33.5.
61. id., 15. 1–3.

CHAPTER 6 Africa: The Limits of the Possible (pp. 115–55)

1. Pliny, *N.H.*, 5.10.51.
2. *Geog.*, 17.1.53.
3. Forts proven archaeologically at Pselchis (Dakkeh).
4. *N.H.*, 5.10.60.
5. id., 5.10.59.
6. *Geog.*, 17.1.48.
7. id., 17.1.3.
8. id., 17.2.1.
9. id., 17.1.54.
10. *RG*, 26.
11. 'Leagues' is a free translation. The total distance was more like 165 miles.
12. M. Speidel, 'Nubia's Roman Garrison', *ANRW*, 2.10.1.
13. M. Speidel, 'The Eastern Desert Garrisons under Augustus and Tiberius', *RFS*, x (1977), 511.
14. Not to be confused with the Syrian Pentapolis.
15. From the Gulf of Sirte the Latin/Greek divide ran through the middle of Sicily, across the heel of Italy, across the Adriatic to today's Albania, across the north of Greece, cutting Bulgaria in half, and ending where the Danube branches to its delta.
16. Procopius, *Buildings*, 62.3.
17. Cornicularnum (Ajdabia), now largely covered by an Islamic fortress.
18. M. Wheeler, *Rome Beyond the Imperial Frontier* (London, 1954), 105.
19. J. T. Swanson, 'The Myth of Trans-Saharan Trade during the Roman Era', *AS*, 8 (1975), 583.
20. Josephus, *The Jewish War*, 2, 382–3.
21. Pronounced 'shot' – in the Middle East, the feature is called *sebkha*.

22. *Antonine Itinerary*, 75.5.
23. Berber *erg* = dune region.
24. P. Trousset, 'Recherches sur le Limes Tripolitanus', *RFS*, x (1974), 114–18.
25. P. Trousset, 'Tours de Guet et Système de Liaison Optique sur le Limes Tripolitanus', *RFS*, xiv (1986), 255.
26. id., 259.
27. P. Salama, 'Les Déplacements successifs du Limes en Mauretanie Césarienne', *RFS*, xi (1976), 577.
28. Near Essaouria, level with Marrakesh.
29. *NH*, 5.1.7.
30. id., 5.1.5.
31. id.
32. *AI*, 13.2 (1924), 441–68.
33. M. Euzennat, *Le Limes de Tingitane* (Paris, 1989), 172.
34. At km 6, just before the fork with *R.P. 36.*, on the left.
35. *Bldgs.*, 6.7.2.
36. Some 17 miles west of today's Batna and 90 south of Constantine, eastern Algeria.
37. Tacitus, *Annales*, 1.17.
38. *CIL*, 8, 2532 and 18045.
39. M. Le Glay, 'Les Discours d'Hadrien à Lambèse', *RFS*, xi (1976), 545.
40. M. Janon, 'Lambèse et l'Occupation Militaire de la Numidie Meridionale', *RFS*, x (1974), 478–85.
41. For fuller texts see M. Grant, *The Army of the Caesars* (London, 1974), 239–41.
42. *Codex Theodosianus*, 7.15.1.
43. Arabists unfamiliar with French transliteration will have gathered that bent = bint, djebel = jebel, oued = wadi, etc.
44. 15–20 miles southwest of Biskra.
45. 'Note sur le Limes romain de Numidie', *AI* (1937), 256–62.
46. L. Deuel, *Flights into Yesterday* (London, 1969), 96.
47. J. Baradez, *Fossatum Africae: recherches aériennes sur l'organisation des confins sahariens à l'époque romaine* (Paris, 1949).
48. Which he would identify as watchtowers.
49. Baradez misunderstood this term.
50. *FA*, 29.
51. *FA*, 30 and 35.

52. i.e. out of sight of intruders from the Saharan direction.
53. *FA*, 35–6.
54. *FA*, 64.
55. P. Trousset, 'Le Camp de Gemellae sur le Limes de Numidie d'après les Fouilles du Col Baradez (1947–50)', *RFS*, xi (1976), 562.
56. The opinion of J. C. Mann, 'The Frontiers of the Principate', *ANRW*, 2.1.508–33.
57. 'Compléments inédits au "Fossatum Africae"', *RFS*, vi (1964), 201.
58. *FA*, 59.
59. *Compléments*, 203.
60. Perhaps added at later date.
61. *Compléments*, 203–4.
62. *Hist.*, 4. 64–5.
63. And an inception, at least for the Saharan sector, predating the imperial visit of 128.
64. *FA*, 171.
65. Eight vols. (1920–28).
66. S. Gsell, *Histoire ancienne de l'Afrique du Nord* (Paris, 1920), 99.
67. *FA*, 356.
68. *FA*, 186.
69. *FA*, 180.
70. E. Birley, 'Hadrianic Frontier Policy', *RFS*, ii (1955).
71. Genesis 4:2 and 4:8.
72. M. Euzennat, 'Recherches récentes sur la Frontière d'Afrique', *RFS*, x (1967), 443.
73. M. Gichon, 'The Roman Defence of Southern Palestine', *RFS*, xv (1989), 321.
74. E. W. B. Fentress, 'Numidia and the Roman Army', *BAR*, 53 (1979), 185–6.
75. *FA*, 359.
76. Euzennat, *RFS*, xi (1976), 543; Salama, id., 592; Fentress, op. cit., 13.
77. *CIL*, 8, 4508.
78. A. R. Birley, 'The Economic Effects of Roman Frontier Policy', *BAR*, 109 (1981), 47–50.
79. W. G. Kerr, 'Economic Warfare on the Northern Limes: Portaria and the Germans', *RFS*, xv (1989), 443.

80. *FA*, 194.
81. id., 362.
82. Nicknamed Antoninus Pius (Antoninus the Good).
83. Dio, 69.23.1–2.
84. *AH (H)*, 25.9.

CHAPTER 7 Antoninus and Marcus: The Test of War
(pp. 156– 83)

1. Pausanias, *Arcadia*, 43.4.
2. A. P. Birley, 'Roman Frontiers and Roman Frontier Policy', *D & N Trans*, 3 (1970), 17.
3. *AH (A)*, 2.1.
4. *AH (A)*, 5.4.
5. *Agr.* 23.
6. G. S. Maxwell, 'Recent Aerial Discoveries in Roman Scotland', *Britannia*, 14 (1983), 167–71.
7. *Vegetius*, 3.8.
8. Commonly approached from Bonnybridge.
9. D. J. Breeze, *Roman Scotland* (Newcastle-upon-Tyne, 1979), 25.
10. Caesar, *de Bello Gallico*, 7.73.
11. H. von Petrikovits, *RFS*, vi (1967), 215.
12. 25 miles west of Stuttgart.
13. *Hist.*, 2.5.
14. J. von Elbe, *Die Römer in Deutschland* (Berlin, 1977) 252–3.
15. *PSAS*, 38 (1904), 454.
16. Followed by Collingwood (1936), Richmond (1963), Frere (1967), Salway (1984).
17. N. Hodgson, 'Were There Two Antonine Occupations of Scotland?', *Brit*, 26 (1995), 31–6.
18. Since 1990 housed in the Palazzo dei Conservatori.
19. Younger kinsman of Hadrian's original heir.
20. Dio, 71.1.3.
21. The Khabur, northern Iraq.
22. *AH (M)*, 14.1.
23. *AH (M)*, 21. 6–8.
24. *AH (M)*, 17. 4–5 and 21. 9.
25. H. Ubl, 'Der österreichische Abschnitt des Donaulimes, ein Forschungsbericht, 1970–1979', *RFS*, xii (1979), 595.

26. *ILS*, 8977.
27. 38 miles east-north-east of Ljubljana, 10 west of Celje.
28. *AH* (*M*), 22.7.
29. Ammian, 31.5.13–14.
30. 80 miles north-east of Bratislava.
31. *CIL*, 3, 13439.
32. Dio, 72.11.3–5.
33. id., 72.15.1.
34. id., 72.16.1–2.
35. id., 72.19.2.
36. In Ovid's Poems of Exile: *Tristia* ('the Sorrows') and *Epistulae ex Ponto* ('Letters from the Black Sea').
37. Perhaps in Vienna, where a street on the site of the fortress has been named Marc Aurel Strasse.
38. Dio, 72.36.4.
39. *AH* (*S*), 20. 4–5.
40. Dio, 73.1., 1–2.
41. *AH* (*Co*), 5.4.
42. Dio, 73.8.2.
43. At the fort of Intercissa, *CIL*, 3, 3385.
44. *AH* (*Co*), 18. 3–4 and 19. 2.
45. *AH* (*Avidius Cassius*), 13. 3.

CHAPTER 8 Septimius: A Prophetic Principate (pp. 184–209)

1. Dio, 75.1.3–5.
2. *AH* (*S*), 7.2.
3. So spelt for convenience. Correctly, *Lepcis* in the early period, *Lepti* in the late.
4. Dio, 75.11.1.
5. Pronounced oz-roe-ay-nay.
6. Dio, 75.3.2–3.
7. S. Gregory and D. Kennedy, 'Sir Aurel Stein's *Limes* Report', *BAR*, 272 (i) (1985), 3.
8. Ammian, 18.7.5.
9. R. Cavenaile, *Corpus Papyrorum Latinorum* (1958), 324.
10. Ovid, *Metamorphoses*, 5.189 and 13.110.
11. F. Cumont, *Fragment de Bouclier portant une Liste d'étapes*, *Syria*, 6 (1925), 1–15.
12. 'Kifrin and the Euphrates *Limes*', *BAR*, 297i (1986), 357.

13. Boswell, *Life of Johnson*, vol. 2, 141.
14. A. R. Birley, 'Septimius Severus, Propagator Imperii', *RFS*, ix (1972), 298.
15. Also written Bou Ngem, Abu Njaym, etc.
16. Documents in ink on pottery fragments.
17. R. Rebuffat, 'Notes sur le Camp Romain de Gholaia (Bu Njem)', *Libyan Studies*, 20 (1989), 155–6.
18. I. B. Cataniciu, 'Nouvelles Données sur le *Limes Transalutanus*', *RFS*, xi (1972), 263.
19. *Fouilles et Recherches Archéologiques en Roumainie* (1911).
20. Cataniciu, op. cit. (1972), 33.
21. *AH* (*S*), 18.2.
22. Herodian, 3.14.
23. A. S. Robertson, 'The Bridges on Severan Coins of AD 208 and 209', *RFS*, xii (1972), 137, suggests the permanent bridge was at York.
24. L. Alcock, 'A Survey of Pictish Settlement Archaeology', *RFS*, xii (1979), 62.
25. Dio, 77. 12–13.
26. id., 77.15.4.
27. id., 77.15.4.
28. id., 73.2.4.
29. Marcus Aurelius Antoninus, nicknamed Caracalla from his habit of wearing a Gaulish cloak, the *cara galla*.
30. Dio, 78.14.4.
31. Gibbon, Chapter 12, 82.
32. Baatz, op. cit. (1974), 210.
33. Federal highway 417, 1½ miles north of the village of Neuhof.
34. *AH* (*S*), 19.6.

CHAPTER 9 Frontiers of Retreat (pp. 210–39)

1. W. S. Churchill, *The Second World War* (New York, 1949), 2, 42.
2. A. H. M. Jones, *The Later Roman Empire* (Oxford, 1964), 23.
3. Ammian, 14.8.
4. S. Lieu, 'Captives, Refugees and Exiles: Contacts between Rome and Persia from Valerian to Jovian', *BAR*, 297, ii (1986), 480.
5. Ammian, 14.8.

6. Near Einod, 5 miles east of Saarbrücken.
7. M. Cary and H. H. Scullard, *A History of Rome*, 3rd edn (London, 1975), 513.
8. *AH* (Probus), 13.5–7.
9. E. Wightman, 'The Fate of Gallo-Roman Villages in the Third Century', *BAR*, 109 (1981), 237.
10. *Hist.*, 8.2.
11. S. Apollinaris, *Epistulae*, 5.14.
12. G. Alföldy, *Noricum* (London, 1974), 217–22.
13. The massive remnant may still be seen outside Rome's railway station.
14. Ammian, 20.8.13 (AD 360).
15. H. Porter, 'Environmental Change in the 3rd Century', *BAR*, 109 (1981), 353.
16. L. Guicciardini, *Descrittione de tutti i Paesi Bassi* (Antwerp, 1581).
17. The Fosse Way, the Highland line, the Stanegate, Hadrian's Wall, the Antonine Wall, the Saxon Shore.
18. Ammian, 27.8.1.
19. id., 27.8.5.
20. See below, pp. 264–266
21. *N.D.*, *Occidentalis*, ch. 28.
22. Vegetius, *Epitoma Rei Militaris*, 4.37.
23. Pronounced with last three letters elided – 'lim'.
24. W. Stukeley, *Itinerarum Curiosum* (1776), 1.132.
25. The author's own expression.
26. *RIB*, 1912: '*Praetorium quod erat in humo copertum et in labem conlapsum et principia et balneum.*'
27. Midway between Ulm and Kempten.
28. Near Lauingen, between Ulm and Donauwörth.
29. 'Der Limes Hispaniens im 4 und 5 Jh.', *RFS*, xii (1979), 384.
30. A deserted site near Vitoria.
31. Singular *gasr*, a variant of *ksar* or *qasr*, from Lat. *castrum* = fort.
32. N. Benseddik, 'La Ferme Romanette (...) Fortins ou Fermes Fortifiées?', *RFS*, 12 (1979), 988–90.
33. G. W. W. Barker et al., 'Unesco Libyan Valleys Survey: the 1989 Season', *LS*, 22 (1991), 34–51.
34. G. Donaldson, 'The *Praesedes Provinciae Tripolitanae*', *BAR*, 274 (1985), 167.

35. D. J. Buck, 'Frontier Processes in Roman Tripolitania', *BAR*, 274 (1985), 186.
36. Ammian, 21.16.3.
37. M. Rostovtzeff, *Rome* (Oxford, 1927), 280.

CHAPTER 10 False Dawn (pp. 240–68)

1. D. van Berchem, 'Armée de Frontière et Armée de Manoeuvre: Alternative Stratégique ou Politique?' *RFS*, x (1977), 542.
2. Ammian, 25.7.9.
3. *Geographical Journal*, 35 (1910), 368.
4. University of Sheffield/British Institute of Archaeology at Ankara.
5. 'The Defence of the Roman and Byzantine East', *BAR*, 297, ii (1986), 516 and 572.
6. S. T. Parker, op. cit. (1979), 871.
7. Ammian, 14.8.3.
8. 'With dried pork, mousetrap and rough plonk', *AH* (*H*). 9, 10.
9. P. Crawford, 'Food for a Roman Legion', in *BAR*, 340, i (1987), 692–3.
10. M. Gichon, 'When and Why did the Romans Commence the Defence of Southern Palestine?', *RFS*, xv (1989), 318.
11. 'The Origin of the *Limes Palaestinae* and the Major Phases in its Development', *RFS*, vi (1964), 190–91.
12. Luxor is from the Arabic *el aksar* = 'the forts'.
13. S. E. Sidebottom, 'A *Limes* in the Eastern Desert of Egypt: Myth or Reality?', *RFS*, xv (1989), 497.
14. *Geog.*, 17.1.5 and 17.1.42.
15. From the Latin *burgus*.
16. M. Reddé, 'A l'Ouest du Nil: une Frontière sans Soldats, des Soldats sans Frontière', *RFS*, xv (1989), 485.
17. *CIL*, 8, 21533.
18. *CIL*, 8, 9725.
19. *Fossatum Africae*, 161.
20. Tile stamps date this example to Valentinian.
21. Romania, 15 miles east of Arad and north of the river Muresh.
22. A. Mócsy, 'Ein Spätantiker Festungstyp am linken Donauufer', *RFS*, viii (1969), 192.
23. S. Soproni, 'Eine Spätrömische Militärstation im Sarmatischen Gebiet', *RFS*, viii (1969), 197–202.

24. K. Horedt, 'Zur Frage der grossen Erdwälle an der mittleren und unteren Donau', *RFS*, ix (1972), 207.
25. For Romanian and Moldovan dykes: R. Vulpe, 'Les Valla de la Valachie, de la Basse-Moldavie et du Boudjak', *RFS*, ix (1972), 267–76.
26. Ammian, 31.3.7.
27. Vegetius, 20.1.
28. E. Stein, *Geschichte des Spätrömischen Reichs*, (Berlin, n.d.), i, 331.
29. e.g. J. Matthew's fine study, *The Roman Empire of Ammianus* (London, 1989).
30. Ammian, 15.7.1.
31. id., 2.16.4.
32. id., 16.12.19.
33. id., 16.12.26.
34. id., 16.12.63.
35. id., 23.5.18.
36. id., 23.3.9.
37. id., 19.10.4.
38. id., 29.4.1.
39. id., 21.11.2.
40. id., 28.10.5.
41. id., 28.5.8.
42. id., 33.4.
43. id., 27.10.3–4.
44. id., 30.1.19–20.
45. id., 29.6.5–6.
46. id., 31.16.8.
47. Zosimus, 5.45.
48. Ammian, 28.2.1.
49. id., 16.12.62., 24.4.6.
50. id., 29.6.2.
51. id., 29.6.8.
52. id., 30.6.3–6.

CHAPTER 11 The Wrath of Mars (pp. 269–93)

1. In reformed spelling Xiongnu.
2. A theory originating in M. Deguignes, *Histoire Générale des Huns, des Turcs, des Mongols, et des autres Tartares Occi-*

dentaux, avant et depuis J.C. jusqu'à present (Paris, 1756).

3. L. Zewen and others, *The Great Wall* (London, 1981), 162.
4. J. O. Maenchen-Helfen, *The World of the Huns* (Berkeley, California, 1973), 174.
5. Deity of travel, beginnings and the new year.
6. ? Marmot.
7. Ammian, 31.2.1–12.
8. id., 31.4.1.
9. The suffixes, *ric, rich, rix,* etc., are from the Latin *rex.* Ermanarich = King Herman.
10. Ammian, 31.3.8.
11. id., 31.4.6.
12. id., 31.6.4.
13. id., 31.3.18–19.
14. St Jerome, *Letter* 60.
15. St Jerome, *Letter* 127, quoting Isaiah 15:1.
16. See above, pp. 123–4.
17. J. Šašel, '*Clausurae Alpium Iuliarum*', *RFS*, v (1961), 155.
18. 35 BC, Octavian, later the emperor Augustus.
19. Pronounced hrooshika, also meaning 'pear tree'.
20. T. Ulbert, *Ad Pirum (Hrušica) Spätrömische Passbefestigung in den Julischen Alpen* (Munich, 1981).
21. Pronounced Lan-eesh-chè (emphasis on first syllable).
22. P. Petru, 'Neuere Grabungen an der *Clausurae Alpium Iuliarum*', *RFS*, vi (1964), 122–4.
23. Today's Vipacco or Wippach.
24. Zosimus, 6.5.
25. id., 6.10.
26. Gildas, *de Excidio Britanniae* ('On the Destruction of Britain').
27. Ammian, 29.5.13, 29.5.25.
28. id., 20.11.15.
29. A. H. M. Jones (1964), 618.
30. Vegetius, 1.20.
31. Zosimus, 4.31.
32. Ammian, 24.3.4.
33. The junction was at Sirmium (near Belgrade).
34. R. M. Harrison, '*To Makron Teichos, the Long Wall of Thrace*', *RFS*, viii (1969), 244–8.
35. *Bldgs.*, 4.9.6.
36. Near Belgrade, AD 452.

37. J. F. C. Fuller, *The Decisive Battles of the Western World* (London, 1954), 95.
38. R. Noll, *Eugippius, das Leben des heiligen Severin* (Berlin, 1963) [Latin text with German trans.].
39. M. Gichon, 'Excavations at En Boqeq, the First Season', *RFS*, viii (1969), 261.
40. *Bldgs.*, 1.1.11.
41. Gibbon, vol. 6, ch. 28, 400–1; Procopius, *The Gothic War*, 1.4.20.
42. D. A. Welsby, 'The Roman Military Defence of the British Province in its Later Phases', *BAR*, 101 (1982), 87.
43. e.g. C. M. Daniels, 'Excavations at Wallsend and the 4th century barracks on Hadrian's Wall', *RFS*, xii (1980), 173, 189.

CHAPTER 12 Fallible Friend (pp. 294–303

1 'In the Old Theatre, Fiesole' (1887).
2. A phrase of Pliny the Younger, *Panegyricus*, 12.3.
3. Gibbon, ch. 3, 118.
4. *NH*, 27.1.3.
5. *An.*, 15.1.

Index

Ancient versions of place names are given in italics, modern versions in the Roman alphabet. Where ancient and modern names are available as alternatives, indexing favours the one which seems to be in commonest usage. Roman personal names remain a vexed question. Here, while lesser characters are usually given under *cognomen* (surname), celebrities are indexed under the name by which they are best known.